POWER *to the* POOR

GORDON K. MANTLER

POWER *to the* POOR

Black-Brown Coalition and the
Fight for Economic Justice, 1960–1974

The University of North Carolina Press · *Chapel Hill*

© 2013 The University of North Carolina Press

Designed and set in Espinosa Nova by Rebecca Evans
Manufactured in the United States of America

The paper in this book meets the guidelines for permanence
and durability of the Committee on Production Guidelines for
Book Longevity of the Council on Library Resources.

The University of North Carolina Press has been a member of
the Green Press Initiative since 2003.

Library of Congress Cataloging-in-Publication Data
Mantler, Gordon Keith, 1972–
Power to the poor : Black-Brown coalition and the fight for
economic justice, 1960–1974 / Gordon K. Mantler.
pages cm.—(Justice, power, and politics)
Includes bibliographical references and index.
ISBN 978-0-8078-3851-8 (cloth : alk. paper)
1. African Americans—Economic conditions—20th century. 2. Hispanic
Americans—Economic conditions—20th century. 3. Coalitions—United
States—History—20th century. 4. Poverty—Political aspects—United States—
History—20th century. 5. Social movements—United States—History—20th
century. 6. Social justice—United States—History—20th century. 7. Political
activists—United States—Biography. 8. Ethnicity—Political aspects—United
States—History—20th century. 9. United States—Economic conditions—
1961–1971. 10. United States—Race relations—History—20th century. I. Title.
E185.8.M19 2013   305.800973—dc23   2012031383

17 16 15 14 13   5 4 3 2 1

To my family,
Christina and Zella
Mom and Dad

When you stand up for justice, you can never fail.
—Dr. Martin Luther King Jr., March 10, 1968

Contents

Illustrations

Abbreviations in the Text

AFL-CIO	American Federation of Labor–Congress of Industrial Organizations
AFSC	American Friends Service Committee
AGIF	American GI Forum
ANMA	Asociación Nacional México-Americana
CCCO	Coordinating Council of Community Organizations
CFM	Chicago Freedom Movement
CORE	Congress of Racial Equality
CSO	Community Service Organization
FBI	Federal Bureau of Investigation
HEW	Health, Education and Welfare Department
JOIN	Jobs Or Income Now Community Union
LADO	Latin American Defense Organization
LULAC	League of United Latin American Citizens
MAPA	Mexican American Political Association
MAYO	Mexican American Youth Organization
MFY	Mobilization for Youth
NAACP	National Association for the Advancement of Colored People
NCNP	National Conference for New Politics
NFLU	National Farm Labor Union
NIYC	National Indian Youth Council
NWRO	National Welfare Rights Organization
OEO	Office of Economic Opportunity
SCLC	Southern Christian Leadership Conference

SDS	Students for a Democratic Society
SNCC	Student Nonviolent Coordinating Committee
UAW	United Auto Workers
UFW	United Farm Workers
UFWOC	United Farm Workers Organizing Committee
UPWA	United Packinghouse Workers of America
YCCA	Young Chicanos for Community Action

POWER *to the* POOR

Introduction

As Reies López Tijerina stepped to the podium in a small but ornate room at Chicago's Palmer House hotel, the charismatic Chicano leader exuded both a supreme confidence and a genuine urgency about the state of his people in the fall of 1967. "The black man is marching in the streets," Tijerina told a mix of supporters and curious observers, emphatically waving his hands. "You think we should sit down and relax?" The land-grant rights leader from New Mexico was in town for the first and only National Conference for New Politics convention, a raucous gathering of New Left activists considering an electoral challenge to President Lyndon Johnson primarily over the Vietnam War.

Although not explicitly a war opponent, the onetime itinerant Pentecostal preacher received an invitation after gaining notoriety for his provocative and unorthodox activism. For the previous four years, Tijerina had applied his penchant for rich rhetoric and publicity to the cause of Mexican American land-grant rights long sought by the descendants of deed owners in U.S. territory that had been Mexico until 1848. For Tijerina and his tens of thousands of followers in New Mexico and throughout the Southwest, honoring the land grants under the Treaty of Guadalupe Hidalgo, which ended the U.S.-Mexican War, was the primary way to alleviate the grinding poverty that many Mexican Americans faced in the United States more than a century later. The convention was a prime chance to spread the word to a new audience of potential allies, especially African Americans, with whom Tijerina believed his people had a shared goal. "The black man has his cause and we have ours," Tijerina reminded his listeners. "It is the same cause—justice."[1]

On the surface, Tijerina's statement could be interpreted as nothing more than a hopeful but largely rhetorical declaration of multiracial solidarity—a desire to ally with people who had comparable histories of oppression in the United States. But Tijerina's declaration actually suggested a more complicated reality, one that prompts several questions. Exactly what does "justice" mean? Is this vague but powerful term enough upon which to build a sustained multiracial alliance among African Americans and Mexican Americans—Tijerina's stated goal for attending a convention of New Left activists? Or is justice actually an obstacle? And how could the Chicano movement have both the "same" and a separate "cause," to quote Tijerina, as the African American freedom struggle? Perhaps his statement simply reflects the bombast he was known for. A talented orator, Tijerina had built a reputation for galvanizing audiences with fiery, fist-pounding speeches that often privileged high-flying rhetoric over exact details, or even reason.

Yet, as Tijerina suggested that weekend in Chicago, "justice" could be an effective way to organize poor people precisely because it had so many definitions. The question was whether these definitions overlapped, or at least complemented, each other enough to allow meaningful coalition. For Tijerina and his followers, restoring the land grants from the nineteenth century was the quintessential definition of justice. Even a little communal land control was better than the "justice (that) depends on a handout of powdered milk," Tijerina noted, referring to more traditional antipoverty approaches. But, he added, justice could take other forms— ones that emerged in the convention's Spanish-speaking caucus, on the plenary floor, and elsewhere, including access to bilingual and quality education, protections from police brutality and urban renewal, public jobs programs and open housing, and the right to welfare and collective bargaining. In its broadest sense, justice included a wide range of solutions to the poverty of the late 1960s that plagued nearly 12 percent of all Americans, one-third of African Americans, and one-fourth of Mexican Americans.[2] And to Tijerina, "while this was no new struggle," the opportunity for Mexican Americans to work with blacks against poverty was ripe. "We must unite," he concluded.[3]

Tijerina had been particularly interested in a partnership with Dr. Martin Luther King Jr. The Chicano leader wanted to establish what he called "a solid alliance between the Spanish-Americans and the moderate Negroes." Such a coalition was "not to support the fight for land grants— we can take care of that ourselves," Tijerina added, but to find common ground among the nation's two largest minority groups, Mexican Americans and African Americans.[4] King gave the keynote address at the National Conference for New Politics convention and even was rumored to be the delegates' top choice as a third-party presidential candidate. But an exhausted and depressed King—deeply disturbed by the violence of urban riots and the Vietnam War and embattled because of his stance on both—made it clear that he had no interest in running for office and left soon after his speech. The early departure allowed Tijerina the briefest of moments to introduce himself at the airport.

Tijerina vividly recalled the short encounter as deeply symbolic. "I suggested to him a coalition between the brown people and the black people. Also the Indians and poor whites," Tijerina said after King's death. "He said it was high time."[5] To Tijerina, it represented the first seed of what would become King's most far-reaching and radical crusade, the Poor People's Campaign of 1968, in which King sought a multiracial army of the poor to demand the nation's rededication to the federal War on Poverty. In reality, the campaign had more complicated origins, and King later did not readily recall meeting Tijerina that day. But the substance of their short time together did reinforce what King already had been thinking—genuine change in America required a grander, more militant coalition than he had ever succeeded in putting together before. People of Mexican descent were essential to any such coalition, King came to believe.[6]

Disappointed that they could not speak at more length, Tijerina had more in-depth engagements with representatives of black power organizations, such as Ron Karenga of the culturally nationalist US Organization and Ralph Featherstone and Maria Varela of the Student Nonviolent Coordinating Committee (SNCC), which increasingly embraced more assertive tactics and rhetoric similar to Tijerina's. These conversations led to a series of coalitions between Tijerina, other Chicano leaders such as Rodolfo "Corky" Gonzales, and African American activists of many backgrounds, including King. And none would be as grand, as instructive, or as complicated as King's campaign to help the nation's poor achieve their own form of justice.

◆ ◆ ◆

Justice and poverty were central to the multiracial coalitions that emerged in the late 1960s. Both issues long had been underlying concerns of post–World War II civil rights activism, but it was the 1960s that witnessed the nation's most concerted efforts to address them explicitly. Federal officials initially believed that the nation could eliminate inequality without massive intervention in the nation's economic and political structure. The government, however, quickly distanced itself from the War on Poverty declared by President Johnson in 1964 before ever really fighting it. In response, activists of the African American freedom struggle, many of whom had pressed the federal government to combat poverty in the first place, attempted to mobilize a broad alliance of poor people and their allies to keep the pressure on. And for the next several years, members of the Chicano movement sought ways to work with their black counterparts—as well as American Indians, Puerto Ricans, and poor whites—to address the discriminatory and structural policies that allowed poverty to wrack their communities in disproportionate ways. But as these individuals discovered, there was nothing natural to a multiracial coalition.

Through the careful examination of antipoverty coalition building among primarily African Americans and Mexican Americans in the late 1960s, this book reveals a relationship between race-based identity politics and class-based coalition politics that was not antithetical, but mutually reinforcing.[7] One could not exist without the other. African Americans' and Mexican Americans' common fight against poverty held the greatest potential for multiracial cooperation at the time, given their similar histories of oppression at the hands of the white power structure. Yet such efforts also exposed the complex dynamics between the nation's two largest minority groups, including distinct definitions of justice that were often fueled further by a variety of other factors: differences in strategy and in the personalities of key movement leaders, a clear activist hierarchy with blacks on top, the power of what could be called "non-blackness" in Mexican American and Chicano identity, and persistent harassment and violence by the state. Ultimately, such collaboration was difficult, rarely sustained, and even symbolic at times. Some meaningful coalition did occur, but it often ironically facilitated productive race-based activism by African Americans and Chicanos in attaining political and cultural power into the 1970s. The development of such power bases, in turn, made multiracial coalitions more possible in the future. Coalition, after all, suggested difference, and difference ultimately relied on separate foundations of power—foundations rooted in strong racial identities.

Thus, historians have exaggerated the characterization of an emerging identity, race-based, or interest group politics of the late 1960s and early 1970s as a sharp declension from the so-called halcyon days of early sixties Kennedy liberalism and the southern civil rights movement.[8] Identity politics did not represent an abandonment of coalitional politics but actually was a necessary element of coalition. Identity and coalition coexisted and reflected important, productive, and complementary impulses in the United States in the decades after World War II. Ultimately, the story of the late 1960s and 1970s is one of neither triumph nor declension. It is a story of social change through empowerment.

One of the best illustrations of this relationship was the era's most high-profile but much-maligned attempt at multiracial collaboration: the Poor People's Campaign of 1968. Envisioned by Dr. Martin Luther King Jr. in the last year of his life, the crusade blossomed into the most ambitious campaign ever undertaken by King and the Southern Christian Leadership Conference (SCLC). The campaign, which King did not live to see, has been dismissed by journalists, scholars, King biographers, and even some activists as either irrelevant or a disastrous coda of the black freedom struggle. One former SCLC official referred to the campaign as the "Little Bighorn of the civil rights movement"—an eye-catching but imprecise analogy.[9] And, in fact, the campaign *was* deeply flawed in many ways and often *was* preoccupied with symbolism. It did not spark a new War on Poverty. It did not reinvigorate nonviolent strategy. And it did not achieve many of SCLC's stated policy goals, including a New Deal-style jobs program.

Yet a closer look at the campaign reveals a unique and remarkably instructive experiment to build a multiracial movement designed to wage a sustained fight against poverty. Even amid the cacophony of assassinations and political turmoil that spring, the campaign captured the nation's attention and imagination. Only in Washington in the spring of 1968 did local, regional, and national activists of so many different backgrounds—from veterans of the labor and southern civil rights movements to activists of the newer Chicano, American Indian, antiwar, and welfare rights struggles—attempt to construct a physical and spiritual community explicitly about justice and poverty that went beyond a one-day rally. By bringing such a diverse array of activists together from across the country, the campaign highlighted how multiracial coalitional politics operated alongside the identity politics of black and Chicano power. That relationship was messy at times and exacerbated by other forces. But, ultimately, activists such as Reies Tijerina and Martin Luther King Jr., Corky Gonzales and Jesse Jackson, Maria Varela and Marian Wright, and thousands of others did not choose either identity politics or coalitional politics at this time. They chose both and participated in both, frequently at the same time.

While the campaign may have been the most prominent example of this phenomenon, there were other multiracial experiments that influenced and reflected the complexities of the era's coalition work. Beginning in 1965–66, Cesar Chavez and what became the United Farm Workers lobbied mainstream civil rights groups to support actively the union's boycott of table grapes—a relationship that continued in some fashion for years. Between 1967 and 1969, Reies Tijerina pursued collaboration with black power and other African American activists, first through the National Conference for New Politics and then in California and the Southwest. In 1969 dynamic Black Panther leader Fred Hampton founded the original Rainbow Coalition in Chicago with Puerto Rican, Mexican American, and white street gangs that had become more explicitly political. And when analyzed alongside the Poor People's Campaign, these collaborative efforts provide invaluable insight into how identity and coalition interacted in the fight against poverty.[10]

◆ ◆ ◆

An analysis of multiracial coalition and how identity impacted it starts with a nuanced approach to the political dynamics between African Americans and Mexican Americans in the second half of the twentieth century. While not designed to exclude other groups, this emphasis reflects the understudied complexity of the interracial and intra-racial politics among the nation's two largest minorities.[11] Black-brown relations long have been the purview of political scientists and sociologists most interested in the formation of contemporary urban political coalitions.[12] Recently, however, this relationship has begun to receive serious attention from historians—efforts that help upend the prevailing and distorting racial binaries that have privileged white power to racial "otherness" in U.S. historical scholarship—not to mention the public memory. From the dominant story of black and white to more recent but similar narratives of brown and white, Indian and white, and so on, such binaries suggest that the past can be understood only through "two irreducible elements, usually oppositional, like: good and evil, mind and body," to quote one Chicana activist and scholar of the civil rights movement.[13] In practice, this black-white dualism denies the fluidity of race and racial formation by flattening everything into two poles and conflating brown with black, Indian with black, Puerto Rican with black. Looking at Mexican Americans' interactions with other racial minorities, as well as whites, best highlights their unique historical experience. Therefore, this field of research is a much-needed corrective.

But while establishing a necessarily deeper context, recent historical studies tend to fall into two distinct camps that risk oversimplifying the complex relationship between black and brown. Some historians focus on moments of cooperation, especially the "rainbow radicalism" of the 1960s inspired by the Black Panthers, and as a result downplay—and at times disregard—deep-seated differences among the supposedly harmonious parties.[14] Other historians emphasize conflict, mostly fed by competition over economic and social resources such as housing, jobs, and local anti-poverty community action programs. Some of these scholars also suggest, rather simplistically, that little more than unvarnished racism is at play.[15] A third much smaller group strives for a balance between conflict and cooperation, such as by highlighting cultural exchange and largely parallel legal actions between Mexican Americans and African Americans that occasionally crossed racial lines.[16]

Of greater concern, however, is that nearly all of these studies, whether focused on conflict, cooperation, or something in between, approach multiracial organizing as if it is inherent. The assumption is that, if only a white power structure that pitted racial minorities against each other for economic gain would step out of the way, these groups could bond along class lines. In contrast, if African Americans and Mexican Americans constructed their poverties differently because of distinct historical trajectories, as Reies Tijerina suggested and this book argues, then moments of cooperation should be viewed for what they were: unique instances worthy of study but not to be held up automatically as the natural and desired outcome or goal of the era's black and brown activists.

In addition to differing definitions of justice, several other factors complicated the relationship between African Americans and Mexican Americans and identity politics and coalitional politics. Although people of Mexican descent had a long history of political resistance and activism, it was not a history that many African Americans, especially those east of the Mississippi River, knew about. As a result, Chicano organizations in the 1960s ran into an activist hierarchy, in which African Americans saw themselves as the most oppressed because of a brutal 350-year history of slavery and segregation, and thus were the most deserving of assistance and political deference. Much has been written on the paternalism of traditional civil rights organizations such as King's SCLC toward women.[17] But such an attitude often applied to their interactions with Mexican Americans as well. Even when civil rights groups such as SCLC or SNCC determined that a multiracial partnership would be in their best interest, internal resistance emerged. This proved especially true in preparation for the Poor People's Campaign, as members of King's inner circle reportedly used "child" and "little brown brother" to refer to some of their Mexican American counterparts.[18]

Modern Mexican American and Chicano racial identities also reinforced an activist hierarchy in the late 1960s. While "whiteness" did play a role in Mexican American legal strategies on school desegregation, its application to Mexican Americans' own identity is less conclusive.[19] Most people of Mexican descent did not see themselves as white exactly. But that did not preclude the persistence of what could be called "nonblackness," or a denial of African roots, in both Chicano and Mexican American identity. The *mestizaje* celebrated so vigorously by Chicanos in the 1960s and 1970s privileged the mix of indigenous and European culture and blood and generally disregarded any African influence. Emphasizing this precise mix even more pointedly was Reies Tijerina, who called himself and his followers *indohispanos*. Although such constructions may be consistent with the racial ideology pursued by Mexicans during and after the revolution of 1910 and by Mexican Americans in New Mexico in the late nineteenth century, it remains striking how Chicanos so well versed in the prerevolutionary Mexican past, such as Tijerina and Corky Gonzales, chose to accept the erasure of Africans from that history. In a symbolic moment, when asked in 1968 about these forgotten roots, Tijerina dismissed black historical influence and argued that they were "absorbed at a very fast rate" in the seventeenth and eighteenth centuries.[20] A distinct African identity did disappear, but only later did Mexicans and Mexican Americans actively deny African contributions to Mexican culture and identity. Such denial helped distinguish themselves from their black counterparts, especially for Mexican American elites seeking to maintain their influence in a newly Americanized New Mexico in the late nineteenth century. Such a move may have been to their political advantage in a white-dominated power structure, but it also contributed to a century of distrust among African Americans.[21]

Such ideologies and binaries even affect the language we use in discussing group identities and their relationships with others. While "African American" and "black" have become generally accepted interchangeable terms for people of African descent in the United States, the terms used to identify people of Mexican descent remain far more contested. In this book, "Chicano" refers solely to those people of Mexican descent who identified with the namesake political and cultural movement of the late 1960s and 1970s. In contrast, "Mexican American" and "person of Mexican descent" serve as umbrella terms for Chicanos, U.S.-born Mexican Americans, and Mexican-born immigrants. "Latino" describes Spanish-speaking people of different nationalities in the United States, including Puerto Ricans and Cuban Americans, rather than "Hispanic," a popular usage today that nonetheless falsely privileges European heritage over indigenous and African influences in the Americas.[22] And because scholars of twentieth-century U.S. history routinely employ "interracial" to mean solely black and white—and thus perpetuate a misleading binary—this book uses "multiracial" to describe interaction among African Americans and people of Mexican descent and any other minority groups. Clearly, these labels are imperfect and the result of inconsistent and often illogical social constructions. Therefore, readers should consider them to be approximations at best rather than objective categories.[23]

If certain forces tended to divide people, at least one definition of justice routinely brought a wide range of Mexican Americans and African Americans together, especially by 1968: a vigorous opposition to state violence, both domestic and foreign. Much has been written about what forms this violence took, from police brutality and harassment to surveillance and dirty tricks, and the role it played in crippling the Black Panther Party and other organizations.[24] But there has been far less study on the level of cooperation that such activities produced among a broad range of poor people, including poor whites. While the misinformation campaigns of the Federal Bureau of Investigation and local police departments' Red Squads, most prominently in Chicago, certainly produced distrust among activists, distaste for strong-arm, undemocratic police tactics encouraged coalitions among the most unusual bedfellows. Incongruously, police beatings produced some of the most poignant moments of the Poor People's Campaign, while opposition to police brutality helped sustain the black, white, and brown youth of Chicago's Rainbow Coalition—at least for a time, until the state's assassination of Fred Hampton.

Unearthing the mutually reinforcing tendencies of identity and coalition politics also complicates the understanding of a "long civil rights movement," a struggle that goes beyond the traditional narrative that closely hewed to Martin Luther King Jr.'s public life.[25] Undoubtedly, as these instances of multiracial cooperation suggest, activism persisted years after the traditional "end" date of the classical civil rights movement, whether it is the 1965 Voting Rights Act or King's assassination in 1968. Participants in the Poor People's Campaign, for instance, viewed economic justice as inextricably linked with their citizenship rights and overall quest for dignity. They were disproportionately women, who struggled with poverty far more than men. They came from places not just in the South but the North and West as well. They included people not normally seen as civil rights activists, including men and women of Mexican and Puerto Rican descent. And many of them did not see a great deal of difference between those seeking civil rights and those advocating black power.

At the same time, critics are correct to argue that the movement does not live forever unchanged, as one pair stated it, "virtually eternal, like a vampire."[26] The antipoverty coalitions of the late 1960s and early 1970s represented a demographic shift from the largely black and white movement activism of the earlier part of the decade. By the mid-1970s, civil rights activism fundamentally changed as the number of African American officeholders skyrocketed, simultaneously giving blacks more inside access to the system while undercutting outsider protests against continued racial inequality. Racial identity politics—bolstered by multiracial cooperation such as the Poor People's Campaign and Chicago's Rainbow Coalition—strengthened the electoral results of African American and Chicano politicians and their middle-class benefactors. But this process also shifted the movement's energy and enthusiasm to the arguably more staid and limiting world of electoral politics.

This book uses several sites to explore the interplay among local, regional, and national activists, recognizing that national events and campaigns influenced grass-roots people's actions as much as local efforts affected and shaped those at the top. The nation's capital, of course, plays a central role as the destination of many antipoverty activists' demands on the state, particularly during the Poor People's Campaign. Yet more than any other city, Chicago threads itself throughout the narrative and analysis here. While known for extensive racial balkanization reinforced by its neighborhoods and a dominant political machine designed to control such disparate parts, the "second city" was also often a laboratory of multiracial collaboration. Not only did King set his sights on Chicago as his first foray into the North; the city also hosted the National Conference for New Politics, became a key organizing and recruiting site for the Poor People's Campaign and farm workers' grape boycotts, and was home to Fred Hampton's (as well as Jesse Jackson's) Rainbow Coalition. Supporters of Harold Washington, the city's first African American mayor, pointed to the coalitions of the 1960s as instrumental in his surprising victory more than a decade later.

Colorado and New Mexico also play prominently here, one of several ways this book expands upon the existing scholarship on Mexican Americans and the Chicano movement. As the home bases for Corky Gonzales's and Reies Tijerina's popular Chicano organizations, these two understudied states offer some distinctions from the predominant Mexican American experiences of Texas and California.[27] The issues of land-grant and treaty rights were not just symbolic but had tangible meaning to Chicanos in Colorado and New Mexico, where most of the original grants were located. While both states had larger Mexican American populations than African American, they also had sizable concentrations of American Indians—far more so than in Texas and California—that contributed to their thinking about multiracial alliances.

Moreover, this study bridges the black freedom struggle and the Chicano movement in broader ways. Chicanos did not simply emulate African Americans, as some scholars emphasize.[28] While they too had their own activist traditions, Chicanos also participated in civil rights campaigns that transformed their lives. From the SNCC activities of Elizabeth "Betita" Martínez and Maria Varela to Mexican American participation in the Poor People's Campaign in Washington, actions sponsored and led by African Americans provided important building blocks to the Chicano movement.

Not surprisingly, a wide variety of sources informs this book. More than sixty oral histories—both conducted by myself and as part of existing collections—have been central to recovering many of the grass-roots stories here. In addition, this book relies on more than twenty manuscript collections, including the recently processed records of Reies López Tijerina and Corky Gonzales and a variety of unprocessed materials, such as documents of the National Welfare Rights Organization. Mainstream and underground newspapers and magazines, including the black and Spanish-language press, play a sizable role, as do select FBI files on King, Tijerina, and many of the other organizations and individuals under police surveillance during this time.

◆ ◆ ◆

Overall, by beginning in 1960 and ending in 1974, this book challenges the traditional time frame placed on the Chicano movement, the black freedom struggle, and the federal War on Poverty by highlighting how multiracial and identity politics reinforced each other throughout this period. Chapter 1 briefly traces African Americans' and Mexican Americans' distinct historical trajectories before 1960 and how civil rights and labor activists influenced the national "rediscovery" of poverty. While both African Americans and Mexican Americans viewed poverty as a dangerous obstacle to freedom and full citizenship, they often desired vastly contrasting solutions to inequality. Their solutions clashed not only with each other but also with federal officials, who had settled on a War on Poverty that stressed elite-driven incremental changes to the economy. Chapter 2 explores the mid-decade transition from mostly separate but parallel black and Mexican American civil rights movements to tentative efforts at multiracial antipoverty coalition building. In late 1965, Cesar Chavez and the United Farm Workers (UFW) reached out to civil rights organizations for assistance. But while Martin Luther King Jr. offered rhetorical support, SCLC did little else to help the grape boycott—this despite King's leadership in the Chicago Freedom Movement, a city where UFW grape boycotts made a lasting impact. In contrast, UFW had relatively more success with SNCC and the Congress of Racial Equality, both of which offered formal material support to the boycott.

By 1967, new powerful forces had begun to alter civil rights activism fundamentally: the anti–Vietnam War movement and the growing prominence of black power. Chapter 3 analyzes how the identity politics of peace and blackness actually reflected and incorporated ongoing concerns around poverty and propelled efforts at multiracial coalition. In particular, the work of prominent Chicano movement leaders, Reies López Tijerina and Corky Gonzales, attracted enough attention to garner invitations first to the white New Left's antiwar National Conference for New Politics and then to the Poor People's Campaign of Martin Luther King Jr. King's vision became the era's highest-profile attempt at creating a multiracial coalition. Yet, as chapter 4 argues, the campaign process tested SCLC organizers' networks and their own capacity to comprehend issues different from their own. One unique result was the so-called Minority Group Conference, held in March 1968, in which King and his aides met with representatives of a broad range of groups engaged in antipoverty work. Despite some palpable tension at times, participants left the one-day conference committed to the campaign and enthusiastic about the "making of a bottom-up coalition," to quote one attendee.[29]

King's assassination in April 1968 did not derail the Poor People's Campaign, but his death did alter its organization, spirit, and composition. Chapter 5 traces the campaign's development as it became increasingly dominated by its African American participants and leaders. The campaign captured the imagination of many marchers and led to numerous instances of multiracial bonding. But after an opening series of rallies in which blacks, whites, Chicanos, and American Indians all played substantive, high-profile roles, SCLC officials—sometimes deliberately, sometimes not—marginalized marchers of other races. At the heart of this process was Resurrection City, a tent city on the Washington Mall envisioned as a symbol of unity among the nation's poor and a pragmatic space to house protesters and launch civil disobedience. While at times a vibrant and dynamic community, Resurrection City also suffered from disorganization, poor weather, and an increasingly hostile press and public. As conditions worsened in the city, SCLC leaders tried to control the situation more and more, reinforcing the activist hierarchy and exacerbating already strained interactions with nonblack marchers. By the time the police knocked down Resurrection City in late June, it had become a racialized all-black space. Yet its demise did not directly impact the hundreds of Chicano marchers who made the cross-country journey to Washington because most had never lived in Resurrection City. In fact, in many ways, their experience proved quite different from that of most of their black counterparts. Chapter 6 argues that Chicanos had a transformational experience in Washington because, more than anything, they deepened ties with each other—many of whom had met for the first time there or on the road to Washington. Living in an experimental high school a few miles away from Resurrection City, Chicanos used their time to prioritize their own interests—and when necessary, to pursue them separately. In the process, the campaign experience empowered individuals, complicated their own analyses, and strengthened the interregional networks that became the backbone of the burgeoning Chicano struggle.

The campaign's Washington phase ended in July amid tremendous condemnation, but marchers did not return to their communities empty-handed. Chapter 7 explores the many lessons and contacts campaign participants brought home with them. Reies Tijerina was just one of several participants to run for public office. Some marchers continued their multiracial efforts, while still others dedicated themselves to building a more cohesive Chicano movement. Calling on many of the men and women he met in Washington, Corky Gonzales and the Crusade for Justice hosted the first Youth Liberation Conference in Denver in spring 1969, which brought together more than one thousand young Chicanos, produced the foundational *El Plan de Aztlán*, and helped set the movement's tone for the next several years, culminating with the founding of the Chicano-only La Raza Unida Party. Even if the Poor People's Campaign itself did not achieve its primary goals, its impact on individuals proved immense. Meanwhile, SCLC officials ramped up their support for an all-black hospital workers' strike in Charleston, South Carolina. Ralph Abernathy and Coretta Scott King called Charleston the second act of the Poor People's Campaign—but unlike the Washington phase, the strike was primarily a gendered labor action championed by African Americans and their traditional civil rights allies. Chapter 8 explores the symbolism of this and other African American activism through the National Black Political Convention in Gary, most of which emphasized racial rather than class unity. This organizing did not preclude moments of multiracial cooperation, such as Fred Hampton's Rainbow Coalition, but it too proved short-lived and unable to overcome internal disputes and state violence. By the turn of the new decade, racial identity among African Americans and Mexican Americans was stronger than it had been just five years before.

The epilogue takes the story past the early 1970s, when commentators popularized what they viewed as a pejorative term for race-based political activism: identity politics. But it was really a new term for a time-tested approach. And rather than a negative, identity politics helped produce the antecedents to a new generation of sustained coalition building—just as it did in 1967 and 1968. Justice and poverty still looked, and looks, different to African Americans and Mexican Americans. Identity, racial and otherwise, remains a powerful force in both productive and not-so-productive ways. A recognition of all of these facts and a willingness to see them as essential to productive coalition remains an important step before setting one's differences aside in order to find commonalities. Recognizing the complex, mutually reinforcing relationship between identity and coalition is a key lesson from this historical era. Although some of the issues and ideologies of the twenty-first century are different, those activists attempting to build antipoverty coalitions today continue to face many of the same obstacles. Perhaps they could learn something from their counterparts of a generation ago.

1 ◆ The "Rediscovery" of Poverty

"Poverty can now be abolished. How long shall we ignore this underdeveloped nation in our midst? How long shall we look the other way while our fellow human beings suffer? How long?"[1] These words from *The Other America*, written by Michael Harrington in 1962, became one of the era's most eloquent calls to action to address the plight of wrenching poverty amid plenty. An estimated fifty million souls, or roughly 27 percent of the population with an even higher percentage of children, lived in destitution compared to their fellow Americans, wrote Harrington. And unlike past eras, "the other America, the America of poverty, is hidden. . . . Its millions are socially invisible to the rest of us."[2]

Harrington, a one-time member of the Catholic Worker movement in New York City before converting to socialism in the 1950s, became "the man who discovered poverty" in what is one of the most enduring creation myths in modern American history.[3] A poignant piece of social criticism that became a bestseller and political and cultural touchstone, *The Other America* was read by some of the most powerful people in the nation, even President John F. Kennedy, the story goes. Believing that poverty indeed could be eliminated, federal officials and liberal economists then set forth with what would become the War on Poverty, conceived under Kennedy's administration in 1963 and pursued, although never fully, by President Lyndon Johnson. While economists such as John Kenneth Galbraith had written about the deceptive and changing nature of the nation's postwar economy, it was Harrington's slim volume of less than two hundred pages that crystallized the thinking of the policy-making intelligentsia around poverty. It later would be called one of the "ten most important nonfiction books" in the twentieth century.[4]

Yet, as appealing as this narrative might be—especially to writers, scholars, and social critics—it distorts the context from which *The Other America* was born. "That book belonged to the movement," wrote Harrington in his memoirs a decade later, "which contributed so much more to me than I to it."[5] Harrington did not go to the South in the early 1960s, but as his biographer states, "The movement . . . gave his politics a depth of human empathy and understanding lacking in the 1950s."[6] Those individuals so often linked to the War on Poverty's origins, like Harrington, did not work in a vacuum, insulated from the growing crescendo of the era's social justice movements, particularly the black and Mexican American freedom struggles and the early student movement. Rather, directly and indirectly, grass-roots activists influenced the ideas and timing of what would become the War on Poverty.

In fact, grass-roots activists of all races had been fighting their own war on poverty for a generation. They just did not call it that. Nor did they necessarily use the term "poverty." They spoke instead of justice and freedom, which commingled issues from voting and equal access to public accommodations to jobs, welfare, and economic opportunity. As Ella Baker, long-term black activist and leading light of SNCC, reported from that organization's initial conference in 1960, the students "made it crystal clear that the current sit-ins and other demonstrations are concerned with something much bigger than a hamburger or even a giant-sized Coke. . . . the movement was concerned with the moral implications of racial discrimination for the 'whole world' and the 'Human Race.'"[7]

Even as the public focused on seemingly narrow demands to end segregation of public schools, lunch counters, and other accommodations in the 1950s and early 1960s, African Americans and Mexican Americans argued that good jobs, open housing, and an end to police brutality were just as essential to their freedom. This line of argument took many forms. African Americans resurrected the "don't buy where you can't work" campaigns from the 1930s, most notably in Philadelphia, while demonstrators in Chicago and cities across the North and West boycotted poor, overcrowded schools and fought discrimination in the lucrative construction industry. Dr. Martin Luther King Jr. wrote of desegregation meaning little if blacks did not have the money to "buy the goods and pay the fees" that middle-class whites routinely did in Birmingham and elsewhere.[8] Even the youth of SNCC, who exercised great caution just to register African Americans to vote in rural Mississippi, used their freedom schools to combat poverty in small ways.

Mexican Americans, disproportionately rural, heavily concentrated in the Southwest, and far from the nation's political power, did not view their poverty quite the same way as their black counterparts. Yet Mexican Americans shared a similar, overarching goal on which much of their activism focused. Whether it was the American GI Forum or Mexican American Political Association, the Community Service Organization or one of the many other civil rights groups across the country, these organizations combated racial discrimination in order to seek greater economic opportunity for people of Mexican descent. This activism included not only fighting racial discrimination in the schools and other industries but also reducing language barriers to Spanish speakers and electing people of Mexican descent to public office. These actions also took the form of labor organizing, especially of landless farm workers through the California-based National Agricultural Workers Union, the Agricultural Workers Organizing Committee, and eventually the National Farm Workers Association. Many activists—Mexican American, black, and white, including Bert Corona, Pancho Medrano, Bayard Rustin, A. Philip Randolph, and Walter Reuther—sought closer ties between civil rights groups and labor unions in order to empower people economically. Rustin and Randolph, in particular, dreamed of a national civil rights–labor coalition—an objective that remained mostly elusive.

A brief exception, however, was the broad solidarity demonstrated in August 1963, when the demand for jobs and economic justice on a national scale culminated in the March on Washington for Jobs and Freedom. The event drew an impressive 250,000 people, and while mostly African American and white, there were a handful of Mexican Americans present—two years before any national civil rights organization had reached out formally to people of Mexican descent. The march gained momentum as a lobbying effort in favor of President Kennedy's relatively narrow civil rights legislation, and is remembered primarily for Martin Luther King Jr.'s "dream." But jobs and other solutions to black poverty loomed just as large that warm Wednesday in August. The march demonstrated how race and class were intertwined and could be the foundation of a broader civil rights coalition, black, white, and beyond. And within months, long before the civil rights bill passed, the government launched the official War on Poverty.

◆ ◆ ◆

The United States in 1960 was in many ways, as one book famously coined it, an "affluent society." But just as economist John Kenneth Galbraith had meant by this phrase, the triumphant postwar nation that flaunted an impressive private affluence also risked very little investment in the public sector and often hid substantial poverty. The rapid economic growth

African American children play amid crumbling houses in Barelas, an overwhelmingly poor community one mile south of Albuquerque's central business district. Largely Mexican American with some black residents, Barelas epitomized the deep poverty of the early 1960s. At 30 percent, New Mexico's poverty rate was the highest outside of the South; poverty figures for African Americans and Mexican Americans were well over 50 percent. (Albert W. Vogel Photograph Collection [000-005-0023], Center for Southwest Research, University Libraries, University of New Mexico)

of the 1940s and early 1950s had been followed by the "Eisenhower Blues" as the economy slipped into a series of wrenching recessions.[9] And the United States' "semiwelfare state"—reliant on more limited iterations of Social Security and Aid to Families with Dependent Children (AFDC, better known as welfare)—was the thinnest in the Western industrialized world, including the nations that lost World War II. As a result, tens of millions of Americans in 1960 lived in poverty. Estimates of poverty ranged widely and, as Michael Harrington pointed out, basic household income figures often did not reflect variations in region or family makeup and size. Some analyses, such as one conducted by the American Federation of Labor–Congress of Industrial Organizations (AFL-CIO), used the generous cutoff of $4,000 a year for an urban family of four to determine poverty; others such as Galbraith, Senator Paul Douglas of Illinois, and economist Leon Keyserling from President Truman's Council of Economic Advisors used lower thresholds, from $1,000 to $3,000 a year. But figures from the Census, Bureau of Labor Statistics, U.S. Commerce Department, and the Federal Reserve reinforced an emerging consensus that at least 40 million and perhaps as many as 60 million Americans—out of 180 million, or anywhere from 22 to 33 percent—lived in poverty.[10]

No matter how imprecise the definition might be, poverty disproportionately afflicted African Americans and Mexican Americans one hundred years after the end of slavery and the nineteenth-century conquest of the West. At least half of all blacks and one-third of people of Mexican descent lived in what was considered poverty in 1960—compared to roughly 19 percent of whites. And it affected rural and urban alike. For the rural poor, poverty might have meant a family of six or more living in a one- or two-room shack made of tar paper and other scraps with no windows or doors. The children of a sharecropping family in Mississippi would have been lucky to have shoes or to attend the local black school six months out of the year. Post–World War II mechanization of agriculture rapidly diminished the need for sharecropping. But those who stayed in agriculture faced arguably worse conditions as part of the nation's one million and growing army of migrant farm workers, whether they were black and Puerto Rican migrants working up and down the Atlantic seaboard or Mexican American workers who circulated through the Southwest and Midwest. Families such as the Blakeleys of Belle Glade, Florida, and the Barreras of McCullen, Texas—featured on national television and in Congress—routinely survived on less than $1,000 a year, while they lived in work camps with straw for beds and no indoor plumbing or screens. Water came from a hand pump, and the bathroom was a hole in the ground. And sustained schooling for migrant children was even less common than for sharecropping families.[11]

In contrast, the urban poor may have had more stable shelter, running water, even working appliances. But living in an impoverished community in Chicago or Los Angeles meant other forms of degradation instead. For instance, in the "second ghetto" of Chicago's West Side, black families lived in run-down two- and four-flat apartment buildings often infested with roaches and rats in neighborhoods rife with crowded and low-performing schools, few job opportunities, drug use, and petty street crime. Youth gangs became both attractive options for high school dropouts and favored targets for police brutality and harassment. More than 14 percent of African Americans on the West Side were unemployed, with many more underemployed. The average family income was just $2,800 a year—far more than their rural counterparts, but well below the national average, especially for expensive city living. Jobless rates in other cities were even higher; unemployment in south-central Los Angeles, or Watts, topped 30 percent. And in both cities, housing stock available to African Americans declined even as the black population continued to increase. The result was an ever-increasing density that magnified an already grinding poverty.[12]

Expert explanations for the persistence and size of poverty varied as much as the definitions of poverty did. While the age-old arguments about the Christian work ethic and self-help remained popular among conservative scholars and commentators, new theories also emerged. Some economists, both conservative and liberal, focused on the rise of automation in American industries, which they argued risked creating a permanent class of unemployed within a society of abundance. Calling the situation "paradoxical," economist Robert Theobald argued, "Because we still believe that the income levels of the vast majority of the population should depend on their ability to continue working, over 20 per cent of the American population is exiled from the abundant economy and this percentage will grow." Theobald became best known for advocating a guaranteed annual income, or a negative income tax, for "the maintenance of human dignity" of all Americans—a proposal embraced by welfare rights activists later in the decade.[13] Others acknowledged such structural deficiencies but also stressed a "culture of poverty." A concept introduced by anthropologist Oscar Lewis in his ethnographic studies of

Mexicans and Puerto Ricans, the culture of poverty suggested not simply economic deprivation but cultural deprivation, too, a "subculture of its own" or "a way of life . . . passed down from generation to generation along family lines." Most poor Americans did not suffer from such cultural deprivation, Lewis argued, but those who did struggled to "take full advantage of changing conditions or increased opportunities which may occur in their lifetime."[14] Conservatives and liberals alike soon would morph Lewis's theory into a way to blame the victims of poverty, but in the early 1960s the concept remained potentially radical in that one method to harness the culture was to organize the poor themselves.[15] In 1962 Harrington popularized this behavioral consideration of poverty with empathy, not condemnation—an approach that received the attention of policy makers in Washington.[16]

While acknowledging that the factors that led to the War on Poverty were not entirely clear-cut, historians still try to explain it largely by giving credit to those "whiz kids" who went on to populate the Kennedy administration. Harrington's message shocked many liberals, even the president. "Kennedy had read it, and it impressed him," one of his aides recalled, adding that Kennedy also had been stunned by the poverty he discovered in rural West Virginia on the 1960 campaign trail.[17] Harrington's concern about the poor echoed what had been stated in more muted terms by economists Galbraith, Leon Keyserling, and Walter Heller, who chaired the administration's Council of Economic Advisors. Reflecting the generally ebullient view of the era's intelligentsia, Keyserling believed that through massive government spending "we can abolish poverty in America within ten years."[18] Lloyd Ohlin, a professor of social work at Columbia University, also joined the administration for a year to direct its Office of Juvenile Delinquency. In his studies on delinquency with Columbia colleague Richard Cloward, Ohlin argued that the lack of opportunity for youth living in urban slums produced such behavior. "To eliminate delinquency," wrote Ohlin and Cloward, requires "the reorganization of slum communities"—an approach they tried in New York's Lower East Side through a demonstration project called Mobilization for Youth (MFY).[19] Initially focused on basic education and job training programs, MFY leaders by mid-1963 had determined that they had made little overall difference in the lives of the poor and switched the agency's emphasis to organizing them to enact institutional change. The reorganization produced several tenant and welfare unions, which then led to rent strikes and other actions against welfare offices in 1964 and 1965. Despite mixed results, such reorganization of the poor became the basis of the War on Poverty's community action programs.[20]

Both domestic and international politics, including the black freedom struggle in the North, played a central role in the administration's pursuit of antipoverty programming in 1963. Designed to pair with a tax cut that would benefit middle- and upper-income Americans the most, initial antipoverty work prioritized conditions in Appalachia and other rural pockets of economic desperation in order for the white poor to "have something to cheer about on election day."[21] But the politics of the movement also forced itself into policy makers' thinking. Time and again, grass-roots protesters had forced the Kennedy administration into reluctant action in 1961 and 1962, whether it was protecting the Freedom Riders and enforcing the desegregation of interstate transportation in the Deep South or persuading state officials to protect James Meredith's entry into the University of Mississippi. President Kennedy and his brother, Attorney General Robert Kennedy, were anxious not to have the southern movement constantly place them in political peril with their white supremacist congressional allies from the South—or create a situation that would risk a new round of Soviet propaganda using the U.S. treatment of blacks to embarrass the nation. But the Kennedys slowly grasped that ignoring civil rights simply was not possible. And if they needed a reminder that the movement must be considered in the administration's political calculus, Martin Luther King Jr.'s campaign in Birmingham, Alabama, in the spring of 1963 ratcheted up the level of African American protest against discrimination and poverty not just in the South but across the nation.[22]

◆ ◆ ◆

Economic justice had been central to the modern black freedom struggle since its emergence in the 1930s and 1940s. Whether it was tobacco workers in North Carolina, packinghouse workers in Chicago, or members of the Civil Rights Congress in California, African Americans routinely connected the fight against Jim Crow segregation with the economic barriers they faced. Labor organizations played up this "civil rights unionism," but so did more traditional civil rights organizations. Activists in the National Association for the Advancement of Colored People (NAACP) in California, for instance, championed fair employment practices commissions to combat racial discrimination by employers and more conservative unions. The NAACP's legal wing, the Legal and Educational Defense Fund, viewed courtroom strategies to expand voting rights and quality education as essential to the widening of economic opportunity. In the West, such efforts also created limited space for cooperation between blacks and Mexican Americans.[23]

But the rise of the Cold War and a virulent domestic anticommunist movement in the late 1940s and early 1950s forced organizations to recalibrate their calls for economic reform or anything their opponents might call pro-Soviet socialism. Otherwise, they risked destruction. As a result, anticommunist red-baiting, coupled with a resurgent white supremacy, gutted many left-leaning unions and groups such as the Civil Rights Congress, which had championed fair employment practices laws, opposed police brutality, and endorsed income redistribution programs. In contrast, those civil rights organizations that thrived in the 1950s, such as the NAACP, Urban League, and Martin Luther King Jr.'s SCLC, carefully framed civil rights in practical, constitutional, and religious ways and avoided the language of economic justice. They emphasized school desegregation, the integration of other public accommodations, and the end of race-based disenfranchisement, primarily on the basis of notions of citizenship and the equal protection clause of the Fourteenth Amendment—and, in the case of SCLC, Christian morality. While nothing short of revolutionary in many ways, this narrower focus on the South's racial caste system nonetheless left discrimination elsewhere to fester. Of course, there were exceptions. In what one scholar calls a "movement without marches," African American women in Philadelphia, and presumably other northern cities, led individualized fights for greater welfare benefits and better housing and against police brutality and job discrimination.[24] Some local chapters of the NAACP, such as Robert Williams's organization in Monroe, North Carolina, did not lose sight of economics. And a few of the nation's most prominent unions—the United Auto Workers and the United Packinghouse Workers of America, to name two—continued to connect civil rights with class. Yet even they tended to focus on narrower workplace issues in the interest of protecting earlier gains in jobs and benefits.[25]

Largely isolated politically and geographically in the Southwest and California, Mexican Americans pursued their own grievances around civil rights and poverty—but they could relate to African Americans' experience during the early Cold War. Much like their black counterparts, Mexican Americans also actively viewed economic justice as essential to their civil rights since the 1930s. Whether it was the radical labor organizers of El Congreso del Pueblo de Habla Español and Asociación Nacional México Americana (ANMA) or the more middle-class founders of the Community Service Organization (CSO), Mexican Americans fought poverty in myriad ways. Performing their own version of civil rights unionism, both El Congreso and ANMA unapologetically criticized police brutality, housing discrimination, deportation raids, media stereotyping, and even U.S. foreign policy in Latin America. The state's treatment of citizens and immigrants of Mexican descent alike was central to their agenda, as the deportations of more than 400,000 people during the mid-1930s, many of them citizens, remained a stark memory among Mexican Americans. But El Congreso and ANMA also partnered with African Americans in the Civil Rights Congress and the NAACP to fight for permanent fair employment practices commissions in California and Colorado, with ANMA's Virginia Ruiz declaring, "The only way to win this fight is to have the closest unity with our strongest ally, the Negro people."[26] Mexican Americans and African Americans also teamed up to fight police brutality, in the wake of the zoot suit riots and the Sleepy Lagoon incident in Los Angeles in 1942–43. Such partnerships proved fleeting, however, as domestic anticommunism took its toll on left-leaning organizations such as ANMA and its union sponsor, the International Union of Mine, Mill, and Smelter Workers.[27]

As a result of the Cold War, Mexican American organizing in the 1950s and early 1960s looked more and more like the activism of the Texas-based League of Latin American Citizens (LULAC). Founded in 1929, LULAC was the nation's most prominent Mexican American civil rights group but had gained a reputation for conservatism through its emphasis on citizenship, whiteness, and patriotism. LULAC's support for strict immigration curbs, in particular, set the tone for the American Federation of Labor's National Farm Labor Union (NFLU), as well as the Community Service Organization and the American GI Forum (AGIF). With its history rooted in the radical politics of the Depression-era Southern Tenant Farmers Union and in organizing some of the poorest, hardest-to-reach workers, the NFLU held great potential for bucking the decade's conservative trend. But while agricultural workers gamely attempted to stop production multiple times, growers effectively counteracted such maneuvers, using a mix of publicity, political influence, and the federal *bracero* guest worker program to break each strike. The bracero program, designed to provide farm labor during wartime shortages, had become a devastating tool to depress wages and undermine collective bargaining as growers simply brought in more braceros and undocumented workers to resume production. Thus, even the NFLU remained silent when the federal government launched Operation Wetback, an oppressive deportation campaign that ensnared more than one million Mexican Americans in 1954 alone. The NFLU never gained sufficient traction and was replaced by the Agricultural Workers Organizing Committee in 1960.[28]

Called "the most important civil rights organization of its kind in the West," the CSO was known for compassionate and effective aid for migrant workers, including undocumented immigrants.[29] Yet, to avoid charges of communism, its leaders often echoed LULAC's rhetoric of citizenship. Founded as a political organization to elect future congressman Edward Roybal as Los Angeles' first Mexican American councilman in the twentieth century, the CSO evolved into a voter registration powerhouse and clearinghouse for migrant services with more than twenty chapters across the Southwest. Invigorated by Saul Alinsky protégé Fred Ross and the funding and precepts of the Chicago-based Industrial Areas Foundation, the CSO went to extraordinary lengths to seek and incorporate grass-roots input in its work. In 1952 Ross discovered a young Cesar Chavez, who after some reluctance became a key organizer. If CSO activists demonstrated a unique devotion to grass-roots relationship building through tools such as house meetings, however, their radical approach rarely translated into equally bold rhetoric or public positions. Rather, throughout the 1950s, the CSO became increasingly narrow in its interests and efforts, offering services such as credit unions more than political empowerment to its constituency and prompting Chavez's departure in 1962.[30]

By the early 1960s, this tepid approach to economic justice began to give way among both Mexican Americans and blacks. They felt emboldened by their frustration with the slow movement of desegregation, the presence of young sympathetic liberals in the White House, and the product of years of incremental but important grass-roots activism. Media coverage of the southern black freedom struggle stressed sit-ins at lunch counters and interstate bus stations—eye-catching and powerful demonstrations against the racial caste system of the South. But activist groups, especially in the North and West, sought much more.

Two of those organizations started to assert antipoverty rhetoric alongside their support for Mexican American civil rights: the Texas-based AGIF and the California-based Mexican American Political Association

(MAPA). Founded by college-educated immigrant, medical doctor, and military veteran Hector P. García in 1948, the AGIF blended a patriotic advocacy for Mexican American military veterans with broader support for jobs and justice. Unlike LULAC, the AGIF had a sizable working-class membership and orientation, which led to a sharper critique of racial discrimination and the lack of quality jobs than the elite LULAC usually could muster. In the late 1950s and early 1960s, the AGIF routinely challenged the segregation of Mexican Americans into poorly equipped schools, the "daily belittlement of Latin" workers and customers in the post office, and the denial of open housing and access to job training in local industrial plants that held government contracts. The AGIF in New Mexico supported grievance procedures for Mexican American sanitation workers, while other chapters provided training grounds and opportunities for future movement leaders, including Corky Gonzales, Francisco "Pancho" Medrano, and San Antonio's Albert Peña Jr. After his old Texas ally Lyndon Johnson entered the White House, García became an enthusiastic proponent of the War on Poverty.[31]

MAPA, founded in 1959 by a cadre of Mexican American leaders including Edward Roybal and veteran labor organizer Bert Corona, took a similar stance to racial discrimination. Explicitly formed to strengthen Mexican American political opportunities in California, MAPA's primarily middle-class professionals strongly opposed Mexican American poverty by challenging workplace discrimination, police brutality, and educational inequality. MAPA tackled job discrimination in a variety of sectors, including the military establishment, auto repair shops, car dealerships, and the California state college system. Mexican Americans, incredibly, could not even secure jobs teaching Spanish regularly. MAPA backed strikes by the multiracial Local 26 of the International Longshoremen's and Warehousemen's Union, which Corona had organized. MAPA also addressed "poor schooling in the Oakland public schools, better housing in the predominantly Latino Mission District, as well as opposing police brutality in that area."[32] And in a series of small California towns, MAPA won the early release of several youths of Mexican descent who had not had proper criminal defenses.[33]

Yet even when issues of interest overlapped, Mexican Americans continued to view the black freedom struggle in the South remotely and pursued their issues in relative obscurity from a national press and federal government on which they had little influence—at least compared to African Americans. Both the AGIF and MAPA proved reluctant to work with African Americans. Respect for the Spanish language and Mexican culture often distinguished Mexican American education claims, as did the kinds of jobs Mexican Americans pursued, such as foreign language instruction and auto repair. And the ideology of "nonblackness" always loomed large. Bert Corona tried to broach the topic within MAPA at a 1960 convention. Corona had deep labor roots in the Popular Front politics of the 1930s as an organizer for longshoremen and a founder, along with Guatemala native Luisa Moreno, of the labor-influenced El Congreso in Los Angeles. These experiences helped make him more open to multi-racial collaboration a generation later. "This generated much discussion," recalled Corona. "Although some delegates were willing to use the term 'Mexican,' they were not prepared to come out front and state that we considered ourselves nonwhite."[34] Two years later, MAPA delegates re-considered as the influence of black protest spread—and won tangible results in California—and decided to make multiracial cooperation orga-nizational policy. Yet MAPA's number one priority remained the election of Mexican Americans and the "betterment of Mexican Americans and all other Spanish-speaking people."[35] For instance, in 1964 MAPA opposed Proposition 14, which was designed to repeal California's landmark open housing law. But Mexican Americans proved unenthusiastic in defending a law they saw as addressing "largely a Negro problem," according to a state advisory committee to the U.S. Commission on Civil Rights. "While there may be a problem for members of these two groups, there is a far greater degree of housing mobility for Orientals and Mexican-Americans in California than exists for Negroes," the committee had concluded in 1961.[36]

In contrast, the AGIF completely avoided collaboration. Hector García not only had advocated the legal strategy of whiteness common in the 1950s but also insisted on his own white identity into the 1970s, even after the Chicano movement popularized brownness. Moreover, García care-fully distinguished AGIF activities by calling it a "charitable" organization rather than a "civil rights" organization. "Personally," he wrote, "I hate the word." Embracing a politics of respectability and citizenship, AGIF delegates routinely opposed such civil disobedience tactics made popular by the black freedom struggle. One exception was a resolution commend-ing the 1960 sit-ins in the Deep South. But in the tumultuous years that followed, the AGIF neither repeated the gesture nor reached out to black civil rights leaders, even those in Texas. Therefore, while the AGIF fought poverty among Mexican Americans around the edges, it drew the line at working with its African American counterparts in the early part of the decade.[37]

Together or apart, civil rights activists by 1963 increasingly drew explicit links between the fight against racial segregation and the presence of economic barriers. Writing in a newspaper column on the eve of the Birmingham campaign in 1963, Martin Luther King Jr. connected the two, arguing that politics "is the key that opens the door of economic opportunity. We must never overlook that the Negro has suffered as much from political and economic exploitation as he has from the more obvious forms of segregation."[38] Others across the country agreed. One of the many practical goals of the movement's citizenship or freedom schools conducted by SNCC, SCLC, and the Highlander Folk School in the early 1960s was to connect learning to political action around economic rights. "We need to think about taxes, social welfare programs, labor management relations, schools and old age pensions," wrote activist Septima Clark in 1963.[39] SCLC had targeted the city nicknamed "Bombingham" because of its history of racial violence, a dynamic local movement led by the Reverend Fred Shuttlesworth's Alabama Christian Movement for Human Rights, and the presence of a perfect villain in arch-segregationist police commissioner Eugene "Bull" Connor. With remarkable success, SCLC famously juxtaposed nonviolent children's marches with Connor's men wielding fire hoses and snarling police dogs to maximum effect. This "good-versus-evil" stagecraft—while damaging to public understanding of the moment's complexity—produced an outpouring of national support for the civil rights demonstrators and helped produce a climate in which President Kennedy felt compelled to unveil civil rights legislation that eventually became the far-reaching Civil Rights Act of 1964. Hundreds of demonstrations occurred in sympathy and solidarity with the Birmingham demonstrators—with a total of 1,412 protests across the country that summer, according to the Justice Department.[40]

While many of these demonstrations explicitly targeted segregation of public accommodations, such as sympathy pickets outside Woolworth's and Kress, most of the rallies and protests focused on a broader range of issues that fueled black poverty, mainly workplace discrimination, educational inequality, and police brutality. One epicenter was Philadelphia, where wrenching black poverty had prompted a variety of actions by African Americans. One harkened back to the long black tradition of "don't buy where you can't work" campaigns in the North in the early twentieth century. In 1959 the Reverend Leon Sullivan and the organization 400 Ministers started a "selective patronage" operation. In three years, Sullivan claimed that the boycotts of businesses that did not hire or promote African Americans—boycotts routinely led by women—had created two thousand "breakthrough" jobs and influenced the hiring practices of another three hundred companies. Black women in the city also had waged more singular fights against racial discrimination in welfare, housing, schools, and health care. But in 1963, these protests became far more public and organized as black protesters challenged the city's segregated municipal construction projects through a series of regularly scheduled, high-profile demonstrations at the mayor's home, City Hall, the Liberty Bell, and building sites throughout the city, including a partially built school in a black North Philadelphia neighborhood. Led by the brash criminal defense attorney Cecil Moore, who had run an insurgent candidacy to become president of the local NAACP, the demonstrators all but discarded the rhetoric of nonviolence in taking on black poverty. "You gotta use a little demagoguery now and then," Moore explained. Whites "have all the money, all the jobs, and all the houses."[41] Moore was able to blend nonviolent civil rights protest with the more nationalist rhetoric of Malcolm X to wring concessions out of building contractors and the city. Philadelphia activists then turned to other issues and targets but always with attacking black poverty in mind.[42]

Similar rhetoric to Cecil Moore's could be heard in Chicago, Detroit, Harlem, and elsewhere, as African Americans pushed for government action to combat economic inequality in more than 150 cities. In Chicago, disorders arose from conditions in Birmingham and at home. In mid-May, thousands of African Americans took to the streets and threw rocks at police after a false rumor that officers had shot two young boys. Even Mayor Richard J. Daley's nephew was beaten up and told that, "This is for Birmingham, Alabama."[43] A rising movement also had developed to protest educational inequality in the Windy City, symbolized by the double shifts and classroom trailers used in predominantly black schools while white facilities sat half-empty. Some 900 demonstrators protested a commencement address by the Chicago school board's most prominent black member, Mrs. Wendell Green, and called her a fraud. "We can no longer allow false representation of Negroes to go unchallenged," stated protest leader Charles H. Jones Jr. of Chicago's Friends of SNCC chapter. "She has no psychological or emotional identity with the Negro community."[44] More than 150,000 people marched in support of better jobs and against police brutality in Detroit in late June, in what was called a "dress rehearsal" for the March on Washington in August. And in Harlem, a coalition of blacks and Puerto Ricans shut down a hospital construction site because only nine of sixty-four workers were minority despite the project being in a black community.[45]

At the same time, left-leaning labor unions fought their own war on poverty, and in a nominally multiracial way. In the early 1960s, the United Auto Workers (UAW), United Packinghouse Workers of America (UPWA), and the Drug and Hospital Workers Union Local 1199 in New York City, in particular, unevenly blended claims to civil rights with their own efforts at higher wages and job security. The UAW and UPWA had helped bankroll civil rights activities in the South, from the taxi service that sustained the Montgomery bus boycott in 1955–56 to the Prayer Pilgrimage for Freedom the following year. In 1963, under pressure by Attorney General Robert Kennedy to bring the Birmingham conflagration to an end, the unions provided bail money for jailed protesters in Birmingham. At the same time, the UPWA and UAW represented hundreds of thousands of workers—white, black, and Mexican American—in negotiation with their industries. Thus, they were a natural place to combine issues of human rights with those of labor rights. As one prominent Mexican American historian reminds readers, "Labor rights are civil rights."[46]

These unions, however, were less likely to challenge discrimination in their own back yards, in the industries, or within the organizations themselves. Although the UAW's Walter Reuther and the UPWA's Ralph Helstein routinely supported civil rights from afar, there were few minorities in union leadership beyond presidents of locals. Blacks and Mexican Americans also received little UAW support to break discriminatory hiring practices for production line jobs. Hank Lacayo became president of the UAW's majority-minority Local 887 in California in 1962, while veteran Texas labor activist Francisco "Pancho" Medrano became an "at-large organizer" for the UAW in 1963. African Americans such as Local 600's Horace Sheffield had risen in the ranks as well, but none to the union's executive board, which prompted several black activists' founding of the Trade Union Leadership Council (TULC) in 1957 to "demand Black entrance into the skilled trades and into the leadership of the UAW."[47] Even Local 1199, whose strike of seven New York City area hospitals Martin Luther King Jr. championed in 1959, had an overwhelmingly white male leadership cadre representing predominantly female black and Puerto Rican workers. The gap between leadership and rank and file, in image and substance, racially and otherwise, proved a stumbling block to more national and comprehensive efforts at fighting poverty. What limited multiracial efforts did occur locally proved to be rare.[48]

This also began to change in 1963. Under pressure by TULC activists, Walter Reuther started to take a firmer stance on racial discrimination in Detroit as well—increasingly tying it to his longtime concerns about automation's impact on industrial jobs. Automation and recession had destroyed 140,000 jobs in the auto industry alone between 1947 and 1963. Even larger changes had occurred in the rail, mining, and meatpacking industries. Reuther also could be found walking side by side with Martin Luther King Jr. at the head of a huge freedom rally on June 23 that Detroit activists called the "Great March," perhaps best known for King's first delivery of the "I Have a Dream" speech. The prominence of Reuther and white liberal Mayor Jerome Cavanaugh, in fact, had been opposed by many of the march's black organizers, including ministers Albert Cleage and C. L. Franklin, both of whom were skeptical of liberal whites' genuine commitment to black equality. They backed down only when the Detroit NAACP threatened to withhold its support, but they maintained a sharp economic message pointed toward whites; in his speech, Cleage called for a boycott of white-owned city supermarkets. The freedom rally that day with 150,000 people—90 percent of them black—turned out to be the largest such march to date in the United States. Such stepped-up public support of a broad civil rights agenda that included economics—now embraced by a leading labor leader such as Reuther—was not lost on the Kennedys, who viewed the UAW president as a key ally in a tough upcoming reelection battle. "There was no organization in the United States," said Robert Kennedy in 1964, "with whom the President was more closely associated and identified than the UAW." The pressure to act on poverty, in the broadest sense of the word, had become that much greater.[49]

Overall, the explosion of protests in the spring and summer of 1963, including the Detroit march, caught federal officials off guard. Attempts to address the media-dubbed "Negro revolt" through public service announcements, meetings with black elites such as entertainer Lena Horne and psychologist Kenneth Clark, and even executive orders prohibiting discrimination in construction projects contracted by the federal government had little effect on the anger and frustration in the streets. That only intensified with the assassination of civil rights hero Medgar Evers in Jackson, Mississippi. That same night, on June 11, Kennedy called for a new civil rights bill in response to the violence not only in Birmingham but also in the North and West. "The fires of frustration and discord are burning in every city, North and South, where legal remedies are not at hand," stated Kennedy. "Redress is sought in the streets, in demonstrations, parades, and protests which create tensions and threaten violence and threaten lives."[50] But when revealed later that month, the legislation emphasized the desegregation of public accommodations, important to the southern struggle but of less consequence to northern and western blacks, not to mention Mexican Americans outside of Jim Crow Texas. The president had downplayed jobs, voting rights, and other issues. Protests continued and plans for a grand march on Washington moved forward, with the Kennedy civil rights bill becoming a primary focus.[51]

For those working on the federal antipoverty program, as well as those projects after which it would be modeled, the economic roots of black protest held implications on whatever would be proposed. In New York City, staff with Mobilization for Youth determined that residents' grievances with housing and the welfare system reflected the same anxiety and anger over jobs and poverty that produced the construction site and tenant union protests in Harlem and Brooklyn that summer. The so-called Negro revolt also seemed to resonate with those putting together the North Carolina Fund, a statewide antipoverty program that federal bureaucrats used to shape the Economic Opportunity Act of 1964. "This cycle of poverty is found in white and Negro neighborhoods alike, but it has affected a far greater proportion of the Negro population than the white," stated a fund proposal to the Ford Foundation that summer. "At the same time as the Negro is demanding better opportunities in education and employment, he is finding that he faces severe cultural and educational handicaps that prevent his seizing those opportunities."[52] While the fund's staff persistently avoided color-coding the program's work, executive director George Esser read not just a steady diet of materials by white scholars on dry approaches to end poverty but also more assertive grass-roots economic arguments by Martin Luther King Jr. and Saul Alinsky. The protests of the moment and the fight against poverty were linked inextricably.[53]

◆ ◆ ◆

On a national level, the summer's protests culminated with the March on Washington for Jobs and Freedom, in which African Americans, whites, and a small number of Mexican Americans made their demands for justice heard. A. Philip Randolph, head of the virtually all-black Brotherhood of Sleeping Car Porters, had dreamed of such a march since

Months before President Lyndon Johnson declares the War on Poverty, civil rights demonstrators at the 1963 March on Washington for Jobs and Freedom stress issues of economic justice as much as voting rights and the end of segregation. The march, however, has been remembered mostly for King's "I Have a Dream" speech. (Walter P. Reuther Library, Wayne State University)

1941, when he first threatened President Roosevelt with the spectacle of thousands of black men descending on the nation's capital in protest of racial discrimination in the defense industry. Determined to avoid such a wartime embarrassment, Roosevelt established the federal Fair Employment Practices Commission to look into and adjudicate claims of racism. Although the agency had little enforcement power, its establishment still represented a triumph for Randolph. But he still wanted a march, especially as it became clear that the long postwar boom did not benefit African Americans equally. In May 1957, on the third anniversary of the *Brown v. Board of Education* decision, Randolph helped preside over and organize the Prayer Pilgrimage for Freedom, a rally that attracted approximately twenty thousand people to the Lincoln Memorial. The rally's culminating speech, "Give Us the Ballot," helped solidify Martin Luther King Jr., fresh off the Montgomery boycott and founding of SCLC, as a national civil rights leader. Despite such success, the rally did not address what was of utmost concern to Randolph: jobs and economic justice for African Americans. He waited another six years to fulfill that dream.[54]

A new national black freedom rally in Washington—one that went beyond the confines of de jure Jim Crow in the South—was born out of the trade union activism of which A. Philip Randolph had long been a part. Labor activists had talked of holding such a rally outside the AFL-CIO's national headquarters for a year, but the idea to launch a broad protest on the National Mall came out of a conversation Randolph had with Bayard Rustin in late 1962. A onetime peace activist and civil rights confidant of Martin Luther King Jr., Rustin had a long but rocky friendship with Randolph, whom Rustin viewed as a mentor. While visiting, the two men agreed that the freedom struggle would benefit from a march on the nation's capital. They slowly began to build support for a march through Randolph's Negro American Labor Council, but their efforts gained momentum only after the events in Birmingham, Philadelphia, and elsewhere, and Kennedy's civil rights speech in response. King, who initially had shown tepid support for a national mobilization on Washington, suddenly saw a mass march as "the greatest weapon" to capitalize on Birmingham.[55] By late June, what were considered the nation's six major civil rights organizations were on board with a new March on Washington that combined the demands of the southern and northern freedom struggles—freedom from segregation and poverty.[56]

Congress, the Kennedy administration, and the mainstream white press responded with alarm to the announcement of a new mass march of up to 100,000 people on Washington. They feared the prospect of violence and mass chaos, which then could be used to scuttle the civil rights bill. Before the 1960s, Washington's mall, memorials, and government buildings did not have today's reputation as the "people's space," where mass demonstrations are commonplace and expected. Rather, the mall was a space primarily for elites, to be protected from ordinary citizens making demands on the government, especially economic demands. The few times in which mass numbers of people marched on the capital—most notably the unemployed men of Coxey's Army in 1894 and the Bonus Expeditionary Force in 1932—the marchers had been greeted with disdain, arrests, even military force. Coxey's Army, which demanded investments in rural infrastructure and monetary reforms to end the depression of the mid-1890s, was only one thousand men. The Bonus Expeditionary Force of six thousand desperate World War I veterans called for early bonuses for their military service three years into the Great Depression.

In the original March on Washington movement, Randolph threatened a protest of thousands of black men in 1941. And even the Prayer Pilgrimage in 1957 was no more than twenty thousand people and just three hours long. That Randolph, Rustin, and other organizers called for five times that number for an all-day event seemed ambitious but also panicked official Washington, who believed that "criminal, fanatical, and communistic elements, as well as crackpots, will move in to take every advantage of this mob," as segregationist Senator Olin Johnston of South Carolina told Rustin.[57] Recalled Kennedy aide Burke Marshall: "The politicians in Washington . . . were scared to death of the march, just totally irrational. I don't know what they thought a march on Washington was going to be. I guess they thought people were going to march down Constitution Avenue throwing stones."[58] After it became clear that the organizers could not be dissuaded and the numbers could be even higher, the government planned for a massive police presence, curfew, and the closure of the federal government beyond essential workers. Officials prepared for a siege.[59]

In the months leading up to the march, organizers maintained a focus on economic justice, jobs, and poverty and made full use of their few labor allies. In a whirlwind of activity as the march's primary organizer, Bayard Rustin recruited thousands of workers, employed and unemployed, with the assistance of mostly left-leaning labor unions, such as the UAW and the UPWA, as well as the National Urban League. Although the nation's largest labor organization, the AFL-CIO, did not endorse the march, individual unions played a central role in transporting thousands of workers to Washington, by train, plane, and chartered bus, while marchers held preprinted placards paid for by the UAW. Union money also helped fund the sandwiches, portable toilets, and other amenities that day. Even organizers of Mobilization for Youth, Lloyd Ohlin's experimental project to combat poverty on the Lower East Side of Manhattan, reserved a train for local youth to go to Washington. Indicative of the march's tight organization, Rustin released two "Organizing Manuals" that laid out in painstaking detail the march's extensive objectives in economic justice. The second revised manual, released in August, included "a massive federal program to train and place all unemployed workers—Negro and white—on meaningful and dignified jobs at decent wages," "a national minimum wage act" of no less than $2 an hour, broadened fair labor and fair employment acts, and "desegregation of all school districts in 1963."[60]

Yet such objectives went largely unmentioned by the mainstream press, who framed the upcoming march in terms of the chance of violence. Throughout the summer, Randolph, union activist Cleveland Robinson, and others spent considerable time assuring reporters that the march would not turn into a frenzy. "There will be no violence in Washington. . . . There will be no lunatic fringe among us," Randolph said at one news conference, adding provocatively that the chance for "the powder keg" to go off among jobless youth would be much greater if the march did not move forward.[61] Despite such assurances, both editorials and news stories remained fixated on violence. "All of these precautions may prove unavailing," warned a *New York Times* editorial, "with results that could prove permanently hurtful to the civil rights movement."[62] Added the *Los Angeles Times*, "A sympathetic nation can only hope the Washington march won't be a step backward."[63] Even President Kennedy's public remarks in support of the march did not help, as he went on to compare the proposed march to the so-called civil rights violence in Cambridge, Maryland, and told demonstrators in no uncertain terms, "Avoid violence."[64]

While August 28, 1963, has been remembered as a surprisingly "orderly" rally of 250,000 people, a "picnic air," and soaring rhetoric about one man's dream, the issues of jobs, economic freedom, and poverty dominated the day's program often through "tough, even harsh language."[65] In the second-most famous speech that August afternoon, SNCC chairman John Lewis repeatedly connected the "starvation wages" that blacks earned as domestics and agricultural workers to larger notions of freedom and justice. "What is there in this bill to insure the equality of a maid who earns five dollars a week in the home of a family whose income is a hundred thousand dollars a year?" Lewis asked. Speaking also for agricultural workers, he claimed that "we have worked in the fields from sun-up to sun-down for twelve dollars a week. . . . The revolution is at hand, and we must free ourselves of the chains of political and economic slavery." Lewis's controversial speech almost was not delivered, because of its stated opposition to the bill and combative language—including allusions to the Union army's "March to the Sea" during the Civil War. That Lewis broached economic issues so boldly, even after being censored by the more moderate civil rights leaders around him, demonstrated how mainstream such a critique was among movement activists.[66]

Speakers from A. Philip Randolph to Roy Wilkins to Walter Reuther also offered a series of economic calls to action. "This civil rights revolution is not confined to civil rights," Randolph said in the day's opening remarks. "We have no interest in a society in which 6,000,000 black and white people are unemployed, and millions more live in poverty." Class and race, he pointed out, were closely linked, as were the policies to address both kinds of discrimination. "Look for the enemies of Medicare, of higher minimum wages, of Social Security, of Federal aid to education," Randolph said, "and there you will find the enemy of the Negro." Wilkins, executive director of the NAACP and a reluctant march participant at first, employed uncharacteristically strong language. Calling the Kennedy bill "so moderate that if it is weakened or eliminated, the remainder will be little more than sugar water," Wilkins highlighted the need for jobs and the end to the physical abuse African Americans faced "all over this land" and the "incomprehensible" acceptance the government seemed to have for such brutality. Wilkins also echoed Randolph in calling for the kind of fair employment practices commission activists had sought in the 1940s. Fine-tuning his call for an interracial "coalition of conscience," Walter Reuther declared, "We will not solve education or housing or public accommodations as long as millions of American Negroes are treated as second-class economic citizens and denied jobs." And he repeated his call for urgency within a rapidly automating economy. But it remained unclear how many Americans outside sight of the Lincoln Memorial heard this message; of all the mainstream media's chronicles of the march, very little about poverty and economics made it into print.[67]

Missing from the official speeches were the voices of women—including those who helped make the march possible. March organizers allowed them on stage for Daisy Bates's brief pledge to support those black men "fighting for civil liberties" and for musical entertainment. Marian Anderson led the national anthem, while Mahalia Jackson, Odetta, and Josephine Baker, among others, offered musical selections between speeches. At most, they offered an innocuous sentence or two after singing. "You can't go wrong," declared Josephine Baker. "The world is behind you." Such sexual "tokenism" infuriated those female trade unionists, such as Maida Springer and Anna Arnold Hedgeman, who had worked so hard to make the march happen, as well as women activists like Dorothy Height of the National Council of Negro Women and attorney Pauli Murray, who argued that poverty particularly affected women amid the growing prevalence of single female-led households. As a result of their exclusion, the march's rhetoric around jobs and economic opportunity took on a male-centric hue. Welfare, for instance, received nary a mention.[68]

Less controversial or surprising was the absence of another set of voices—those of Mexican Americans. Concerted efforts to include people of Mexican descent in the larger freedom struggle were still a few years away. Mexican Americans did not have the relative historic clout in Washington that African Americans such as King, Randolph, Roy Wilkins, or the Urban League's Whitney Young could wield on occasion. And what became the most famous Mexican American organization, the National Farm Workers Association, had been founded only a year earlier and remained poor, small, and far from the eastern corridors of power, despite the efforts of its spokesman, Cesar Chavez. March materials did not list any Mexican American organizations, or Puerto Rican groups for that matter, despite interest in bringing a contingent of New York's "Spanish" workers to Washington. Yet at least some Mexican Americans made it there as part of a trade union or simply on their own. Pancho Medrano went as a UAW activist and the only Mexican American veteran of the Montgomery boycott. MAPA's Bert Corona could not attend but remembered other members going. A handful of activists in the American GI Forum, Community Service Organization, and Texas-based Political Association of Spanish-Speaking Organizations unofficially went as well. In contrast, LULAC drew up a resolution denouncing the March on Washington. Members were even more proud, according to some, that LULAC had zero representation in Washington that day. The last thing these Mexican Americans wanted was to be identified with African American civil disobedience methods and notions of justice.[69]

◆ ◆ ◆

The March on Washington for Jobs and Freedom may not have been the "Farce on Washington" that Malcolm X so derisively called it, but the one-day rally also did not have the demonstrable effect on the trajectory of the freedom struggle that American public memory insists upon. The march did not greatly alter the probability of the Kennedy civil rights bill's passage. Nor did it significantly impact other civil rights activities, in the South, North, and West that fall. Yes, the march became an iconic moment in American history because it surpassed everyone's expectations in its size, spirit, and rhetoric. And undoubtedly, King's dream speech represented a high water mark in the rhetoric of hope and helped establish his role as a statesman. But most importantly, the march symbolized where the movement stood in 1963. It illustrated the ever-increasing importance of poverty and economic justice to the freedom struggle. It suggested what great lengths it took to unify the message of African Americans and their liberal white allies—a task that had become more and more difficult as the movement struggled to address the grinding poverty and its by-products outside of the South. And it captured how fleeting the reprieve from violence—state and extralegal—really was. Just weeks later in Birmingham, the bombing of the Sixteenth Street Baptist Church by Klansmen killed four young girls and sparked a melee in which two more black youths were murdered.[70]

The violence continued in November. An assassin's bullet guaranteed that President Kennedy would not live to see his civil rights bill become law or a War on Poverty declared. Instead, newly sworn-in President Lyndon Johnson moved quickly to enact and expand upon his predecessor's programs. Those working on the poverty program, which Kennedy had requested of his aides only that spring, scrambled to put something coherent together. What emerged was a series of demonstration projects, based upon David Hackett's earlier delinquency program and the North Carolina Fund, in which a central component was the poor's empowerment to challenge entrenched power. Called a "community action program," this potentially radical approach became not only the most controversial aspect of the War on Poverty but also the part least understood by the new president or many of those who implemented the broad program. Nonetheless, just six weeks after Kennedy's assassination, on January 8, 1964, during the State of the Union address, Johnson unveiled the new initiative: "This administration today, here and now, declares unconditional war on poverty in America."[71]

In their own ways, both African Americans and Mexican Americans contributed to the president's bold new effort. Although these two distinct minority groups may have worked separately for the most part, both valued economic justice and opportunity, good jobs and wages, and dignified treatment in the workplace and welfare offices, and they saw these issues as inextricably linked to their larger pursuit of first-class citizenship. In the years to follow, the fight against poverty offered the greatest potential for new, more muscular coalitions among the nation's dispossessed, especially for African Americans and Mexican Americans. The other Americans, as Michael Harrington dubbed them, would continue to raise their voices—but this time in unison.

2 ◆ First Experiments

Soon after his union won a breakthrough contract in 1966, Cesar Chavez received a telegram from Martin Luther King Jr. lauding Chavez's victory through perseverance. "Our separate struggles are really one—a struggle for freedom, for dignity and for humanity," wrote King. "You and your valiant fellow workers have demonstrated your commitment to righting grievous wrongs forced upon exploited people. We are together with you in spirit and in determination that our dreams for a better tomorrow will be realized."[1] Chavez did not respond, perhaps because a contract with one grower, while important, simply represented just the first step for the United Farm Workers Organizing Committee (UFWOC). Much of the hard work lay ahead, requiring Chavez to stay focused on the fields of California and not risk any distractions that threatened the farm workers' strike and boycott—including an alliance with the nation's best-known civil rights leader.

Two years later, Chavez hinted at having a few regrets. In the summer of 1968, he lamented the fact that he and King never had the opportunity to sit down with each other. "I never met him," Chavez told activist Eleanor Eaton of the American Friends Service Committee (AFSC). "In fact, I have never met any of the top SCLC staff." Andrew Young, who led a small SCLC contingent during the four-hundred-mile Texas UFWOC march to Austin in September 1966, did not cross paths with Chavez there. Nor was King able to make a scheduled meeting with Chavez in March 1968 in preparation for the Poor People's Campaign; King canceled in order to address striking sanitation workers in Memphis. Eaton found this missed opportunity "extraordinary and tragic" given the two men's similar strategies and objectives. To Eaton, who knew both men, "There is no one . . . who best exemplifies the twin commitment to poor people and nonviolence for which Martin Luther King was fighting than Ceasar [sic]."[2] This does seem remarkable, considering popular comparisons that often portrayed Chavez as the "Dr. King" of Mexican Americans. Such a parallel was clumsy at times, considering the two men's dissimilar class backgrounds and personal organizing styles. Yet their use of nonviolent protest strategy, their strong Christian faith, and their role as heroes to African Americans and Mexican Americans convinced many people—even King's widow, Coretta Scott King.[3]

That Chavez and King never met—despite being so often mentioned in the same breath in the public memory—carries great symbolism. And this missed opportunity speaks to more than just the complexities King and Chavez faced as their movements' most revered leaders. It is also emblematic of the difficult balance black and brown activists attempted to strike between their own narrower movements and a broader coalition. While federal officials declared a War on Poverty and began to sketch out what that initiative might look like on the ground, both Mexican American and African American civil rights organizations continued to pursue their own ways of defining and addressing poverty. But that process also included considering what new allies might be needed to achieve long-term goals of economic justice and security. For the UFWOC, formed in 1962 as the National Farm Workers Association (NFWA), that meant reaching out to those more seasoned civil rights organizations willing to listen to and help the union pursue collective bargaining in the fields.

National civil rights groups responded to this call in several ways. At least initially, the NFWA found its most willing partners in SNCC and the Congress of Racial Equality (CORE), both of which threw their rhetorical and material support behind the farm workers' cause. But this backing proved deceptive. While African Americans in those organizations' home offices in Atlanta and Chicago signed off on such endorsements, it was mostly white activists in California who actually worked side by side with the farm workers. In what was a harbinger of the alliance's future, SNCC activist Marshall Ganz went to work full time for the NFWA, while SNCC itself pursued other agendas. Rather than develop a relationship that might lead to greater cooperation between Mexican American farm workers and black civil rights activists, as some had hoped, the NFWA, SNCC, and CORE increasingly viewed their trajectories as incompatible.

Martin Luther King Jr. also offered rhetorical support to the farm workers. But despite scholarly claims about King's alliance with unions, SCLC had a poor track record of aiding local union efforts.[4] The civil rights organization's response to the farm workers was no different, as SCLC did little else to support the NFWA's consumer boycotts of Schenley liquor products and, later, table grapes. Chicago offers a stark case study. Starting in 1965, King led a spirited fight against housing and job discrimination through the Chicago Freedom Movement and Operation Breadbasket and even attempted for the first time to reach out to Latinos in an organized way. NFWA-UFWOC organizers meanwhile managed to make Chicago one of the nation's most successful boycott cities, even targeting some of the same grocery stores that Breadbasket had. Yet overall, the union received very little help from civil rights organizations and instead tapped into predominantly white labor and faith circles to sustain the boycott.

In the spring of 1967, King abandoned a Chicago movement that had achieved far less than activists had hoped and increasingly turned his attention to U.S. war policy in Vietnam—a turn that altered the organization's ability to build ties with Mexican Americans. Culminating with a speech at the Riverside Church in New York City, King positioned himself as one of the war's highest-profile opponents and tied the war's end to a renewed effort against poverty. But while King's vocal opposition to the war certainly had roots in his belief in nonviolence, this position did not build a new bridge to Cesar Chavez, who opposed the war but did not make it central to his organizing. Instead, King's bold criticism of the war ironically positioned him to find common ground with the more radical voices of the emerging Chicano movement who incorporated opposition to the war into a larger critique of the U.S. system.

◆ ◆ ◆

In the mid-1960s a much tougher critique of American society had begun to emerge among people of Mexican descent, one that looked and sounded different from those offered by the AGIF, MAPA, or CSO. While these organizations certainly viewed poverty as a scourge in the nation's Mexican American communities, they tried to address the lack of economic opportunity through more incremental and traditionally political means. On the leading edge of this more biting critique were workers, particularly the men and women of the National Farm Workers Association, which developed a movement culture under the leadership of Cesar Chavez, Dolores Huerta, and others in the fields of central California. After years of quietly building their strength among the workers, the NFWA called its first strikes. In May 1965 it acted against rose growers and then in September in solidarity with its predominantly Filipino counterpart, the Agricultural Workers Organizing Committee (AWOC). Charging the growers with unsafe and unjust labor practices, the NFWA endorsed AWOC's goals of a written contract and a minimum wage of $1.40 an hour—a modest demand that the growers rejected, prompting the five-year Delano Grape Strike for which the union became famous.[5]

The NFWA—renamed UFWOC in 1966—was no ordinary union.[6] In many ways, what became known as La Causa was as much of a movement as it was a labor organization. Using nonviolent strategy from picketing to fasting, as well as promoting consumer boycotts of grapes, the NFWA developed a national following that made Chavez one of the best-known Mexican Americans in the United States. The struggle, and particularly its diminutive leader with his straight black hair and indigenous features, attracted people for a myriad of reasons. As a spiritual man, Chavez deftly used religious imagery from the Virgin of Guadalupe to pilgrimages to build bonds with his overwhelmingly Roman Catholic workers, as well as sympathetic communities of faith elsewhere—all while keeping a healthy distance from the church as an institution. As a labor leader, Chavez demonstrated a patient and steely grit while organizing people around work and the basic demands of their dignity and fair wages. And as a racial leader, Chavez embraced the language of civil rights and the analysis that race- and ethnic-based discrimination was an evil that must be overcome—to the point that the media viewed him as not just a spokesman for Chicanos but for blacks, Puerto Ricans, and Indians as well. Concluded one journalist, "To the saint-makers, Chavez seemed the perfect candidate."[7]

As recognizable as the farm worker struggle was, however, it was ironic how it became the symbol of the era's burgeoning Chicano movement. In many ways, neither the farm workers nor Chavez himself was as radical as the students whose imaginations were sparked by the struggle. While he viewed himself as a "truth teller" more than anything else, Chavez was a union leader interested in improving the economic power of hard-working but perpetually put-upon people. This became clearer as the Chicano moment began to fade, and Chavez worked to consolidate UFWOC's gains. "Effective political power is never going to come, particularly to minority groups, unless they have economic power," Chavez told one biographer. "And however poor they are, even the poor people can organize economic power."[8] Recruited by Saul Alinsky disciple Fred Ross in 1952, Chavez became an organizer with the CSO and spent most of the next ten years building relationships with Mexican Americans, including farm workers, in the San Joaquin Valley and making small but substantive changes in their lives, from voter registration to the establishment of credit unions. But when Chavez proposed organizing farm workers after he became national director in the late 1950s, leaders of the increasingly conservative, middle-class CSO balked. Increasingly disillusioned, Chavez eventually left the CSO in 1962 to organize those same workers.[9]

In many ways, such "slow and respectful" work among the people—work that viewed regular folks as a movement's most valuable source of ideas and energy—was actually quite radical, similar to SNCC's nonhierarchical democratic vision in the early 1960s in the South. But as a labor organizer, Chavez had never fully embraced the cultural nationalism that many of his Chicano followers and counterparts, such as Reies Tijerina and Corky Gonzales, espoused. Rather, he saw nationalist language and symbolism as both a way of motivating his followers and a means toward a more just society—one that treated the overwhelmingly Mexican American farm workers he represented with respect and dignity, as evidenced by a decent wage and humane working conditions. This helps explain Chavez's willingness to work with mainstream politicians such as Robert F. Kennedy—and the comparisons between Chavez and Martin Luther King Jr. Theirs was a shared devotion not only to nonviolent, Christian activism but also to what Chavez himself called a "culture of social justice."[10]

Yet it was the freedom struggle's predominantly student-based organizations, not King and SCLC, that most rapidly came to the farm workers' aid. In late 1964 and early 1965, SNCC and CORE initiated contact with the NFWA and soon became the first black civil rights organizations to endorse the farm workers' activities in California. Initially prompted by Bay Area SNCC members and sympathizers, the alliance emerged from a belief that the NFWA's cause was analogous to the struggle in the South. Recalled SNCC activist Terry Cannon: "The core of the connection [between SNCC and the NFWA] was the similarity in treatment of blacks in the South and Latinos in the West and Southwest."[11] That resemblance actually worried some people who advised Chavez. "People warned me, 'Look what happened to the Civil Rights Movement,'" Chavez recalled, referring to the risk of volunteers muddying the movement with their own "hidden agendas," such as opposition to the war in Vietnam. But, according to Chavez, the "cross-fertilization" was worth it: "If we were nothing but farm workers in the Union now, just Mexican farm workers, we'd only have about 30 percent of all the ideas that we have. . . . It's beautiful to work with other groups, other ideas, and other customs."[12]

And Chavez was right. By the middle of 1965 when the California Migrant Ministry assisted farm workers in a rent strike in Tulare County, SNCC began providing valuable support including nonviolence training. "They were very good at teaching nonviolent tactics" to staff people who did not "thoroughly understand the whole idea of nonviolence," recalled Chavez.[13] Volunteers also shared some radios and a car or two. Perhaps most importantly, the SNCC chapter produced valuable publicity through the *Movement* newspaper, which was distributed to progressive organizations across the nation. Such support increased in the fall after the NFWA joined AWOC in the first grape strikes. CORE also provided individuals and training in the strikes of 1965. But CORE's assistance quickly declined as it tackled new projects and witnessed substantial organizational upheaval, including longtime director James Farmer's departure, the move of its national office to Durham, North Carolina, and a reorientation toward black nationalism. These all made the farm workers' cause less relevant to CORE's central mission of empowering African Americans. In contrast, SNCC support of NFWA strikes and boycotts increased steadily into early 1966.[14]

The backing of both organizations was misleading, however, at least in its reflection of black-brown coalition building. With the exception of African American activists Hardy Frye and Dickie Flowers, whites facilitated SNCC's partnership with the NFWA. Mike Miller, Terry Cannon, George Ballis, and Marshall Ganz, all white, became SNCC's key liaisons to Chavez and the farm workers. CORE's two most prominent volunteers with the Tulare rent strike, Bob Sokolow and Bob Fisher, were also white. Even Flowers, who had been on SNCC's Greenwood, Mississippi, staff, went to California primarily to work with the small percentage of African Americans—mostly in Bakersfield in the southern end of the San Joaquin Valley—because many local blacks seemed opposed to the strike. In fact, the SNCC-NFWA partnership won the approval of African Americans in the national office in Atlanta well after the fact, in November 1965. Chavez went on to charm Stokely Carmichael, Ralph Featherstone, and Cleveland Sellers during their trip to California the following month— but it was Miller and Ganz who facilitated the meeting in the first place, made the pitch to the national office to support the NFWA, and, months before, committed the San Francisco chapter of SNCC to the cause. This decision even created some confusion initially when the national office in Atlanta denied any knowledge of the grape boycott in September and October.[15]

In the end, SNCC's expertise proved indispensable to the NFWA's early successes, while the farm workers' campaign simultaneously offered a sort of refuge for whites in a changing civil rights organization. From the famous 340-mile march from Delano to Sacramento to the national boycott of grower Schenley Industries, the mostly white SNCC volunteers helped the fledgling union operate on a national stage. Mike Miller and Jim Drake of the California Migrant Ministry coordinated the Schenley boycott with the help of SNCC offices across the country, while Marshall Ganz helped manage march logistics. Terry Cannon, editor of the *Movement*, became the campaign's press secretary—a vital role given the march's objective of generating publicity and sympathy. In April 1966 the campaign succeeded as Schenley agreed to the union's first contract. Yet SNCC's new partnership and support for the pilgrimage was set on a backdrop of increasing disillusionment among SNCC activists in the Deep South. From the betrayal by white liberals at the 1964 Democratic National Convention in Atlantic City, to growing internal tensions along gender, class, regional, and racial lines, SNCC found itself in the middle of an extended identity crisis—one that emerged in ways that especially confused those not based in the South. For Mike Miller, inconsistent and contradictory communication from Atlanta and Mississippi made his job increasingly difficult. "What the H is going on in Atlanta?" Miller wrote SNCC's national coordinator, Karen Whitman.[16] By the end of 1966, nearly all white members of SNCC had left, ushered out by a series of charged decisions in December. Ganz became a full-time employee of the farm workers union, as did Bob Sokolow of CORE, while Cannon continued to edit the *Movement*, which severed its ties from SNCC. Miller left town completely. But at a significant moment in the young union's existence, SNCC played an instrumental role in transforming the NFWA into a national cause.[17]

In contrast, King and SCLC demonstrated little interest in the farm workers in 1964 and 1965—and nearly all labor-based causes for that matter. King had earlier lent his support to striking black and Puerto Rican hospital workers in their battle to join Local 1199 of the Drug and Hospital Workers Union, which he later dubbed "my favorite union." In 1964 he backed a national boycott of Scripto pens in support of seven hundred striking black workers in Atlanta. "We must join the war against poverty and believe in the dignity of all work," he told workers, many of whom attended his home church of Ebenezer Baptist—a fact that may have explained his vigorous support for their cause.[18] Ironically, King's intervention in the Scripto strike actually undermined the process when he negotiated with the company's president without the knowledge of the union leaders or workers. But this did not stop two allies from hoping that King meant it when he said, in terms of his involvement in labor disputes, there "will be many more to follow."[19] After King's triumphant spring of 1965 championing voting rights in Selma, Cleveland Robinson of the Retail, Wholesale, and Department Store Union invited the civil rights leader to join an organizing drive of four thousand mostly black and Puerto Rican department store workers. L. D. Reddick, another confidant, pitched a more universal class-based vision, imploring King that African Americans must join "all the disadvantaged . . . the American Indian, the Puerto Rican, the Mexican and the Oriental" to address the nation's poverty.[20]

But King declined these invitations, and while he may have known about the grape strikers, he remained detached from their cause. This stemmed at least in part from his overall skepticism of organized labor, which, with a few key exceptions such as the Congress of Industrial Organizations (CIO) of the 1930s, had been historically indifferent if not hostile toward African American workers going back to the nineteenth century. More recently, AFL-CIO actions fueled his discomfort through its anticommunist aversion to fight racial injustice or deep-seated poverty in any genuine way. Despite the prominent role of the AFL-CIO's United Auto Workers and other unions, King focused on how the union federation refused to endorse the 1963 March on Washington for Jobs and Freedom, demonstrating how "organized labor, not only on the national level but frequently on the local level as well, is lacking today in statesmanship, vigor and modernity."[21] This fed King's unwillingness to become involved in grass-roots organizing drives and a belief that other organizations and means proved more effective. Highly conscious of the media's influential role in making the violence of Selma and Birmingham a national story, King hinted at a more tactical reason in a discussion with Stanley Levison. In response to another entreaty to become involved in a labor dispute, King argued that organizing southern laundry workers simply did not produce the kind of news coverage he and SCLC needed to push the national civil rights agenda forward. The same could have applied to the grape strike, which, early on at least, appeared little more than another desperate effort by farm laborers to receive better wages and conditions. The history of the South was full of failed attempts, the most recent being the short-lived Mississippi Freedom Labor Union in 1965. King declined to support that one as well. Of course, one consequence of rejecting labor unions as an organizing model or vanguard was a missed opportunity to work with Mexican Americans.[22]

Rather than pursue closer ties to labor through workplace-based events, King chose higher-profile ways to address economic justice. When Cleveland Robinson sought King's help in a union election at a Coca-Cola bottling plant in Selma, King was in southern California—but not in support of the farm workers. Rather, he went there in August 1965 to try and make sense of the Watts rebellion. Exploding just days after the signing of the Voting Rights Act, the rebellion demonstrated how the civil rights victories of the South had no tangible effect on already enfranchised African Americans in the North and West. Certainly aware of the violent potential of simmering anger in the nation's cities, King believed that Watts was mainly "an economic conflict between the haves and have-nots" and could be alleviated through greater funds, local control of the antipoverty board, and a civilian police review panel.[23] He also preached about the effectiveness of nonviolent strategy to a clearly skeptical audience, some of whom believed that fire had won the day. Indeed, Mexican Americans, most of whom steered clear of the rebellion despite some similar grievances, perceived a positive government response to the conflagration in the form of antipoverty programming for African Americans. MAPA chose not to weigh in on the violence, but other outraged Mexican Americans responded to the shooting deaths of three Mexican Americans during Watts by looking for new local organizations. One would become the Young Citizens for Community Action, the predecessor of the Brown Berets.[24]

For King, Watts strengthened his resolve to take his organization north to tackle the problems of a northern ghetto. After considerable deliberation and despite the protests of his aides who were leery of such a different context, King took on what the U.S. Commission on Civil Rights had called "the most residentially segregated city" in America: Chicago.[25] There, King's experience demonstrated not only the difficulty of combating racial discrimination outside of the South but his lack of preparation to do so—including the limited way in which he considered Mexican Americans and other Spanish-speaking people part of the larger struggle for freedom.

◆ ◆ ◆

King did not "bring the movement North," as is the stubbornly popular perception of the Chicago Freedom Movement (CFM).[26] Nor did he leave the city's freedom struggle in a permanent shambles, as many historians argue.[27] Instead, he came to Chicago at the invitation of the Coordinating Council of Community Organizations (CCCO), and built on the city's already energetic movement led by the CCCO, the United Packinghouse Workers, the Saul Alinsky–inspired Woodlawn Organization, and myriad other community groups. In the early 1960s, a fragile coalition of mostly blacks and whites, plus a few Mexican Americans and Puerto Ricans, had formed to challenge the power of Democratic Party machine boss and mayor Richard J. Daley, particularly the policies of Daley's school superintendent, Benjamin Willis. Few cities in the nation were more balkanized than the Chicago of the 1960s, where Daley's political machine deftly manipulated minority representatives to either fall in line with City Hall, accepting patronage perks along the way, or face swift political marginalization. Daley's police department, particularly the Subversive Unit, or Red Squad, also maintained political discipline through surveillance, infiltration, and intimidation. As a result, blacks on Chicago's South Side had sent African American Democrats to Congress and the city council since the 1930s, yet witnessed little substantive change in their subpar living conditions. The black- and Latino-dominated West Side was even worse. By the 1960s, Chicago's reputation as a promised land for African Americans had waned. But relative to the Deep South, the city still offered better opportunities for social, political, and economic mobility for blacks, who continued to migrate there in the hopes of something better.[28]

In 1961 frustration over persistently poor conditions in the city's black communities, especially its woefully crowded schools, boiled over. While many white students attended underutilized facilities, an ever-growing population of blacks and Latinos struggled to receive quality education in jam-packed schools using double shifts and portable classrooms dubbed "Willis wagons." Benjamin Willis and the city's board of education claimed that such measures were necessary and any disparities reflected de facto, or voluntary, residential segregation. Of course, African Americans knew that state-sanctioned discrimination in federal and local housing policy had helped create such segregation and that school board attendance policies perpetuated it. Chicago Urban League research reinforced this with one report in 1962 concluding that class sizes in predominantly African American schools were 25 percent bigger while per pupil expenditures were 33 percent lower than those for whites. In the summer of 1961, the local NAACP sued the school board over its discriminatory policies to deny transfers to black students. Less than a year later, both middle- and working-class African Americans staged sit-ins and other protests in South Side and West Side neighborhoods such as Vernon Park, Woodlawn, and North Lawndale. The CCCO emerged out of these demonstrations, as organizations ranging from the NAACP to local Parent-Teacher Associations and community groups such as the Woodlawn Organization sought to pool their resources and fight for quality education.[29]

Between 1961 and 1965, the Chicago movement became particularly vibrant as organizations across the city launched campaigns to improve living conditions for African Americans. Some called for opening more jobs to African Americans, fighting housing discrimination, and even challenging prejudice within Roman Catholic institutions. Students for a Democratic Society (SDS) made Chicago one of its target cities for the Economic Research and Action Project (ERAP), in which it aimed to organize poor whites, Puerto Ricans, and American Indians in the Uptown community "to protest the inadequacies of social and economic life which we face every day," from jobs and welfare to exorbitant rents and the lack of playgrounds.[30] And despite the decline of union influence as a result of deindustrialization and anticommunist politics, Chicago remained a stronghold for activist labor unions, particularly the United Packinghouse Workers and the United Steel Workers. But quality education remained the number one issue. In late 1963, Benjamin Willis resigned in a dispute with the school board over integration. White residents threatened to march themselves, and the board quickly rescinded Willis's resignation, prompting 225,000 students to boycott schools in October 1963 and another 175,000 in February 1964. During the next eighteen months, thousands of marchers led by the CCCO and former teacher Al Raby periodically tied up schools and downtown streets in an attempt to sway Daley and his allies to take their concerns seriously. When such protests continued to fall on deaf ears, Raby filed a formal complaint with the U.S. Office of Education, charging the school board with operating a segregated public school system. At stake was $32 million in federal funds.[31]

Chicago's version of the War on Poverty, also worth millions in federal dollars, emerged in 1965, and added fuel to an already roaring fire. A key component of the new Economic Opportunity Act was a clause calling for the "maximum feasible participation" of the poor in local community action programs' decision making and implementation. Personally, Daley believed the federally funded empowerment of the poor was crazy. "It would be like telling the fellow who cleans up to be the city editor of a newspaper," Daley said. In his frequent communications with a White House indebted to Illinois's most powerful Democrat, Daley gave President Johnson and his advisers an earful. "What in the hell are you people doing?" Johnson aide Bill Moyers recalled Daley as saying. "Does the President know he's putting money in the hands of subversives . . . money to bring him down?"[32] Such a program, Daley believed, even could be an existential threat to the Chicago machine itself. But the mayor did like the idea of millions more in federal spending coming into the city—as long as he and his allies could control it. As a result, Chicago's new antipoverty agency, the Chicago Committee on Urban Opportunity, had a seventy-five-member board chaired by Daley and stacked with machine loyalists, city bureaucrats, and other members of the mayor's coalition. A laughably low seven board members came from poor neighborhoods. For the agency's executive director, Daley chose Deton Brooks, a sociologist, former Cook County official, and black Daley loyalist. Brooks in turn named the politically connected directors of twelve neighborhood service centers, who then tapped local residents for advisory panels. While this provided a façade of participation by the poor, Daley insisted that everything be made by appointment, which ensured that the machine retained control of the program and funding.[33]

Neighborhood antipoverty activists cried foul. In what had become a pattern with antipoverty projects since at least the 1930s, local activists complained of being shut out of the process as political elites and machine partisans enriched themselves. Most critics also connected the antipoverty program's deficiencies to the unresponsiveness of school district and urban renewal officials. Chicago's antipoverty effort "is only more of the ancient, galling war against the poor," argued the Reverend Lynward Stevenson of the Woodlawn Organization, which had applied for funding for a variety of programs. One rejected program proposed developing local leadership in West Side neighborhoods; another to run a daycare center. "We want the federal law on maximum feasible local participation enforced in Chicago," Stevenson told members of Congress, adding that "grass roots organizations" are the best hope for the poor, not "men who drive Cadillacs, eat 3-inch steaks and sip champagne at luncheon meetings."[34] Others made similar arguments. Chester Robinson, director of the West Side Organization, grumbled about "dishonest local politicians" who "tie up programs meant for the poor." Added another spokesman for the group, "If a city doesn't operate the program to really help the poor—

but just to use them—(OEO director Sargent) Shriver should cut off the funds."[35] Several studies backed up critics' claims. Federal investigators determined that more than 70 percent of the city's antipoverty funds went to pay the salaries of bureaucrats, most of whom were connected to the machine. Moreover, more than a quarter of those students in Head Start, one of the signature antipoverty programs, came from families well over the legal income limit.[36]

Predictably, Daley defended his city's community action program (CAP). "Local government has responsibilities it should not give up," Daley contended. "What's wrong with a Democratic committeeman sending a capable man or woman when the test is on the person's qualification and not who sends him?"[37] Daley emerged as the spokesman for several other big-city mayors who had similar tightly controlled programs, such as Sam Yorty in Los Angeles and James Tate in Philadelphia. Office of Economic Opportunity director Sargent Shriver also came to Daley's defense. Once at odds with Daley's rather loose interpretation of maximum feasible participation, Shriver attended an antipoverty conference in Chicago hosted by Daley. Rumored to be interested in running for political office as a Democrat in Illinois and thus needing Daley's approval, Sargent Shriver hailed Chicago's program as "the model CAP in the country." He went on to point out the demonstrators protesting in the lobby outside as evidence that the program was somehow working. "As you can see today," Shriver said, "even our critics are given a platform to denounce, deplore and decry everything we have accomplished and are trying to accomplish."[38] Activists just shook their heads in disbelief.

◆ ◆ ◆

By July 1965, Martin Luther King Jr. had homed in on Chicago for a variety of reasons. Despite the community's prolonged, enthusiastic response to inequalities, activist momentum had begun to wane. Black comedian Dick Gregory had been leading marches several times a week—to the point of saturation—and many in the CCCO, including Al Raby, believed that the Chicago movement desperately needed an adrenaline shot of some kind. There already was an existing movement apparatus, and despite a lengthy negotiation about how the SCLC-CCCO partnership would work, no other city's local people were as excited about an SCLC campaign. "The Southern Christian Leadership Conference," Raby declared, "will always be welcome here in Chicago."[39] King, according to some observers, also believed that Daley's mythical control over Chicago made the preacher's task easier—convince the mayor to embrace nondiscrimination, institute it through the machine, and civil rights forces would win. Besides, as Bernard Lafayette recalled, "something like forty-two percent of the blacks in Chicago were either first or second generation from Mississippi . . . so there was a good deal of appreciation for what we were doing."[40] Certainly they would support a nonviolent campaign in their adopted city to prevent another Watts. "Chicago is a symbol of de facto segregation," King declared during an initial visit. "I feel there is a very critical situation here that could grow more serious and ominous unless the city's leaders are eternally vigilant."[41]

As it turned out, that risk was quite real, as Chicago saw its share of uprisings during the next several summers, the largest coming after King's assassination in 1968. But, as many of King's allies feared, the city's potential to embrace nonviolent strategy was not as real as even Birmingham and Selma. Bayard Rustin, in particular, was blunt. "You're going to get wiped out," he told King.[42] Whether or not SCLC intervention only prolonged the slow collapse of the CCCO as a viable organization and the city's freedom struggle in general, King underestimated the level of prejudice held by working-class whites in the North, as well as the wiliness of Richard Daley and the strength of his political machine. Other scholars have offered exhaustive detail about the Chicago Freedom Movement— ranging from Daley's political cunning to the remarkable level of white violence toward black marchers, violence that included King being struck by a rock in suburban Gage Park.[43] But it remains important to note that, at each step, King and his aides seemed taken aback by the sheer intensity of white ethnic hostility to calls for open housing. "I have never in my life seen such hate," King said, perhaps with some hyperbole. "Not in Mississippi or Alabama."[44]

They were also surprised by the sophistication of the Daley machine in mobilizing black hostility to King's presence and by local activists' ferocious accusations of being a "sellout" at the eventual settlement King and CFM negotiators made with Daley and the real estate industry over open housing. The so-called Summit Agreement in August 1966 ended freedom marches in residential areas in exchange for a vague set of official promises to combat housing discrimination and the establishment of an organization, the Leadership Council for Metropolitan Open Communities, to monitor open housing progress. SCLC allies on the poorer West Side condemned the settlement. Calling the agreement a bunch of "empty promises," Chester Robinson of the West Side Organization vowed to move ahead with march plans in all-white Cicero—a move supported by the local chapters of CORE and SNCC. The march occurred on Labor Day weekend, and apocalyptic warnings of violence went unfounded, thanks to three thousand police officers protecting the marchers. But King's one-time allies still felt betrayed. Labor and community activist Timuel Black called the agreement "the most unkind cut of all," adding that, "With his Negro and white Judas Iscariots the Mayor had taken on the great Dr. Martin Luther King and . . . won."[45] Such feelings intensified as city officials backed away from almost every point of the agreement in the following months.[46]

Yet, though many accounts portray the Chicago movement as unable to produce national reform as the Selma campaign did, the CFM did offer a few tangible results that went beyond local circumstances. They included the lessons learned between SCLC and the disaffected young black men in the city's notorious gangs. With the assistance of CCCO activists, SCLC aides held training and listening sessions with gang members early on, winning praise from the trainees and producing somewhat incongruous images of them holding hands and singing freedom songs. "Martin Luther King is a heavy stud," asserted one young man. But in a lot of ways, gang members' actions taught King as much as he could teach them. In the broadest fashion, "the Chicago riot," as one historian argues, "was a turning point in King's radicalization."[47] For three days in July 1966, Chicago police officers battled African Americans, including many gang members, on the West Side, leaving two blacks dead and many more injured after shutting off a fire hydrant in hot weather and precipitating a revolt. Open hydrants routinely took the place of swimming pools on hot summer days in poor neighborhoods. On the last day of the uprising, young black men—many of them gang members—met with King and Andrew Young and talked of fleeting job opportunities, terrible schools, and police brutality, and it dawned on the preachers that the solution to ghetto misery was empowerment in any way possible. "A lot of people have lost faith in the establishment," King concluded. "They've lost faith in the democratic process."[48] As a result, "frustration generates aggression. . . . Violence is but an expression of his present life," King wrote in his column that month. As long as violence remained within the "colony" through fatal gang fights, society turned a blind eye. Only when it spilled outward has "our society . . . been willing to recognize him as a doer and not as a victim. . . . Although the rioting actively involved only a small percentage of Chicago ghetto population, a large number of persons vicariously felt that they were striking out against the oppressor."[49]

This did not dissuade King of his own belief in nonviolence but rather provided a deeper level of comprehension as he attempted to persuade young black men to consider the alternatives to aggression in Chicago and future campaigns. Such efforts did get some gang members, despite their suspicions of traditional civil rights leaders, involved in nonviolent work for a time. More importantly, they found ways to become more political. Blackstone Rangers provided security for a march through a hostile and violent crowd in Gage Park. "I saw their noses being broken and blood flowing from their wounds," King recalled, "and I saw them continue and not retaliate, not one of them, with violence."[50] During the next two years, gang members involved themselves in the War on Poverty with the Woodlawn Organization and then the Poor People's Campaign. In 1968 members of the Rangers and Egyptian Cobras went to Washington and worked in recruitment and security as part of the campaign's Chicago contingent, the largest of any city. Unaffiliated men such as Billy Hollins, who had been sleeping in his car with little direction in 1965, also found their calling during the Chicago movement. "When SCLC came to town, I begged" for a job, recalled Hollins, who became a field staffer for years, including a key coordinator for the Poor People's Campaign.[51] In addition, SNCC and AFSC veteran Bernard Lafayette's work coordinating Chicago activists, including gang members, led to his eventual naming as the campaign's national director.[52]

The Chicago campaign also represented the first time that SCLC tried to reach Latinos as part of its mobilization, both because of the city's growing Puerto Rican and Mexican American presence in or near many black neighborhoods and because the campaign needed every possible ally. Chicago's industries had attracted thousands of Latinos in the first half of the twentieth century, particularly in the 1940s. While some lived in majority-white areas such as Uptown, Lincoln Park, and South Chicago, both ethnic groups faced similar constraints to African Americans in where they were allowed to live without harassment. By the late 1950s and early 1960s, neighborhoods in which Puerto Ricans and Mexican Americans were the majority had emerged—culturally vibrant but highly segregated from much of the city's wealth and quality schools. Urban renewal also had a significant impact on both groups, forcibly removing Mexican Americans, for example, from the future site of the University of Illinois, Chicago Circle. As a result, Latinos had formed social and political organizations such as Los Caballeros de San Juan and the Spanish Civic Committee, as well as "fighting" youth gangs like the Spartans, Marquis, and Young Lords, all of which formed to protect neighborhood turf amid shifting racial boundaries. Although primarily African American, the school boycotts also involved a small number of Latinos.[53]

SCLC officials hoped to build on this activism. In mid-1965, SCLC officials indicated that "several" leaders "have committed themselves to work with the movement." But while early documents suggested a detailed game plan in the predominantly black communities of North Lawndale and West and East Garfield Parks on the West Side, strategy proved far vaguer in the neighboring and predominantly Latino communities of Humboldt Park and Little Village. Spanish-speaking liaisons did plan what they called "community leadership training classes," met with Latino youth groups, and distributed Spanish-language publicity materials. Obed Lopez Zacarías, a Mexican American activist with the Fair Play for Cuba Committee and founder of the Latin American Defense Organization, recalled handing out fliers for the movement's large kickoff rally at Soldier Field. And at least a few Latino gang members participated in nonviolent training sessions. Latino enthusiasm, however, was limited for what was seen as a primarily black movement, dominated by traditional civil rights groups like SCLC, CORE, and the NAACP, as well as the Blackstone Rangers, a gang seen as hostile toward its Latino counterparts.[54]

Events in the Puerto Rican community along Division Street soon provided SCLC a unique opportunity to reach out. Whereas African Americans had received some attention in Chicago through the machine and civil rights activities, Puerto Rican concerns over rent, education, and police brutality long had been ignored. Frustration boiled over on June 12, 1966, when police officers shot twenty-year-old Cruz Arcelis, an incident that sparked three days of rioting and left sixteen people injured and more than fifty buildings destroyed. The conflagration prompted Obed Lopez and "two dark-skinned Puerto Ricans" he knew to step away from the Chicago Freedom Movement and embrace more community-specific activism, but not before Lopez invited James Bevel and SCLC organizers to come observe a "social phenomenon."[55] Hundreds of Puerto Ricans marched five miles to city hall a few days later and made formal demands about police brutality and a general lack of services in their neighborhoods. In addition, Puerto Ricans and Mexican Americans formed the Latin American Defense Organization (LADO) and the Spanish Action

Committee of Chicago as explicitly political organizations willing to use direct action protest to better the community.[56]

SCLC tried to capitalize. "Those who praise the efficient work of riot-control trained policemen and dogs should also be vocal in their denouncement of those city agencies which ignore dangerous social conditions caused by deprivation," King declared a few days later. "It is ironic that the power structure will not listen . . . until an atmosphere for violence threatens to blight the whole community." He went on to call for all "Latin-American residents of Chicago to join me . . . to demand of the city fathers an open city for all men, regardless of their race, religion or national origin."[57] James Orange was even more direct: "You suffer from the pressures and pains of prejudice because you are darker," emphasizing that "we're dark, too."[58] But perhaps this was too opportunistic. Although Lopez found the rally a few weeks later to be inspirational, King did not speak directly to Latino concerns, mentioning them exactly once. In the end, as Puerto Ricans and Mexican Americans in Chicago feared, they were bit players in a larger struggle, even after their attention-getting rebellion.[59]

Operation Breadbasket, CFM's most lasting and most economically driven enterprise, also signaled a willingness to work with Latinos. Tapping into a long tradition of African American selective-buying campaigns, Breadbasket modeled itself most closely after the work of Philadelphia's Leon Sullivan. In 1962 SCLC started a similar campaign dubbed Operation Breadbasket in Atlanta, which produced an estimated five thousand new jobs for blacks in a five-year span. Persuaded by Jesse Jackson that Breadbasket could involve Chicago's black ministers in the CFM without their participation in mass street action—and avoid the fury of Richard Daley—King in January 1966 announced the formation of a Chicago chapter to secure "jobs, jobs, jobs."[60] And while employment for African Americans was Breadbasket's highest priority, one of the organization's first actions was to endorse the NFWA's national boycott of Schenley Industries liquor products at the farm workers' request.[61]

During the next year, as SCLC and CCCO officials organized open housing marches, a small group of ministers, including Jackson and fellow seminarians Gary Massoni, David Wallace, and Calvin Morris, spearheaded campaigns against several businesses serving the inner city but notorious for hiring few if any blacks. Following a procedure of information gathering, public education, negotiation, and then direct action, if necessary, Breadbasket received assurances for more aggressive minority hiring from a range of businesses with local and regional headquarters there—including Borden, Country's Delight, and Hawthorn-Mellody dairies; Jewel, Hi-Lo, and National Tea groceries; and soft drink giant Pepsi. Sometimes company officials agreed only after scores of people picketed their stores—a harbinger of the successful grape boycotts of 1967–68 in Chicago and elsewhere. But quickly, business officials learned to make promises to avoid demonstrations. Looking back, Massoni considered the early victories of 1966 and 1967 as "more genuine and successful" than later ones, because the organization had a consistent follow-up mechanism in place.[62] Not unlike in Birmingham and later in the Summit Agreement, the risk of broken promises remained high. At least one business, Hi-Lo, went bankrupt before complying with its hiring assurances. But while cynicism set in among activists over King's settlement with Richard Daley, observers viewed Breadbasket as a lasting highlight of the CFM.[63]

The same dynamic that strained the Chicago Freedom Movement's relationship with Puerto Ricans applied to Cesar Chavez and the farm workers as well. While the CFM ramped up in early 1966, the city also had become a key boycott target for the NFWA's campaign against Schenley. Both Breadbasket's early endorsement and the founding of the Chicago Citizens Committee to Aid Delano Farm Workers by Al Raby, Bob Lucas, and C. T. Vivian suggested some coalescence between the two movements. A veteran of the Selma campaign and an Illinois native, Vivian was perhaps SCLC's most enthusiastic labor supporter. But, in the end, similar boycott tactics did not make for the same goals. While both organizations aimed to shape businesses' decisions, the boycotts inspired by the farm workers' struggle pressured companies to alter their inventory, not the far more fundamental change in hiring practices that Breadbasket sought. Thus, despite early commitments from civil rights groups, Chicago boycott leader Tony Orendain credited others for UFWOC's eventual success in the city. In addition to the support of the "entire Spanish-speaking community," the Roman Catholic Church's "Archbishop's Committee and local unions are putting steam in the boycott," reported Orendain, a California native that Chavez assigned to Chicago. Even Congressman Roman Pucinski, an ally of Daley and critic of the War on Poverty, "is setting up a special committee of Congressmen to help the farm workers."[64] While such congressional actions went nowhere, such claims suggested how broad the farm workers' coalition was—and had to be—to be successful in Chicago. After the Schenley victory in the spring of 1966, Orendain left Chicago to assist UFWOC efforts in Texas, where he fought for farm worker rights the rest of his career. Eliseo Medina replaced him a year later to lead the grape boycott in Chicago. And as Orendain had found, Medina determined that the farm workers could rely the most on labor and faith groups, such as the city's liberal-leaning Protestant and Roman Catholic churches, Quakers, the Chicago Teachers Union, UAW, UPWA, and dozens of other unions.[65]

Ultimately, while SCLC did not go beyond rhetorical cooperation with Mexican Americans and Puerto Ricans, it was the civil rights organization's allies in the CCCO and CFM that found more solid common ground in 1967. In general, the poor people of the Near West, Northwest, and North Sides of Chicago demonstrated a greater willingness to pursue a multiracial organizing model built on mutual respect and the recognition that everyone's issues were not the same. While the Chicago Freedom Movement had stressed open housing more than anything, activists banded together to fight for welfare rights and school and police reform. "We made contact with the welfare rights organizations from the West Side, like the West Side Organization," recalled Lopez, LADO's founder. "LADO from day one had in mind that we needed to develop relationships to the Appalachian whites and to the Afro-Americans, but it had to be at the grass-roots level, at the level of welfare rights organizations."[66] Both the West Side Organization, led by Chester Robinson, and the SDS-founded JOIN [Jobs Or Income Now] Community Union in Uptown had success teaming up with whites, Mexican Americans, and Puerto Ricans by protesting the welfare system's treatment of its beneficiaries. Small multiracial groups of activists picketed and jammed city welfare offices to air their grievances, actions met with strong-arm tactics by the police aimed at intimidating them. "It is essential that we be unified," concluded Marilyn Katz of JOIN. "We must not be forced to keep reacting to situations as individual groups who come together only at the moment of crisis."[67] Similar statements were made when African Americans and Latinos staged school walkouts that echoed ones from years before—and foreshadowed the so-called "blowouts" by Mexican Americans in Los Angeles, Denver, and Texas—to challenge the district's desegregation policies. Yet such coalitions remained difficult to maintain. Activists in the welfare unions, for instance, sniped at each other, questioning each other's motivations and associations at times. And the Chicago Police, particularly the department's secretive Red Squad, did its best to foment divisions among grass-roots activists through surveillance, misinformation, and intimidation.[68]

◆ ◆ ◆

King's relationship with Mexican Americans began to change only after his departure from Chicago and his rise as a vocal opponent of the Vietnam War. King left the city in early 1967, radicalized by the depth of the black frustration, white racism, and liberal cynicism he witnessed there. Concluding that the imperialist and capitalist roots of racism had to be attacked, King weathered the criticism that SCLC's campaign was an abject failure on the national level. His influential status as a civil rights leader, Nobel Peace Prize winner, and moral conscience of the nation had been tarnished, even jeopardized. And his emergence as a vocal critic of the Vietnam War—a natural step after the Chicago experience—just compounded the impression among elite opinion makers, journalists, and most politicians that his most influential days were behind him. Yet, in fact, the decision to speak out more forcefully against American actions in Southeast Asia created new opportunities for King, including organizing with Mexican Americans. His more strident Vietnam stance may have closed some doors with old movement allies, but it simultaneously opened up others, especially within the Chicano movement.

King and SCLC had been on record against U.S. involvement in the war in Vietnam since 1965, when the American presence swelled from 3,500 to 200,000 soldiers and commenced daily bombing raids of North Vietnam. Citing his commission as a Nobel Prize winner, King believed it was his duty to "take forthright stands against the escalation of war and for a negotiated settlement. . . . The time is so potentially destructive and dangerous that the whole survival of humanity is at stake." SCLC's executive board endorsed the statement initially. But by late 1965, King backed down from his most strident critiques of the war as the board grew squeamish amid increasing criticism, including from allies such as Bayard Rustin, who believed mixing civil rights and peace would doom the movement. Only after the Chicago setback, a year of lackluster War on Poverty funding, the war's official condemnation by CORE and SNCC, and King's own exposure to disturbing images of disfigured Vietnamese children in *Ramparts* magazine did SCLC's leader decide to step up his criticism of the war.[69]

In February and March 1967, King participated in his first antiwar

In early 1967, Martin Luther King Jr. marches with Al Raby and Bernard Lee in an anti-Vietnam War parade along State Street in Chicago. Jack Spiegel of the United Shoe Workers is to King's right. King increasingly found it difficult to separate civil rights activism from opposition to the war. (Copyright © Jo Freeman / www.jofreeman.com)

marches in Chicago and Los Angeles, neither of which caused much concern or extensive press coverage. The former, for instance, was even seen as an extension of his Chicago campaign. But the response to his speech at New York City's Riverside Church on April 4, 1967—exactly one year before his death—proved quite different. King had taken his nervous advisers' counsel and agreed to speak to the respectable antiwar group Clergy and Laymen Concerned about Vietnam in order to neutralize his potentially risky presence at the upcoming and much larger Spring Mobilization against the War in New York City.[70] Instead, King's speech represented his most blistering attack on war policy to date. Rather than make vague links between cuts in War on Poverty programs and the war effort, or deliver a peace message based on a philosophical pacifism, King proved more combative—directly criticizing the Johnson administration, speaking rhetorically from the perspective of a Vietnamese peasant, and consistently linking the peace movement with the larger struggle for freedom. Speaking of the angry urban rioters with whom he had engaged in Chicago, Watts, and elsewhere, he repeated a question they had posed to him. "But they asked—and rightly so—what about Vietnam?" King said. "They asked if our own nation wasn't using massive doses of violence to solve its problems, to bring about the changes it wanted. Their questions hit home, and I knew that I could never again raise my voice against the violence of the oppressed in the ghettos without having first spoken clearly to the greatest purveyor of violence in the world today—my own government."[71] He told the crowd of more than three thousand that he could not stay silent about the war any longer, and that they should not either.[72]

The directness of the speech left King in good spirits, even if it meant a potential decline in SCLC fundraising from white liberals and institutions such as the Ford Foundation. He anticipated criticism from the Johnson administration; one aide told the president that the "stupid" and "inordinately ambitious" King had "thrown in with the commies."[73] But what he did not expect were the virulent attacks on him by the many liberals not ready to cut ties with the White House and uncomfortable with his calls for draft resistance. Nearly every major newspaper, including the *New York Times* and *Washington Post*, severely criticized his logic and understanding of the issues. Calling some of his statements "sheer inventions of unsupported fantasy," the *Post* declared that King "has done a grave injury to those who are his natural allies" and "even graver injury to himself."[74] Although King expected the national offices of the NAACP and Urban League to distance themselves from his statements, he found criticism by fellow Nobel winner Ralph Bunche and onetime pacifist Bayard Rustin more disconcerting. Both publicly counseled that the civil rights and peace movements should remain separate. "In my view, Dr. King should positively and publicly give up one role or the other," Bunche said. "The two efforts have too little in common."[75] Black columnist Carl Rowan, apparently encouraged by the White House, delved into King's relationship with Stanley Levison, and later in the year published a piece calling King a communist "dupe."[76] It was clear the most vocal critics either had close ties to the Johnson administration or, in the case of Rustin, held out hope that the White House would rededicate itself to the cause of black civil rights.

King was not universally criticized, however, as he gained a substantial amount of credibility among peace and student activists, not to mention at least some grudging respect from black power advocates and others who had over the years sarcastically called him "de Lawd" for his paternalism. Together with a sprinkling of "dove" senators, these war critics applauded King's sharp critique of U.S. policy in Vietnam. Letters of support flooded SCLC offices and mainstream newsrooms, while other national leaders such as CORE's Floyd McKissick welcomed King's new message: "Dr. King has come around and I'm glad to have him with us, no question about that."[77] King's stance on the war also overjoyed Stokely Carmichael, who believed the SCLC president would have arrived at the position eventually. "You know, the statement was, 'We're going to beat them with nonviolence and love,'" he said, speaking of King's larger message. "It was clear that his philosophy made it impossible for him not to take a stand against the war in Vietnam."[78] Other activists, such as Marian Wright and Michael Harrington, were also supportive. "The prophet has moved out of the back of the bus," declared Harrington in a *Washington Post* opinion piece. "Dr. King obviously could not take the advice to segregate his moral principles to one question."[79] With such encouragement, King talked of launching a "Vietnam Summer" in 1967.[80]

A summer dedicated to ending the Vietnam War did not come to pass, nor did the issue bring King into closer contact with Cesar Chavez. The UFWOC president, while philosophically opposed to the war, remained careful to keep his movement's focus on the growers and La Causa. He did not want to undermine the union inadvertently with any kind of perceived radical statements he might make about U.S. foreign policy. Besides, much of his constituency still supported the war, a reflection of, as one scholar puts its, "a venerable Mexican American civil rights tradition that had emphasized ethnic-group patriotism, especially as manifested through military service, in the hopes of obtaining first-class citizenship."[81] This reality came as a shock to the SNCC and CORE activists who volunteered in the early months of the Delano strike. "Farm workers are ordinary people, not saints," Chavez told the volunteers, warning them not to allow any outside issues to derail the cause. Thus, the somewhat surprising result was that even a pacifist stance on Vietnam did not bond the era's arguably two most famous men of peace.[82]

But unlike a year earlier, King did not let such circumstances or resistance from friend or foe—including the summer urban uprisings in Newark, New Jersey, and Detroit—quiet his criticism of U.S. involvement in Vietnam or pretend to see these phenomena as unrelated. The war remained central to his thinking about what he saw in Chicago, including how to quell urban violence, address the rising expectations and subsequent frustrations of many African Americans—especially young, unemployed black men—and reinvigorate the nation's War on Poverty. As King began to consider launching a new campaign for all poor people, he contemplated the impact of the war on the most impoverished Americans, through depleted federal budgets and underfunded programs, the lost and maimed lives of disproportionately working-class soldiers, and a society facing an unquantifiable but apparent moral decay.

Even if Cesar Chavez did not allow himself to become embroiled in such issues aloud, many other Chicanos did. They pondered the disproportionate level of sacrifice made by people of Mexican descent, whether it was home amid the fields of Delano or abroad in the killing fields of Southeast Asia. When would they be able to partake fully in a nation that asked them to do so much? Was fighting other people of color the only way to become a citizen of the United States? What did they get out of this in the end? Among the new voices posing such questions were two of the most confrontational Chicano leaders, Reies López Tijerina and Rodolfo "Corky" Gonzales. By the end of the summer of 1967, the disparate parts of the larger movement—from King, SNCC, and CORE to the organizations of the Chicano movement to the white members of the New Left—would go to extraordinary lengths to find common cause and build a new political movement. They called it the "new politics."

3 ◆ War, Power, and the New Politics

As the United Farm Workers celebrated its first triumphs over California grape growers, other activists dreamed of a much larger victory in national politics. Championing what it called the "new politics," a cadre of mostly white, male organizers from the anti–Vietnam War movement began laying the groundwork for what they hoped would become a multiracial coalition to challenge the establishment liberalism of President Lyndon Johnson at the ballot box. Arguing that "it is now abundantly clear that the cost of the war has doomed hopes of any meaningful attack on our slums and ghettos," organizers including William Pepper of SDS and former SNCC chairman Julian Bond sought a new national coalition of black, white, and increasingly brown to fight poverty, racism, and U.S. involvement in Vietnam.[1] By linking the three issues so closely, proponents of the new politics rejected not only Johnson's liberal political assumptions but even those of the recently unveiled Freedom Budget, written by A. Philip Randolph and Bayard Rustin, endorsed by Dr. Martin Luther King Jr., and predicated on using a greatly expanded welfare state to eliminate poverty without altering war spending.[2] A war against poverty and injustice, new politics adherents charged, can never be won if the United States remained in Vietnam.[3]

After more than a year of discussion, recruitment, and the occasional endorsement of challengers to establishment liberals in the 1966 congressional elections, the National Conference for New Politics (NCNP) held a convention to prepare for the 1968 presidential campaign and to "end the reign of Lyndon Baines Johnson." From August 30 to September 4, 1967, the convention took over the famed Palmer House hotel in Chicago—symbolically important as the city of Johnson ally and "old politics" titan Mayor Richard J. Daley. More than 3,200 delegates from about 200 political organizations attended to hammer out a strategy to defeat Johnson, perhaps through a third party led by someone deeply respected in the antiwar movement, such as King or celebrity pediatrician Benjamin Spock.

Although a reluctant King did deliver the convention's keynote address, he made clear that he had no interest in running for office.[4] And, in contrast to press reports, delegates viewed a third party as just one of several alternatives that also included intense local organizing and selection of local- and state-level presidential tickets.[5]

Rather than produce a unified strategy to defeat the president and permanently alter the nation's politics, however, much of the NCNP convention became a verbal brawl over African Americans' role in the organization. While making up no more than 20 percent of voting delegates, members of the convention's Black Caucus insisted that blacks control a full 50 percent of the vote, or they would walk out. They also demanded that the convention accept thirteen black power principles without amendment, including reparations for African Americans and the condemnation of Israel's Six-Day War that summer.[6] Delegates averted a potentially catastrophic racial split when enough whites accepted the argument that such an approach was the only way to alleviate black fears of co-optation by the white-dominated antiwar movement. Whites "are just a little tail on the end of a very powerful black panther," explained white delegate Bertram Garskoff, alluding to the Oakland-based black self-defense group and symbol of black power. "And I want to be on that tail—if they'll let me."[7] But many participants dismissed the result as an undemocratic farce and the worst example of white guilt. To such critics, including much of the press, the NCNP lost credibility as a serious force, and they were not surprised that the organization collapsed just months later. A disgusted SDS leader Todd Gitlin declared, "The main moral of the happening is that it should not have happened at all."[8] Accordingly, the NCNP often disappears from scholarly analysis of the era.[9]

Yet, while the NCNP failed to become a major force in the 1968 campaign, it did serve as a significant moment for the small contingent of Chicano activists present. Both Reies López Tijerina, land-grant rights leader from New Mexico, and Rodolfo "Corky" Gonzales, a Democratic Party operative turned radical Chicano spokesman from Denver, left Chicago with distinct impressions of where the burgeoning Chicano movement needed to go. On the convention's last day, Tijerina orchestrated the passing of a vague resolution in support of the Mexican American struggle. But Gonzales was struck overall by how invisible the Spanish-speaking contingent remained, despite the importance of antiwar and antipoverty activism to Chicano activists like himself. When efforts to form a united Latino caucus at the convention failed to materialize, Gonzales departed believing they needed to be more assertive in making Chicano voices heard amid the cacophony of black and white. That meant, Gonzales and Tijerina concluded, both emulating black power and reaching out to its advocates—all while carving out a unique Chicano identity.[10]

The first and last convention of the National Conference for New Politics demonstrated the mutually reinforcing relationship between coalition and black and brown power politics. Both encouraged cooperation with like-minded activists of other races. But the resulting coalitions also reinforced the need for ever-stronger identity, as Gonzales and Tijerina determined. And the NCNP was far from unique in playing this role. Activists of all kinds began to take what were once isolated moments of multiracial cooperation on a local issue and attempted to translate them into national politics. Many nascent multiracial efforts were made possible because of—not despite—the rise of the black power and antiwar movements, both of which encouraged coalitions more racially diverse than that of the traditional civil rights movement.[11] Nearly all of these experiments fell short of their goals and were often pulled apart, ironically, by the same forces that brought them together.

Yet this process could be productive, not destructive. Fleeting attempts at coalition building became practical stepping-stones to future organizing, such as the regional and national expansion of activist networks. This certainly was the case for Tijerina's 1967 land-grant rights convention, Corky Gonzales's early antiwar activism, and even the casual interactions between black power icons and the Chicano youth group called the Brown Berets. Multiracial efforts also highlighted how distinct racial groups defined their solutions to poverty. Sometimes these solutions overlapped, such as opposition to state violence in the form of police brutality and harassment and their role in perpetuating economic inequality. More often, these solutions were quite different. In the case of the NCNP, for instance, what some interpreted as tyranny propped up by white guilt was simply justice to people long disempowered.

◆ ◆ ◆

When SNCC chairman Stokely Carmichael uttered the words "black power" during James Meredith's March against Fear in 1966, the phrase sent reverberations throughout the nation. For a lot of whites, including the journalists covering the movement, the words seemed menacing, reflective of a supposedly new era of militancy that embraced what *Time* magazine called "the new racism."[12] To many African Americans, the opposite was true. As demonstrated by blacks' boisterous echo of "black power" that June day in Canton, Mississippi, the phrase was a liberating expression of black frustration and anger with the glacial pace of racial change. It was also an expression of pride. The concept, if not the phrase, had deep roots. From Absalom Jones and David Walker to Marcus Garvey and Malcolm X, blacks long had demonstrated a strong desire to control their fate by managing their own political, religious, economic, and social institutions. In the past, this had led to strong black churches, businesses, social and political organizations, and schools and colleges. In the context of the mid-1960s, this muscular and emergent form of black nationalism often meant firm control of their own movement, and a defense of it and themselves by any means necessary.[13]

What black power did not mean, however, was an inherent hatred of nonblacks, especially whites. Certainly, some African Americans viewed whites as "blue-eyed devils," to quote Malcolm X from his early Nation of Islam days, or at least with a healthy skepticism, as became apparent at the NCNP convention. But most saw black power as love of, pride for, and confidence in people of African descent. No characteristic linked the many factions of black power more than the belief that "black is beautiful." While this may have made coalition building with whites untenable in many cases, black power organizations in principle had fewer qualms organizing alongside and at times partnering with other racial minorities also viewed as victims of white supremacy. Many of these connections were little more than a vague model for organizing and rhetorical dexterity in poor Chicano, Puerto Rican, Indian, or Asian neighborhoods. But occasionally, black power ideology translated into more hands-on cooperation and support for activists of other racial groups who embraced such tactics. One example was black nationalists' embrace of Reies López Tijerina and the Chicano land-grant rights movement in northern New Mexico and southern Colorado.

In many ways, Tijerina was an unlikely hero for black power supporters. A Texas native and itinerant Pentecostal minister prone to vivid religious visions, Tijerina discovered the poverty of northern New Mexicans in the 1950s and its relationship to the century-old loss of Spanish and Mexican land grants—parcels under the *ejido* land system that had been privately held but communally used. After a short-lived attempt to establish an illegal religious commune in rural Arizona called Valle de Paz, or Valley of Peace, Tijerina became a fugitive from the law and began to research the land grants as the embodiment of a Bible commandment to serve the poor. During the next several years on the lam, Tijerina researched the history of the 1848 Treaty of Guadalupe Hidalgo in archives and with land-grant descendants in the Southwest and Mexico. Applying to the treaty the same sort of literal interpretation he accorded the Bible, he became convinced that white Americans "had legally stolen the land of many Mexican families through . . . lawyers and Anglo politicians" after the U.S.-Mexican War of 1846 to 1848, in clear violation of the treaty.[14]

To win the land back, Tijerina in 1963 founded the Alianza Federal de Mercedes, or Federal Alliance of Land Grants, in Albuquerque, modeling it somewhat after the much older Abiquiú Corporation, a small, secretive New Mexico organization dedicated to land rights litigation. He also borrowed organizational ideas from the Nation of Islam's Elijah Muhammad, with whom he met for a week in 1961 and whose emphasis on the importance of land resembled Tijerina's. Alianza quickly became viable as it attracted thousands of rural, religious, inherently conservative Mexican American families living in poverty and hoping to regain control of land lost a century before. In addition, Alianza expanded land rights organizing beyond slow-moving litigation to include a letter-writing and public awareness campaign—and eventually the direct action protests that not only attracted more youthful members but also brought the organization national attention.[15]

For Tijerina, the land-grant struggle spoke to an almost obsessive need to please God and a strong belief, based on his periodic messianic visions, that he was somehow anointed to lead the charge. "Everything that I do on behalf of my blood brothers and sisters, the divine hand of the God of Justice is what guides me," Tijerina wrote in May 1965, after he had converted to Roman Catholicism. "I . . . understand the task and responsibility that the hand of Destiny had rested on my shoulders, [and] nailed in my heart." He also compared himself to Moses and Joshua, who "distributed lands to the Israelites, the Hebrews. Well that's just the way it is in our case."[16] But it was also a struggle that animated people of Mexican descent who lived throughout the territory ceded to the United States in the Treaty of Guadalupe Hidalgo. This land became known to activists as Aztlán, referring to the mythical place of origin of the pre-Columbian Aztec people. It represented many things to Mexican Americans, from an identity independent of European influence to a culture of economic independence based upon herding, weaving, and communal property. The loss of that land not only translated into a decline in wealth but also endangered a cherished way of life. Despite being a charismatic preacher far more than an organizer, Tijerina managed to harness the long-stand-ing bitterness regarding the land grants. In the words of activist-scholar José Angel Gutiérrez, Tijerina became the "first architect of Aztlán" who "did what Malcolm X and the Black Panthers only talked about," by art-fully creating a vision of Chicano activists' mythic home through literal land possession, citizen's arrests of top officials, early multiracial coalition building, and internationalization of Chicano politics.[17]

While black power activists undoubtedly would disagree with Gutiér-rez's characterization of their own lack of action, Tijerina's assertiveness in 1966 and 1967 garnered the land rights leader plenty of admirers. Frus-trated with the unresponsiveness of state and federal officials to their demands for legal action, including a face-to-face meeting with Demo-cratic governor Jack Campbell of New Mexico, Tijerina and his followers stepped up their activism with the brief takeover of the Echo Amphithe-ater campgrounds at the Kit Carson National Forest. The action included a mock trial and sentencing of two "trespassing" park rangers and the declaration that 500,000 acres of the forest would be returned to the land grant's heirs and fancifully renamed the Independent Republic of the San Joaquín del Río de Chama. The incident led to a ratcheting up of hostili-ties between the Alianza and state officials, whose opinion of Tijerina had changed from tolerant curiosity to deep concern. Land-grant claimants had "had their day in court," argued state archivist Myra Jenkins, who charged that the Alianza pursued nothing more than "a con game." The state's Mexican Americans, claimed one newspaper columnist, were "em-barrassed and annoyed" by Tijerina and the Alianza.[18]

Increasingly negative rhetoric from their opponents prompted alarm among Alianza members. Rumors circulated that District Attorney Alfonso Sánchez in the northern New Mexico county of Rio Arriba planned to round up Tijerina and other Alianza leaders on false charges—with some reports even suggesting that the state police planned an "ac-cident" in which Tijerina could be killed. In response, twenty followers of Tijerina's went to Tierra Amarilla, the dusty county seat of Rio Arriba, to place Sánchez under citizen's arrest. Sánchez, however, was not at the courthouse, and, in their frustration, the Alianza members shot up the place and wounded a jailer. Tijerina's role in the raid has come under some dispute. While Sánchez tried to pin the jailer's wounding (and eventual death) on Tijerina, it is not even clear if the land rights leader was in Tierra Amarilla that day, let alone one of the shooters. There was little doubt, however, that Tijerina hatched the raid idea.[19]

No matter what his role was, the courthouse raid briefly transformed Tijerina into a nationally recognized figure—a hero to some and a pariah to others. Already someone who used bold rhetoric and spectacle to inspire, Tijerina embraced the criticism of reluctant onetime allies such as U.S. senator Joseph Montoya of New Mexico—who had called Tijerina an "exploiter, fraud [and] discredited charlatan"—to fashion himself into a martyr and was successful at it for a time.[20] Yet this maneuver also resulted in him becoming a caricature in the public eye—depicted as a fundamentalist kook, a dangerous communist, a Wild West "bandido," or a courageous spokesman for the little man.[21] More likely, Tijerina embodied a little of all these identities, as early biographer Richard Gardner tried to capture: "He was a man of contradictions, with myriad flaws and failings and a number of hidden conflicts. But . . . beneath the tangle of contradictions there was a pattern . . . a central core of compulsive determination." Tijerina was able to channel those conflicting energies into shaping some of the most popularized and galvanizing narratives of Chicano history.[22] It was this ability that made him arguably the most controversial of Chicano movement leaders—and one of the most attractive to many activists on the left.

In the weeks that followed the courthouse raid, Tijerina and the Alianza gained interest, even praise, from activists of different stripes. Cesar Chavez, Bert Corona of California's Mexican American Political Association, and Corky Gonzales of the Crusade for Justice all made pilgrimages to New Mexico. During his visit, the often cautious Chavez even hugged Tijerina and announced that, if he had been a resident of New Mexico, he would belong to the Alianza. The San Francisco–based *Movement*, until recently the official newspaper of SNCC, featured glowing coverage of the land-grant movement in its August 1967 edition. Written by Jim Kennedy, founder of Albuquerque's Marxist W. E. B. Du Bois Club, the supplement drew several parallels to rhetoric and assumptions of black power, categorizing New Mexico as a colony, calling Tijerina "a Mexican Malcolm X," and suggesting that black-brown cooperation was inevitable. "This urge, this growth, for unity of la raza with the Negro cannot be resisted," Tijerina told the reporter. "It will come because it must."[23] Organizers of the NCNP, desperate to find even the most roundabout ways to reach out to African Americans, also began to pay attention. Maria Varela, a Mexican American literacy coordinator for SNCC in Mississippi, recalled a phone call from Julian Bond, in which the NCNP cochairman and former SNCC communications coordinator asked her to escort Tijerina at the fall convention in Chicago. "We don't even know if the man speaks English," Varela recalled Bond as saying, "and we want him to feel comfortable. Would you come?"[24]

Tijerina made full use of his English when he went to Chicago. Interested in capitalizing on his notoriety among civil rights and black power activists, he spent much of his time in Chicago making contacts with African Americans and inviting them to Alianza's October convention. These efforts included a chance airport encounter with a fatigued Dr. Martin Luther King Jr., who Tijerina viewed as a "sort of philosopher . . . who weighs his words very much before making his statement."[25] He also met with activist-comedian Dick Gregory and had a private visit with the Nation of Islam's Elijah Muhammad, whom Tijerina had met six years before and was the one black leader with whom he seemed most enamored. Tijerina enjoyed his largest stage during the convention panel on "Spanish-speaking interests," where he made the case for black-brown unity despite inherent differences. "The situation of the Mexicans and Puerto Ricans is similar to that of the Negro people, but is not the same," Tijerina declared. "We have to fight for the right to speak our language. Even the demand of the Puerto Rican for independence is different from the Mexican's demands. But we must unite."[26]

Of course, Tijerina's interest in coalition building was calculated—based upon his own identity and experiences in New Mexico. Rather than a romanticized class-based unity, Tijerina saw successful black organizations as ones to emulate as well as to associate with in order to build his own credibility. Tijerina acknowledged as much in one interview in late 1967. "The reason I met with all the leaders—I don't care about their cause and their ideas but I wanted an alliance for moral support and a mutual push for the pursuit of justice," Tijerina said. "The primary thing is to avoid future frictions between the Negro and the Spanish American."[27] He knew how debilitating such frictions could be from the indifference the small minority of African Americans in Albuquerque held for the Alianza, which blacks often viewed as narrow and unconcerned with the issues of urban poverty.

Tijerina also distanced himself from black concerns by emphasizing his curious self-identity of *indohispano*. A combination of Spanish and indigenous, *indohispano* was a narrow racial ideology that became popularized during the Mexican Revolution of the early twentieth century. "We are not Spaniards, not Indians, as the history will state and prove," Tijerina argued. "We are a new breed that for the last three hundred years has been multiplying at a very fast rate."[28] While this identity allowed Tijerina to differentiate himself from those New Mexicans who embraced whiteness fully as so-called "Spanish Americans," it excluded the well-documented African roots of *mestizaje*. Many Mexican Americans, of course, could be given the benefit of the doubt regarding their history; Mexican narratives stressing indigenous and European influences inundated the culture on both sides of the border since at least the Mexican Revolution. But given Tijerina's exhaustive research of Mexican history, law, and culture in U.S., Mexican, and Spanish archives dating back several hundred years, this identity most likely reflects a deliberate calculation on his part. Perhaps Tijerina was simply prejudiced. However, admitting any African influences also could undermine his legitimacy, especially among the conservative land heirs in the Alianza. As a result of this identity and ideology, Tijerina's primary allies on land issues in New Mexico were not the most racialized of minorities in U.S. society but the Hopi Nation and its spiritual leader, Thomas Banyacya. The Hopis had similar interests in protecting their land and culture in western New Mexico.[29]

These experiences may help explain why the most substantial contact Tijerina made in Chicago turned out to be Maria Varela. While asked to be there by SNCC, Varela attended the conference for other reasons as well. By 1967, Varela decided that it was time to explore a new direction of activism. She first had come to the South from Michigan at the behest of Students for a Democratic Society activist Casey Hayden and soon landed in Selma, Alabama, in 1963. SNCC staffers Bernard Lafayette and Frank Smith believed her Roman Catholic background would help facilitate SNCC support for a local black Roman Catholic pastor who had opened his parish to the movement. She also worked with Lafayette's successor, Worth Long, to develop a voter literacy program, and then in 1965 she went to Mississippi to produce educational materials for local organizers including voting guides, farmers cooperative materials, children's readers, and film strips. But as SNCC slowly turned away from interracial grass-roots organizing by late 1967, funding for such programming had dwindled. After meeting in Chicago, Tijerina prompted a letter exchange in which he invited Varela to join the Alianza. "So glad to know that you are a true fighter and a very brave girl," he wrote a bit condescendingly to the young woman activist. "It would be very nice if you could come to Albuquerque and spend some time among our people."[30]

This connection briefly led to an organizational relationship between the Alianza and SNCC. Long an admirer of SNCC, Tijerina also wanted to learn about that organization's approach to publicity, in hopes of replicating it with the land rights movement. In a letter to Tijerina less than a week after the convention, Varela laid out a strategy of what Alianza could convey to African Americans, including the many parallels in experience between Mexican Americans in the Southwest and blacks in the South, as well as Tijerina's "alliance" with Elijah Muhammad of the Nation of Islam. "I found (her black brothers) had very little knowledge of the struggle of la raza much less the struggle of the Alianza," Varela wrote Tijerina. "Some black people seem to feel they are the only ones who suffer from discrimination and poverty." In private conversations with Tijerina, she added that many African Americans might have considered him white, and thus not entirely trustworthy, an assertion that surprised him. While he made no mention of any possible African ancestry in being *indohispano*, Tijerina certainly did not consider himself white either. He saw his actions as fighting the Anglo as much as African Americans did. The question became, Were racial discrimination and a common enemy enough upon which to build a coalition? The experience at Alianza's fifth annual convention suggested it just might be.[31]

◆　◆　◆

Delegates to the 1967 convention began to arrive in Albuquerque on October 20. It was "a gathering," one observer noted, "the likes of which hadn't been seen in the Southwest since the days of the discoverers, Cabeza de Vaca and the black slave Estevan; of the explorers, Coronado and his wily Comanche guide, the Turk; of long-past fiestas and trade gatherings, where priest and medicine man, soldier and painter warrior, mountain man and runaway slave had mingled and palavered on the crazy-quilt frontier."[32] While certainly over the top, the writer's description also reflected genuine surprise and the recognition that people were witnessing something historic that weekend in New Mexico. Varela, who had gone to Albuquerque under the auspices of SNCC but traveled separately from the rest of the civil rights group's delegation, was "astounded" by the scene. "I was just struck by all the different faces that I saw there," she recalled. There were American Indians such as Thomas Banyacya; mostly older northern New Mexican villagers "with distinctive faces and features," who made up the majority of the Alianza membership; visiting Mexican Americans from California and Texas, including Corky Gonzales, Bert Corona, and José Angel Gutiérrez; African Americans from the

From left, Hopi spiritual leader Thomas Banyacya, SNCC's Ralph Featherstone, Ron Karenga of the US Organization, and Reies López Tijerina share the stage at the historic 1967 Alianza convention. These men signed the highly symbolic Treaty of Peace, Harmony, and Mutual Assistance at Albuquerque, a pact that included a list of vague promises to respect the faith and culture of the signing members' organizations and to not attack each other verbally or physically. (Peter Nabokov Collection [PICT 000-093-0017], Center for Southwest Research, University Libraries, University of New Mexico)

South and West, many of whom sported the late 1960s dress code of afros, dashikis, and sunglasses; and a smattering of whites, from local Alianza members to journalists and not-so-undercover FBI agents.[33]

In all, African Americans made up no more than fifty of the approximately four hundred people attending the convention at the Albuquerque Civic Auditorium. But their presence altered the dynamics of the convention, by shifting some attention away from Reies Tijerina and even the singular message of land rights. Tijerina had invited Martin Luther King Jr., Stokely Carmichael, and newly elected SNCC chairman H. Rap Brown to address the convention, all of whom declined, citing previous commitments. The most prominent black leaders that did attend were Maulana Ron Karenga, founder of Los Angeles' cultural nationalist US Organization; Ralph Featherstone, SNCC's program coordinator; and Walter Bremond of the Los Angeles–based Black Congress. In addition to Featherstone and Varela, SNCC sent Willie Ricks, Ethel Minor, and Freddie Greene to represent the civil rights group. SNCC had become somewhat desperate to build new partnerships after its turn toward black nationalism all but eliminated its white funding sources and staffers, including those who had facilitated the organization's relationship with the United Farm Workers. Meanwhile, Karenga, interested in Tijerina's most practical goal of reducing tensions between blacks and Mexican Americans, brought an entourage of eleven, including a young Angela Davis. Several other mostly black power organizations were also represented, such as the Black Panthers, Black Youth Congress, Congress of Racial Equality, Black Students Union, and Black Anti-Draft Unit.[34]

Alianza members did not completely know what to make of the situation. Surprised by how many out-of-state visitors were present, the largely Mexican American audience remained initially quiet and attentive during the convention's plenary sessions as its black guests shared the stage and lectern with Tijerina and other Chicano leaders. Some FBI agents interpreted the crowd's calm as unease, an impression reinforced by Tijerina's own statements earlier reassuring Alianza members that blacks would not take over their convention and even be asked to leave on certain days. Yet the latter did not happen, and most observers read the audience's silence as respect for African Americans' plight and appreciation of their support for Alianza. "The blacks were magnificent politicians," reported one FBI informer. "They mingled with the people, spoke with them, and politicked very well, and visibly moved the convention to acceptance of them."[35] Ethel Minor and then Karenga addressed the convention in Spanish, the latter calling for a new movement by people of color. "¡Viva Tijerina!," he shouted in a shrill and heavily accented Spanish. "¡Vivan los indios! ¡Vivan los hombres de color!" Following Karenga, Featherstone approached the podium and raised his fist, declaring repeatedly, "¡Poder Negro!" which prompted a standing ovation and enthusiastic response of fist-pumping "black power" chants from the audience. If the aging farmers and ranchers were uncomfortable at the convention's start, it disappeared among the deafening calls for black-brown unity.[36]

The African Americans present saw their hosts as both welcoming and intriguing. "We found this to be an interesting group of people," said Ethel Minor, SNCC communications director. "It was a family. . . . It wasn't just young college students," as she and her colleagues from SNCC were accustomed to. They also were not recent immigrants, for the most part, which also surprised the SNCC delegation. This U.S.-born family atmosphere—"from grandparents to babies," Minor recalled—offered a different sort of tenor to the convention and to their entire visit. This proved especially true when their hosts took them to see Tierra Amarilla and a few of the families who lived there. One family they met had a scrapbook full of clippings about the Nation of Islam and Elijah Muhammad—a discovery that thoroughly impressed Minor, who had close ties to the Nation to the point that she ate dinner regularly with Muhammad when she was in Chicago. Rural New Mexico "was the last place I expected to see anything about the Nation and Muhammad," she said, although it made sense in retrospect, given the Nation's and Alianza's shared emphasis on landownership. Despite the links between property ownership and relative black independence in the Jim Crow South, SNCC had not made land a central tenet of its activism, even after the turn toward black nationalism. While Minor grasped the importance of land, others from SNCC did not. What they did understand, however, was the potential bond SNCC had with an Alianza willing to use any means necessary to make their case. Thus, appropriately, Alianza members insisted that SNCC staff members pose for a series of photographs while in Tierra Amarilla—on horseback and holding rifles.[37]

Despite such memorable experiences, it remains debatable whether the convention accomplished much beyond a superficial spectacle of black and brown together. The largest tangible accomplishment in coalition building arguably was the Treaty of Peace, Harmony, and Mutual Assistance at Albuquerque, an agreement that made a variety of vague promises to respect the faith and culture of the signing members' organizations, as well as to not attack each other verbally or physically. Signers included Tijerina, Karenga, Banyacya, Featherstone, Bremond, Eliezer Risco of *La Raza* newspaper, Anthony Babu of the Black Panther Party and Black Student Union, and James Dennis of CORE. But while the treaty may have had some symbolic importance, the secretive process of drafting and signing it proved off-putting to many there. Ethel Minor and Maria Varela, for instance, were furious that the signing took place behind closed doors at the Alianza headquarters with no women present, per Karenga's request. For reporter Peter Nabokov, the treaty also represented a "tone of hardness" underlying the entire convention. Yet the agreement remained so vague that it did not delve into the participating groups' ideologies beyond nebulous references to culture and the "CRIMES and SINS of the Government of the United States." Land was not mentioned once.[38]

Although much of the attention and publicity focused on the African Americans in Albuquerque, the convention actually had a marked impact on those trying to build a network of Chicano activists. For Maria Varela, the convention allowed her to see the Alianza and northern New Mexico up close. Not completely sold on the effectiveness of Tijerina's organizing style, Varela was moved by what she saw in Tierra Amarilla. "I met some incredible people," she said, and not just the men and women trying to make a living on the land in northern New Mexico. She also made initial contact with members of the Chicano Press Association, especially Eliezer Risco, editor of Los Angeles–based *La Raza*. In talking with Risco and a few other Chicano journalists, she learned of the strength and breadth of the Chicano Press Association, made up of more than thirty community newspapers and for which she eventually wrote and took photographs.[39]

Although not many Chicano youth made it to the convention, those who did began to sketch out their own network of communications to flesh out some of the early "problems" of the movement. One of those issues, not coincidentally, was how should Chicanos relate to other oppressed groups. Their more immediate action was to invite all young Chicano activists to El Paso the following week, on October 28, to protest the Johnson administration's Cabinet Committee Hearings on Mexican American Affairs. Although designed to highlight Johnson's concern for Mexican American interests, the conference instead demonstrated his disregard for some of the biggest issues by snubbing Tijerina, Corky Gonzales, and representatives of the local El Paso Federation of Spanish-Speaking People.[40] Along with the leaders of the Mexican American Youth Organization, Tijerina and Gonzales led a protest and rival conference of six-hundred people, which produced *El Plan de La Raza*, a forerunner to the formation of the Chicano party called La Raza Unida. While reaching out to African Americans, the Alianza convention managed to affix another building block to the Chicano movement itself.[41]

Tijerina's efforts to connect with African Americans continued after the convention, even as his legal troubles mounted—and sometimes because of them. After being convicted and sentenced to two years for assault and destruction of federal property stemming from Echo Amphitheater, Tijerina received support from several high-profile leaders, including Karenga and Martin Luther King Jr. SNCC chairman H. Rap Brown was most active, writing Tijerina twice and speaking on his behalf in another telegram to New Mexico governor David Cargo. Free during the appeals process, Tijerina was able to return the favor soon after by joining Stokely Carmichael, Walter Bremond, and others in rhetorical support of jailed Black Panther Huey Newton and black-brown cooperation more generally at a "Free Huey" rally in California in February 1968. In early March, Tijerina returned to California to meet with black state senator Mervyn Dymally of Los Angeles and MAPA's Bert Corona to discuss a new multiracial coalition. And just days later, Tijerina responded to Martin Luther King Jr.'s call for activists of all sorts to join him in his new crusade, the Poor People's Campaign. Whatever his disparate motivations, Tijerina had become a pivotal figure in advocating a nascent national coalition among African Americans and Mexican Americans, one that strengthened brown power at the same time.[42]

◆ ◆ ◆

Another advocate of coalition and sometime ally of Tijerina's was Rodolfo "Corky" Gonzales. A self-described "trouble-maker" in the mid-1960s, Gonzales also had far more practical political experience than Tijerina did, stretching back nearly twenty years.[43] The son of a migrant sugar beet picker, Gonzales emerged in the 1940s as a charismatic featherweight boxer with a clean-cut image among Denver's white elites. Asked if making the sign of the cross helped him win, the devoutly Roman Catholic Gonzales quipped, "Sure, if you know how to fight."[44] He parlayed his success in the boxing ring first into business and then into community activism in the city's impoverished and racially mixed Eastside in the early 1950s, eventually becoming active in several local civil rights organizations, including the Colorado GI Forum and the Antipoverty Program for the Southwest. This also led him into local Democratic Party politics, knocking on doors for reformist mayor Quigg Newton's reelection. Increasingly concerned about the state of the community's Mexican American youth, Gonzales ran for city council in 1955 and lost narrowly to an African American in a district evenly divided among whites, blacks, and "Spanish-Americans," who were mostly of Mexican descent. As a prominent and seemingly "safe" Mexican American in the eyes of white Democrats interested in expanding their base, Gonzales became a party ward leader in 1956 and chairman of Colorado's Viva Kennedy chapter four years later. Although known for his unpredictably outspoken manner, Gonzales proved to be an effective political operative among Mexican Americans.[45]

This reputation only grew during the next few years. While Gonzales received official appointments as local director of the Neighborhood Youth Corps and then chairman of Denver's War on Poverty Inc., he and several other men also founded an organization called Los Voluntarios in 1963. Designed to advocate for Spanish-speaking people in Denver, the group initially portrayed itself as strictly reformist, reflected in its mission statement to "not only inform, but advise the public on political issues, educational advantages, social acceptance."[46] But what sparked their actions most was city officials' repeated disregard of allegations of police brutality and other civil rights violations of Mexican American and black youth. In 1964 Gonzales and others protested after the beating of nineteen-year-old Alfred Salazar, who died a day after an officer fractured his skull while detaining him for resisting arrest and disturbance. Local chapters of CORE, SNCC, and the AGIF also protested the death and joined Los Voluntarios in calling for a formal investigation. At a public meeting, Gonzales threatened a march of thousands on City Hall and criticized Mayor Tom Currigan for reneging on a campaign promise to establish a civilian police review board. "If in four days we can raise 500 people to show up here, we can raise 5,000 when we march on City Hall," Gonzales said.[47] Yet he remained a popular force within the Democratic Party, which led to the mayor's appointment of him as chairman of the local War on Poverty board. The former boxer was characteristically combative: "I'm an agitator. . . . That's my reputation," he said at the time. "They didn't buy me when they put me in this job."[48]

This seemed clear when, in 1966, the conservative local daily *Rocky Mountain News* published unsubstantiated charges by a Gonzales aide that the poverty program director exhibited undue favoritism toward Mexi-

Corky Gonzales, head of Denver's War on Poverty agency in the mid-1960s, sympathizes with protesters highlighting the hypocrisy of persistent Mexican American poverty despite great sacrifices on the battlefields of South Vietnam. Gonzales became increasingly vocal about the connection between war and continued poverty after leaving the post and starting the Crusade for Justice. (Howard Oda photo / Denver Public Library)

can Americans. A rapid series of events followed. "If a kid comes along from a family of ten children where the income is $2,000, he gets a job quicker than a kid from a family of four with $4,000 income," Gonzales responded. "If that's favoritism, then let it be that way."[49] The newspaper continued its critique, prompting Gonzales to organize a boycott and picket around the newspaper's building—an unusual step for a local government official. Mayor Currigan agreed, calling the move inappropriate and demanding that Gonzales resign or be fired. To protest the forced departure, members of Los Voluntarios staged a rally at Denver's Civic Center, where twelve hundred people heard Gonzales declare that it was only the beginning of "a crusade for justice."[50]

Over the next year, Gonzales's estrangement from the political establishment seemed to complete itself. He renounced his membership in the Democratic Party, challenging its corruption as "a world of lackeys, political bootlickers, and prostitutes."[51] He rejected repeated invitations to join a labor-liberal coalition, calling the AFL-CIO, except for the United Farm Workers, "part and parcel of the power structure."[52] He then wrote "I Am Joaquin," an epic Chicano poem that pays homage to Mexican history, heritage, and identity and remains a standard of the Chicano literary canon. "I must choose between the paradox of victory of the spirit, despite physical hunger," wrote Gonzales, "or to exist in the grasp of American social neurosis, sterilization of the soul and a full stomach." Meanwhile, Los Voluntarios evolved into a new, more radical self-defense organization called the Crusade for Justice. Mirroring Gonzales's own transformation, the organization rejected mainstream politics and blended the needs of urban Mexican Americans, especially youth, with the cultural rhetoric of Aztlán and an invigorated Chicano identity.[53]

Similarly to Tijerina, Gonzales also omitted any African roots in his evolving identity. He may not have had quite the breadth of Mexican historical knowledge that Tijerina had developed, especially the close readings of nineteenth-century laws and treaties and their impact on people of Mexican descent. But Gonzales still demonstrated a strong grasp of the popularly constructed mythologies of *mestizaje* that privileged Spanish and Indian. For instance, in "I Am Joaquin," Gonzales provided a lyrical, fast-paced history of the Chicano experience, starting with the sixteenth-century clash and mixing of cultures and continuing through a narration of the independence movements of Mexico, from Spain, France, and then the authoritarian regimes of the late nineteenth and early twentieth centuries. Throughout the poem, the indigenous Mexican survives, even triumphs:

The Indian has endured and still
Emerged the winner,
The Mestizo must yet overcome,
And the gachupín [Spanish settler] will just ignore.

In contrast, Gonzales makes just one oblique mention of Africans—not as slaves but as would-be conquerors: "Part of the blood that runs deep in me could not be vanquished by the Moors." While this could be a clever way to suggest the absorption of African influence into Mexican (and European) history, culture, and identity, it more likely reflects the focus on indigenous survival amid Spanish and European conquest. Similar constructions of Chicano identity reinforcing "nonblackness" also showed up in his speeches from the era and the popular play he penned in 1966, *The Revolutionist*.[54]

Yet while both circumstances and Corky Gonzales's strong personality may have taken his work in a particularly nationalist Chicano direction, some of the former prizefighter's most reliable allies in Denver were white and black activists in the evolving antiwar movement. This made sense given the Crusade for Justice's unofficial identity as an antiwar organization—and the increasing role of peace in the Chicano movement more generally. Gonzales routinely spoke at antiwar rallies, arguing that the state's economic health cynically depended upon war and the tremendous sacrifices made by the poor. "Check the casualties, check the injured, check out the entire number of drafted young men," he told an antiwar crowd in August 1966, "and then compare the financial status of their parents and check the ethnic background, check to see which minorities are dying for a cause they cannot see or understand. Then you will understand why economics plays a major role in this and any war."[55]

Refusing the draft and, instead, fighting at home also became a central theme of Gonzales's rhetoric and spoke to the Crusade's popularity among young Chicano men and teenagers. Speaking to followers of Reies Tijerina in New Mexico, Gonzales argued that, "If you must shed your blood, it's better that it be shed in Tierra Amarilla fighting for what is yours."[56] When nineteen-year-old Ernesto Vigil decided to join the Crusade and evade the draft, *El Gallo*, the Crusade's newspaper, prominently featured the story on the front page, hyperbolically declaring, "First Chicano in Southwest refuses to kill in Vietnam." Gonzales and Esequiel "Kelly" Lovato, a founding member of the Crusade and contributor to *El Gallo*, routinely used its pages to encourage Mexican Americans to attend antiwar demonstrations. Lovato also tied participation in antiwar protests not only to a new definition of Chicano manhood, rejecting military service, but also to all racial and ethnic minorities' fights against police brutality at home. "By not supporting a rally you show your support for 'the man,' the same guy who beats you, jails you and sends you up or shoots your brother in the back," Lovato wrote. "All of this is true of our black brothers, too. Wake up minorities, unite."[57]

Indeed, this stance against violence both home and abroad made peace activists such as Lauren Watson, founder of the local Black Panthers and a former CORE member, an occasional ally of Gonzales. For instance, in

July 1967 the separate shooting deaths of Eugene Cook and Louis Pinedo by police brought members of the Crusade, the Panthers, and other nationalist groups together to protest ongoing violence against minority youth, no matter what color. In an illustration of their independence from each other, both the Crusade and the Panthers requested march permits. But when city officials approved only the Panthers' permit in what may have been an attempt to drive a wedge between the two groups, Gonzales and the Crusade joined the Panthers' march to City Hall. "We will no longer be shot in the back and take it lying down," Crusade Vice Chairman Emilio "Zapata" Dominguez told those gathered, referring to the teens' deaths. Protests condemning the violence at home and in Vietnam continued throughout the fall, as police shot several more young Chicanos under suspicious circumstances.[58]

Despite Gonzales's emergence as a potent voice of the Chicano movement, it was the Crusade's antiwar activism that led to his invitation to the National Conference for New Politics convention. Gonzales was Denver's sole field staffer for Vietnam Summer, a Massachusetts-based organization founded by older antiwar activists interested in mobilizing students to build a new middle-class coalition against the war. In fact, Vietnam Summer and NCNP records reflect Reies Tijerina as a late addition filed under Gonzales's name. Gonzales chose to attend but not necessarily to support a third-party movement. Rather, he and Emilio Dominguez went to Chicago to build momentum for a national Chicano—or, even better, Latino—conference. They did meet with the two dozen or so other Latinos there, including Puerto Ricans from New York and representatives of the Latin American Defense Organization in Chicago. But their efforts to form an influential Latino caucus at the conference fell short.[59]

Instead, Gonzales and Dominguez witnessed black power forces successfully dictate terms to the white majority, and they were impressed. "The black power advocates demonstrated to me the reality of a group united in pride and purpose," wrote Dominguez admiringly. "Aware that there are many of their own who do not agree with their philosophy . . . they continue in their fight to regain the culture snatched from them centuries ago." The parallels to the radical and culturally nationalist Crusade for Justice were clear, even if the specific issues diverged at times. And, to these two men, also similar were the tactics needed to make a difference. Thus, they left Chicago concluding that the power demonstrated by the NCNP's Black Caucus—while abhorrent to many white observers—was something Chicanos must emulate.[60]

Chicano students had begun to draw similar conclusions. Inspired by the farm workers' demonstration of unity and identity in action, these often first-generation college students from the Mexican American barrios of California, Texas, and elsewhere also paid close attention to the rising influence of black nationalism and antiwar fervor and contemplated how best to harness other movements' tactics in their own burgeoning activism, including cross-racial cooperation. By the fall of 1967, high school and college students in California brought an increasingly education-centered and confrontational critique to local Mexican American activism. In the Los Angeles area, students formed several organizations, including the Mexican American Student Association at East Los Angeles Community College, the United Mexican American Students at Loyola University, and, perhaps the best-known, the Young Citizens for Community Action (YCCA), which eventually became the Brown Berets.

The YCCA, in particular, developed some ties to black activism and politics. Emerging out of a local government-sponsored youth conference in response to the 1965 Watts rebellion, the YCCA initially offered a reformist agenda. Its initial members, including Vickie Castro, David Sánchez, and Ralph Ramirez, all students at East Los Angeles' Roosevelt High School, viewed the War on Poverty and electoral politics as the ways to bring change. Helping Mexican American Julian Nava win a seat on the Los Angeles County school board, the YCCA criticized the negative treatment and lack of recognition of Mexicans in U.S. history books, rules against speaking Spanish in classes and interracial dating with whites, and an overall school system that ignored Mexican culture and identity. Their work in electoral politics and with other groups such as the Community Service Organization elevated their visibility in East Los Angeles as well as their ethnic and racial pride. By mid-1967, the YCCA had changed its name (with the same initials) to the Young Chicanos for Community Action. And with the help of Episcopal priest John Luce, the YCCA opened La Piranya, "a coffeehouse for the community, for the youth, where they could go and indulge in political activities, cultural activities," recalled Ralph Ramirez. The coffeehouse, inconveniently next door to a California Highway Patrol station, quickly emerged as a magnet for Chicano youth culture in East Los Angeles. Afternoons that started with a visit by a Chicano leader such as Chavez ended with an evening jazz set by a band "composed of Japanese Americans and African Americans, playing for a very small wage." Ramirez recalled La Piranya as where one could find

East Los Angeles' vibrant black-infused jazz and rock scene, as well as visiting black power activists such as Stokely Carmichael, H. Rap Brown, and Bunchy Carter.[61]

The YCCA's similarities to the Black Panthers, in particular, attracted Los Angeles sheriff's deputies, negative attention that increasingly radicalized the students. Deputies constantly harassed patrons of the coffeehouse, arresting them for minor infractions and placing the small storefront under near-constant surveillance. Gloria Arellanes remembers "all the lights would be off inside . . . the sheriff's (deputies) outside, with their lights shining in" and her standing still, petrified to move. Frustrated by the harassment, David Sánchez and younger activists became increasingly vocal in their opposition to police brutality. Donning military-style khaki clothing and their trademark berets in January 1968, the newly named Brown Berets embraced a tone similar to that of their black power counterparts, calling for "brown power" and armed self-defense in Mexican American neighborhoods. They eventually released a ten-point program, similar in substance (and the number of items) to the Black Panthers' own agenda, and founded their own community survival programs including a free health clinic. And unlike many Chicano students still protective of their patriotism, the Berets actively attended antiwar protests alongside black and white demonstrators. In March 1968 Chicano high school students ratcheted up their criticism of the school district's policies toward Mexican Americans, including a high forced dropout rate, decrepit facilities, and racist teachers and administrators. To display their frustration, more than a thousand Mexican Americans, along with dozens of black and Asian sympathizers, walked out of the East Los Angeles schools in what became known as the "blowouts." While the Brown Berets did not plan the walkouts, they did play an "advisory" role, offering the coffeehouse as a staging area for protests, as well as providing physical protection for the younger students. Suddenly, Chicano students—and particularly the Brown Berets—grabbed the nation's attention.[62]

A vibrant Chicano movement among youths also emerged in Texas, symbolized by the state's best-known student organization, the Mexican American Youth Organization (MAYO). Alienated by the older, more conservative Mexican American leadership of LULAC and the American GI Forum, a cadre of students at St. Mary's College in San Antonio hoped to re-create the 1963 spirit of Crystal City, when Mexican Americans won a majority of the city council. Calling themselves Los Cinco after the five winning councilmen, the students founded MAYO in 1967. Much like the Brown Berets, MAYO brought similar criticism of the educational system's treatment of Mexican Americans, as well as of police brutality and harassment of Chicano youths. The latter provided opportunities to team with African Americans, most notably with the Houston chapter of SNCC. "When we could support each other, we would," said José Angel Gutiérrez, one of the five founders of MAYO, "as in the case of Lee Otis Johnson," a black SNCC organizer sentenced to thirty years in prison in 1968 for a minor first-time drug charge. Gutiérrez, as a self-described "soldier" of Tijerina's land rights movement, studied SNCC from afar—and had chances to meet SNCC officers at the 1967 Alianza convention and stay with them in Atlanta in preparation for the Poor People's Campaign.[63]

But, in contrast to California, the extent of cooperation among Chicano student groups and black civil rights organizations in Texas took on a different hue, a reflection of that state's demographic concentrations, a more codified racial caste system, and the continued importance of military service among the state's Mexican Americans. Far less emulation of black organizing occurred in Texas. "I find it most curious to read now that we were heavily influenced by the activities of blacks in our pursuit of civil rights," wrote Gutiérrez, once known for his "acid tongue," to quote one scholar. "We seldom saw or read about them in our area newspapers," he added. Instead, "they followed our lead." Certainly knowledge of the larger black freedom struggle influenced MAYO but usually from afar, not locally. Only in Houston, where African Americans were the dominant minority group, did Chicanos take more of their cues from black activists in SNCC and the Black Panther Party. In addition, memories of how whiteness had been routinely used to distinguish between Tejanos and African Americans, as well as the import of military service to the former, maintained a certain level of distrust. Despite personal misgivings about the Vietnam War, leaders of MAYO—at least early on—expressly forbade its members from identifying themselves with the organization during antiwar protests, or otherwise risk further marginalization among Mexican Americans who still viewed the military as an honorable path to demonstrate or attain citizenship. In contrast, African Americans by late 1967 did not have such qualms.[64]

◆ ◆ ◆

During the last several months of 1967, Corky Gonzales and Reies Tijerina often pursued their distinct but overlapping agendas together. At least early on, the two men seemed to like and respect each other. And even while Gonzales brought a far more urban and secular understanding to the Chicano experience than Tijerina, he recognized the practical and symbolic importance of the land rights movement and the quirky preacher's leadership. "Tijerina is one of our men," Gonzales said when he went to Albuquerque to help in wake of Tijerina's legal troubles that summer, "a man who puts everything on the line for his people, even his life and family."[65] His is a just and honorable cause, Gonzales added. In support, *El Gallo* routinely provided coverage of land rights in southern Colorado and northern New Mexico and encouraged Crusade members and followers to assist however they could. It is less clear if Tijerina felt the same way about Gonzales and his concerns, especially for Mexican American youth in the barrio. Tijerina normally spoke of only the Treaty of Guadalupe Hidalgo, the white-dominated police state, and, to a lesser extent, Vietnam. In fact, a marked rivalry between the men began to emerge as early as 1968.[66]

But in late 1967, they were staunch allies. In October alone, the two men shared the stage at least four times—at a meeting sponsored by the United Mexican American Students at California State College, at an anti–Vietnam War rally in East Los Angeles, at the Alianza's annual convention, and at a protest in opposition to President Johnson's Cabinet Committee Hearings on Mexican American Affairs in El Paso. After federal officials did not invite them to the El Paso hearings, Gonzales, Tijerina, and MAYO leaders organized a protest and a "rump" conference immediately after the demonstration. While very little substantive policy emerged from the formal cabinet hearings, the El Paso protest experience inspired Gonzales to contemplate how to capitalize on the movement's energetic and enthusiastic youth, whom he saw on full display. As MAYO used the demonstrations to launch a new party, Gonzales dreamed of a youth liberation conference.[67]

With the help of the black power and predominantly white antiwar movements, both Tijerina and Gonzales looked to strengthen their distinct fights against poverty in 1967. So did Chicano students, especially those in California. In December, the best chance yet to gain greater regional and national exposure for a brown power movement and Chicano solutions to economic inequality came from another coalition with African Americans and a few whites. But this time, it was a more traditional civil rights organization—one trying to navigate the changing landscape of the late 1960s that the black power and antiwar movements had helped create. As if answering Chicanos' prayer for a national stage, an embattled but hopeful Dr. Martin Luther King Jr. announced a new, multiracial poor people's march on Washington and invited not just blacks and whites but people of all races to join him.

4 ❖ Poverty, Peace, and King's Challenge

On December 4, 1967, Martin Luther King Jr. formally announced SCLC's much-anticipated program of mass civil disobedience for the upcoming election year. The Poor People's Campaign aimed to dramatize poverty in the United States, by leading "waves of the nation's poor and disinherited to Washington, D.C. . . . to secure at least jobs or income for all," King stated. During the following spring, he continued, "we will be petitioning our government for specific reforms and we intend to build militant nonviolent actions until that government moves against poverty."[1] At the heart of the plan was King's notion of "militant nonviolence," illustrated through a series of planned marches, rallies, demonstrations, and sit-ins designed to tie up federal agencies and Congress—all emanating from a central, semipermanent campout of poor people on the Washington Mall.[2] If such "massive dislocation" failed to move decision makers in Washington, then demonstrators would take their protests home to cities and smaller communities across the country, as well as to the two major party political conventions in Miami Beach and Chicago in the summer of 1968. One way or another, King promised, the poor would be acknowledged in the richest nation in the world.

King's vision of an "army of the poor" was ambitious, to say the least. Other activists such as Reies López Tijerina had envisioned and pursued parallel efforts to reach across the seemingly impenetrable ethnic, racial, and cultural lines that so often divided the country's poorest. But King's proposal surpassed these actions in both scope and potential, by envisioning the transformation of an already-evolving black freedom struggle into a genuine national movement of, by, and for poor people.

Whether SCLC was equipped to handle such a daunting task remained an open question. Undoubtedly, SCLC boasted two advantages: an unparalleled access to financial resources, particularly through organizations such as the Ford and Rockefeller foundations, and the continued rhetorical star power of King and aides such as the Reverend Jesse Jackson.

Even after the withering criticism of his Chicago Freedom Movement, his position against the Vietnam War, and his commitment to nonviolent protest, King's articulation of a new campaign against poverty garnered wide attention, even cautious admiration.

But just as SCLC challenged the country to take poverty seriously, this new campaign challenged the venerable civil rights organization itself in several fundamental ways. Much has been written about SCLC's lack of practical organization and communication, especially in regard to the day-to-day conduct of the campaign.[3] Much also has been said about SCLC's struggle to counter adequately the rhetoric and strategy of black power.[4] Without question, mobilizing thousands of people into a multiracial alliance, while balancing the competing interests, objectives, and rhetoric of several movements *and* also adhering to the tenets of nonviolent protest in a time of uncertainty and rising expectations, would have proved daunting to any organization. But journalists then and historians since have been preoccupied with SCLC's disorganization and the viability of nonviolent action and, in the process, have neglected the ideological challenges SCLC encountered in early 1968.

These challenges were laid bare as SCLC prepared for the campaign, and particularly as it confronted issues raised by activists of Mexican descent in the rapidly changing landscape of the late 1960s. A reliance on a charismatic paternalism that stressed mobilization and speech making left SCLC ill-equipped to smooth the tensions inherent to the broader coalitions King sought. The paternalism displayed by SCLC toward women had long been criticized. "It's a man's organization," longtime activist Septima Clark stated bluntly, "and I don't think women's words had any weight whatsoever."[5] Ella Baker and other women leaders of the movement had similar perspectives. Yet the organization also relegated nonblack minorities to the status of "junior partners." The practical result was that most Mexican American activists and others did not respond to SCLC overtures until King himself intervened. He did so by convening a historic multiracial gathering of community leaders in Atlanta on March 14, 1968. Only during this Minority Group Conference did the campaign begin to break new ground in earnest, suggesting the campaign's great potential to build a class-based alliance for the first time. Yet what put those individuals in the room was King.

Ultimately, this reality both reflected and contributed to the continued tentativeness of the era's coalition building. The limits of racial identity seemed to encourage coalition—for both King and his Chicano counterparts. But the same identity also could hinder that same coalition, as SCLC's extensive efforts at collaboration exposed multiple competing and counterproductive hierarchies at work. And these hierarchies were not just within the internal pecking order of King's dynamic cadre of aides. These complex relationships also occurred with other black advocacy organizations and Chicano groups, which were seen by some blacks as less established, less legitimate, and less worthy. The result was genuine enthusiasm for the potential of such a coalition and grave doubts that African Americans and Mexican Americans really could work together beyond the abstract.

◆ ◆ ◆

King had pondered launching such a campaign for months—publicly since a call for action during SCLC's annual convention in August 1967 and privately well before that. Prompted by the devastating uprisings in Detroit and in Newark, New Jersey, in which at least sixty-nine people were killed, King had appealed to President Johnson and Congress to act.[6] In a telegram to the president, King argued that the violence stemmed from a lack of real economic opportunities and that more disorder could be expected. "There cannot be social peace when a people have awakened to their rights and dignity, and to the wretchedness of their lives simultaneously," King wrote. "If our government cannot create jobs, it cannot govern. It cannot have white affluence amid black poverty and have racial harmony."[7] Official commissions seeking explanation of the uprisings, including the Kerner Commission, drew similar conclusions.[8] Even a large majority of the public, polls suggested, supported further federal action "to give jobs to all the unemployed."[9] Yet recalcitrant members of Congress—many of whom viewed more urban spending as rewarding rioters, during a war no less—refused to authorize even an inexpensive rat control program.[10]

In his August speech to SCLC convention delegates, largely written by lawyer and close aide Stanley Levison, King sharpened his critique of the country's economic structure and its unwillingness to address poverty seriously. Replacing what one historian calls the "rhetoric of hope" with a more hard-edged "rhetoric of power," King proposed a massive campaign of nonviolent protest in northern cities.[11] Acknowledging the perceived power of black street violence to enact short-term gains, King contended, "To dislocate the functioning of a city without destroying it can be more effective than a riot because it can be longer-lasting, costly to the society, but not wantonly destructive. Mass civil disobedience can use rage as a constructive and creative force." Marchers would not just walk to the courthouse or Capitol in an orderly fashion with the protection of a parade permit. Rather, they would lead mass school boycotts—much like those in Chicago—but for weeks, not just single days. Protesters could hold "mass sit-ins . . . inside and at the gates of factories for jobs" while "thousands of unemployed youth camp in Washington."[12] He mused later that "militant nonviolence" could include tying up area hospitals or bridge traffic into Washington, or even the safe evacuation and burning of a "slum that was unsafe and beyond repair."[13] But in his attempt to harness the anger simmering in the cities in order to address the injustice of poverty, King led SCLC into uncharted territory. And he remained vague and, privately, unconvinced that such hardball tactics actually could work.[14]

Indeed, the risks were great—street and state violence, political backlash, irrelevance—as several newspaper editorials dutifully pointed out. "To paralyze a city's economy and movement hardly sounds like the redemptive suffering Dr. King used to speak of," stated King's hometown paper, the *Atlanta Constitution*. "It sounds like a threat and an invitation to violence." The *New York Times* called it a "formula for discord," arguing that the result could very well be an even more conservative Congress and president in the near future: "Whether or not Dr. King goes ahead with his perilous project, its mere announcement will give added strength to the powerful Congressional elements already convinced that the answer to urban unrest lies in repression rather than in expanded programs for eradicating slum problems." The *Chicago Tribune*, known for hostility to civil rights, interpreted King's proposal as a desperate attempt to elude irrelevance. "The commander in the paper hat has waved the wooden sword," the paper declared. "Who will follow him in the charge against Cemetery Ridge?"[15] Meanwhile, King's statements sparked little public comment among government officials but considerable maneuvering behind the scenes, particularly by J. Edgar Hoover's FBI, which continued to plot ways to undermine the civil rights leader. By the end of the year, King's pronouncements landed him on the bureau's "agitator index" and made him a target of its counterintelligence program known as COINTELPRO. Other targets included the Black Panther Party, Nation of Islam, and any organizations deemed "militant." The new designation placed King at risk of extensive wiretapping and surveillance.[16]

To address his critics as well as his own qualms, King spent the next several months discussing the merits of a massive civil disobedience campaign with a variety of people, from his inner circle to opinion makers such as the editorial board of *Time* magazine. King had considered bringing poor people to Washington since at least October 1966, when some two thousand welfare rights activists staged a one-day Poor People's March on the capital.[17] But it was Marian Wright, a young NAACP attorney and confidant of King, who helped transform King's vague notion into a concrete idea. As a board member of the antipoverty Child Development Group of Mississippi, Wright appeared before the Senate Labor Committee's subcommittee on poverty in March 1967 and challenged the senators to see the poverty and hunger in rural Mississippi for themselves. "They didn't quite believe me when I talked about how the conditions of life, the poverty, was getting worse and the people really didn't have enough to eat in Mississippi," she recalled. "So they came, and [Senator] Bobby Kennedy came with them, and while they were there to examine the impact of the poverty program on Mississippi blacks and whites, I used it as an opportunity to tell them about growing hunger in the Delta."[18] Kennedy, she claimed, was shocked by what he saw and later that summer suggested that Wright advise King, "Tell him to bring the poor people to Washington" because that would bring a "visible expression of the poor."[19] Wright did so at an SCLC retreat in September, adding her own twist by suggesting a fast and sit-in by King and a handful of poor people and civic leaders at the Department of Agriculture.[20]

Stanley Levison proposed an even more ambitious crusade. Reaching back to the 1930s, Levison envisioned a level of drama akin to the Bonus Army March. In 1932 up to six thousand World War I veterans descended upon Washington to demand an early payment of their war bonuses. After being rebuffed by President Hoover and the U.S. Senate, marchers responded by setting up nine camps across the city to lobby the government and sway public opinion. Within weeks, the camps swelled to more than twenty thousand veterans and their family members, risking unruliness and spooking authorities. After a month, federal troops under General Douglas MacArthur tear-gassed and burned down the camps, a heavy-handedness that helped seal Hoover's reelection defeat as well as legitimize the political strategy of marching on Washington. While the marchers did not receive their bonuses for another three years, Levison viewed the event as an effective form of political theater.[21]

King also received encouragement from more unlikely sources. Soon after the September retreat, a young grass-roots "NAACP militant" unex-

Marian Wright, an NAACP Legal Defense Fund attorney, tells skeptical senators during a hearing on poverty in 1967 to come visit Mississippi, where she served on the board of the antipoverty Child Development Group of Mississippi. Her experience there prompted her to tell Martin Luther King Jr. to bring poor people to Washington—an impetus for the Poor People's Campaign. In the 1970s, she launched the Children's Defense Fund. (AP Photo / Henry Griffin)

pectedly buoyed King's spirits in New York City. According to Andrew Young, the youth did not reject nonviolence as a quaint and outdated strategy. Rather, he stated, "We had not used nonviolence massively enough and disruptively enough in New York and in the North generally for its full impact to really be felt."[22] And despite journalists' overall negativity, at least the editors of *Time* agreed with King that some bold action needed to be taken to combat poverty.[23]

Not everybody within SCLC's circle was in agreement. The most prominent critic in King's inner circle was James Bevel, who made an impassioned plea at the retreat to prioritize antiwar activism. In the spring, Bevel had taken a leave of absence from SCLC to help organize the Spring Mobilization against the War (Mobe) in New York, which he believed represented the future of the civil rights struggle. As "Mobe" organizers had hoped, Bevel persuaded King to raise his visibility in the antiwar movement. But despite staunch opposition to the war, most SCLC aides and board members recalled clearly the firestorm King's raised profile created in the spring and remained skeptical of the wisdom of placing peace at the top of the new campaign's agenda. King and others at the retreat also believed that a "stop the draft" movement, as Bevel had proposed, was impractical. At the time, more than four months before the massive Tet Offensive eroded public support, most Americans still backed the war. While the war could be linked to the summer's uprisings, as King, Stokely Carmichael, and other activists had in public, King believed that the real momentum was for antipoverty causes. Vietnam could be addressed, as one aide suggested, through the "back door." Tensions over the war, however, only became worse over time.[24]

Bevel was not alone in his skepticism. Hosea Williams, a blustery organizer who had worked most recently in Selma, wanted to see a renewed commitment to voter registration in the South. He complained that the Selma office "consists of one person, the Director. . . . I couldn't hardly get gas money down the street."[25] Jesse Jackson, the director of SCLC's Operation Breadbasket in Chicago and a rising star in the organization, saw his operation's use of boycotts of individual industries and businesses as a more productive method to create jobs for African Americans. A Washington campaign not only could distract from local affairs, Jackson argued, but also relied too much on the federal government.[26] Bayard Rustin, onetime adviser to King, also saw the campaign as fraught with peril. Although in agreement with King on the nation's economic needs, Rustin believed that traditional coalitional politics, not protest, were the real "lessons of the long hot summer." "There is in my mind a very real question as to whether SCLC can maintain control and discipline over the April demonstration," he warned, "even if the methods are limited to constitutional and nonviolent tactics."[27] Prominent SCLC board member Marian Logan echoed this sentiment, even after the board reluctantly endorsed the campaign in February 1968. "This bringing of poor people to the seat of government was like throwing it in their faces," she recalled, adding that, in an echo of media predictions, the campaign guaranteed the election of a conservative president and Congress even more hostile to the poor.[28]

These voices, however, did not dissuade King from forging ahead. By the time King spoke in late October to the Kerner Commission, he was convinced that a massive civil disobedience campaign was the viable "middle road between riots and timid supplication of justice." Nonviolence could still work, he contended, because there was no other peaceful alternative. King advocated a new "bill of rights for the disadvantaged" during the hearings, including $20 billion a year for a guaranteed annual income, slum eradication, and housing improvements—the same figure estimated to be saved if the United States withdrew from Vietnam. He then unveiled to the press his determination to have a "camp-in" in Washington to dramatize the issue of poverty and opportunity. Although it was another six weeks before he formally announced the campaign, King publicly committed SCLC that day in late October.[29]

As King's initially vague proposal for massive civil disobedience began to take shape, journalists renewed their attacks on what they viewed as King's new militancy. Calling his words "an appeal to anarchy," the *Washington Post* cautioned, "Those who conjure up mobs to force the suspension of Government itself are talking about revolution—even if they call it 'passive resistance.'"[30] For the next several months, the *Post* and the rest of the national media maintained a steady drumbeat of criticism, issuing dire warnings that the SCLC plan, no matter how well intentioned, played into the hands of militants and likely would result in more chaos.[31] King contended that it was inaction that guaranteed such a result.

Yet the media made at least one important observation: SCLC's new campaign indeed was its most radical to date. But its radicalism did not lie in the potential for conflict or massive disobedience that bordered on the tactics of "any means necessary." Rather, the Poor People's Campaign's most striking militancy came in the form of an aggressive inclusion and recruitment of nonblack minorities. When unveiling the campaign in December, King declared, "We also look for participation by representatives of the millions of non-Negro poor: Indians, Mexican-Americans, Puerto Ricans, Appalachian whites, and others."[32] Such rhetoric became boilerplate in King's public discussions of the campaign during the next several months. And behind the scenes, King made it clear that he wanted a complete cross section of the poor, not just blacks and whites. According to Bernard Lafayette, SCLC's national campaign coordinator, these other minorities were central to King's thinking. "I asked Dr. King, 'Do you mean all the poor people?'" Lafayette recalled. "And he said, 'Are they poor? . . . Then we want them involved.'"[33] But most observers, particularly reporters, did not take this new multiracial dimension seriously and instead focused on their own more sensational definition of militancy.[34]

In one sense, media skepticism was understandable. As a result of his more vocal stance against the Vietnam War, King maintained a strong network among African American activists, stretching from his home base in Atlanta and the Deep South to the far reaches of Los Angeles and the West Coast. He could still speak to moderates such as Bayard Rustin as well as to black power advocates such as Stokely Carmichael, with whom he shared a deep respect and friendship. He had begun to strengthen relationships with peace activists. And despite the unpopularity of his Vietnam position among the mainstream media, polls ranked King as the nation's most "influential" and "trusted" black leader. But when it came time to build a multiracial coalition that included Mexican Americans, Puerto Ricans, and American Indians, King and SCLC had painfully few contacts.[35]

King stayed abreast of Cesar Chavez's activities and was held in high esteem by Chicano movement leaders in general, but King did not know any of them well. In addition to the handful of telegram exchanges with the United Farm Workers leader, King briefly met Reies Tijerina and Corky Gonzales during chance meetings in Chicago during the National Conference for New Politics. Moreover, SCLC efforts in Los Angeles, Texas, and Chicago never succeeded in—or in most cases even tried—penetrating Mexican American communities. Admiration from a distance did not translate into the concrete relationships necessary to organize such an ambitious campaign.[36]

Overall, of all the challenges the campaign posed to SCLC while King was alive, mobilization was the most difficult. Admitting that the campaign would tax his organization greatly, King simultaneously made several personnel moves, hiring William Rutherford and Bernard Lafayette in order to strengthen SCLC's finances and administration in preparation for it. Rutherford, a Chicago native and a skilled public relations manager, was charged with tightening SCLC's loose organizational and financial ship, which he did right away and much to the chagrin of some staff members. But most of the burden of the Poor People's Campaign—and, specifically, mobilization—fell on the young shoulders of Lafayette.[37]

Brought in as SCLC's program administrator, Lafayette had a long resume of organizational and personal affiliations essential to making King's multiracial vision a reality. As a student at the American Baptist Theological Seminary in Nashville, Lafayette interacted with fellow seminarian James Bevel, helped coordinate the sit-ins there in 1960, and went to work with SNCC in several of the movement's most recognizable flashpoints, including the Freedom Rides, Birmingham, and Selma.[38] In 1964 he joined the American Friends Service Committee (AFSC) and went to Chicago, where he later became a key ally of SCLC during the Chicago Freedom Movement. He then helped Bevel coordinate the National Mobilization against the Vietnam War in the spring of 1967 in New York City—again coinciding with King's own rhetoric, this time on the war. That fall, King asked Lafayette to join SCLC and quickly placed him in charge of the Poor People's Campaign, confident that Lafayette's legitimacy among both peace activists and grass-roots civil rights organizers would help form the broad progressive foundation the campaign sought. That antiwar protest had begun to emerge as an important unifying element of the developing Chicano movement also made Lafayette a logical choice to reach out to Mexican Americans—although it is not clear that King knew this. Lafayette's antiwar contacts, however, remained mostly in the East and Midwest, a mix of white, black, and a few American Indians. Other than Maria Varela, with whom he worked in Selma briefly, Lafayette proved to have just as few ties with activists of Mexican descent as King and other prominent aides.[39]

A month later, this lack of networking with Mexican Americans had become apparent. In mid-January 1968, when announcing their plan to bring three thousand organizers trained in nonviolent protest to Washington, King, Lafayette, and Hosea Williams listed target cities only in the East, Midwest, and South. Although Detroit and Chicago did have Mexican American communities, campaign memoranda on both SCLC staff assignments and supporting organizations included only a handful of nonblack activists such as Grace Mora Newman, a Puerto Rican coordinator of the Fort Hood Three Committee, a Bronx-based antiwar group. Places such as California, Texas, Colorado, and New Mexico, where the majority of Mexican Americans lived, went unmentioned. When asked about other minorities' participation in January, King assured the press that, "This is a march of poor people on Washington. . . . Naturally, it will be predominately Negro . . . because the Negro is the poorest of the poor in proportion to his size in the population. But . . . it will not be an all black march."[40] Behind the scenes, however, the campaign looked very much all black.[41]

To address this situation, Lafayette hired two young assistants to help reach organizations and individuals not in the SCLC rolodex. Tom Houck, Coretta Scott King's former chauffeur, and Ernie Austin of the Appalachian Volunteers had a daunting task ahead of them, particularly for an organization better known for building on others' work in the grass roots. From the end of January to the beginning of March, Lafayette, Houck, and Austin directed an effort to contact literally thousands of people to compile a list of interested organizations and individuals. Lafayette recalled a "real fast" process that promoted superficial relationships. At first, they relied on lists and contacts from organizations that early on had agreed to participate, including the American Friends Service Committee, the United Church of Christ (of which Andrew Young was a minister), the World Council of Churches, and the antiwar Spring Mobilization Committee. The AFSC proved particularly helpful because of its deep contacts among American Indians and Mexican Americans. Its presence in Denver, for instance, helped bring on board Indian activist Tillie Walker and eventually Corky Gonzales, while in the Pacific Northwest the organization's long support for tribal fishing rights provided yet another conduit to nonblack minorities.[42] The AFSC also was a prominent supporter of the United Farm Workers' grape boycott. Meanwhile, the Highlander Folk School's Myles Horton and Guy Carawan, activists who had worked with SCLC since the 1950s, proved indispensable in reaching poor whites in Appalachia. Houck said that, by mid-March, they had written what seemed like ten thousand letters and telegrams and had made "a couple of thousand dollars worth of phone calls."[43]

Even though SCLC characteristically put three men in charge, women were the linchpins in campaign recruitment and organizing on the ground. The AFSC's Barbara Moffett, Pam Coe, and Eleanor Eaton worked tirelessly behind the scenes to publicize the campaign and connect potential organizers and other participants with SCLC. Tom Houck singled out Tillie Walker as one of the most enthusiastic early leaders they had contacted: "Tillie would call me every day to find out what I was doing."[44] To Walker, a Mandan-Hidatsa living in Denver, poverty was poverty. "I saw that if you are poor in Mississippi and you are poor in North Dakota, it's all the same thing," she recalled. "You're fighting the same battle." Although she did not necessarily see herself as an "Indian leader," Walker had extensive ties among American Indians and Mexican Americans as the director of the United Scholarship Service in Denver, which assisted mostly Mexican Americans and American Indians to gain admission to elite preparatory high schools. From her post, she knew many young Indian activists who became involved in the National Indian Youth Council, such as Clyde Warrior and Mel Thom, and believed that they were best suited and most willing to spotlight the wrenching poverty on Indian reservations for a national audience.[45]

King, however, remained concerned that mobilization was moving too slowly and that, more alarmingly, organizers had recruited mainly middle-class leaders and not poor people. During an action team meeting in early February, he chastised Lafayette and others on their recruiting. "We have not recruited twenty folks that are people who will go and stay with us," King said. "I am disturbed about the fact that our staff has not gotten to the people we are talking about—not young people, middle-class people, etc., but the hard-core poor people. . . . We can get a lot of people there; that is not the problem. But the much greater thing is for us to get the poor people who will be demanding something because they have been deprived."[46] If mobilization did not improve, King said that he would consider canceling the march. One outcome of his entreaties was the proposal to bring together representatives from interested organizations—particularly nonblack groups—to discuss the goals of the upcoming campaign.

◆ ◆ ◆

Goals had been an issue since King had sketched out his plans in December 1967. Questions regarding what King really wanted to accomplish infused early press coverage. For instance, the *Los Angeles Times* mused whether Washington political circles were correct that King mostly sought to outflank black power adherents, while other editorial pages wondered if King really had thought through his proposal.[47] But while journalists narrowly focused on debates over strategy, the risk of violence, and the misleading binary between nonviolence and black power, potential campaign participants asked more substantive questions. Would the Poor People's Campaign call for peace and make explicit connections, as King had before, between the war in Vietnam and the listing War on Poverty? Would it demand government jobs, assistance in attaining private-sector employment, or welfare reforms? How would it incorporate the objectives of Mexican Americans and other minorities, not quite the same as SCLC's perceived goals? Would it have explicit goals at all?

Finding answers to these questions grew in urgency as recruitment efforts intensified, especially among the nonblack poor. Historians have suggested that much of this debate took place behind closed doors—a battle among King and his mostly male advisers.[48] Indeed, James Bevel, Jesse Jackson, and Bayard Rustin continued to criticize the project as overly provocative, unworkable, and, in the case of Bevel, not sufficiently antiwar. Even Bernard Lafayette, the campaign's national coordinator, believed its policy goals needed to be more specific than a vague call for "jobs or income."[49] Yet the sharpest questions initially came from SCLC's future partners in the campaign, groups such as the AFSC and the National

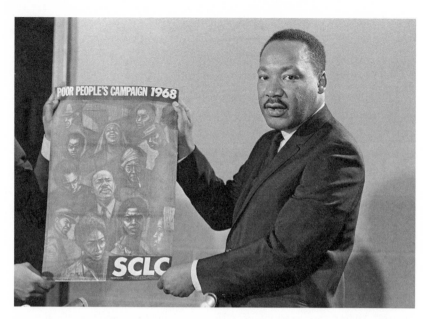

Dr. Martin Luther King Jr. unveils Poor People's Campaign materials in March 1968. Worried that mobilization of actual poor people had been slow, King spent much of March recruiting participants in the Deep South and elsewhere—including Mexican Americans and other minorities. Unfortunately, much of the campaign's promotional materials did not represent the rainbow of people King sought, reflecting the lack of commitment by some within SCLC to include people of other races. (AP Photo / Horace Cort)

Welfare Rights Organization (NWRO). Their demands for expansive but precise policy objectives put march organizers on notice and forced them to hone the campaign's message—a sometimes painful, humbling process that previewed the even greater challenges leaders of the Chicano movement brought to the table.

SCLC had turned to the AFSC immediately because, as Bill Rutherford described it, the Quaker organization "is the only group in America with whom we can identify totally in terms of their devotion to nonviolence and the struggle for freedom."[50] Indeed, not only did the longtime pacifist organization founded during World War I adhere to nonviolence as a central philosophy, but its members were often the few whites in southern towns to champion civil rights early, particularly on open housing, voting rights, and school desegregation.[51] The AFSC saw its participation in the campaign as a continuation of a "common cause . . . to build the same kind of society, one that does violence to no man; one that recognizes the brotherhood of all men," stated Colin Bell, the AFSC's executive secretary. "There is no doubt that Dr. King is addressing himself to a sickness in our society."[52]

In the early stages, AFSC officials were the only outside representatives asked to participate on every level of the campaign, from the Research Committee to grass-roots recruiting. And they often proved quite blunt in their critique of SCLC plans. Although the organization did not come on board officially until February, AFSC officials were intimately involved from the beginning. In December 1967, Marjorie Penney, director of the AFSC's Fellowship House in Philadelphia and an old friend of King's, complained that James Orange, the local SCLC coordinator, offered "unbelievably confusing" presentations and "gave widely differing pictures of his mission and SCLC plans for coming here. The total effect has been one of unusual irresponsibility."[53] AFSC officials also raised concerns over SCLC's initial unwillingness to include nonblack participants in decision making, as well as the location of the Minority Group Conference in Atlanta rather than a more central location such as Chicago or Denver. During the next two months, King and his aides responded to such criticism by offering the AFSC's top officials unprecedented access to discussions of the campaign's organization, publicity, and goal setting. This established the AFSC as a key partner in the campaign's preparation.[54]

Yet by mid-February, campaign goals remained too unfocused for AFSC leadership. Calling the campaign's priorities "disastrously confused," Barbara Moffett offered a five-page memo responding to an SCLC-authored "manifesto" on the campaign. The memo detailed the manifesto's shortcomings, including the lack of a clear-cut statement, "not subject to distortion, of the reasons for the campaign and goals of this army of the poor"; little explicit language on how the poor would be involved in the planning and implementation of policy changes; and no recognizable framework to make concrete demands. Most egregious to Moffett and AFSC officials was the lack of a clear position on Vietnam, one that linked the war to the lack of domestic resources. "It seemed to us that this draft . . . puts SCLC in a position of accepting the inevitability of continued American fighting in Vietnam," Moffett wrote King, when the organization should declare, in unambiguous language, that "in the name of America's crying needs, in the name of morality, and in the name of peace, we say: Stop the War."[55]

For the NWRO, the campaign message became an issue for different reasons. Founded in 1966 as a national federation of local welfare rights groups, the NWRO had advocated for a variety of poverty-alleviating measures, including expanded welfare budgets, more equitable and respectful treatment of welfare recipients, the right of recipients to have private store credit, and an income maintenance program.[56] In September 1966, the predecessor to the NWRO, the Poverty/Rights Action Center headed by former CORE officer George Wiley, sponsored its own one-day Poor People's March, in support of the embattled Office of Economic Opportunity. For more than a year, leaders of the grass-roots-oriented NWRO tried to create a dialogue with the well-established and financially connected SCLC regarding their shared interest in economic justice. But while SCLC had endorsed a guaranteed annual income in 1966, King and his aides did not respond to NWRO queries until campaign planning had begun. By that time, Wiley, chairwoman Johnnie Tillmon, and other NWRO leaders were infuriated with King's promotion of one of their key issues without demonstrating an interest in the details of welfare policy. His sudden championing of the issue risked marginalizing the NWRO and years of hard work by poor black women.[57]

In response to King's request for campaign support in January 1968, NWRO officers demanded that King come to Chicago and hear for himself what the organization's goals and strategies were. After NWRO activists rejected King's attempt to send his "fourth lieutenants" to Chicago, King, Lafayette, Ralph Abernathy, Andrew Young, and Al Sampson met with Tillmon and other female activists of the NWRO on February 3. There, the hosts challenged King immediately, participants recalled later. "How do you stand on P.L. 90-248?" asked Etta Horn, referring to legislation that added a mandatory work program to Social Security and was dubbed "the anti-welfare bill" by activists.[58] "Where were you last October," demanded Beulah Sanders, "when we were down in Washington trying to get support for Senator Kennedy's amendments?" After much hemming and hawing by the increasingly uncomfortable preachers, Tillmon stated, "You know, Dr. King, if you don't know . . . you should say you don't know," to which a puzzled and chastened King responded, "We don't know about welfare. We have come here to learn."[59] From there, the women gave the ministers several lessons on welfare policy—including an explanation of "the anti-welfare bill" mentioned by Horn and Robert Kennedy's attempts to amend it—as well as how important it was that the NWRO and its hard work be recognized.[60]

From there began a fruitful conversation in which the NWRO eventually agreed to participate fully in the campaign, but with a number of conditions designed to protect its autonomy within the larger structure of the Poor People's Campaign. The NWRO leaders not only wanted "prime responsibility for policy, negotiation, and public statements on welfare issues, public law 90-248," and "in negotiations with government agencies around these issues"; they also insisted on taking the lead on welfare rights workshops, both in recruitment cities and eventually in Resurrection City.[61] In addition, the NWRO's planned Mother's Day march on May 12, headlined by Coretta Scott King, would continue to be a welfare rights action, not one shared with SCLC or under the larger umbrella of the Poor People's Campaign. And under no circumstances would they get themselves arrested. "Don't you go talking about putting any of us in jail," declared Beulah Sanders of the New York City-Wide Coordinating Committee. "We have children to take care of. You men, you go to jail."[62] King agreed to all of their demands, but this did not stop SCLC's relationship with the NWRO from being primarily competitive in the months to come.[63]

The NWRO's endorsement of a guaranteed annual income, or income maintenance, also demonstrated just how treacherous a path campaign organizers took when setting more specific policy goals. When demanding "jobs or income" in his campaign rhetoric, King had meant primarily restoring good-paying jobs to poor men. "What does it profit a man to be able to have access to any integrated lunch counter when he doesn't earn enough money to take his wife out to dine?" asked King in a standard refrain.[64] But through a federally funded income maintenance program, female welfare rights activists sought expanded definitions of work, workplace, and even producer. Argued one NWRO activist from Milwaukee, "I think that the greatest thing that a woman can do is to raise her own children, and our society should recognize it as a job. A person should be paid an adequate income to do that."[65] Making a direct payment to every citizen whose income fell below a certain level made philosophical sense to King. Politically, it was another matter. Yet SCLC's partnership with the NWRO translated into a vigorous endorsement of income maintenance and thus posed a substantial risk to building the kind of coalition King sought.[66]

That risk included the further estrangement of labor organizations, most of which had not weighed in on the campaign. While a black-labor alliance had proved rare throughout his public career, King had believed that he could count on substantial support from organized labor in his push against poverty. Instead, most union leaders reserved judgment or outright rejected the campaign. The refusal to endorse by the board of the

American Federation of Labor and Congress of Industrial Organizations (AFL-CIO) came as little surprise to campaign organizers, given AFL-CIO president George Meany's close political ties to the Johnson administration.[67] More surprising was the reluctance of UAW president Walter Reuther. Scholars have blamed labor's lack of enthusiasm on King's Vietnam position.[68] But while King's war pronouncements contributed to organized labor's inaction, the campaign's downplaying of Vietnam and the increasing opposition to the war among rank-and-file union members suggest there are other reasons.[69] The campaign's prominently expanded definition of "work" could be one explanation. According to one "high official" in the AFL-CIO, "Support for this kind of plan just doesn't exist and couldn't exist in a work-oriented culture."[70] This was a problem for most workplace-based organizations. While UAW leadership championed a guaranteed income for idled factory workers, it also drew the line at a federal income maintenance program. Even after the UAW, the United Steel Workers of America (USWA), and other progressive unions eventually endorsed the campaign in April, they took pains not to mention income maintenance in their internal coverage and publicity of the march.[71]

For Cesar Chavez, who did not endorse the campaign, the calculus was different. In addition to being weakened physically by a protracted fast that spring, the UFW leader risked losing the goodwill of grape boycott supporters if he endorsed something seen as not directly applicable to the farm workers' plight. Indeed, the boycott strategy in cities such as Chicago rested precariously on the shoulders of not just labor unions but also white suburban housewives. Chavez feared that making a high-profile endorsement of an assertive black-led crusade such as the Poor People's Campaign could imperil his operation. Thus, with the notable exception of a few predominantly female unions such as the American Federation of Teachers and Local 1199 of the Drug and Hospital Workers Union—the latter with many blacks and Puerto Ricans—organized labor did not devote vast resources to the campaign. Endorsement of seemingly radical policies like income maintenance contributed to this reality—a situation that increasingly worried SCLC officials.[72]

The unexpected clash between the rhetoric of work and that of welfare was just one more example of the complexity of SCLC's challenge in 1968. Three months after the first phase of planning had begun, organization and recruitment for the Poor People's Campaign sputtered. Yet, thanks to such eye-opening experiences as the NWRO confrontation, it had become clear to King that he could not just set a few goals and say paternalistically,

Senator and presidential candidate Robert F. Kennedy visits a fast-weakened Cesar Chavez in March 1968. Despite embracing some rhetoric from the Chicano movement, Chavez maintained ties with mainstream Democrats such as Kennedy and declined to participate in the Poor People's Campaign. (Walter P. Reuther Library, Wayne State University)

"Come, march with me," and people would come—particularly among nonblack minorities. Perhaps some of his aides truly believed, referring to Reies Tijerina in a March strategy meeting, that "we were the parents and he was the child," but clearly Tijerina did not.[73] And increasingly neither did King. Despite garnering respect among Mexican Americans for his movement leadership, King had to work to persuade Chicano activists that they were welcome and full partners in the endeavor. That also required convincing his aides that real concessions would need to be made. According to José Angel Gutiérrez of MAYO, he and his fellow activists assumed that the campaign had not been designed for their participation. "Is this another black-white thing," he remembered asking, "or are we involved?"[74] This may explain why so many Chicano activists interviewed years later did not recall the campaign as an idea until March 1968. Despite King's early inclusive rhetoric, it was not until then that

King himself made the effort to speak with nonblack minority activists, understand their issues, and learn how they understood their own poverty and the solutions to overcome it.

But if King's awareness of such inherent tensions had changed markedly, his decision to keep goals vague had not. If anything, such tensions reinforced his decision not to have a concrete list of demands, beyond the broad "jobs and income" motto designed for the media. He believed that Congress would not respond to proposals of specific legislation: "Underneath the invitation to prepare programs is the premise that the Government is inherently benevolent—it only awaits presentation of imaginative ideas." Remaining flexible was key. "You can say that the goal of this campaign will be to expose Congress," he told a writer for the *New York Times Magazine*. "We will escalate the campaign on the basis of the response we get."[75] He also believed that a complicated list of policy goals and proposals would turn off the very poor people he wanted to attract. Doing any of these things was, in the words of Andrew Young, "building in failure."[76]

Instead, King's hope was that, through meetings such as the Minority Group Conference, he could explain the reasoning behind the campaign, listen to potential participants' issues, and then persuade them to accept some flexibility in the campaign's approach—all in the hope of encouraging genuine poor people to make the trip to Washington. Here was where his charm and charisma might make the difference. This was how he could build trust.[77]

◆ ◆ ◆

With that in mind, SCLC invited some eighty representatives of the nonblack poor to meet for the Minority Group Conference on March 14 at Paschal's Motor Hotel—considered Atlanta's "black city hall"—to discuss this budding multiracial coalition. Several more people came than were invited, and, as many of the participants would say afterward, the conference proved to be a historic occasion.[78]

The Minority Group Conference was just one day at a motor lodge, but in many ways, it was the most unheralded triumph of King's last weeks and of the Poor People's Campaign in general.[79] For a rare moment, activists from several dozen organizations gathered on more or less equal terms to discuss the merits of SCLC's proposed campaign and what exactly, as a unified group, they wanted to achieve. Every sort of social movement organization on the left was represented in the room: civil rights, student, labor, peace, religious, welfare rights, middle class, working class, Chicano, American Indian, Puerto Rican. And so the list of attendees included some of the better-known movement and antipoverty activists in the country. Joining King and his aides were Myles Horton of the Highlander Folk School, Tom Hayden of Students for a Democratic Society, Carl Braden of the Southern Conference Education Fund, former SNCC coordinator John Lewis (representing the Southern Regional Council), Richard Boone of the Citizens Crusade Against Poverty, and Bert Corona of MAPA.[80]

Many other attendees represented a younger generation of up-and-coming activists, hitting their stride in their own communities but unfamiliar to King and other veterans of the movement. Mexican Americans and Puerto Ricans made up the largest delegation beyond SCLC itself. In addition to Reies Tijerina and Corky Gonzales, others included José Angel Gutiérrez of MAYO, Leo Nieto of the Austin-based Texas Council of Churches, Miguel Barragan of the Bishop's Committee for Spanish-Speaking in San Antonio, Oliverio Morales of the South Florida Migrants Council, and New York Puerto Ricans Gilberto Gerena-Valentín and Grace Mora Newman. Mel Thom, Hank Adams, and Tillie Walker helped represent American Indian interests, while Charles "Buck" Maggard and Bob Fulcher hailed from white Appalachia. In all, only a few invited guests did not make the trip, including the fast-weakened and skeptical Cesar Chavez.[81]

King stood at the center of the gathering. But while his prestige put leaders in the room, King had to persuade his guests that the campaign was worthy of their participation. Considering the ideological debates surrounding the campaign's goals, this was a tall order. As the delegates ate a meal of soul food, King made his pitch for the "radical redistribution of political and economic power." Participants recalled that much of the speech focused on a sharp but familiar critique of the nation's economic system and the Vietnam War, as well as the need for jobs or income for the nation's poor. But in a rare rhetorical gesture, King also discussed the denial of land as a source of people's poverty. Although his example focused on newly freed slaves in the Reconstruction South, such a reference also attempted to bind the cause of African Americans with those Mexican American and American Indian champions of land and treaty rights. Imploring the delegates to join what was "now a human rights movement," King concluded that the "nation has mixed up priorities" and that "we must think of the David of truth against the Goliath of injustice. . . . The Poor People's Campaign was designed to get the nation right side up." But, he said, it was possible only if the people in the room joined SCLC that spring.[82]

After King received modest applause, the "bull session" that followed showcased the anxious energy and unanswered questions of the activists present—not to mention the vastly different ways those present sought to combat poverty. Echoing the concerns of José Angel Gutíerrez and others, Bert Corona asked, "Do you want just our support or do you want our demands to include in the whole ball of wax?" Corky Gonzales characteristically was even more pointed, arguing that if King wanted to "confer" with Chicanos, he must understand that "conferring is a two-way street." That included nonblack representation in decision making and policy making, as well as the inclusion of their issues. Tijerina repeated such concerns and then captivated the room with a fist-pounding, table-rattling, stem-winding defense of the land-grant struggle, the Treaty of Guadalupe Hidalgo, and the distraction that debates about violence and armed self-defense posed. "Whites are afraid of their own crimes," he cried. "They are not afraid of violence. . . . The Liberty Bell cracked in rebellion against the betrayal of the aims of this country." He concluded by asking Ralph Abernathy, standing in for King that evening, if the civil rights leader supported the treaty. Couching his answer slightly, an unsure Abernathy responded that they were "with him in spirit"—and the room exploded with applause.[83]

Although some delegates grumbled at the ambivalent response of Bill Rutherford and other SCLC officials who maintained a fierce ownership of the campaign, most nonblack participants were pleasantly surprised by SCLC's openness to hearing their issues. These civil rights veterans listened intently as Hank Adams explained American Indians' pursuit of fishing rights in ancestral waters of Washington State and the obstacles to organizing together posed by "anti-Negro" tribal governments. White Appalachians talked of the ongoing fight against coal companies' degradation of the land and water supply and the "powerful economic and political managers who want to keep us down."[84] Puerto Ricans stressed independence for the island commonwealth, while more urban Chicano leaders sketched out issues of police brutality, educational inequality, and language barriers to services. Whether King and company fully understood the importance of these issues—and several observers believed they did not—participants gave them credit for listening. "He always exhibited a sensitivity to the needs of Mexicanos," remembered Bert Corona. "He understood our particular historical conditions, but he also stressed that we needed to struggle together to correct common abuses. He was very sympathetic and supportive."[85] Tijerina went one step further, saying that King had made a leap "from civil rights to human rights," which in his interpretation meant "from jobs to land claims. . . . What I understand from what Martin Luther King said, he is now committed to all the poor peoples."[86]

As afternoon became evening, tensions began to ease as delegates shared another meal of soul food and began deliberating their level of engagement in the coming campaign. Even when Peggy Terry, a self-proclaimed hillbilly active in Uptown Chicago's Jobs Or Income Now (JOIN), admitted that she had once supported the Ku Klux Klan before hearing King speak, her fellow delegates chose to recognize the long journey she had taken. As Gutiérrez said about organizing back in Texas, when white folks were present, you assumed they were radical, for better or worse.[87] That assumption held. As delegates ate, they continued their conversations and shared a bit of their respective cultures. For instance, Father Miguel Barragan of San Antonio, one of the first and most enthusiastic activists to respond to SCLC overtures, led the singing of several Mexican folk songs during dinner. Attendees then broke into caucuses roughly delineated by race and ethnicity to decide whether they would participate in the campaign. To the relief of the organizers, almost all agreed to move forward.[88]

That evening, conference-goers immediately set to work. One task was the creation of a national steering committee, made up of two representatives from each ethnic group. Designed to placate Chicano concerns over decision making and goal setting, the committee was charged with monitoring the campaign's progress, as well as choosing the Committee of 100, a vanguard that eventually took the poor people's demands to Congress. The steering committee had some influence, but worked primarily as an advisory board to King and SCLC, much to the disappointment of other ethnic leaders. Conference participants also tentatively decided upon a series of caravans—loosely based on the Selma-to-Montgomery and Delano-to-Sacramento marches of 1965 and 1966—that would carry poor people across the country while it built momentum and publicity for the campaign. Only after conference participants sketched out this structure did the marathon meeting end—well past midnight with a rousing rendition of "We Shall Overcome."[89]

Not everyone agreed to participate, but the skeptics still left the conference finding the experience beneficial. Baldemar Velásquez, the youthful head of the Farm Labor Organizing Committee (FLOC) in Ohio, said that King's words resonated with him—a story he still told forty years later while traveling the country as FLOC's president. "His comment was when you impede the rich man's ability to make money, anything is negotiable," Velásquez recalled. "I came away with that line branded in my brain."[90] Even Gutiérrez, wary of King's nonviolent strategy and religious training, said the conference allowed him and fellow MAYO activists a chance to stay with their counterparts in SNCC, still based in Atlanta. "The SNCC people were very much in solidarity," he said. "We had group cohesion instantly, even though we were just meeting each other. . . . We contacted them, and said we're going to go to this thing, and we need a place to stay. So they opened their doors. . . . We tried to interpret to them . . . what the Chicano movement was all about. . . . And vice versa, we'd ask them about black culture, and why not all blacks were militants. . . . We were always constantly inquiring of each other for learning experiences."[91] Most black power organizations, such as SNCC and Stokely Carmichael's Black United Front in Washington, did not endorse the campaign. But they did agree not to interfere with King's Washington efforts, another sign that the media obsession with the rivalry between black power and nonviolence seemed misplaced at best, dishonest at worst.[92]

After returning to Tennessee from the conference, Myles Horton, founder of the Highlander Folk School and longtime trainer of grassroots organizers, penned a letter to King and Andrew Young. In it, he expressed a cautious but real optimism for the campaign's potential. "I believe we caught a glimpse of the future," Horton wrote. "We had there in Atlanta authentic spokesmen for poor Mexican-Americans, American Indians, blacks, and whites, the making of a bottom-up coalition." But he also recognized that this potential could be fulfilled only if SCLC took a different approach, not only by making the end of the Vietnam War a part of the organization's basic program but also by encouraging other groups' autonomous activities. "This, as you know, would require not only sharing of planning but sharing of the publicity where the mass media will be primarily concerned with SCLC," Horton wrote. "Martin, and those of you close to him, will have to spearhead the putting together of grass roots coalitions for the Washington demonstrations. This could lay the groundwork for something tremendously exciting and significant . . . a bona fide coalition. No other organization has this opportunity and therefore, this responsibility."[93]

Horton's warning proved prescient. Despite preaching an increasingly radical democratic vision, based upon an aggressive empowerment of women, Mexican Americans, and other nonblack minorities, King and his organization found it difficult to take the necessary ideological and organizational steps to allow such a loosely controlled coalition to emerge through a campaign that SCLC began. Such actions fundamentally challenged the organization and philosophy SCLC had honed for eleven years, forcing the civil rights institution either to change or to invite conflict among its new partners.

Recognition of this tension, however, did not sink in right away. Rather, by mid-March, a guarded hope slowly began to replace the anxiety felt by King and his aides concerning the campaign. Despite the challenges that the campaign posed to the organization—from competing, even contradictory objectives to questions over the relevance of nonviolent tactics—the Poor People's Campaign took on the appearance of viability. An energy and enthusiasm around the campaign had emerged, buoyed by declarations of support by key religious and civil rights organizations, a surge of volunteers, the recommendations released by the Kerner Commission, and the campaign's endorsement by a rainbow of activists at the Minority Group Conference. In a week's time, four religious organizations from Washington, D.C.—the Council of Churches, Catholic Archdiocese, Jewish Community Council, and the Washington City Presbytery—added their support.[94] And in a more surprising development, the NAACP's national board endorsed the campaign—despite the wishes of Executive Director Roy Wilkins—because it gave "an opportunity for the poor people to lobby for themselves."[95]

The recruitment of individuals willing to march on Washington also showed signs of improvement. "Philadelphia already has 600," Andrew Young told Stanley Levison. "Mississippi has five or six hundred. Every place is running over."[96] Although this last statement was an exaggeration, given King's own continued concerns about recruitment, even unsympathetic FBI informants confirmed that the number of volunteers had increased in many locales and that organizers rapidly had begun to fulfill the two-hundred-person quotas set by SCLC for each city. This was particularly true in the strongholds of SCLC or its partners such as Philadelphia, Chicago, Alabama, and Mississippi. In Alabama, confidence in SCLC's old stomping grounds translated into a met quota of three hundred, while in Mississippi, King's "people-to-people" tours had tapped into a strong following among rural folks such as Mae Bertha Carter, a former sharecropper and now civil rights activist from Drew. Adoring crowds in Mississippi and elsewhere greeted an exhausted yet resilient King, who was sometimes moved to tears by devastating personal stories of poverty and many individuals' willingness to tell their stories in Washington personally.[97]

The despair and frustration he saw and heard on these tours echoed the recently released conclusions of the Kerner Commission, which warned of "a nation . . . moving toward two societies, one black, one white—separate and unequal" and laid the blame at the feet of "a white society . . . deeply implicated in the ghetto. White institutions created it, white institutions maintained it, and white society condones it."[98] Although the commission's report framed the disorders and the racism from which they stemmed solely in terms of black and white—ignoring, for instance, the impetus behind the high-profile uprising of Chicago's Puerto Rican community in 1966—King made sure to connect its findings and recommendations to the upcoming campaign.[99] "This report reveals the absolute necessity of our spring campaign in Washington, D.C., for jobs and income and the right to a decent life," he argued. "Our experience is that the Federal Government, and most especially Congress, never moves meaningfully against social ills until the nation is confronted directly and massively."[100] The question, he asked rhetorically, is to what means would the nation finally respond?

The participation of Mexican Americans and other minorities also contributed to the campaign's new energy. Members of the steering committee chosen by Minority Group Conference delegates met a week later to work out their communities' campaign commitments and potential demands. Not surprisingly, activists were at different stages in their commitments to the march, often based upon their own groups' strengths and organizational prowess. During the meeting, Grace Mora Newman spoke of printing up to 100,000 leaflets in Spanish and assured everyone that New York's Puerto Rican community would send several busloads to Washington (although not necessarily the fifty to one hundred buses exuberantly promised by fellow organizer Gilberto Gerena-Valentín). Chicago welfare rights activists Dovie Coleman and Peggy Terry of JOIN said they were busy recruiting "all poor people," including Puerto Ricans, poor whites in Uptown, and Mexican migrants in East Chicago. Hank Adams and Tillie Walker expressed similar initial support among their fellow American Indians but stressed that "the tribal councils . . . want to make sure that this isn't just a NEGRO movement." Both also added that they already had begun to contend with antiblack sentiment in their communities—a fact several SCLC officials found surprising and disconcerting.[101]

Other steering committee members remained more noncommittal, sensitive to the obstacle of deep-seated prejudice. Cliston "Click" Johnson, a disabled white Kentuckian with nine children was one skeptic. "It's up to the people to decide what kind of a part they want to play," Johnson said. "We just came here to try to get a better idea."[102] He then explained how challenging communication and coordination was in the region, a problem inherent to the geographically isolated towns of the mountains. He also openly discussed the black-white divide and his concerns that it could scuttle local participation. In response to an SCLC offer to send a recruiter to the area, Johnson implored officials to "send someone intelligent. Not someone who's going to stir up trouble between colored people and white. . . . The power structure would like nothing better than to have us fall out among ourselves."[103]

Chicanos were the most enthusiastic of SCLC's new partners in late March. Several attended the steering committee meeting, including Lares Tresjan, a farm worker activist from New York State. Tresjan briefly captivated the committee with horror stories of farm worker treatment, from poor health standards to seventeen-hour workdays. Not only must the farm workers demand Washington's attention, she concluded, "we want to bring Chautauqua County (New York) to the attention of God." And the committee agreed to do its part, entertaining several of Tresjan's ideas on promoting better work conditions. But it was Tijerina again who dominated much of the meeting. Mixing criticism and praise of SCLC and his fellow Chicanos, Tijerina applauded the campaign's broad vision but also questioned organizers over why the Alianza continued to receive such short notice for strategy sessions. It was an imperative to explain the march to Mexican Americans and include them in the decision making; otherwise, march organizers risked undermining support among people of Mexican descent. And to other Chicanos, Tijerina hinted at the underlying tensions created by competition by scolding them to not jeopardize this golden opportunity. "We were invited," Tijerina reminded the Mexican Americans present, including Tresjan and Corky Gonzales. "Dr. King initiated this great plan . . . it was born in his heart and we must NOT question that," Tijerina said. ". . . The last time we were here I noticed that some of the Puerto Ricans and Spanish-Americans were trying to demand too much equality. . . . We must not let jealousy blind our reason."[104]

Despite such enthusiasm, many Americans, even in civil rights circles, remained unconvinced of the campaign's viability.[105] Only some larger dynamic could shift opinion in favor of the Poor People's Campaign—a very real possibility in a volatile political year in which the Tet Offensive shook public confidence in the war and President Lyndon Johnson nearly lost the New Hampshire primary to a little-known senator. The worst in terms of violence and political turmoil was yet to come, and the Memphis sanitation strike was at the epicenter.

◆ ◆ ◆

In several conspicuous ways, the Memphis strike epitomized what King had been discussing in preparation for the Poor People's Campaign. In one labor dispute, the issues of class, race, and gender came crashing together: a nearly all-black sanitation work force demanding not only union recognition—and the improved wages and benefits that usually came with it—but also recognition of the workers' basic dignity as human beings and as men. "I am a man" became a rallying cry for the striking sanitation workers and their supporters because, as one scholar notes, "it publicly articulated long-standing critiques of racial servitude, dependency, and dehumanization." For their working-class supporters, especially women, the slogan addressed their dependence on public assistance through welfare and even "underscored their assertiveness as women."[106] Memphis also seemed like a throwback to SCLC's heyday in the early 1960s. Rather than requiring the careful navigation of complicated multiracial politics or the construction of a new national movement, both inherent to the Poor People's Campaign, the Memphis strike appeared to King as a simpler black-white affair rooted in a long tradition of grass-roots activism. Not only did the strike pit an interracial coalition of civil rights and labor activists versus a white paternalistic mayor and his reactionary supporters, but King also believed he could drop in, make a speech, and then leave without diverting SCLC's already stretched resources. When the Reverend James Lawson, a veteran organizer of the Nashville sit-ins, invited him to speak on March 18, 1968, King accepted.[107]

King's initial decision to go and then his deepening commitment to Memphis, however, highlighted far more than his insistence on transforming "civil rights into human rights," as scholars have illustrated.[108] It yet again demonstrated SCLC's insular decision-making process and how others with vested interest were often left out of the discussions when strategy was ultimately determined—even when Memphis increasingly affected staffers' planning and challenged King's own commitment to the march on Washington. This began immediately as King failed to anticipate several things: the unusually high level of enthusiasm for and exhilaration over his visit, the wild card that the youth gang Memphis Invaders represented, and how outraged King's aides were at his decision to go at the height of their Washington campaign organizing. Andrew Young captured his and other aides' frustration. "I had been down that road enough times to know that to become involved in any way in the garbage workers' strike in Memphis would really mean taking on another campaign," Young recalled. "We had been through this too many times to think Martin could just go to Memphis, make a speech, and leave. Albany had started with one little speech. The Meredith march had taken nearly a month out of the middle of our Chicago campaign. I was constantly in the position of urging Martin to focus our limited staff resources and resist the temptation to respond to every worthy cause."[109]

Young and Lafayette begged him not to go to Memphis, citing his already packed schedule and the campaign's need for King himself to shore up its sometimes shaky support. The campaign's launch already had been delayed once to April 22—just a month away—to coincide with the end of Congress's Easter recess, and King's itinerary for the rest of the month appeared daunting, taking him to towns across Mississippi, Alabama, and Georgia, as well as to New York City, Newark, Baltimore, and Washington. He had just returned from a West Coast trip and had promised his new Mexican American and American Indian partners that he would make more visits to the West, including to reservations and migrant labor camps. But the weary King also was convinced that "Memphis is the Washington campaign in miniature."[110] He was going whether his aides liked it or not. And those racial and ethnic minorities who committed their own resources to the Poor People's Campaign just a few days earlier would have to read about it in the newspapers.[111]

King's first trip to Memphis reaffirmed his decision. Overwhelmed by a packed house of roughly fifteen thousand at the Mason Temple in Memphis, an exhilarated King spoke for an hour. He declared that "all labor has dignity," called for a general strike, and then vowed to return and lead a march, which he did ten days later.[112] But instead of demonstrating the strikers' strength and a unified community, the King-led march ended in turmoil as impatient, disaffected youths stripped protest placards down to three-foot wooden clubs and smashed storefronts. Police responded with overwhelming, often unnecessary force. Aides whisked King away to an upscale hotel out of the riot zone, which only added to the criticism that soon cascaded down on SCLC. Those already inclined to oppose the Poor People's Campaign pounced on the chaos in Memphis, arguing that such unrest proved their suspicions all along—that SCLC could not prevent black street violence from occurring in the nation's capital. Even sympathetic newspapers cast doubt on the campaign. "Small groups over whom the demonstration organizers have no control could and may well be planning to exploit things for their own selfish purposes," wrote the *Los Angeles Times*. "The planned activities of Dr. King . . . can only be negative in terms of accomplishing civil rights progress."[113] Not only did King clearly not have control over the marchers, critics charged, he escaped the scene to what journalists called a "plush" hotel, a far cry from where his constituency lived—be they sanitation workers or the nation's poor. The *Commercial-Appeal* in Memphis even challenged his manhood, running an infamous editorial cartoon entitled "Chicken a-la-King" that showed the SCLC leader literally running away.[114]

The events in Memphis emboldened other critics, particularly those in the federal government. Viewing Memphis as an affirmation of his placement of King on the "agitator index," FBI director J. Edgar Hoover took the opportunity to ratchet up the agency's surveillance of King's organization within COINTELPRO, including a formal request for wiretaps of SCLC's offices in Atlanta (which was denied by Attorney General Ramsey Clark). Meanwhile, congressional critics excoriated King and the upcoming campaign on the Senate floor. Leading the charge was West Virginia senator Robert Byrd, chair of the U.S. Senate Appropriations Subcommittee on the District of Columbia. Calling Memphis "a preview of what may be in store" for Washington "if this self-seeking rabble-rouser is allowed to go through with his plans," Byrd challenged his colleagues and the White House to do something: "It is time for our Federal Government—which in recent years has shown itself to be virtually spineless when it comes to standing up against the lawbreakers, the hoodlums, and the Marxist demonstrators—at least to let the nation know . . . that it will not allow this Nobel Peace Prize winner to create another Memphis."[115] Senator John Stennis, who made a career of wrapping southern white supremacy in a softer shell than his better-known Mississippi colleague James Eastland, suggested that marchers should be stopped at the city limits and allowed to send only a small delegation to the Capitol.[116] Edward Brooke of Massachusetts, the Senate's only African American, echoed the concerns of more cautious black leaders in questioning whether the march could remain nonviolent. Inside the White House, Cabinet members and presidential aides continued a heated debate over how to blunt the campaign, from blocking the campaign's park permit to reminding the public how much the administration had already accomplished for the poor.[117]

Unbeknownst to the many activists who had committed to the Poor People's Campaign, even King began to waver on its future, telling both Stanley Levison and Ralph Abernathy that he was thinking of calling it off. Abernathy recalled King saying, "Maybe we'll have to let violence run its course. Maybe people will listen to the voice of violence. They certainly won't listen to us."[118] Neither man accepted such talk, arguing that it was King's exhaustion speaking. Despite his fatigue, King stayed up late the night of the Memphis violence, expressing a mix of frustration and resentment to a series of intimates, including his wife Coretta, Hosea Williams, and Bernard Lee. In his conversations with Levison, he even toyed with the idea of fasting to prevent further violence, as Cesar Chavez had earlier in the month—and, as a *New York Times* editorial stated the next day, Mahatma Gandhi had in India.[119]

On March 29, King was encouraged by a productive meeting with Charles Cabbage and members of the gang suspected of starting the riot, and he told the press that the Poor People's Campaign was still on. But first, he would return to Memphis and lead, this time, an SCLC-organized march.[120] Many of his closest aides did not agree with this decision, arguing that a return to Memphis meant canceling, or at least postponing, the march on Washington. An emergency strategy session turned into, at least for a while, a rehashing of earlier concerns. Uncharacteristically, King exploded in anger and walked out, leaving Young, Abernathy, Levison, Lafayette, and a few others to work out their differences and achieve a consensus plan to return to Memphis. Admittedly an early skeptic, Young concluded that another march *had* become essential: "Memphis had become a necessary stepping-stone to Washington and the successful launching of our Poor People's Campaign."[121]

It is unclear how close King actually came to canceling the Washington campaign. Two days later, on March 31, King hinted publicly that he would consider canceling it if President Johnson, who had just announced his intention not to run for reelection, wanted to negotiate. King added, however, that, "I don't see that forthcoming."[122] Tom Offenburger, SCLC's public relations director, said that the executive staff never seriously considered such a step; instead, staffers were opposed to returning to Memphis.[123]

But it remains striking that a powerful activist hierarchy, rooted in black identity and paternalism, still appeared to be at work. Real strides toward genuine understanding had been made that spring, as had numerous commitments in time, energy, and resources to the campaign by Chicano, welfare rights, Appalachian, and other activists. Yet, none of the discussions of canceling the march went beyond the confines of King's inner circle, according to SCLC documents, FBI surveillance reports, and records of the other key participants. Rather than discuss the campaign's suddenly unclear future with the national steering committee or the Committee of 100, SCLC's "junior partners" instead had to learn of the campaign's fluid status through the press—on the eve of the campaign.

5 ✦ Race and Resurrection City

Dr. Martin Luther King Jr. returned to Memphis on April 3 triumphantly, delivering the powerful and soulful "Mountaintop" speech in which he seemed to predict his own death. Less than twenty-four hours later, stunning the nation and the world, an assassin's bullets martyred the civil rights leader at age thirty-nine. Among those trying to comprehend was Kay Shannon and her colleagues at the Washington office of the Poor People's Campaign, all of whom at first believed the news to be a cruel joke. Informed by an anonymous caller, she accepted it only after talking to an SCLC representative in Atlanta—sparking a mix of tears and resentment among the staff members present. "The girl next to me, who was black, started to cry and I put my arms around her because I was feeling the same way," Shannon recalled. "She turned to me and she saw that I was white and she immediately turned away, and I had this . . . ache because I knew that we were going to be confronted with that situation from then on."[1]

Indeed, King's assassination on April 4 in Memphis threatened to disrupt not just fragile black-white relations but most of what he had sought in the last months of his life—new alliances, increased public sympathy toward the poor, and a renewed dedication to nonviolent strategy. In the days that followed, black anger and frustration boiled over in more than a hundred cities. Of course, the mistrust and rage of African Americans toward whites and the "system" had translated into civil disorders every spring and summer since Harlem erupted in 1964. But King's death compounded that anger and frustration. While less deadly than Watts and Detroit, the unrest of April 1968 touched more cities and produced more property damage, arrests, and injuries than any other time in the 1960s. Chicago, Baltimore, and the nation's capital, once deemed "riot-proof," were particularly hard hit.[2]

Conventional wisdom might suggest that King's death and the ensuing street violence should have prevented the campaign as planned from ever moving forward.[3] This was certainly the position taken by Washington media outlets. Obliquely referencing the smoldering ruins of black neighborhoods just blocks from the White House, the *Washington Post* proposed changing the march's direction: "Let us have a march, by all means. But why not turn it around and have its route run from Washington to where the poverty is."[4] *U.S. News & World Report* gave congressional critics space to call for the march's cancellation. "There is no legitimate reason for the march on Washington," said West Virginia senator Robert Byrd. "It can hardly serve a constructive purpose. . . . And it carries with it the potential for additional civil disorder and violence."[5]

While both street and state violence did change the dynamics of the Poor People's Campaign, it did not derail the effort. In fact, the response to King's assassination suggested an unusual window of opportunity: the public proved far more willing to support the campaign after his death. Just hours after the assassination, King's successor, Ralph Abernathy, assured the public that "we are going to carry through on Dr. King's last great dream—the Poor People's Campaign."[6] And in the weeks that followed, thousands of people donated time, money, and material to the campaign—including many people who initially had remained aloof or opposed. Mourning SCLC officials welcomed the belated embrace, viewing the surge of support as an affirmation of their plans. An initial visit to Washington by representatives of the poor went well, which helped instill SCLC organizers with desperately needed confidence as the campaign neared. Perhaps the slain leader would be vindicated in death.

The campaign's instant popularity, however, also held real dangers—especially to the careful coalition building and the nonviolent training that organizers had begun to nurture. Ironically, the sudden tremendous interest in the campaign became a burden on an organization already strained by its daunting logistics. This became most obvious in Resurrection City, a tent city on the Washington Mall envisioned as not only a symbol of unity and resolve among the nation's poor but also a pragmatic space to house protesters and launch marches, demonstrations, and, if need be, massive civil disobedience. While at times a vibrant and dynamic community determined to encourage multiracial unity and cultural exchange, Resurrection City more often proved to be a great distraction to campaign organizers—a fact exacerbated by the flood of people who came to visit, see, or live in the shantytown on the Mall. The makeshift town as spectacle threatened to overwhelm the campaign, as much of the mass media chose to focus on the disorganization, conflict, and poor weather that plagued Resurrection City.

As conditions worsened, the multiracial alliances that King had begun to work so hard to build became mired in the city's intractable mud and SCLC's paternalism. SCLC leaders, especially Ralph Abernathy, tried to control the situation and message more and more—with limited success. These efforts, often inadvertently, reinforced an activist hierarchy with primarily African American organizers dictating the campaign's course with little input from others. Whether it was a specific issue to demonstrate around or the simple logistics on when and where to go, nonblack marchers concluded that they actually had little say in the campaign's organization. It may not have been about egotism or even disrespect, many marchers concluded. But the outcome was the same. Most Mexican Americans (and American Indians) believed their history of lost land, culture, and livelihood had been overshadowed by a black-dominated campaign narrative of jobs or income. Thus, they arrived in Washington in anonymity and chose to live somewhere other than Resurrection City. And as a result, the shantytown on the Mall did not become a symbol of the challenges of the poor. It became a symbol of the black poor.

♦ ♦ ♦

There had been a moment of great promise, however, even amid the chaos immediately after April 4. "I noticed it a day or two after the assassination," recalled James Edward Peterson, a staffer in SCLC's campaign headquarters as the capital's riots raged outside. "The phone started ringing; we were sort of barricaded in the switchboard room. Tear gas was being thrown around and the white people were being told that they could leave."[7] Added Kay Shannon: "The black community started calling and saying, 'We want to help, we want to help.'"[8] This was new. Up to that point, many middle-class African Americans in the Washington area had been wary of the campaign, driven by class politics, fear of unrest, and skepticism of its success. The campaign had some official support in black Washington, ranging from the Urban League's Sterling Tucker and Julius Hobson of the Black United Front to members of the D.C. Federation of Civic Organizations. But many local black activists had stood on the sidelines as suburban whites dominated early planning in the capital. Kay Shannon, a peace activist through the Committee for a Sane Nuclear Policy and the United Nations Association, attended a packed meeting in mid-February at which she was surprised to see just two African

A few days after the assassination, dignitaries from the civil rights and labor movements join Coretta Scott King in a march in Memphis in honor of Martin Luther King Jr. From left are: Harry Belafonte, King's children Yolanda, Martin III, and Dexter, AFSCME's Jerry Wurf, Bayard Rustin, Mrs. King, Ralph Abernathy, Walter Reuther, Andrew Young, AFL-CIO's Don Slaiman, and Rabbi Abraham Heschel. (Walter P. Reuther Library, Wayne State University)

Americans, including the AFSC's Tony Henry. Only after King's death did many local faith leaders, politicians, and other volunteers support the campaign. And even then, SCLC organizers came to question their motivations. As Peterson recalled, they "always wanted their name to be on the program."[9] But overall, there was a noticeable and sustained surge of support in the city that would become the campaign's epicenter.[10]

A similar pattern played out across the nation, as activists once dismissive of the campaign reconsidered. Suddenly, local organizers reported hundreds of people interested in attending, including those skeptical of the campaign's nonviolent approach. Lauren Watson, a Black Panther and an antiwar activist from Denver, initially viewed nonviolent strategy as a waste of time. Only after attending King's funeral did Watson change his mind on the campaign. "I . . . felt that as my personal tribute to Dr.

King that I would go ahead and do it," said Watson.[11] In the weeks that followed the assassination, the local Panthers joined a multiracial coalition of political and civil rights activists and marched on the Colorado capitol to demand civil rights legislation in King's name. Watson also took a leadership position in the campaign, using his extensive network among peace activists in the West to recruit participants and organize the Western Caravan from Denver. But his participation did not mean he had changed his mind on the use of armed self-defense, he added: "There's always room for [my] kind of thinking."[12]

That turned out to be true. Although some of the biggest names in black power, such as Stokely Carmichael, Floyd McKissick of CORE, and H. Rap Brown of SNCC, remained uninvolved beyond a few supportive words, many of their followers made deep commitments—often to honor King.[13] Members of the Black Panther Party, especially in the San Francisco Bay Area and other parts of the West, were well represented, including a last-minute funding drive by Bobby Seale and Mark Comfort's agreement to coordinate the San Francisco Caravan. Milwaukee's NAACP Youth Council, which had become a leading radical voice for open housing, chose to go after reconsidering the advice of mentor Father James Groppi, while Los Angeles' Black Congress, an umbrella organization for the city's black organizations, enthusiastically endorsed the campaign. Promising opportunities to provide "security" as marshals in Resurrection City, SCLC recruiters also persuaded several gangs to participate including the Commandos, a Milwaukee gang affiliated with the youth council, and the Blackstone Rangers, Egyptian Cobras, and Disciples, all from the South Side of Chicago. Even Charles Cabbage and the Invaders, blamed by SCLC officials for the March 28 violence in Memphis, were invited, reflecting King's recognition that all these young men wanted was inclusion and respect.[14]

Some of the campaign's loudest detractors in more mainstream civil rights and media circles also tempered their criticism. NAACP executive director Roy Wilkins, who had called for the campaign's cancellation just a day before the assassination, recognized the groundswell of support and dropped his opposition. Meanwhile, onetime King confidant Bayard Rustin not only endorsed the campaign but also offered to replicate his organization of a climactic rally at the Lincoln Memorial, as he had in 1963—an offer SCLC organizers initially accepted. Several newspapers once critical of the campaign reconsidered its wisdom and either offered tepid approval or refrained from further criticism. For instance, the *Atlanta Constitution*'s editorial page questioned its earlier concerns of violence, adding, "How mild that threat now seems in light of the disorders that have erupted in more than a hundred cities." Calling the campaign "inevitable . . . until Congress adopts an economic declaration of freedom," the *Constitution* declared that "jobs, housing, a chance for dignity . . . are the goals now."[15] Even the *Chicago Tribune*'s editorial page, long a sharp-tongued critic of King, remained silent in the weeks after his death.[16]

National fundraising for the campaign also spiked, and necessarily so as the increased interest in the campaign placed even more financial pressure on SCLC. In the Los Angeles area, for instance, celebrities and blacks of means began giving heavily to the cause. Celebrities from television's Robert Culp and Lorne Greene to the big screen's Marlon Brando, Jack Lemmon, and Barbra Streisand opened their wallets and mouths in support of the campaign. Others formed a Hollywood Support Committee and held a highly publicized benefit at the Hollywood Bowl. SCLC officials had learned during past campaigns that it was important to take advantage of such moments; the Birmingham campaign in 1963 had produced substantial financial support but only for a few months. And the upsurge in fundraising proved well-timed, as SCLC records and FBI documents both demonstrate that the organization did not have enough money to transport everyone to Washington who wanted to attend, especially from the West Coast. Ironically, if fundraising improved, recruitment would progress that much more—a development predicted by J. Edgar Hoover.[17]

King's death deeply saddened Chicano activists and reinforced the desire to reach out to their African American counterparts. This often took the form of eulogies and poems in Spanish and English. Words from Bert Corona and Cesar Chavez were secular. King's example proved that we all could "live together and work together to gain a place in society which we merit as men," Corona wrote. "We have a debt to Dr. King, a debt larger than to any living man."[18] But many more were religious, likening King to Moses or even Jesus Christ, consoling African Americans and reminding Mexican Americans that he spoke for them as well. "The Prince of Peace is dead," declared *El Gallo*, while another eulogy called King the new Messiah, "the Moses of the blessed scripture [who] carried his people to the promised land, resplendent in colors, all the colors and all the races."[19] Many Chicanos also attended King's funeral—including Reies Tijerina, Corky Gonzales, and Leo Nieto, a South Texas minister who drove through the night and survived a freak car accident with a bull to witness the funeral procession.[20]

In a series of interviews, Tijerina stressed that King's death demanded, if anything, greater efforts by Mexican Americans to connect with their black counterparts—but not necessarily through nonviolent strategy. "We're going to strengthen our ties, our unity. We have no other choice," he told African American commentator Elsa Knight Thompson.[21] But what that unity looked like beyond the Poor People's Campaign remained unclear. In a more animated appearance with interviewer Della Rossa, Tijerina said that he noticed a change in the thousands of African Americans who attended King's funeral and watched the procession go by. Characterizing the funeral's mood as "fantastic" because "the people were angry," Tijerina suggested that King's death "was the end of the peaceful approach and nonviolence. It was the greatest mistake the militant right-wingers have made."[22]

This potential for conflict worried prominent Chicano activists—at least enough for one to back out of the campaign. After King's assassination, Baldemar Velásquez of the Ohio-based Farm Labor Organizing Committee said that he "lost hope. I didn't think anyone could pull it off. . . . To pull together a cross-racial, cultural united front around class, it was going to take an extraordinary ability to articulate that. I think Martin had that. I didn't think anyone else had that."[23] Not even Cesar Chavez, Velásquez suggested. And Chavez never committed to the campaign beyond vague verbal support. Despite several pleas from Abernathy and campaign participants to come to Washington, Chavez responded that physical ailments and the sheer organizing challenge of the grape boycott required his undivided attention to the work of the United Farm Workers. He later told an AFSC staff member that "he had felt it would be immoral for him just to go and make a speech and then go back to California, that if he had come to the Poor People's Campaign he would have to stay and be part of it."[24] That he disapproved of Tijerina's sometimes bombastic behavior and worried that a failure in Washington, D.C., could cost goodwill among middle-class supporters of UFW boycotts probably played a role as well. Whatever the reason, the best known Chicano leader—and the one most identified as an advocate of nonviolence—stayed away from Washington that spring.[25]

The risk of violence also remained the most oft-repeated critique from congressional critics, who introduced more than seventy-five bills to block the campaign. While Senators Robert Kennedy and Eugene

McCarthy, both Democratic presidential candidates, expressed their support for SCLC's effort, their voices momentarily were drowned out by southerners in their own party. Led by Senators Robert Byrd of West Virginia, Russell Long of Louisiana, and John McClellan of Arkansas, Senate proceedings became venues for attacks on the campaign. Inflammatory remarks praising "shoot-to-kill" policies to quell demonstrators and looters who got out of hand, or charges of communist influence were commonplace. In a tirade on the Senate floor, McClellan charged that "militant advocates of violence" would infiltrate the march—information based upon an informant deemed unreliable by the FBI.[26]

Congressional opponents, in fact, had become increasingly isolated as the once-reluctant Johnson administration began to cooperate with SCLC organizers, including eventually allowing a permit to camp out on the Washington Mall. President Johnson already had signed the swiftly passed Civil Rights Act of 1968, which outlawed racial discrimination in housing, a week after the assassination. When it became clear that the new law had not persuaded SCLC to call off the campaign—and public support for the effort in fact had grown—administration officials decided to remain "flexible" and try to dissuade the poor by giving "them 'small victories' if possible."[27] During a hearing of Arkansas senator John Mc-Clellan's Permanent Subcommittee on Investigations, Attorney General Ramsey Clark and Interior Secretary Stewart Udall refused to take a hard line against the campaign, much to the chairman's dismay. And while the president privately remained "appalled" at the prospect of Resurrection City, a consensus began to emerge in favor of allowing the permit.[28] In a memo to senior Johnson aide Joe Califano, White House staff member Matt Nimetz reminded Johnson's right-hand man that the government not only had supported the 1963 March on Washington but also granted a permit for the more controversial 1967 March against the Pentagon. By mid-May, presidential aides were reading historian Arthur Schlesinger's account of the 1932 Bonus Army march and the government's uncooperative response, which about guaranteed President Hoover's electoral loss to Franklin Roosevelt. Nimetz concluded, "We can learn from their mistakes."[29] That led to the administration's approval of a thirty-seven-day renewable permit for Resurrection City.[30]

◆　◆　◆

Before Resurrection City could be constructed, however, campaign organizers had to figure out how to harness the newfound resources and enthusiasm for the Poor People's Campaign. For instance, how should they involve volunteers such as Victor Charlo, a Bitteroot Salish and antipoverty program employee from Utah who decided, after King's death, that he "had to do something"?[31] Reversing course from King's initial thought to keep such goals vague, SCLC organizers believed that the first step was for the poor to formulate and deliver their specific policy demands as a "last chance" for official action. If the demands were not met, as expected, the poor would begin to march en masse on Washington. Thus, after burying their friend and mentor, a fatigued but determined SCLC staff renewed its recruitment across the country as a campaign steering committee formulated demands to take to Congress and federal agencies.[32]

Records of these internal deliberations are scarce, but the final list of demands was comprehensive, reflecting the broad multiracial range of issues discussed initially at the Minority Group Conference in March. Numbering forty-nine pages, the demands were organized into more specific statements to individual cabinet secretaries, agency chiefs, and members of Congress, but they also echoed five broad requirements of any governmental action to "set poverty on the road to extinction," including:

1. A meaningful job at the living wage for every employable citizen
2. A secure and adequate income for all who cannot find jobs or for whom employment is inappropriate
3. Access to land as a means to income and livelihood
4. Access to capital as a means of full participation in the economic life of America
5. Recognition by law of the right of people affected by government programs to play a truly significant role in determining how they are designed and carried out

Such rhetoric, backed up by specific policy initiatives, was the campaign's most inclusive to date and clearly reflected the concerns of those Mexican Americans and American Indians engaged in treaty and land rights and cultural and tribal sovereignty—as well as those of the NWRO and SCLC's more traditional black partners.[33]

For both the NWRO and SCLC, goals that were alien to black organizers just two months earlier seamlessly appeared throughout the list of demands. In addition to universal concerns over welfare rights, access to quality education, health care, housing, fair employment practices, and

poor people's full input in antipoverty policy decision making and implementation, the demands highlighted issues specific to these communities.
For Mexican Americans, they included requests for special housing programs for Spanish-speaking people "in line with their cultural habits,"
withdrawal of "all subsidies, . . . contracts and services from farm employers who employ illegals or 'green card holders' during a strike," and the
Justice Department's full investigations of "illegal jailings, brutal beatings
and even killing of Mexican-Americans by the police." A reevaluation
of the Treaty of Guadalupe Hidalgo headlined a list of foreign policy
requests to Secretary of State Dean Rusk that also criticized U.S. cooperation with the governments of South Africa, Israel, and South Vietnam.
Similarly, for American Indians, demands called for investigations of
police brutality on reservations and "action to protect the hunting and
fishing rights of Indians." And in further reaffirmation of century-old
treaty rights, demands for the Department of the Interior and the Bureau
of Indian Affairs stressed recognition of Indians' unique autonomy as
"separate and equal communities within the American system.[34]

But the importance of the Committee of 100—made up of one-third
steering committee members and two-thirds recruited poor people—was
not just rhetoric. The initial Washington "lobby-in," as much of the press
called it, represented the campaign's best effort at physically projecting
an integrated multiracial vision. Led by Ralph Abernathy, this vanguard
arrived in Washington on April 28 and was remarkably diverse—not only
racially but also in terms of class and gender. More than 30 percent of the
protesters were Mexican American, Puerto Rican, or American Indian
and roughly half were women. "The committee was multiracial and multiethnic," recalled Andrew Young. "We did not appreciate it at the time,
but with Martin's death, the Poor People's Campaign became the venue
through which his coalition of conscience came together."[35]

The first morning, Abernathy led the Committee of 100, singing freedom songs, out of the Church of the Reformation and to their first stop at
the Department of Agriculture. There, Abernathy delivered an opening
statement calling the existence of hunger in the United States "a national
disgrace." But as would become the norm during the next three days,
Abernathy then introduced a series of other people to speak for the nation's dispossessed. Chicanos blended the problems of the poor with their
own needs. Speaking to Attorney General Ramsey Clark later that day,
Miguel Barragan, a Roman Catholic priest from Texas, called for the end
of police harassment of Mexican Americans, whether they were migrant

workers or Reies Tijerina. Just two days before, Tijerina had been arrested on twenty-four counts related to the Tierra Amarilla courthouse raid, preventing the land-grant rights leader from going to Washington.[36] Maria Varela, a SNCC veteran who recently joined Tijerina's Alianza, spoke in his place. The next day, Lares Tresjan of the United Farm Workers and the Crusade for Justice's Corky Gonzales addressed the Senate Subcommittee on Employment, Manpower, and Poverty. A former local poverty program director himself, Gonzales criticized the performance of such initiatives in Denver. "Your pilot programs are merely another method of helping municipalities hire people to wash and clean their floors, clean their windows, and pick the weeds and papers," charged Gonzales. Calling them "'window dressing' for the establishment," Gonzales argued that the programs needed to be sensitive to "culture and . . . ethnic identification" to be most productive in the nation's barrios.[37]

American Indians also played prominent roles during the three days in Washington. On leave from his position with Utah's Indian Community Action Project, Victor Charlo read an initial statement to the Office of Economic Opportunity's Bertrand Harding, requesting greater participation by the poor in programs designed to help them. And Mel Thom, a Paiute from Nevada and executive director of the National Indian Youth Council (NIYC), delivered the committee's introductory remarks to Interior Secretary Stewart Udall and Commissioner of Indian Affairs Robert Bennett, whose agencies had primary jurisdiction over the nation's Indian reservations. "We ask to be heard, not just listened to, or tolerated," Thom said. "The oppressed can be oppressed only so long."[38] Epitomizing that sentiment was Martha Grass, a Ponca from Oklahoma who was arguably the Indian delegation's most powerful voice. The mother of eleven and wife of a disabled veteran, Grass told a U.S. Senate subcommittee and Secretary of Labor Willard Wirtz of her family's vicious circle of poor education, few job opportunities, and hunger. "We are not educated because we do not have the money," Grass reminded senators. "You talk about education funds. Who gets it?" Earlier, she had told Wirtz that, "My son can get work all right. He can pitch hay for two cents a bale. We don't want government handouts. We want work. We don't want bosses telling us they won't hire us because we're Indians. And we don't like having to beg for what was once ours, after all."[39]

Of course, blacks and whites were also part of the Committee of 100 and spoke their minds—too much for some observers. From African American welfare rights activists Alberta Scott and Dovie Coleman to unemployed white coal miners Robert Fulcher and Click Johnson, the poor offered their specific prescriptions to alleviate their plight, whether it was urban Chicago or rural West Virginia. Puerto Rican activist José Ortiz also spoke, representing youth in New York City. Issues of respect repeatedly arose amid the calls for more resources and control over their own lives. "A man should be refunded or taken care of to where he can hold up his head in dignity," said Fulcher, who worked in the mines for more than twenty years before becoming disabled, "not in shame, but in dignity, that an industry that he gave his life to is able to protect him and care for him."[40] Most of the poor delivered pointed but respectful statements—although not all and not always to the official with the correct jurisdiction. While the press did highlight African American voices, they were often the angriest voices. One black man told officials, somewhat menacingly, "Baby, you better come on down to earth, because if you don't, there ain't gonna be no more earth."[41] Philadelphia meat-wrapper Karen Allen blasted Attorney General Ramsey Clark on the limitations of existing government programs and their impact on people's diet and dignity. "You look down on people who live off welfare," Allen told Clark. "You say how could we be poor and look so fat. . . . We eat boiled potatoes for breakfast . . . fried for lunch . . . baked for dinner . . . Sure you get fat. When you train people for jobs, you train them for menial jobs nobody wants. Why doesn't the Government train them for work they want and will enjoy?"[42] Newspaper reports also framed Abernathy's periodic lateness as disrespectful and his response when questioned as flip: "We've been waiting on the white man for 100 years, and today we just decided to let them wait on us."[43] It also illustrated his inclination to speak in racial instead of class terms.

Despite such reporting, the Committee of 100's visit to Washington—designed for media consumption—garnered some of the campaign's best publicity. To government officials and media observers, this resulted from the vanguard's overall "orderly and peaceful" demonstration of democracy, as constituents respectfully proposed changes to their government representatives.[44] Organizers, however, were more proud of the vanguard's success in presenting a genuinely multiracial effort by poor people. The press, however, did not always cooperate in that sense. Most of the mainstream media, including the *New York Times*, quoted and photographed only Abernathy and the chastened politicians.[45] But there were notable exceptions in periodicals ranging from the *Washington Post*, the newspaper of the capital elite, to the black working-class *Jet* magazine—both of which featured a rainbow of faces and voices in the name of the poor. And despite few written details, the *Los Angeles Times* printed a front-page photograph of the multiracial contingent linked arm-in-arm.[46] Thus, the activists left Washington pleased with their opening salvo, putting the government on notice while portraying the poor as not just black but of many races and ethnicities. Little did the Committee of 100 know that this initial visit would prove to be the campaign's high water mark of multiracial unity.

◆ ◆ ◆

On May 2, 1968, Coretta Scott King laid a wreath where her husband had been killed, pledged her "eternal loyalty and dedication" to the work "he so nobly began," and officially launched his last crusade. After a brief memorial service, Ralph Abernathy, wearing jeans and a denim shirt, started the Freedom Train caravan to Washington with more than one thousand marchers and two mules pulling a wooden cart. The caravan, started from Memphis, traversed Marks, Mississippi, and the Delta, and then wound its way through the rest of the Deep South on its long march to Washington. It was joined by eight other caravans: the Southern, Eastern, Midwestern, Western, and San Francisco caravans, the Indian Trail, the Appalachian Trail, and the Mule Train.[47]

Born out of the Minority Group Conference and reminiscent of SCLC's 1965 Selma-to-Montgomery march and the UFW's Delano-to-Sacramento action in 1966, the caravans offered the dramatic spectacle favored by SCLC—but not always to its favor. The caravans certainly provided an opportunity to recruit and build momentum along the way. City after city, communities warmly received them, orchestrating sympathy rallies and marches and contributing supplies and people.[48] The caravans themselves, carefully coordinated at times and wildly disorganized at others, took on their own distinct personalities as they crept across the country.[49] But while they created interesting publicity, the caravans also reinforced a narrow portrait of the campaign. The mainstream and alternative media were interested primarily in the caravans from the South, filing daily reports as they traveled through several civil rights "flashpoints," including Montgomery on the day that Alabama governor Lurleen Wallace's body lay in state. Photographs of blacks marching and Ralph Abernathy in overalls dominated news coverage.[50]

Of particular interest was the use of mules, especially in the Mule Train.[51] Featuring fifteen mule-driven wagons, this caravan dramatized the abject poverty of rural Mississippi by using a universal symbol of sharecropping. Nearly scrapped because of its inherent impracticality, the mules offered moments for showmanship, as Ralph Abernathy— wearing an armband trumpeting Nina Simone's call to arms, "Mississippi Goddam"—explained to a laughing crowd that two mules were named after Mississippi's white supremacist senators, John Stennis and James Eastland. Not surprisingly, the mules became an instant hit with photographers, journalists, and the public. But as vivid as the Mule Train was, it also risked reinforcing a racialized and regionalized understanding of poverty. The three southern-based caravans were overwhelmingly black, with just a few whites and Indians participating. In the end, the Mule Train became symbolic of the larger campaign's logistical challenges as well; thanks to long delays, the mules arrived in Washington two days after the campaign's climactic rally in late June.[52]

In contrast, the Eastern and Midwestern caravans, with their more diverse, urban constituencies, received far less attention. Starting with fifty participants in Brunswick, Maine, the Eastern Caravan added blacks, whites, and the campaign's approximately three dozen Puerto Rican participants as it moved through the major cities of the East Coast. By the time it reached the outskirts of Washington, the caravan totaled nearly one thousand people in two dozen buses. Dubbed the most suspicious and potentially violent by the FBI, the Midwestern Caravan also passed through several cities and boasted five hundred disproportionately young participants, many of whom belonged to gangs in Chicago, Milwaukee, and Cleveland. Only when violence broke out did either caravan receive much notice from the press. Both the *Los Angeles Times* and *New York Times* made front-page news of the minor assault on Josef Mlot-Mroz, a self-described "Polish freedom fighter" and campaign critic in Boston. Similarly, those marching from the Midwest showed up in the media only after police and marchers scuffled in Detroit, knocking down Milwaukee's activist priest James Groppi.[53]

The first of the southern caravans, the Freedom Train, arrived in Washington on May 12, in time for a Mother's Day march led by Coretta Scott King and welfare rights activists. Keeping a promise made before the assassination, SCLC officials took a backseat to the NWRO and other women's organizations that sponsored the march and wanted to emphasize welfare rights specifically. A few dozen NWRO activists even had held a small demonstration on the campaign's original start date weeks before in tribute to Dr. King. But on May 12 a much larger crowd of several

In Washington, activists with the National Welfare Rights Organization hold a Mother's Day march on May 12, 1968—a day before Resurrection City opens. Coretta Scott King headlines the march, which NWRO officials insisted on organizing independently from SCLC and not under the umbrella of the Poor People's Campaign. (Jack Rottier Collection, Special Collections & Archives, George Mason University Libraries)

thousand, including Betty Friedan and Ethel Kennedy, joined King as they walked through rain in the neighborhoods damaged by riots after her husband's death the previous month. Speaking at a rally at the end of the march, King stressed women's roles in perpetuating the use of non-violence and helping the poor. "I firmly believe," King said, "our last and best hope for a future of brotherhood and peace lies in the effective use of woman power."[54] Given poverty's disproportionate impact on women, organizers delighted in the march's symbolism. But a symbol of what? Men, in fact, outnumbered women at the march's culminating rally. And other than the conspicuous presence of Clifton Hill, a Creek from Oklahoma, the crowd was overwhelmingly black and white. Such perceptions did not change as the campaign's most potent symbol, Resurrection City, began to rise in West Potomac Park on the Mall.[55]

To a crowd's joyful shouts of "freedom" the next day, Ralph Abernathy drove the first stake into the ground at Resurrection City and officially began the tent city's role as symbol of the entire campaign. Organizers originally had called the new settlement the City of New Hope, until officials at a California hospital of the same name complained. In its conspicuous location adjacent to the Lincoln Memorial and the Reflecting Pool, the camp naturally attracted attention from journalists and dignitaries to curious photo-snapping tourists. But first and foremost, the city had the pragmatic function of housing, feeding, and organizing up to three thousand poor people and their allies. Sketches by University of Maryland architect and local activist John Wiebenson envisioned an orderly city of about five hundred A-frame "homes" of plywood, two-by-fours, and canvas, running along two streets and supplemented by several larger structures to house the city's governing council, health and dental clinic, cafeteria, freedom school, cultural exchange center, and other services expected in a town of comparable size. Engineers planned to tap into old sewer and water lines, once used by temporary Navy Department buildings during World War II, for modern toilet and bath facilities, as well as food preparation. As architectural drawings often do, the sketches of Resurrection City took on an almost surreal look—stripped of the chaos and messiness so often found on a city street, particularly what would be found in the real Resurrection City.[56]

In reality, orderly would not describe the city, which ran into problems almost immediately. Shortages in funds slowed the construction of Resurrection City shelters, forcing the diversion and delay of several of the caravans to temporary quarters in suburban churches. Four days after Abernathy sank the first stake, housing for seven hundred residents had been completed. But at least eight hundred more marchers stayed elsewhere and another fifteen hundred marchers were expected within a few days. And even with some of the A-frame huts ready, the rest of the city's infrastructure was not. Rather than dig the necessary trenches to lay electrical and phone lines and hook up pipes to the sewer system before marchers arrived, such work remained weeks after people were living there. This was both the result of a late request and granting of the park permit, and Abernathy's insistence that the symbolic first stake go into pristine ground. According to Tony Henry, deputy coordinator of the campaign, Abernathy "wanted to be the first man to drive in the stake and wanted nothing done to the land before he did that and wanted the people to move in immediately afterward, so we had to try to do it that way."[57] This produced considerable inconvenience for those living there, as well as the ill-advised decision by top SCLC officials, including Abernathy, to live temporarily in the Pitts Motor Hotel—a move roundly criticized as hypocritical when it became public.[58]

Bernard Lafayette, the campaign's national coordinator, compounded these issues by holding a disorganized and uninformed press conference in which he exaggerated the campaign's financial challenges. Predicting that the absurd number of one million people would descend upon the capital by month's end, Lafayette announced that the campaign needed $3 million in order to finish construction of Resurrection City, adding that the building might be halted until the organization raised at least some of the money. The media responded to these numbers with incredulity, with good reason, as SCLC's Andrew Young clarified the next day: SCLC needed $3 million for the entire campaign, much of which it already had received in donations, while marchers probably would not exceed fifty thousand. "I talked to Bernard and he just goofed," Young explained, but the press conference left a lasting impression that SCLC officials might be in over their heads and wasting the nation's time.[59]

That attitude seemed increasingly prevalent among journalists in the first days of Resurrection City, which trumped the campaign's larger message of poverty. The press had been deeply skeptical of the campaign from its announcement the previous year, giving SCLC organizers only a brief reprieve in the weeks after King's assassination. But this fleeting sympathy rapidly dissipated amid the misinformation and consistently late-starting press conferences. According to Charles Fager, an early chronicler of the campaign, "most newsmen were getting fed up with the petty harassment they continued to encounter from the (security) marshals and with the now obvious runaround by staff at the camp." The press began to feed hostile editorial desks the kind of negative stories editors sought, added Fager.[60] But while some of SCLC's poor management might have been inexcusable, anyone who had covered the movement— especially the previous campaigns of SCLC—should have been prepared for disorganization, even chaos. As one scholar of SCLC notes, the organization always had been "a study in confusion."[61] Most of the Washington press corps had not covered the movement before and were thus overly distracted by logistics. "The press never did get into the real substance of why we are here," lamented Tom Offenburger, SCLC's director of public

For forty-two days, Resurrection City occupies West Potomac Park, immediately southwest of the Lincoln Memorial and the Reflecting Pool on the National Mall. At its height, the encampment was home to approximately twenty-five hundred people and had many of the services and amenities of a small city, including a city hall, daycare center, health clinic, cultural center, and even its own zip code. (Jack Rottier Collection, Special Collections & Archives, George Mason University Libraries)

information and a former reporter himself. "The press . . . is ready to write a story about something they can see with their own eyes and don't have to interpret or understand much."[62]

In response to the increasingly negative publicity surrounding Resurrection City, SCLC made a concerted effort to "sell" Abernathy as the civil rights organization's new leader, to make it clear he was in control. This often meant pushing Abernathy to center stage, to the detriment of the campaign's multiracial leadership. SCLC's effort also translated into trying to overcontrol the campaign's message, by providing numerous news conferences and press releases, while limiting press access to Resurrection City. The move backfired. Rather than reassure observers, it invited even more comparisons between Abernathy and his charismatic predecessor. In contrast to the urbane and intellectual King, Abernathy reflected his humble roots from rural Alabama and often more readily identified with the black working class than King did. Abernathy's speeches had their own charm and power in their plain-spokenness. But after King died, some observers believed that Abernathy tried too hard to fill his friend's shoes with grand rhetorical flourishes that ultimately fell flat. Therefore, while accurate, such observations by journalists, politicians, and even some SCLC insiders often served as a critique of a man not considered as polished and therefore acceptable to white liberal donors.[63] "Has he the requisite intellectual tools to attain the prominence necessary for . . . effective leadership on a national scale?" the *Chicago Defender* asked. "It is an acid test."[64]

Shifting media focus to Abernathy ironically threatened to overshadow the development of a thriving community in Resurrection City, which, despite its difficulties, had become home for almost twenty-five hundred people at its peak in late May. Described by one magazine as a "revival meeting within a carnival within an army camp," Resurrection City took on "a unique throbbing personality" through a rich diversity of people and a high level of creativity.[65] Residents identified the grassy "streets" between tents with names such as Love Lane and Abernathy Avenue; homes became the Sugar Shack, The Great Society, the Cleveland Rat Patrol, and Venceremos. Doctors with the Medical Committee on Human Rights made "shanty calls," barbers cut hair, and marshals tried to keep the peace. Children played in a daycare center named after Coretta Scott King, while men played checkers. If residents did not meet during periodic demonstrations at a federal agency or a meeting with a member of Congress, they saw each other in line for food or chemical toilets. A newspaper written solely by the camp's inhabitants, *True Unity News*, began to publish, and seemingly every night the entertainment was "the finest in town." With freedom singers and revivalists plus top-flight entertainers like Muddy Waters, Diana Ross, and Gladys Knight and the Pips, Resurrection City quickly became a renowned concert venue. The tent city even had its own ZIP code, 20013—in part to allow for residents' receipt of government benefits.[66]

Resurrection City also witnessed intentional efforts to foster a sharing of different cultural styles and knowledge, particularly through the Many Races Soul Center and the Poor People's University. The Soul Center, located in the small so-called white section of Resurrection City, fostered intercultural exchange among the campaign's diverse participants, especially through music and dance. Coordinated by the Highlander Folk School, the Smithsonian Institution, and SCLC's cultural committee, the center organized activities ranging from historical discussions to live performances. While organizers sponsored some well-known folk artists such as Pete Seeger, of particular importance was finding "musicians and artists from among the residents themselves"—just as *True Unity News* inspired poetry and other writing by the residents.[67] "When the rain started, a shelter was built above the fire where coffee was always boiling and around which good conversation or singing was always taking place," wrote Myles Horton, who as Highlander's founder long had encouraged cultural understanding through music and art. "The scheduled sessions soon gave way to an 18-hour round of informal discussions, arguments, music, singing, coffee drinking and eating."[68] Visiting entertainers found their way there for informal sing-a-longs. From movement icon Bernice Reagon singing freedom songs to Miguel Barragan performing traditional Mexican ballads, the Soul Center hosted a daily symphony of sorts. Reagon, who helped found the SNCC Freedom Singers, recalled an evening at the Soul Center as one of her earliest moments of multiracial cultural exchange: "I saw musicians relating and shifting their material because they were acknowledging the relationship between who they were and who somebody else was."[69]

Organizers had similar aspirations for the Poor People's University, which featured twenty-five lectures and workshops in Resurrection City, as well as activities at nearby George Washington University. Speakers included Michael Harrington, radical journalist I. F. Stone, and pacifist and future Chicago Seven member David Dellinger, while classes ranged from a welfare-rights-sponsored Ethics of a Guaranteed Annual Income to Mexican history and culture taught by Corky Gonzales. As one official explained it, the university was designed to expand folks' horizons beyond "another pair of shoes," and, indeed, at least one observer witnessed a class on Gandhi transform itself from a dull lecture "into an outdoor marketplace of ideas."[70] Some classes kept people's attention, such as Gonzales's discussion of Chicanos' indigenous heritage. But much of the programming struck some observers as boring, unproductive, and too dominated by middle-class whites. Thus, discussion leaders found their audiences constantly shifting, sometimes exacerbated by people leaving in midstream for demonstrations. Hostility among the students was also palpable. For instance, Michael Harrington felt demoralized because a black man, "I think with emotional problems, decided that I was the incarnation of white racism. . . . I became concerned that he could physically attack me. The meeting . . . came to a very unhappy ending, where my message didn't get across."[71] The sharing of knowledge certainly occurred but not always through formal classes. As D.C. teachers' union official Charles Cheng said: "The whole Resurrection City experience was a Freedom School."[72]

Despite press restrictions, at least a few more enterprising journalists were able to dodge the marshals controlling access to the camp to find out why folks were there and get a taste of their experiences in Washington. And what they found was that many poor people saw Resurrection City in empowering yet practical terms. "It ain't no fun riding buses day in and day out and it ain't no picnic living here," said Mary Hyde, who came from Chicago with one of her seven children. "But we think it's worth it because we've lived with trouble all of our lives and we're here to stop trouble. I came here . . . because we got to straighten out these Congress people's values." Resurrection City "shouldn't have to exist" in the richest nation in the world, added Aleah Omeja of New York. But those questioned seemed willing to deal with the inconvenience of living in the tent city if it translated into better opportunities and greater dignity in the long run. Dempsey Price was fired from his job as a coal handler when he told his supervisor that he was going to Washington. "I'll tell you why I'm here," said Price, who was African American. "I'm here because I'm 59 years old and there are people who still call me 'boy.'"[73] That that kind of disrespect proved largely absent from Resurrection City was an accomplishment of sorts—and allowed some people to call the ragged tent city on the National Mall "the only real home they had ever had."[74]

While the drama of Resurrection City and the Mule Train played out under the glare of the national media spotlight, those about to embark on the caravans in the West remained in relative obscurity.[75] Yet it was on the dozen or so buses of these caravans—distinctive in their rich diversity and distance traveled—where the campaign's dynamic multiracial relationships, both productive and destructive, were best on display. The Western Caravan began May 15 in Los Angeles, wound its way through Arizona and New Mexico to El Paso, through Albuquerque and Denver—where it linked up with the San Francisco Caravan—and then east to Kansas City, St. Louis, Louisville, and finally Washington. In eight days, the caravan covered more than thirty-two hundred miles and eleven states. Meanwhile, a smaller caravan called the Indian Trail left two days later from Seattle and moved along the northern edge of the country through the reservations of Montana, North Dakota, and Minnesota before eventually arriving in Washington. After spending so much time on the road together, in both exuberant rallies and intimate living quarters, large sports venues and personal homes, a community took shape on those buses. Yet barriers between people of different races remained, a reminder of the fragility of such coalitions.

Reies Tijerina and Corky Gonzales remained the most prominent voices on the Western Caravan. And as a result, those few accounts that do address Chicano participation generally allow these two men to speak for everyone.[76] For the embattled Tijerina, the campaign brought not just the chance to trumpet the land rights issue, but also the opportunity to bolster his personal legitimacy amid legal troubles from the Tierra Amarilla raid. "The more I was accepted by the world as a voice of the oppressed people of the United States, the more that (U.S. senator Joseph) Montoya's bosses became irked," Tijerina said, referring to the white supporters of New Mexico's Mexican American senator and a Tijerina critic. "Anglos in power in the United States did not want me to be seen next to King" or his successors.[77] Similarly, Gonzales saw the campaign as a chance to raise the profile of a burgeoning but still fractured Chicano movement. To the political establishment that dominated media coverage and federal policy, Chicanos remained nearly invisible. After receiving the invitation to participate, Gonzales postponed his own plans for a regional Chicano youth conference to make fruitful contacts with his black counterparts, other Chicano activists, and even sympathetic members of the white power structure, be they journalists or public officials. Gonzales also believed that "the real work, building bases of power, would remain when the activists returned."[78] Therefore, joining the campaign was just as much about tactics and national exposure as it was a shared ideology about class and poverty.[79]

But Mexican Americans (and American Indians) had reasons for participating that went well beyond those of Tijerina and Gonzales—or their black counterparts. Marchers viewed the campaign as the fulfillment of a variety of dreams and goals, from putting democracy into action to witnessing the shutdown of the nation's capital. While some concerns matched those of African Americans, many did not. The Reverend Leo Nieto, of the Migrant Ministry of the Texas Council of Churches, remembered that the campaign offered the potential of "seeing real democracy at work" and transforming a "glimmer of hope" into a greater federal commitment to the nation's poor, no matter what color. "That's what was exciting about it," Nieto recalled. It was "almost . . . utopian. . . . Wow, this world could be better?" The notion that a multiracial group of poor people could meet with members of Congress and federal agency officials fired his imagination about American democracy. As the son of a pastor called to help the poor, Nieto had seen his share of poverty growing up in San Antonio and ministering mostly to migrant workers in the lower Rio Grande Valley. When SCLC called, Nieto was impressed with the campaign's plans. Most importantly, Nieto "felt that [blacks] were listening" to Mexican American needs as well, a first in his own experiences in west Texas.[80]

For some, the campaign was about only one issue: land rights. Rafael Duran, a longtime member of Tijerina's Alianza in northern New Mexico, viewed going to Washington as a dream come true. "Since I was a kid, my grandfather used to tell me how we were robbed of land by the U.S. government," the sixty-seven-year-old said at the time. "I was always looking for a way to come to Washington to get it back. It was taken by fraud." Similarly, many American Indian activists viewed their participation as a chance to lobby for tribal sovereignty through the issue of native fishing rights, once protected by treaties with the national government but since encroached upon by local governments. Hank Adams, a wonkish NIYC activist, had convinced skeptical members of the Survival of American Indians Association, such as veteran fisherman Al Bridges and his daughter Suzette, to send a contingent to lobby the federal courts directly, in order to "keep fishing and keep living."[81]

Some marchers saw treaty rights and other issues as interrelated. Roque

Garcia of Santa Fe had been a member of the Alianza for several years and had set fire to fences to publicize the land rights issue. Losing the land was inextricably linked to poverty among Mexican Americans, he argued. But he also viewed the trip to Washington as a chance to protest urban renewal efforts in Santa Fe, in which low-income people were paid below-market value for their homes and then shuttled into public housing, which he called "concentration camps for la raza."[82] He hoped to take this issue, in addition to welfare rights, vocational programs, and child care, to officials in Washington—as did many other New Mexicans, including Gregorio Ruiz, Piedad Padilla, and Guadalupe Luna, all of whom struggled to survive on meager welfare benefits. As a welfare rights activist in East Los Angeles, Alicia Escalante also saw the campaign as a way to serve multiple constituencies, all of whom were poor and somehow touched by the welfare system. She took to Washington "the issue of civil rights, of police brutality, of welfare abuse by administration, on and on and on," she stated. "My hopes were that things could change within the welfare system so that women got training to go to work, child care which was non-existent," and overall enforcement of laws that were on paper but rarely put into practice. And key to this transformation was the recognition that not all welfare-eligible people had the same needs or could speak or read English well.[83]

Not all activists were as optimistic about making a claim to the government—or, for that matter, interested in the more accepted methods of lobbying politicians. According to Ernesto Vigil, he and many members of the Crusade for Justice, including Corky Gonzales, were attracted to King's original militant language regarding protest strategy in Washington. King said they "will shut this system down. We will bring Washington to a standstill until it addresses the demands that we're going to place before the power structure in D.C.," said Vigil. "And if you're not responsive, we will shut the city down in massive civil disobedience and challenge the conscience of the country and the world to do something. . . . Yeah, we'll do it nonviolently, but we're going to do it. That's what we all looked forward to participating in, and that particular vision and that particular rhetoric coincided with the views that the organization was evolving in anyway. It struck a chord with the core activists of the Crusade for Justice."[84] Campaign organizers, including King before his death, had stopped mentioning the most extreme forms of massive civil disobedience after initially suggesting that marchers might block traffic on the Potomac River bridges or clog emergency rooms. But while such suggestions had been condemned widely, some activists still held out hope for such tactics.

Others like Carlos Montes made a spontaneous decision to join the campaign. Montes and several of his fellow Brown Berets in East Los Angeles were still dealing with the legal aftermath of the massive March 1968 "blowouts," in which the Berets assisted and advised hundreds of students to walk out of school in support of quality education. Eliezer Risco, editor of the local *La Raza* newspaper, called Montes and asked him if he wanted to go to Washington. Although "we idolized Malcolm X, we still respected King," Montes recalled. "It didn't take much else to convince us to say, 'Hell, yeah, let's go.'"[85] Montes, Ralph Ramirez, Berets president Dávid Sanchez, Gloria Arellanes, and three others literally ran to make one of three buses leaving Will Rogers Park in Watts on May 15. Montes and his friends, part of forty-seven Mexican Americans from the Los Angeles area, joined a predominantly African American bus, and joked that the Mexicans would ride in the back. He remembered the trip as a "good experience," one in which he bonded with fellow Chicanos, like Alicia Escalante and her daughter Lorraine, as well as with African Americans. At least for Montes, it was also a return to his time growing up in Watts when he interacted with blacks on a daily basis, going to school with blacks in Boyle Heights, and eventually working in a predominantly African American janitor crew. There, he learned about the conditions in Watts that led to the 1965 uprising. "That influenced me later on" in his relationships with African Americans, an experience his friends from East Los Angeles did not always have because they grew up in what he called a more insular community. "Some of the Chicanos were prejudiced against blacks," Montes admitted, adding that he believed riding in the caravan was eye-opening for them.[86]

Funding shortages and paternalism threatened to reinforce such attitudes. Only 123 people arrived in Phoenix as part of the Western Caravan because a lack of money prevented at least 80 people from coming.[87] While it was a positive sign for the campaign that interest outstripped available seats, turning away any poor people sowed distrust, especially among Mexican Americans. Tijerina gave voice to the distrust, suggesting that promises were broken and that SCLC might be limiting the number of nonblack marchers deliberately. Campaign organizers denied that, but SCLC heavy-handedness made that charge seem plausible. Long suspicious of SCLC tactics from her days with SNCC in Alabama, Alianza staffer Maria Varela recalled one campaign official (most likely Minority Group Coordinator Tom Houck) coming to New Mexico and trying to redo the extensive logistical work she had conducted. "We got into a terrible argument, 'cause he was coming in doing the typical SCLC—he was a white boy . . . telling us what to do," Varela stated. "I remember—I must have had . . . a lot of rage in me. I remember grabbing his shirt and his neck and pushing him against the wall, and saying, 'Look m.f., you're in our country now . . . so back off.' I just reamed him out, and he turned whiter."[88] Although perhaps an over-the-top response, Varela acknowledged, it worked; he backed down. Similarly, when Tijerina threatened to pull all Alianza members from the campaign—the second time he had done so—march officials scrambled to find the money.[89] But the threat also gave SCLC officials reason to doubt Tijerina's commitment to the larger campaign and to a broader coalition.

Despite funding issues and the early departure of some marchers, the caravan added people at each stop—and in the process a community was built. Phoenix, Albuquerque, and Denver all saw rousing rallies on overnight stays, while El Paso brought people together in a different way. After a festive gathering in Phoenix, where Montes remembered meeting SNCC chairman H. Rap Brown, the Western Caravan continued on to the Texas border town. There, bomb threats—which marchers believed were whipped up by provocative news coverage—prompted the cancellation of a community rally. Instead, marchers were "imprisoned" in the El Paso Coliseum, encircled by police and Texas Rangers supposedly for their protection. To campaigners, this rang false. Gloria Arellanes remembered the Rangers casually drinking beer as they were hustled into the arena and being warned not to look into the men's eyes because "that was a challenge . . . the invitation to get your head beat."[90] Journalists observed authorities that "turned away friends of the poor, even those who came to bring food."[91] Rather than sleep in houses and more intimate venues as they did in other cities, marchers spent a sleepless night on cots on the arena floor and ate bologna sandwiches. Yet the fear actually bonded the marchers with each other in a new way.[92]

The next stop in Albuquerque, if anything, reinforced such bonds. Speaking to a multiracial crowd of more than twelve hundred people, Tijerina called them "a beautiful garden with all those wonderful colors of black, brown, red, and white. It makes a beautiful bouquet."[93] Joining Tijerina and Abernathy at the head of the procession was an ecumenical rainbow of sorts, including Roman Catholic priest Luis Jaramillo, Alaskan Archbishop Joseph T. Ryan, and the Reverend Lee Hobart. The march wound its way for nearly five miles through the city's poorest neighborhoods to the city's historic Old Town district. Even local Roman Catholic Archbishop James Peter Davis, who had earlier questioned Tijerina's role, marched and called on people "to look beyond Mr. Tijerina and what he stands for, to approve the march and hope that it will be successful despite his connection with it."[94] In the square, several hundred more people met the marchers and attended a rally with an almost festival-like atmosphere, food, entertainment—including Hollywood actor Marlon Brando—and speeches featuring Abernathy, Tijerina, Tuscarora chief Mad Bear Anderson of New York, and a reportedly 120-year-old Hopi named Katchongva. Several other Indian leaders attended, including Thomas Banyacya, a Hopi and close ally of Tijerina's, and Beamon Logan, a Seneca.[95]

Marchers had a similar experience in Denver, where they rallied on the state capitol steps and, for the first time, met their counterparts from the equally diverse San Francisco Caravan.[96] Ernesto Vigil had never seen anything quite like it. It was "a swirl of activity and excitement," he remembered. "Black Panthers strutting around. And these farm people out of northern New Mexico, wearing their cowboy hats and their worn-out jeans. And (then) the hippies."[97] After enjoying the hospitality of local churches, the Crusade for Justice, and the local chapter of the American Friends Service Committee the previous night, marchers joined nearly five thousand others in front of the Colorado Statehouse—an energy that reminded one marcher of a Depression-era demonstration by unemployed coal miners. Speech after speech by ordinary poor people, as well as Tijerina, Gonzales, and Bernard Lafayette, prompted shouts of "¡Viva!" from many in the crowd, even Bert Yellow Wolf, a Mandan chief from North Dakota. Indians played a particularly prominent role in Denver, thanks to Tillie Walker's contributions. "Nobody knows what poor is like the Indians," declared Fred Carr, a Crow from Montana, to a nodding crowd. "Nobody has seen horses starving and dead in their own land. The only reason I grew up is because I am mad."[98] Such vivid imagery, anger, and energy led one reporter to conclude that the scene was "a tableau the likes of which Sunday benchwarmers in Civic Center had never seen and most likely never will again."[99]

Even as the marchers celebrated the caravan's diversity, however, the experience in Denver also strengthened intra-racial relationships, especially among Mexican Americans. For Ralph Ramirez, a Brown Beret in his late teens at the time, it was enlightening. "Just coming into contact with all of these people . . . the Tijerina people" was a real education, he said.[100] While not all liked what they saw in Tijerina's melodramatic and at times autocratic style, Chicano activists like Montes, Ramirez, Escalante, and Varela also received their first up-close impressions of Corky Gonzales and the Crusade. The charismatic Gonzales played emcee, deftly managing the sometimes unwieldy rally, while female Crusade activists served traditional Mexican food—called the "best meal of the whole trip"—at the Annunciation Catholic School. Some marchers also were housed in Crusade members' homes. Overall, the Crusade's hospitality made a lasting impression on their Chicano counterparts from Los Angeles and elsewhere and led Gonzales to invite the Berets to ride on an all-Latino Crusade bus for the rest of the trip. Significantly, the Berets accepted—an understandable response to new friends but one that also worked to undermine the multiracial image of unity the campaign attempted to project.[101]

The six-hundred-mile ride to Kansas City highlighted the role the buses themselves could play in building community and bonds among marchers. As eighteen buses and a series of cars and trucks rolled east, riders turned to many things to pass the time. "Riding hour after hour," one marcher wrote, ". . . we sing, hold philosophical discussions, make elaborate signs for our stopping place in Washington, play checkers, and learn Spanish."[102] As labor and civil rights activists had found for generations, singing was particularly effective in bringing people together and fighting boredom. Leading the chorus on the Crusade buses were longtime Denver activist Juanita Malouff-Dominguez and her husband, Emilio, who one acquaintance called "the heart and soul of our contingent."[103] Noting that most of the songs during the city-based rallies were old civil rights and labor classics, such as "Which Side Are You On?," Malouff-Dominguez "took melodies that everybody knew from the (Mexican) Revolution, and changed the words" to fit the moment. Most popular were new renditions of "La Cucaracha," "La Adelita," and others that made references to the poor and Washington. The entire ride, Malouff-Dominguez recalled, "was a great learning experience in sharing."[104]

But, as the buses slowly closed in on Washington, interracial tensions repeatedly surfaced over whose issues received the most attention. At a sparsely attended rally in Kansas City, it became clear early on that the program planned by local black leaders stressed the plight of poor African Americans locally without addressing, even obliquely, the interests of the nonblack marchers. It is not clear what instructions, if any, campaign organizers gave the local speakers, but Mexican American and American Indian marchers felt excluded, prompting an irritated Corky Gonzales to take over the program briefly to allow them to share their stories. Then Gonzales told the mortified hosts, "You can have your program back now."[105] Similarly, in St. Louis—where several buses from Texas joined the caravan—Gonzales led a multiracial walkout of some four hundred marchers before several nonblack people were allowed to speak. Later, a debate ensued over who should lead a symbolic procession east on foot over the Mississippi River bridge, long seen as the white gateway to the West. Gonzales and the Mexican Americans present insisted that American Indians do so, as the most dispossessed group, but Lauren Watson, Mark Comfort, and other Black Panthers challenged that notion. The Chicanos won out and the nearly nine-hundred-person contingent walked across the bridge, sat down briefly at its apex, and continued to the buses waiting on the other side. Witnesses pointed out that the moment resulted in a "togetherness right at this point" and "an atmosphere of brotherhood and good feeling."[106] Yet the two disputes in Missouri contained warning signs. Not only did they foreshadow future quarrels over what Crusade for Justice chaplain Craig Hart called "superficial things . . . who will speak first at the microphone," but the disagreement also demonstrated a willingness by Mexican Americans to make stark distinctions from their black counterparts.[107] It challenged African Americans' activist hierarchy in which they were the most oppressed (and thus most deserving) and linked Chicano interests with those of American Indians. And since the Chicano leaders already identified themselves as partly indigenous—or as Tijerina called it, *indohispano*—such efforts reinforced their difference from blacks.[108]

An overnight stop in Louisville did little to change such perceptions. Originally scheduled to rendezvous with the Indian Trail, the Western Caravan went to Kentucky after lodging could not be secured in Chicago. Instead, marchers spent the night at Churchill Downs, home of the Kentucky Derby, which the children enjoyed but adults found "insulting" as a place to sleep.[109] Compounding these conditions was campaign coordinators' discovery in Louisville that the Chicano contingent—having read reports of slow construction in Resurrection City—had secured alternative housing, at least temporarily, in Washington. SCLC aides feared the decision would be interpreted by outsiders as voluntary segregation, while several Panthers viewed the decision both as a slight and as a sign of Mexican Americans' unwillingness to live among the shantytown's largely black poor. According to Tom Houck, the campaign coordinator of non-black minority groups, "the black group didn't like this. They wanted to be together, and they said that as long as this was our last chance . . . they were going to stay together, rather than part and become enemies. . . . It split everybody up, which was probably, I think, the greatest factor that we had disunity."[110] Ralph Ramirez recalled it a bit differently. "A lot of the rank and file understood," he said. "Their attitude was if we could stay in a place like that we would do it too."[111] Ironically, residents of Resurrection City leveled the same charge at Ralph Abernathy and other SCLC higher-ups who stayed in the Pitts Motor Hotel for most of the campaign. Even some of the Black Panthers, such as Lauren Watson, stayed elsewhere. But campaign officials knew how devastating it could be if the largest contingent of nonblack marchers chose to avoid Resurrection City.[112]

◆ ◆ ◆

As the Western Caravan arrived May 23, so did the heavy spring rains that transformed Resurrection City from a disheveled but lively city into an uncomfortable, unsanitary bog. "The weather didn't give us a break at all," Watson recalled. "It rained like in the Bible."[113] Indeed, it rained heavily more than half of the days Resurrection City existed, climaxing with more than two inches falling in a twenty-four hour period on June 12–13. As a result, people's attitudes soured as the mud and water dramatically reduced mobility around the camp, making everything more difficult, from organizing protests to providing meals. Rain and heavy winds in late May knocked down the main dining hall, and campaign officials temporarily evacuated more than a thousand people. Medical experts worried that the encampment's subpar conditions, due to poor drainage, contaminated water, and inadequate shelter, risked an influenza epidemic or worse. A major outbreak of illness never occurred, leading Dr. Edward Madzique of the campaign's medical services committee to observe that "it may have been the terrible conditions in which the poor residents lived normally that prevented" an epidemic.[114]

SCLC officials could not be blamed for the torrential weather, of course, but there did not appear to be a plan for such a scenario. Surviving records of the campaign, including those of Al Gollin, chairman of the campaign's General Services Administration Committee, demonstrate a remarkable amount of detailed preparation for Resurrection City. From food preparation to block controls for security and fire protection to a

Families and most other residents—including Jesse Jackson (center in background)—evacuate Resurrection City briefly in May after days of rain turn the encampment into a muddy swamp. It rained nineteen days out of thirty-one between mid-May and mid-June, making conditions unbearable and raising the concern of medical experts about possible outbreaks of disease. None happened, however. (AP Photo / Bob Daugherty)

sanitation system that included daily house cleaning and garbage removal, campaign organizers had created a small bureaucracy from whole cloth. But not having a weather contingency plan was a major oversight. No one involved had built or run a city of a few thousand. Jesse Jackson, the shantytown's first city manager, was a protest leader and seminarian known for his charisma and rhetoric, not his administrative skills. Al Gollin was a demographer and chief sociologist for the federal Bureau of Social Science Research. His chief deputy in charge of city planning, Michael Finkelstein, was a postal worker on leave. "I didn't know the first thing," said campaign official Bill Moyer, only half-jokingly. "I can't even drive a nail."[115] As a result, the logistical task simply overwhelmed an organization still reeling from the challenges of the last month.[116]

The absence of King should not be underestimated. While his death may have sparked renewed interest in the Poor People's Campaign, it dev-astated his immediate staff psychologically—a fact that really emerged when the rains came. The staff was "in a daze," recalled Andrew Young, "functioning on autopilot."[117] Maria Varela remembered vividly how "awful" campaign officials looked. "I don't know how they got up in the morning," she said. "Bags under their eyes—they all looked just ter-rible."[118] In fact, one of the only surviving health forms from the medical services committee is for Ralph Abernathy, who suffered from physical exhaustion throughout the campaign. Needless to say, the protest strat-egy for which SCLC was known, including mass arrests and actions that prompted sympathetic media coverage, struggled to compete with the day-to-day governance of an increasingly problem-ridden city.[119]

When the Western Caravan entered Washington, most of the march-ers affirmed what had become clear in Louisville: that they would not move into Resurrection City. "We didn't see what we had hoped to see," said Ernesto Vigil of the Crusade for Justice, "clearly for understandable reasons. Martin Luther King had been assassinated." But "we figured, well okay, if they don't have their shit together, we wish them the best of luck. Meanwhile, we have to get on with what we want to do during the time that we're here."[120] What they had to do was take Chicano demands to federal officials, demands that often differed from those of African Americans, such as land rights and access to bilingual education. In the process, Gonzales and Tijerina hoped, the Chicano movement would receive greater recognition nationally. And if they could build a strong network among themselves and with American Indian activists, that was a bonus.

Thus, nearly everybody in the Western Caravan and Indian Trail—including up to five hundred people of Mexican descent—went straight to the Hawthorne School, a private experimental high school about two miles from West Potomac Park, to set up their own camp.[121] It would be at Hawthorne where a true "multiethnic community" developed, in the words of one resident, and where most of the notable protests of the next month emerged, including a dramatic demonstration outside the Supreme Court building.[122]

The nearly two months following the assassination of Martin Luther King Jr. demonstrated the complex relationship—the possibilities and the tensions—between race and class constituencies during the Poor People's Campaign. Its organizers and participants made great strides in produc-ing, at least at times, a unified multiracial voice for the poor. From the

Committee of 100 to the caravan rallies, people of all colors came together under one banner. Even the early days of Resurrection City held promise in encouraging cross-cultural dialogue and exchange. But by the end of May, only a relative handful of whites, American Indians, Mexican Americans, and Puerto Ricans had moved into Resurrection City. What had become the dominant symbol of the campaign signified exactly what organizers had not wanted: that "poor" was just another word for "black."

6 ◆ Multiracial Efforts, Intra-racial Gains

On May 29, symbolism of a different sort played out in front of the U.S. Supreme Court building. After a boisterous demonstration against a recent ruling on American Indian fishing rights, hundreds of protesters had begun to trek back to the Hawthorne School, when local police officers attacked. Prompted by what the media called lewd gestures by Chicano teens, officers on motorcycles set off a scuffle when they attempted to break marchers' ranks and nearly ran over several small children in the process. While the horrified crowd watched, officers then beat and arrested about a dozen young men protecting the children, including Ernesto Vigil of the Crusade for Justice and Danny Tijerina, one of Reies Tijerina's sons. Bloodied and disoriented, the men then were taken to jail for the afternoon, leaving the remaining protesters shaken and angry about what they considered an unprovoked assault. Yet activists like Corky Gonzales, Ralph Abernathy, and Hank Adams were not surprised by the viciousness. They had seen it before.[1]

But for many of the younger Chicanos present, such as nineteen-year-old Gloria Arellanes, this experience was new. Certainly, the Brown Beret had heard about police brutality, but she never had seen such an attack by the authorities. "It was the first time I had ever (seen) anybody brutally beaten," Arellanes said. "Looking into the faces of these police officers, you could see so many different emotions. I remember one young man, just so embarrassed. You could see his pain."[2] In fact, this was just one of many new things Arellanes encountered in Washington, her first time to the nation's capital. Before that spring, she had met very few Chicana or Chicano activists outside of her immediate world in East Los Angeles and El Monte, California. Nor had she seen white people so poor. But this all began to change when she and her fellow Brown Berets joined the campaign with enthusiasm after hearing Martin Luther King Jr.'s vision for a new multiracial alliance of the poor.[3]

Ernesto Vigil of the Crusade for Justice attempts to get up from the ground after being hit by a Washington, D.C., police officer. The incident occurred as Vigil walked back from the Supreme Court where he had protested in support of native fishing rights. The experience helped galvanize participants—especially Chicanos—according to Vigil. (Photo: © Maria Varela)

For Arellanes, the few weeks that she spent among the poor and their allies in Washington became a turning point personally. "I always told people, I learned more about people on that march than ever," she recalled. "I saw so many things," it was an experience that changed her life permanently.[4] At times, Arellanes witnessed the best of people—the kindness of "the most wonderful" African American hosts while in St. Louis and the camaraderie developed at Hawthorne. But she also saw the worst, from a black woman "clutching her daughter with . . . fear in her eyes" during the bomb threat in El Paso to the hypocrisy of a Chicano leader "trying to live like a king" by eating steak while everyone else had canned rice and beans. All were invaluable lessons that she took home and that helped her become an increasingly sophisticated member of the Chicano movement, in large part because of the folks that she met in Washington, with whom she ate, stood in line, and demonstrated. From land rights activists and students from New Mexico and Texas to Corky Gonzales and the Crusade for Justice, Chicano participants in the campaign earned her respect and affection—and inspired her emergence as a leader, first in the Brown Berets and then, more generally, as a leading voice of Chicana feminist nationalism.[5]

Gloria Arellanes's experience during the Poor People's Campaign was not unusual. Whether they went for months, weeks, or just a day or two, many marchers left Washington enlightened, if not transformed. Most Chicano accounts of the campaign treat it as nothing more than a momentary distraction before activists returned to the business of movement building. At best, scholars view the campaign as an attempt by Reies Tijerina, Corky Gonzales, and other movement leaders to widen national awareness of the Chicano struggle by voicing their concerns in front of the Washington press corps and the rest of the East Coast–centric establishment media.[6] But because journalists all but ignored their participation in the campaign—with the occasional exception of Tijerina—Mexican American issues received little national exposure. Nor did Chicano activists achieve their officially stated priorities in the campaign—particularly U.S. recognition of their claims to land grants dating to the mid-nineteenth century.

Rather, the Poor People's Campaign (PPC) played a more important role in the lives of individual activists, which in turn had a collective impact on the movement itself. Away from Resurrection City and most SCLC and campaign officials, primary plans for some of the most dynamic and memorable protests, including the demonstration outside of the Supreme Court, formed within the confines of the Hawthorne School. The centrality of Hawthorne was no coincidence. It was in this space where for two months during the height of the campaign, people of Mexican descent lived with and interacted daily with African Americans, American Indians, Puerto Ricans, poor whites, and each other. This experience became a key building block for the developing Chicano movement, increasing its sophistication and strength by building and deepening relationships among activists. Not only did it empower individuals and complicate activists' own analyses, but the campaign experience also strengthened intraregional networks. Moreover, their time in Washington shaped the Chicano movement by placing tensions between rural and urban Chicano activists in sharp relief, especially the role of Reies López Tijerina. While Tijerina's leadership as a "memory entrepreneur," to quote one scholar, remained intact, his legitimate status among his peers as a leader and organizer of direct action protest had declined considerably.[7] Instead of a moment of triumph for the rural land rights leader, the Poor People's Campaign led to Tijerina's marginalization and bolstered the organizing and reputation of his rivals, Corky Gonzales, and others. The campaign also helped set the table for some of the intra-racial cooperation that sustained the Chicano movement in the years to come, highlighting how coalition led to the most positive kind of racial identity politics.

✦ ✦ ✦

The caravans from the West, carrying most of the campaign's Mexican Americans and American Indians, arrived in Washington the evening of May 23 with little fanfare. Going straight to Hawthorne, they became immediately isolated, as their SCLC-funded buses departed for Resurrection City and the rains came down. The newcomers there were left to fend for themselves, without even an official greeting. Campaign officials literally were swamped. The next day, spokesmen for the nonblack contingents lashed out. They included Fred Connor, an Assiniboine-Sioux from Montana, who reported from St. Augustine's Episcopal Church, where Indians had moved after the first night to have their own space. Connor told a reporter that tribal elders Mad Bear Anderson, Clifton Hill, and Beamon Logan threatened to leave the march because they felt "ignored" and "abused" by SCLC leaders. They sought "an apology from SCLC, an extended hand," said Connor. "We have yet to have a say in what is planned or . . . our place in the Poor People's Campaign." Myles Horton and Guy Carawan, speaking for poor whites within Resurrection City, expressed their own concerns about being segregated and disregarded, which was one reason many Appalachian whites also opted to stay in Hawthorne, at least for a while.[8]

Not surprisingly and much to the consternation of campaign organizers, Tijerina appointed himself the spokesman for all nonblack delegations. Although he echoed concerns about being cut out of decision making by SCLC organizers, Tijerina stressed that this was less about egos and more about the marginalization of their issues. "We will not move to Resurrection City if Mad Bear and the other chiefs are not accepted," Tijerina told a reporter at Hawthorne. "I think our participation is very important to the Poor People's Campaign." When Tijerina's comments sparked little more than an oblique response from Ralph Abernathy about land rights, Tijerina called his own press conference—the first of many—this time in front of Resurrection City. After a shouting match with SCLC's Rudolph Thompson in front of dozens of rapt journalists, Tijerina repeated his earlier charges and added that his search for Mexican Americans in Resurrection City had proved "fruitless" and that the Puerto Ricans there felt equally marginalized. Tijerina then insisted that Abernathy come to Hawthorne. Tijerina's maneuver had the desired effect—Abernathy showed up at the school, where the two men spent an hour and a half hashing out their differences privately. And while they emerged smiling and conciliatory, the rift mended at least momentarily, the interactions not only placed campaign officials on the defensive but also established Hawthorne as a clear base of power for its nonblack marchers.[9]

The Hawthorne School stood two stories tall and, like most secondary schools, had basic food preparation, toilet, and shower facilities. Although certainly crowded for several hundred fatigued marchers fresh from a cross-country trip and then daily demonstrations in a steamy Washington spring, the conditions in Hawthorne's basement proved far better than in Resurrection City: it was warm and dry. Sent as a scout a week early, the Crusade for Justice's Richard Romero worked with local ministers and eventually located Hawthorne as a suitable housing alternative. For the private school's founders, Eleanor and Alexander Orr, allowing poor people to live there reflected the school's progressive hands-on learning philosophy. Nothing could be more "real" than the campaign's participants, who periodically visited classes and talked to the students that spring. In addition, the Orrs had a connection to northern New Mexico in that they once ran a camp for teenagers in Taos. And for Mexican Americans far from home, staying at Hawthorne ensured that their contingent remained together. "How do you take poor people into inhumanity?" asked Nita Jo Gonzales, Corky's eldest daughter, in explaining her father's rationale for choosing Hawthorne over Resurrection City. "You cannot ask people to come and not provide a place that was not more humane than what they left."[10] To be fair, most Mexican Americans had not seen the shantytown before it became a crowded bog. But the comparison between the two locations, if anything, propelled the school's new residents even more to create a community amid the cots, cold sandwiches, and institutional walls—a community that heightened the humanity of the poor rather than compromised it.[11]

In contrast to depictions by the press, which framed Hawthorne as a one-dimensional facility of racial segregation, the school was multiracial from the beginning and remained so throughout the campaign.[12] While predominantly Mexican American, Hawthorne also housed a sizable number of Appalachian whites and African Americans from the West, as well as most American Indians for a night or two. "By it being initially a multiethnic contingent, word then spread about here's this place that's not going to be inundated by rain," Vigil said. "Provisions have been made for food . . . so people sort of gravitated towards it because it was better organized. . . . We were not going to run people off because they were the wrong color."[13] Nor was there racial segregation inside the facility. Instead, campaign participants separated themselves on the basis of family status, with single men staying in one area and families in another, usually the basement. Although the average campaigner was in his or her twenties, both Mexican Americans and American Indians were more likely to bring their entire families and thus had a greater age range. For every young Brown Beret in his or her late teens there was an older Mexican American with family. Viewing the campaign as fundamentally a family affair, Corky's wife, Gerry, insisted that she and the children come along; five of their eight kids made it. Their eldest, Nita Jo, who had stayed behind, ended up quitting her job and flying to Washington after seeing police threaten her parents on national television. Hawthorne had a higher percentage of women than Resurrection City, although men outnumbered women in both places. With the exception of head cook Emilio Dominguez of the Crusade for Justice, women in Hawthorne took the lead in organizing meals and sleeping arrangements—something mostly left to men in Resurrection City. Some Hawthorne residents, men and women, credited this gendered division of labor as one explanation for the tight-knit community there.[14]

Of course, some tensions existed at Hawthorne, particularly in the first few days when the newly arrived campaigners were hesitant to leave the school until the rain subsided. According to observer Linda Avena, "people were unable to leave the building, unable to clean their muddy clothes . . . and perhaps most importantly, were unable to do any kind of demonstrating." A feeling of isolation also proved acute. The school was almost two miles southeast of Resurrection City—far enough away to feel out of the loop. SCLC officials compounded the marchers' decision to bypass Resurrection City and stay indoors by momentarily forgetting them. The result was considerable testiness and somewhat of a let-down for folks ready to confront the government.[15]

As the initial rains stopped, considerable multiracial cooperation began to blossom within the confines of the Hawthorne School. Sometimes this took the form of a cultural exchange, such as the impromptu jam session Ernesto Vigil witnessed in a Hawthorne common area. A white man from Appalachia "starts playing this kick-ass boogie-woogie on the piano, and all of a sudden, these poor white Appalachians were kicking their heels, black folks jump in, and Mexicans sit around tapping their toes," he recalled. "You had an interesting cross-pollination. You can't structure that."[16] Rudy Gonzales, one of the Gonzales's sons, found it invaluable in his later years to have played with kids of many backgrounds and ethnicities during their stay at Hawthorne. "We had a blast," he recalled, but it also took some adjustment to interact with very poor whites. "I had never seen poor whites before. I mean dirt poor. Some hardly had shoes."[17] And despite his young age, Rudy was not alone. Nearly all of the Chicano activists interviewed echoed this sentiment. To them, whites were typically rich elites who suppressed the rights of others and ran the nation's power structure; they certainly were not *more* impoverished. But when the contingent from Appalachia arrived, Mexican Americans were shocked. "I thought I was poor until I got there and saw some of these people," said Roque Garcia from Santa Fe, who had grown up without indoor plumbing or a regular diet of meat.[18] Gonzales recalled that one initial response by the Mexican Americans there was to gather the extra shoes and jackets they had brought for the trip and to give them to their white counterparts.[19]

Such interactions produced a more sophisticated way of viewing poverty. Corky and Gerry Gonzales had been exposed to poverty of all kinds and knew—at least vaguely—about the rich organizing tradition of poor Appalachian whites. But it gave younger activists something to think about. "It was the first time that a lot of us had any contact with Puerto Ricans, with Appalachian whites," recalled Ralph Ramirez of Los Angeles. "When you never have been out of the state . . . never like even over one hundred miles from where you were born, to come in contact with all these people and these different cultures and these different subcultures" was an education.[20] For Carlos Montes, it helped crystallize some concepts: "I went through a political change, from what I would call a nationalist to more of an international perspective, where I saw the struggle here at home. . . . My rhetoric changed."[21] Rather than vilifying white men, he began to criticize the capitalist structure and its most common defenders, *rich* white men—a change that would prove invaluable to him, first as an activist in the Chicano movement into the 1970s and then as a labor organizer.[22]

Years later, Corky Gonzales credited the campaign as one source of deepened ties with American Indian, white, and black activists, albeit not SCLC. He developed relationships with American Indian activists, adding substance to his rhetoric of indigenous identity, and after meeting James Groppi, Gonzales invited the radical white Milwaukee priest to visit Denver, which he did at least twice. But perhaps more importantly—at least for Gonzales's short-term vision—activists' time at Hawthorne and the campaign in general expanded their networks and strengthened their bonds among themselves. "When would we have gotten together with the Crusade?" asked Carlos Montes, referring to Corky Gonzales's group. "Lived with them? Shared bread with them? Marched every day with them?"[23] For Montes and other young activists, the campaign proved a unique opportunity—on someone else's dime—to spend a month or more with Chicano counterparts they otherwise might not have met. Ernesto Vigil rattled off all the people he met for the first time during the campaign, folks that he would come to know well in the next several years at the Chicano Youth Liberation Conferences and the 1970 Chicano Moratorium: Brown Berets, UFW activists, Leo Nieto of the Texas Council of Churches, Ernesto Cortes of the Industrial Areas Foundation, Tijerina and members of the Alianza, and Maria Varela and Betita Martinez, both SNCC veterans of Mexican descent. Alianza member Gilberto Ballejos's conversations with Brown Berets helped inspire him to found a chapter of the organization when he returned to Albuquerque. And as a result of their contact there, welfare rights activist Alicia Escalante went to Denver to work with the Crusade for Justice, while Nita Gonzales met a Puerto Rican campaigner she would eventually marry—briefly expanding the Gonzales's extended family into a larger Latino alliance.[24]

Living and eating together was part of this bonding experience, but so was being arrested and even beaten together. The Mexican Americans in Hawthorne did not participate in every demonstration organized by SCLC, nor did they wait for SCLC permission to have their own marches. In fact, the protests most opposed by Ralph Abernathy and his aides turned out to be the campaign's most memorable and instructive, including the demonstration outside the Supreme Court building and its violent aftermath, which, if anything, drew activists closer together.

Hank Adams did not live in Hawthorne, but it would be his vision that produced one of the more vivid experiences for the men, women, and children living there. Called the "most important Indian" by activist-scholar Vine Deloria Jr., Adams had emerged as "the key man behind the scenes, the crucial individual who held the line through knowledge, perseverance, and hard work" during the height of American Indian activism in the 1960s and 1970s.[25] Born in Fort Peck, Montana, and raised in Washington State after his mother married a Quinault, Adams became politically active as a fourteen-year-old in response to rising state control of their reservation, which ended tribal alcohol bans and empowered what was seen as a hostile white police force. The articulate Adams emerged as an unlikely spokesman, and tribal leaders began to groom him for bigger things. Becoming disillusioned with their staid leadership in the early 1960s, however, Adams was drawn to the newly founded National Indian Youth Council, which under Clyde Warrior, a Ponca from Oklahoma, had begun to experiment in its own forms of direct action. Emulating the sit-in movement they saw on television, the NIYC and the Washington State–based Survival of American Indians Association began to stage "fish-ins" in 1964 to prompt publicity through confrontation, with Adams conducting much of the behind-the-scenes planning. Four years later, fish-ins continued as the Supreme Court upheld the conviction of twenty-four Nisquallies and Puyallups for fishing in "usual and accustomed places" with their traditional gill nets. The latest decision came down May 27 and prompted Adams—who by this time had become a self-taught expert in treaty law, including the arcane world of fishing rights—to organize the protest outside the nation's highest court.[26]

Adams first brought the idea of a court protest to SCLC's Hosea Williams, who refused to disturb a sleeping Abernathy and called the proposal an ill-considered gambit that would lead to everyone's premature arrest. Adams then turned to Tijerina. "Request your assistance in bringing full support of SCLC, Resurrection City population, and Black community to this active presentation of issues," Adams wrote in shorthand, adding that he "would hope for central focus on these Indian issues tomorrow—limiting other PPC activities as much as possible." Eventually, Tijerina, Gonzales, and the NWRO's George Wiley persuaded a reluctant Abernathy to sanction the rally, although neither Adams nor Mad Bear Anderson wanted SCLC or the Alianza "leading" the way. The SCLC concern about arrests was real, as Adams warned that "most of the Indian group—all of Northwest—prepared to go to jail for sit-in or any such action."[27] Abernathy's experience also told him that protesting outside

American Indian activists spend hours in front of the Supreme Court building to protest a recent ruling against native fishing rights in ancestral waters. The demonstration, a campaign highlight for those who attended, was roundly condemned by mainstream media organizations as an embarrassment. (Karl Kernberger Pictorial Collection [PICT 2000-008-0116], Center for Southwest Research, University Libraries, University of New Mexico)

of the court—complete with a slow, mournful banging of drums and the smoking of elaborate pipes—would not produce the desired response. Left unsaid at the time was Abernathy's discomfort with other leaders calling the shots and emphasizing what he saw as "a private agenda."[28] Abernathy preferred using the small Indian presence symbolically—and some said comically—such as asking a headdress-wearing chief to grant marchers permission to use the Mall. In the end, while some blacks attended the Supreme Court protest, many more joined a Jesse Jackson–led rally outside the Department of Agriculture.[29]

Of all the images produced by the campaign, none perhaps was more arresting than that of hundreds of protesters milling around the U.S. Supreme Court building, banging on its doors, breaking windows, and singing Indian chants and "La Cucaracha." Although not immune from lively demonstrations, the high court generally received more public respect than its executive and legislative counterparts and, with that, often a little more decorum when people did disagree with court decisions. But on this late May morning, the crowd was especially animated in its protests against the court's recent affirmation of curbs on fishing rights. Demanding a meeting with a representative of the court, the protesters eventually chose a delegation including Adams, Abernathy, Gonzales, Tijerina, and sixteen other Indian activists to speak with Chief Clerk John Davis. They presented Davis with a petition of grievances over how state fishing laws and quotas denied certain tribes the ability to sustain their communities through traditional tribal means and violated century-old treaties with the U.S. government. The meeting ended hours later with no resolution.[30]

Ignoring the protest's substance and the central organizing role played by American Indians, journalists overwhelmingly condemned the demonstration. Calling it "foolish," "illegal," and "violent," editorial pages concluded that if campaign participants did not recognize the protest as a bad idea, its leaders should have.[31] "Poor people have poor ways," wrote the *Washington Post* condescendingly, but Abernathy, the editors argued, should have known better.[32] Front-page news stories emphasized conflict, such as the arrest of three people for lowering the U.S. flag in the court's plaza to half staff and the breaking of five basement windows. Moreover, press reports liberally quoted Abernathy and Tijerina far more than their Indian counterparts. The *Washington Post* cited Hank Adams, but called him "a white leader for Indian rights."[33] Perhaps his glasses and English-sounding name, plus the absence of a headdress, confused the reporter. Indeed, the few images of people identified as Indians from the protest

Press and onlookers throng American Indian activist Mel Thom, Ralph Abernathy, Hank Adams, and Reies López Tijerina outside the Supreme Court. Many of the protests during the Poor People's Campaign took on a circus-like atmosphere, as reporters crowded around charismatic leaders instead of speaking to the poor people that came with them. (Karl Kernberger Pictorial Collection (PICT 2000-008-0084), Center for Southwest Research, University Libraries, University of New Mexico)

were of older men and women such as George Crow Flies High wearing headdresses and other traditional garb.[34] Scholars subsequently have echoed much of their media counterparts' treatment of the protest.[35]

Scoffing at the negative publicity, Reies Tijerina called the Supreme Court protest a "monumental victory" because regular people forced someone of status to listen to Indian concerns.[36] Perhaps, but the demonstration that day represented another kind of accomplishment as well: a clear assertion by nonblack leaders that they occasionally could place their issues at the top of the protest agenda in Washington and achieve the subsequent activist bonds that such cooperation could create. This was especially true when police violence occurred on the return to Hawthorne and became a unifying issue for Chicanos, blacks, or Indians. The perpetrators who broke five basement windows appeared to go unpunished. Abernathy claimed that government saboteurs must have broken them, but Ernesto Vigil laughingly admitted years later that he and a few others were the actual culprits. Perhaps the tactical police squad knew that, sparking the police assaults that so horrified Gloria Arellanes and her fellow marchers.[37]

The aftermath of the beatings strengthened Chicano camaraderie. "You really find common cause when you sit in the same god-damned jail cell," stated Vigil, on the hours he spent behind bars with young Chicanos from New Mexico and California.[38] After authorities released them later that evening, a multiracial crowd at the John Wesley AME Zion Church greeted them as heroes. We "received a thunderous reception, black folks standing up . . . after we were bonded out and marching in," Vigil recalled. "It was really a tremendous time which we could have capitalized on." Unfortunately, the moment of unity proved fleeting. As the crowd of black and brown sang freedom songs, several Black Panthers from Denver including Lauren Watson challenged Ralph Abernathy and his aides, arguing that they had paid too much attention to these other marchers. After considerable awkwardness and hurt feelings, Abernathy smoothed over their differences, at least publicly. The Panthers' "power play," as Vigil called it, further damaged the already-frayed relations among some marchers. Yet this exchange also ironically strengthened bonds among Mexican Americans, who concluded that they could not fully trust some of their black brethren—even those from their hometown.[39]

A few days later, a similar scenario again forced Abernathy to intervene on behalf of SCLC's nonblack partners—this time in response to Bayard Rustin. The civil rights veteran and onetime pacifist had been hired to organize the campaign's climactic Solidarity Day, a one-day rally set for June 19 in front of the Lincoln Memorial. As the behind-the-scenes organizer of the 1963 March on Washington and an advocate of a pro-Johnson administration labor–civil rights coalition, Rustin retained considerable respect among journalists and politicians. Calling him a "realist" and "pragmatist," the *New York Times* applauded his "outstanding credentials as an organizer of massive marches" and experience as "a jail-going pacifist and civil rights militant when Abernathy was still in grade school."[40] And when Rustin released a concrete set of demands for Solidarity Day, a *Washington Post* editorial expressed cautious optimism: "With the formulation of some definite goals, the Poor People's Campaign can now turn to sympathetic members of Congress and the Administration with hope for effective action."[41] Similar to Rustin's Freedom Budget from 1966, the

"Call to Americans of Goodwill" included specific "attainable" legislative and policy solutions, including a recommitment to the Employment Act of 1946, adoption of a pending housing and urban development bill, repeal of punitive welfare restrictions, extension of collective bargaining rights to farm workers, and a restoration of earlier budget cuts to various social programs.[42]

Rather than build unity and a firm foundation of organization and discipline, however, Rustin's goodwill message rankled SCLC officials and other marchers. Soon after Rustin unveiled his Solidarity Day plans in a solo news conference, SCLC's Hosea Williams called Rustin's rationale "a lot of foolishness," saying he had "no business" issuing any objectives without prior approval.[43] Offended, Rustin demanded a clarification of his authority from Abernathy, who, in gentler language, agreed, calling Rustin's statement "not comprehensive enough." Not only did the statement drastically lower expectations; it also excluded several issues of utmost importance to the campaign's nonblack participants. Despite language of "black and white, brown and red," the declaration left out demands for land rights, fishing rights, greater prosecution for police brutality, and an immediate negotiated end to the Vietnam War—the latter a position Rustin publicly opposed. As a result, the list infuriated SCLC's partners in the campaign, especially because Reies Tijerina had made such a spectacle a week before.[44]

But Abernathy's principled stand was at a cost. Denied full control of Solidarity Day, Rustin resigned, and the mainstream press audibly groaned. In what one chronicler called a key turning point for those shaping public perceptions of the campaign, many reporters turned on the entire endeavor. Linking Rustin to the 1963 march's moral authority, they painted his resignation as a fatal blow to a hopelessly disorganized campaign. Capturing that mood, the *New York Times* editorial board wrote, "In rejecting Mr. Rustin and his program, the divided Southern Christian Leadership Conference has thrown away its best chance to rally broad national backing for a worthy but faltering crusade."[45] "Get it together," demanded a *Post* editorial, while the paper's news reports labeled the campaign a "fiasco" with a "leadership crisis."[46] Renewed questions emerged over Abernathy's ability to lead, and whether SCLC could survive without King. Even the black press, which had been consistently supportive, echoed the mainstream media's condemnation of the campaign's leadership. "The Poor People's Campaign lost, fired, dissembled, and threw out Bayard Rustin and a good deal of its momentum," wrote the *Chicago Defender*.[47] As the campaign slogged on, Abernathy and campaign organizers found themselves in an unenviable position.

◆ ◆ ◆

For the next several weeks, as campaign officials prepared for Solidarity Day under the new leadership of the Urban League's Sterling Tucker, marchers used the Hawthorne School as a staging area for protest. Only a few gained much media attention. But each demonstration seemed to produce small enlightening, even inspiring, moments that many marchers believed were the most enduring legacies of the campaign. Many involved a rich multiracial mix of participants, reinforcing the notion that a broad understanding of poverty could bring people together at times even if individual definitions of justice varied or leadership and communications broke down.

One of those marchers was Luís Diaz de León of Laredo, Texas. A member of that state's small, multiracial delegation, de León repeatedly referred to Hawthorne as the "Freedom School." Not only did he have the opportunity to travel and live with several African American activists from Houston, but he and other Mexican Americans also had their own moment of multiracial unity. For instance, Reies Tijerina briefly suggested that the black Texans move to Resurrection City, reflecting the limits of his own multiracial commitment—and even a latent prejudice. But de León, Leo Nieto, and others balked. "We said, 'Hey, we're all coming together from Texas and we stay together,'" de León remembered. "'We're . . . one delegation.'" After securing Ralph Abernathy's help with Tijerina, "they stayed with us all through the . . . (campaign)."[48] De León also received what he called his "Vietnam antiwar education" while living at Hawthorne. After backing out of participating in a draft-card burning outside of the White House and weathering a little verbal abuse from his younger peers, de León bonded with Sal Candelaria, a Black Beret from San Jose, who had taken part in the protest and been on the painful end of a police beating. "Later that night *llegaron* [they arrived] and I was in . . . the kitchen, the cafeteria eating supper. *Y este Sal* had a white dirty T-shirt here in his hand. And he came over to where I was and he took it out and he said, 'Do you still think I'm chicken shit?' And, and there was blood coming out of this big cut. And that was the best education that I ever had for starting to read on the Viet Nam War and getting some kind of orientation that, hey, I'm antiwar."[49] Candelaria received nine stitches total, while at least five other protesters suffered minor injuries.[50]

Chicanos often were surprised by how much they had in common with the others staying at Hawthorne, especially poor blacks and whites from Appalachia. "People were just bowled over that there were poor whites in this country," recalled Mike Clark of the Highlander School.[51] That reaction was magnified when Chicano marchers learned how the Appalachians wanted to resolve their impoverished state. "I was just talking to a lady from West Virginia," explained a Chicana to a reporter, "and I asked her about their demands and she said, 'WE ARE DEMANDING OUR LAND'. That's the same thing we're demanding."[52] Indeed, not unlike Chicano (and Indian) demands, many poor whites from eastern Kentucky and West Virginia viewed local control of land as the best way to end coal companies' environmental degradation of their communities through strip mining. Other issues also motivated Appalachian marchers, such as regressive taxation and treatment of "black lung" disease, but opposition to surface mining and absentee land owning was at the heart of the region's antipoverty activism.[53]

Such connections encouraged many Chicanos to join poor Appalachians in a protest outside of the house of West Virginia's powerful U.S. senator Robert Byrd, a vocal campaign critic. A white widow with eight children broke down crying after sharing how her family struggled to survive on a dwindling welfare check and part-time job when she was well enough to work. "It was one of the few times I have seen a group of whites and blacks want to protect somebody as much as they wanted to protect her," reported Joe Mulloy, a veteran activist from the region.[54] A crowd of 150 whites, Chicanos, and a few African Americans then piled into several buses and went to picket Byrd's home in suburban North Arlington, Virginia, and present a twenty-five-foot-long list of demands. Byrd was not there, but "to everyone's surprise, the door flew open and (an) angry-faced Mrs. Byrd appeared, crossly greeting the protestors," wrote another observer.[55] Declaring that the senator worked "seventeen hours a day for you people," his wife traded shouts with Robert Fulcher and a few other protesters before retreating into the house. Cheering, dancing, and chanting, the gleeful marchers left "fired up," wrote Mulloy. "They had the feeling of belonging to something larger."[56]

Similar stories emerged from subsequent demonstrations. Carlos Montes told of one controversial protest at the Department of Interior's cafeteria in which black food workers showed their solidarity by offering approving nods and letting protesters walk out with trays of food without paying. During a cold and drizzly all-night vigil outside the State Department, the Commandos, a black gang from Milwaukee, surprised Pedro Archuleta, Modesta Martinez, and some fifty other marchers from New Mexico with blankets, coffee, and sandwiches. Maria Varela, who photographed much of the campaign, described the interactions she witnessed between younger Chicanos as "critical in forming some of the New Mexico folks who" came from remote rural areas and "were more isolated than the others."[57] Even the assassination of Senator Robert F. Kennedy, on June 5 after he won the Democratic presidential primary in California, prompted more unity than anger as participants remembered the prayer service, respectful suspension of campaign activities, and tearful silence as they watched his funeral procession slowly pass Resurrection City en route to Arlington Cemetery.[58]

For the most part, the mainstream press ignored such moments—to the point that the media itself became the focus of campaign demonstrations. During one afternoon press briefing, a frustrated Hosea Williams stepped in front of the journalists assembled and erupted, accusing them of participating in a "conspiracy to poison the mind of America" by exaggerating the campaign's shortcomings and ignoring its accomplishments. "Most look only at what's bad," Williams said. "They sneak around like an underground assassin, looking for dirt and filth." He went on to question openly whether journalists had a class bias. They "go around with their bellies filled with food like a bigot filled with hate, who go home at night to their big houses and plush carpets while we die of exposure to the weather," he exclaimed. "Are you part of the system? Are you promoting it?"[59] Abernathy and SCLC's Tom Offenburger made similar laments, albeit in less colorful language. Concluded Abernathy, "If people could pay as much attention to the demands of the poor as what was going on in Resurrection City, the campaign could get somewhere."[60]

Chicanos and American Indians took their protests one step further with a boisterous demonstration outside the National Press Club building. Prompted by the press's narrow coverage of the Supreme Court demonstration, the Indian delegation declared in a press release that "the real issues are avoided so that White America does not have to test their consciences. . . . Instead of reporting to the American Public about the real issue that involves the right of Indian tribes to fish for their basic subsistence, the press headlines about the broken windows. . . . The windows can be replaced at a small cost in comparison to the human suffering caused by the ruling of the Supreme Court."[61] Marchers also repeated the long-term critique that racial minorities were represented through only the worst stereotypes in popular culture—the silent Indian in full regalia or the fiery "bandido," a label used to describe Reies Tijerina in the *Washington Post* the very next day.[62] Not surprisingly, only a few press outlets even acknowledged the demonstration, and those that did buried the story deep inside campaign reports on protests at the Justice Department.[63]

As Solidarity Day neared, more and more people poured into the nation's capital—but not necessarily into Resurrection City. With the shantytown struggling to recover from days of rain, mud, and general disorganization, a new Appalachian group of nearly five hundred people negotiated temporary housing at Hawthorne. While the trip organizers recalled the good times they had two weeks before, this second time was different. Even with classes out of session by mid-June, Hawthorne proved hopelessly crowded for a few days with not enough food to go around. The accommodations worked for some who "had a ball talking with other people at Hawthorne," wrote Eric Metzner, an organizer from Pineville, West Virginia. But others became extremely frustrated with SCLC being "completely out of touch with itself, much less other groups." Long delays in paying expenses prompted a group of disabled miners to drop out before leaving West Virginia. SCLC mismanagement also led to a food shortage at Hawthorne for three days and prompted cook Emilio Dominguez to scramble for independent donations. According to Metzner, the Appalachians left Washington early and more disappointed than when they came—something they blamed on SCLC inefficiencies and their own unrealistic expectations of what could be accomplished.[64]

Puerto Ricans, in contrast, made the best of their visit to Washington and to Hawthorne by embracing their Chicano counterparts. Excluded from initial speaker lists and unable to mobilize masses of working people to go to Washington on June 19 because it was a Wednesday, Puerto Rican organizers held their own rally of more than four thousand people the Saturday before Solidarity Day. Called by one scholar "the most significant prelude to the 'New Awakening'" of Puerto Rican radicalism in the late 1960s, the rally at the base of the Washington Monument symbolized their independence and "outsider" status at the campaign.[65] But while a primary concern was independence for the commonwealth of Puerto Rico, most activists' demands overlapped with those of other Spanish-speaking urban residents, such as adequate housing, "urban renewal, not removal," "decentralized public services based on local ethnic and language conditions," bilingual education, credit unions and consumer unions, and recognition of Spanish in voter literacy tests. Bused in overnight from East Harlem, Philadelphia, Chicago, and other industrial cities, they rallied with speeches, songs, and banners, mostly in Spanish. Many participants wore sombreros as they enjoyed the music and poetry of performers like Pepe and Flora Sanchez. In addition to Puerto Rican speakers such as New York City activist Gilberto Gerena-Valentín—who called for a one-day general strike by Puerto Rican workers—Reies Tijerina and Corky Gonzales addressed the marchers, tying the island's struggle to Chicanos' efforts for land rights and better field labor conditions on the U.S. mainland. The campaign, concluded one Chicago newspaper, "was the first time that Mexican Americans and Puerto Ricans had come together to show support for each other."[66]

While the march's new coordinator, the National Urban League's Sterling Tucker, released a much more inclusive list of policy demands, including a negotiated end to the Vietnam War, other decisions regarding Solidarity Day continued to marginalize nonblack marchers. Incredibly, Chicanos, American Indians, and welfare rights activists also did not appear on the original speaker list. Mexican Americans and American Indians had not been part of the original decision to delay the culminating rally from May 30 to June 19, much to their irritation. Even the new date emphasized the African American experience: June 19 was also Juneteenth, a day of commemoration marking the announcement of slavery's abolition in Texas in 1865. Some members of the press mistakenly referred to the rally as a Juneteenth celebration.[67]

Rather than hold their own rally as Puerto Ricans did, other nonblack activists took power into their own hands and forced their way onto the program, making it one of the most diverse events of the campaign—far more than the 1963 March on Washington, with which Solidarity Day routinely had been compared. After Tijerina spoke of "cultural genocide" against poor people of color, Corky Gonzales offered a coherent list of demands that reflected the myriad protests started at Hawthorne over the past several weeks. Known as *El Plan del Barrio*, the list became a model for later Chicano movement documents. Declaring that "poverty and city living under the colonial system of the Anglo has castrated our people's culture, consciousness of our heritage, and language," Gonzales listed policy goals in the areas of housing, education, job development and economic opportunities, law enforcement, farm labor, and land reform.[68] Miguel Barragan appeared on stage with his guitar to play Mexican folk songs during an unscheduled break, while the Appalachian contingent invited Emilio Dominguez to the stage to present him with a signed white cross for his generosity of spirit as Hawthorne's primary cook.[69]

Most striking about Solidarity Day was the number of women of different races it featured. The campaign had "'gotten itself together' and won new life," declared the *Chicago Defender*, partially because of women speakers' hopeful yet hard-hitting tone.[70] Although Ralph Abernathy was the headliner, his long-winded talk proved unmemorable, as did remarks by James Bevel and the United Auto Workers' Walter Reuther. Rather, it was speeches by Coretta Scott King, National Council of Negro Women president Dorothy Height, American Indian activist Martha Grass, white welfare rights organizer Peggy Terry, and black singer Eartha Kitt that stole the show—and perhaps appropriately so, considering how poverty disproportionately affected women, especially women of color. Stating it was women's moral duty to oppose the Vietnam War, King linked increased poverty spending with the war's end just as her husband had in the last year of his life. "If we stop the war four months and one day sooner . . . we could create 400,000 new jobs," she said. "One hour of war could buy your community a new school, hospital, or cultural center." She ended the speech with the familiar refrain of "I Have a Dream," the crowd drowning her out with the last line and a standing ovation.[71] Concluded the *Baltimore Afro-American*, "Some may call it 'Soul Power,' others may scream 'Black Power,' and yet others may say 'Poor Power,' but whatever the phrases may be, it was crystal clear that above all else, there was 'Woman Power.'"[72]

Overall, organizers and some observers deemed Solidarity Day a success. It attracted anywhere from 50,000 to 100,000 participants, many of them white middle-class housewives from the suburbs. Vice President Hubert Humphrey and Minnesota senator Eugene McCarthy, both Democratic candidates for president, were among the dignitaries on hand. Moreover, the rally was orderly, producing impressive images of thousands of people surrounding the Reflecting Pool. But such images also seemed familiar, contributing to the many comparisons with 1963 that worked to undermine the march's modest accomplishments. Even though the political and cultural context was far different from what it had been five years earlier, Solidarity Day did not compare favorably in the eyes of the press. Missing, according to the *New York Times*, were the camaraderie, the Protestant establishment, the "exhilarating hope and promise." Replacing them were a "cool anger," "apocalyptic messages," and signs that read, "This is your last chance for nonviolence."[73] Other publications made similar observations and added their own list of march deficiencies. "The program ran two hours behind schedule," noted the *Los Angeles Times*, while the *Post* pointed out how much smaller it was than in 1963. "Solidarity Day 1968," concluded *Newsweek*, "was no match for the 1963 March on Washington."[74]

Although organizers vowed that the campaign's most militant stage was just beginning, it appeared that Resurrection City's days were numbered as crime and rumors of crime wracked the camp. The government had extended the permit for just one week to allow the staging of Solidarity Day. It was set to expire at 8 P.M. June 23, and Department of Interior officials had no plans to grant another extension. Authorities justified the decision by citing an uptick in crime in the shantytown, including at least one hundred assaults since mid-May, as well as a number of armed robberies—at least one by a youth gang member serving as a city marshal. Press coverage of the city increasingly had emphasized violence by residents, especially after an assault on a journalist in early June. When the young male marshals still tightly monitored security, including the snow fence that ringed the city, they routinely applied the rough tactics they had used, and police used against them, in the streets of Chicago, Memphis, and Milwaukee. For instance, marshals enforced rules to protect residents' privacy after 6 P.M. by "snatching" cameras, even from journalists. Burglaries of the city's unsecure "houses" were also common. And as conditions worsened in the city and security slacked off, tensions rose. "This is a great Campaign and a just one," said former marshal Alvin Jackson, but SCLC officials "just won't allow any kind of discipline in the camp."[75]

Yet such claims also became a convenient excuse for the city's detractors, prompting campaign officials to argue vehemently that while crime among the poor should be expected, the reports were exaggerated. Responding to Jackson's charges of rampant, unchecked violence, Ralph Abernathy called the man a government plant. But he also acknowledged that some acts of violence had occurred and were understandable, if regrettable. "I am certain that one can understand that often, the pent-up hostility and frustration which poor people possess are inflicted on whites and members of the press who they feel are a part of the oppressive structure," Abernathy told a skeptical press.[76] James Orange, in charge of the city's security, unconvincingly characterized rape claims as mostly consensual sex. But too often, rumors of rampant robberies, assaults, rapes, and rape attempts were treated as if fact. "If there was one thing for sure," wrote one journalist, "it was that Resurrection City was a city of rumor."[77] Overall, the claims of violent crime—especially the well-worn specter of black men raping white women that lurked beneath the surface of many rumors—did not reflect the experiences of most campaigners. "We weren't at all afraid," said Tillie Walker, who never had anything stolen and routinely walked around the camp at midnight.[78] There were exceptions, but most residents of Resurrection City were far quicker to complain about cold food and mud than their physical security.[79]

The rising tensions during the city's last days just reinforced officials' decision not to extend the permit. As demonstrations—most notably outside the Department of Agriculture—sparked scores of arrests, near altercations between the authorities and residents happened every evening, prompting police to lob tear gas into the encampment at least once to avert what they feared would be a full riot. "Now the conditions in the city—themselves symbolic of the wretchedness of the poor—are hampering the main order of business," stated a *Washington Post* editorial summing up what had become obvious. SCLC officials "are going to have to accept the inevitability of closing it down."[80]

That occurred on the rain-darkened morning of June 24. After asking George Crow Flies High, a Hidatsa from North Dakota, to give the campaign symbolic permission to remain on the land, SCLC officials prepared for mass arrests. In an overwhelming show of force, hundreds of heavily armed civilian and military police officers dressed in riot helmets and flak jackets swept through Resurrection City. They encountered little resistance, finding fewer than 100 people—almost all of whom were with James Bevel, singing freedom songs in the Many Races Soul Center. Another 250 marchers—black, white, and Indian—walked arm-in-arm with Ralph Abernathy to the edge of the U.S. Capitol grounds, where they were arrested for unlawful assembly. Abernathy, the first to be detained, flashed a peace sign after boarding a bus for a city jail, where he would stay until mid-July. By late afternoon, workers were readying the site for dismantlement.[81]

Resurrection City's fall prompted a mix of feelings from marchers and observers alike. "In one sense, whoever it was who ran us out of there did us a big favor," said Andrew Young, SCLC executive director.[82] The city had been characterized as "an enemy to the cause," "a jungle at night," and simply a "mudhole."[83] But it also had been home to many people, as some journalists discovered in their profiles of the city. "I'm living better here than I ever did" in Marks, Mississippi, said Josie Williams, a mother of seven who could find employment back home only as a domestic.[84] And despite its challenges, the city still represented hope, as radical journalist I. F. Stone recalled other temporary homes for the downtrodden. "Resurrection City is supposed to have been a mess," Stone wrote. "I found it inspiring. It reminded me of the Jewish displaced persons' camps I visited in Germany after the war. There was the same squalor and the same bad smells, but also the same hope and the same will to rebuild from the ashes of adversity. To organize the hopeless, to give them fresh spirit, to see them marching was truly resurrection."[85] The meaning of Resurrection City, it seemed, was as complicated as poverty itself.

◆ ◆ ◆

Mexican Americans, other than a brief appearance by Reies Tijerina, were conspicuously absent from the events surrounding the tent city's last days. Other than a protest outside the Justice Department with a group of American Indians, people of Mexican descent remained at the Hawthorne School or went home. Corky Gonzales, anxious to build on the new contacts he made in Washington, returned to Denver after Solidarity Day in order to start planning what would become the first Chicano Youth Liberation Conference. Others such as Brown Berets Carlos Montes and Ralph Ramirez put off facing charges in Los Angeles stemming from the March blowouts by joining new Puerto Rican friends in New York City. Still others stayed in Washington to form what they hoped would be a more permanent multiracial effort on behalf of poor people, called the Poor People's Embassy.

If the campaign had achieved anything positive by the time Resurrection City fell, according to white Appalachian organizer Al McSurely, it was that "the idea and the actions" of a multiracial coalition of the poor "caught our imaginations."[86] To capitalize on this, a diverse mix of about fifteen activists gathered at Hawthorne on June 25, to devise a plan to keep the campaign's multiracial spirit, however flawed, alive. A few came from Resurrection City after it closed down, but most had been living at Hawthorne for the duration. They included Hank Adams, Reies Tijerina, Alianza deputy Wilfredo Sedillo, Leo Nieto, Mike Clark of the Highlander School, welfare rights organizer Dovie Thurman, SCLC's Andrew Young, and black antipoverty workers Frank Roberts and Cornelius Givens. What these original attendees determined was that America's poor needed its own "embassy" in Washington.[87]

Through nearly unanimous votes during two meetings in late June, the delegates laid out a basic structure for a new poor people's coalition, an organization in which the campaign's five primary racial groups stood on relatively equal ground. Tijerina described the new creation as "a national institution by the poor and for the poor," with a mission "to secure food, clothing and property, plus adequate education and honorable jobs for the poor, with no strings attached from any individual, corporation, or governmental organization."[88] An interim leadership structure included the oddly named Supreme Council made up of Tijerina, Givens, Mad Bear Anderson, Grace Mora Newman, and Click Johnson, and a National Council of fifty, consisting of ten members from each racial group. Plans were then made to continue the conversation throughout the summer, with periodic meetings of the two councils, to establish firmer objectives, as well as to conduct the more mundane work of forming an office and seeking reliable funding sources. Although SCLC's Young participated, it was clear that members of other organizations and racial groups—particularly Chicanos and white Appalachians—drove the conversation.[89]

As McSurely suggested later in a memorandum to the "leaders of the Poor People's Coalition," there were organizing lessons to be learned from the campaign, especially in regard to timing and message. "We see the dangers in having the timing of a campaign dictated by the liberal establishment, instead of by the people and their proven leaders," McSurely wrote, arguing that SCLC and the "rich liberals" that funded the organization were too preoccupied with affecting the presidential primaries and national party conventions. "Whenever you have the 'leadership' and the grassroots organizers working at cross purposes, you have . . . chaos," he stated. "While many of us were dedicated to working out a coalition, which takes time, planning and mutual experience, many others . . . involved in the Campaign were dedicated to getting some heads beat on TV." Therefore, a new organization's actions should heed the poor's experiences, take its time, and "not bite off more than we can chew," an allusion to Resurrection City. In the end, "we must not depend on anyone but ourselves. To meet the needs of the poor in this country, we cannot rely on the consciences of the rich. . . . We can only depend on ourselves—and our organizational strength." To McSurely and the others involved, the group's diverse makeup of grass-roots community leaders held that promise.[90]

During the next several months, a planning committee of activists met in Washington and at the Airlie House retreat in Virginia to develop the coalition's purpose and structure—with the result demonstrating how difficult it was to avoid entanglement with the so-called liberal establishment. What emerged was less a poor person's congressional lobbying group than a clearinghouse designed to provide informational, networking, and strategic support to local community groups interested in class-based, multiracial alliances at home. In a funding proposal to the Ford Foundation—a symbol of that very establishment—the Poor People's Embassy proposed creating national demonstration programs to break down "several fundamental barriers" that "still continue to hamper successful coordination and cooperation between minority and poverty groups." Those barriers included a lack of "sufficient intergroup knowledge as to who constitutes minority leadership, . . . adequate dialogue between minority leadership on both primary and secondary levels, . . . necessary experience and understanding between minority group leadership, resulting in less than adequate concern among the various minority groups for the culture, values and traditions of other groups, and . . . specific information regarding the types of programs that various minority groups have operating in their regions." Programs would consist of workshops, seminars, and research projects designed to "create new program development techniques, minority tactics for social change, community action research methodologies, new program funding techniques," as well as to "re-educate" the middle class in "techniques for the resolution of intergroup conflicts and value confrontations."[91] In proposing an initiative rooted in educational seminars funded by a liberal foundation, the plan relied heavily on the middle-class presumptions so often criticized by activists such as McSurely. Yet, for those who eventually wrote the grant proposal, it represented an intellectual rationale with which foundation decision makers might be comfortable and on which activists could later build.[92]

Such compromise did not bother Reies Tijerina. For the land-grant rights leader, the Poor People's Embassy provided a vehicle for his continued pursuit of multiracial alliances in one form or another. And this proved especially important, as Tijerina's own stock faded among Chicano activists outside of New Mexico. Tijerina's participation in the Poor People's Campaign was not just one more chapter in his activist career, as historians normally portray, but the high water mark of his prominence and popularity within the Chicano movement.[93] His 1969 conviction for

Reies López Tijerina emphatically makes a point during a press conference in the Hawthorne School as Hank Adams, Al Bridges, Ralph Abernathy, and an unidentified woman watch. By the end of the campaign, many fellow Chicano activists had tired of Tijerina's bombastic style and love for the camera and microphone—despite their continued support for the land-grant rights cause. (Karl Kernberger Pictorial Collection (PICT 2000-008-0131), Center for Southwest Research, University Libraries, University of New Mexico)

criminal assault on a federal officer and destruction of property from the occupation of the Echo Amphitheater in 1966 contributed to his disappearance from the scene, but this decline began at the Hawthorne School in 1968.

Ever since Martin Luther King Jr. made it clear that SCLC wanted Mexican Americans to participate fully in the campaign during the Minority Group Conference, Tijerina had been a larger-than-life presence. From his passionate pleas for cooperation behind closed doors to his demands that the interests of nonblack marchers be given equal consideration in public, Tijerina had a knack for captivating an audience with his rhetoric and energy. His attention-getting activities attracted the media, which saw his sometimes incendiary words as good copy, if nothing else. This was a deliberate strategy of Tijerina's. "For him, any media attention was one more brick in the wall or stepping stones to build power," observed Maria Varela, who worked for the Alianza for more than a year. "That's what he thought his job was. He wasn't an organizer. He was a preacher.

And preachers need an audience."[94] Indeed, the invitation from SCLC—an organization that knew a thing or two about media manipulation—to participate in the campaign could be attributed to Tijerina's deft use of hyperbole and spectacle. Without the citizen's arrest of a park ranger, the destruction of fences, the raid on the Tierra Amarilla courthouse, and all of the speechifying that accompanied them, Tijerina may have remained an anonymous preacher from New Mexico.[95]

Instead, Tijerina was the one Chicano activist who received consistent attention from the media—albeit usually in the context of ethnic and racial conflict. While Tijerina at times genuinely represented some westerners' interests in terms of land rights and their own unique understanding of poverty, Mexican American marchers came to question both Tijerina's effectiveness and motivations. His declarations about stolen land and cultural pride solidified the land grants as part of the Chicano narrative and animated young Chicanos from afar. Yet, given the opportunity to work closely with the eccentric activist, many were left unimpressed. "Tijerina was hard to reach," according to Miguel Barragan. "He was pretty much into his pontificating."[96] Corky Gonzales refused to criticize Tijerina publicly, saying that, "Any fights within our family, we keep within the family."[97] But behind the scenes, he came to believe that Tijerina's harangues and public spats were counterproductive, according to Gonzales's children, Varela, and FBI informants. Tijerina "did some incredible things in New Mexico, and some great things that needed to be done," acknowledged Rudy Gonzales. "But he had no sense of organization."[98]

Similar to the disappointment marchers had with Ralph Abernathy's decision to live in a motel for much of the campaign, others close to Tijerina saw a real gap between his public and private personas. Maria Varela, the daughter of a Mexican immigrant, questioned her association with Tijerina after he referred to a judge as a *mojado*, or "wetback," and again when he showed no concern for young Chicanos who had followed him from New Mexico and subsequently were jailed for a land rights protest. SCLC lawyers, at the urging of Corky Gonzales, posted their bail, but Varela said, "I thought to myself what am I doing here?" Calling the incident "the final straw," she quit the Alianza in the middle of the campaign and joined forces with others, including Gonzales.[99] Residents of the Hawthorne School reported that Tijerina routinely ate better food—steak versus rice and beans—and had better accommodations than the other marchers. Even the many children who had traveled with their families offered their own devastating critique, calling him Reies "TV-rina" because of his penchant to literally chase television cameras. (The same kids called SCLC's leader Ralph "Blabber-nathy.")[100]

Yet many of those who criticized Tijerina found the case for land-grant rights compelling. So much so that Maria Varela, on the basis of her experience with the Alianza and later conversations with Corky Gonzales and Cesar Chavez, believed they recognized the primacy of the land rights movement and had been prepared to lead their organizations' support for Tijerina and land grants. Chavez, with his close ties to Senator Robert F. Kennedy and the liberal wing of the Democratic Party, offered supportive words to Tijerina, while keeping a distance from his perceived tactics. In the wake of the Tierra Amarilla raid, Chavez wrote cordial, carefully worded telegrams backing land rights, and in late 1967 the union leader attended an Alianza meeting.[101] He told reporters later that, if he had lived in New Mexico, he would certainly be a member of the Alianza. Gonzales, who had cut his ties to the Democratic establishment, endorsed Tijerina's actions more wholeheartedly. To support "this just and honorable cause," Gonzales raised money for the Alianza, attended its 1967 convention, and even worked out of the organization's New Mexico office for several weeks in 1967 while Tijerina dealt with legal troubles.[102] Another sign of support came from the Chicano Press Association newspapers, especially the Crusade's El Gallo, which covered the land rights movement with enormous sympathy and as central to the larger Chicano struggle.[103]

Thus, even as activists backed away from the leadership of Tijerina, many of these more urban Chicanos recognized the importance of incorporating land reform and rights into their agenda more fully because of his efforts. This inclusion proved tricky at times, given the different nature of the struggle in northern New Mexico and southern Colorado—one that privileged cultural and economic independence through the restoration of land rather than an expansion of government benefits or civil rights. But activists such as Gonzales increasingly embraced both the practical and symbolic importance of land rights because it not only combated poverty but also reinforced cultural pride in the mythical homeland of Aztlán. Some of this work occurred during the Poor People's Campaign. Gonzales included land reform in El Plan del Barrio, while members of the Crusade, the Brown Berets, and more urban Chicano groups marched on the Department of State in support of Tijerina's petition regarding the Treaty of Guadalupe Hidalgo. In turn, Alianza members from New Mexico helped advocate for issues that were considered more urban, such as fighting police brutality. It was these sorts of gestures that led Ernesto Vigil to conclude that the urban and rural impulses of the Chicano movement, albeit real and contentious at times, took a step toward understanding each other during their time in Washington.[104]

◆ ◆ ◆

The Washington phase of the Poor People's Campaign sputtered into early July. Most observers began to write the campaign's obituary, even those few sympathetic to the cause and certain of the media's own complicity. "Poor people goodbye," wrote reporter Robert Terrell in *Commonweal*. "The press did you in."[105] But some activists took the flattening of Resurrection City as the opening of a new militant chapter in the campaign. "I don't care whether we are arrested—I'm from Selma," declared Leona Jackson.[106] Others murmured more menacingly that this might be their last nonviolent march. Trying to emulate his predecessor's famous letter from Birmingham, a jailed Ralph Abernathy implored supporters to continue their protests and spark arrests through his "Letter from a D.C. Jail" and then a Cesar Chavez–style fast. Abernathy's aides echoed his call for action, as did the "Young Turks" of the NAACP, who challenged Roy Wilkins and that civil rights organization's old guard to "pack and go to Washington" during its annual convention.[107]

While many people went home, about a thousand stayed to work on the Poor People's Embassy or lead marches from area churches or Hawthorne, whose directors had refused to comply with city demands to evict their guests. The most prominent actions were a 600-plus-person circle around the Capitol, a Quaker Action Group vigil, and a 125-person hunger strike in a Virginia jail. Simultaneously, sympathizers set up miniversions of Resurrection City in other parts of the country. In Virginia, a few dozen people, calling themselves the "Refugees of Resurrection City, USA," sought a new place to encamp, hold workshops, and build the movement. Eventually settling on ten acres of land provided by civil rights veteran Amelia Boynton in rural Alabama, the group intended to "build a city of love, freedom, equality, peace and justice for all people."[108]

Another tent city was in Washington State, where a few dozen American Indians and their allies pitched tents on the grounds of the state capitol in Olympia. Dubbed "Resurrection City II" by Tulalip tribe leader Janet McCloud, the camp was set up to protest the state's violation of treaty and fishing rights under the 1854 Medicine Creek Treaty, as well as the jailing of black comedian and civil rights activist Dick Gregory during a recent fish-in. Used as a base for demonstrations, the camp took on many of the characteristics of its namesake, including internal security guards and an outpouring of assistance from the public. Supported by members of the Students for a Democratic Society, the Peace and Freedom Party, and the Black Panthers, Hank Adams and local Indians led multiracial demonstrations for more than three months, prompting arrests and publicity before reaching a compromise with authorities. Resurrection City II eventually faced the same fate as its cousin—being unceremoniously knocked down by police.[109]

By the time Ralph Abernathy finished his twenty-day sentence in jail, the campaign's Washington phase was all but over. Abandoning efforts to launch economic boycotts in forty major cities, Abernathy declared that the Poor People's Campaign would continue with small groups of people "well disciplined in the philosophy of nonviolence" outside the Republican and Democratic National Conventions later that summer. He added that, while Congress has "failed to move meaningfully against the problem of poverty," the campaign had prompted several achievements—most importantly "that the poor posed the issues of poverty and poverty will never be again ignored in this nation."[110] Abernathy did not comment on SCLC's former Mexican American and American Indian partners. This included, most notably, Reies Tijerina, who delivered a parting shot toward SCLC as the Washington campaign came to an end. "The poor have been completely mocked" by SCLC, Tijerina told reporters. "Never have I seen the poor so betrayed."[111] A week later, Tijerina then returned to New Mexico and, in a public about-face, praised the campaign for its achievements. Such opposing hyperbolic summations, in a way, represented his schizophrenic public nature—and also of the campaign itself.

Indeed, it could be concluded that the poor were "betrayed" by both their leaders and the federal government. Yet amid many vague promises made by government officials to "look into" a variety of complaints, a few concrete policy and budgetary changes stood out—particularly toward fighting hunger—as a result of the Solidarity Day spectacle and the intense behind-the-scenes lobbying conducted by Marian Wright, the NWRO's George Wiley, and others. Such policy changes included a $100 million program for free and reduced-price lunches for poor children; the immediate release of surplus commodities to the nation's one thousand poorest counties; $25 million for Office of Economic Opportunity (OEO) and Head Start programs in Alabama and Mississippi; the hiring of more than thirteen hundred poor people by OEO agencies; a mild expansion of the food stamp program, reducing its cost to recipients; and a streamlining of some federal welfare guidelines, including those regulating the male partners of women welfare recipients. Such changes seemed minor compared to campaign organizers' ambitious objectives of "jobs or income for all." However, as one independent observer argued, "it must be stressed that nothing had worsened in the fields of welfare and employment, that the PPC had been a remarkably successful holding action against the forces of reaction in a time when the country was clearly turning more and more conservative. Head Start and school lunch programs had actually been slightly strengthened at a time when many commentators foresaw the probability of their being seriously crippled or killed."[112]

Claims of mild policy success came not just from loyal SCLC adherents or left-leaning academics but also from more unlikely sources inside the Johnson administration and the media. Indeed, despite President Johnson's quiet but furious opposition, his most influential aides had argued that assisting the campaign in small ways best served the president. As aide James Gaither put it, "I have little doubt that history will acclaim the objectives of the Poor People's Campaign, irrespective of the means chosen and the violence caused."[113] Other members of the administration lamented that the government never determined a clear, consistent policy on the campaign. "Some kind of uniform approach would have been better" and could have assured a successful campaign, argued Ralph Huitt, assistant secretary for legislation at the Department of Health, Education, and Welfare (HEW).[114] Instead, the result was a limited amount of cooperation behind the scenes—and even faint praise—after it became clear that Ralph Abernathy would not be persuaded to cancel the march. Attorney General Ramsey Clark was the most vociferous defender of the campaign's right to demonstrate. Marian Wright also developed a kitchen cabinet of agency bureaucrats to vet policy proposals, including Roger Wilkins of the Justice Department, Carl Holman of the Civil Rights Commission, Lisle Carter of HEW, and John Schnittker of the U.S. Department of Agriculture. Even HEW secretary Wilbur Cohen, generally critical of the campaign, begrudgingly gave it credit for many of his department's efforts in the last days of the Johnson administration. Progress had been made in the realm of legal services for the poor, recipients' participation in advisory committees on welfare programs, and teacher training for both bilingual education and programs for disadvantaged children. These were promises, of course, from a lame-duck administration.[115]

But arguably the campaign's most important, long-term legacy was its inadvertent strengthening of the Chicano movement and its unique form of identity politics. Amid the attempts at multiracial action—and sometimes because of them—people of Mexican descent built and deepened relationships with each other and with their American Indian brothers and sisters that would help sustain the movement in the years to come. This experience left these activists empowered with more complex understandings of the world around them. It strengthened intraregional networks, connecting people in Denver and Los Angeles to New Mexico, Texas, and beyond. Moreover, the experience shed light on whose leadership skills best suited the movement. This became even clearer as Chicano activists from Alicia Escalante and Gloria Arellanes to Ernesto Vigil and Gilberto Ballejos returned home.

7 ◆ The Limits of Coalition

Gilberto Ballejos returned to Albuquerque in July 1968 inspired and ready to build local bases of power. "A lot of nice things, humorous things, enlightening things occurred" in Washington, Ballejos recalled. Alianza members, young and old, "came back and were very different, and better for it. People I still talk to, it was the highlight of their lives." And despite being a little wiser and more experienced at age thirty-two than some of his younger counterparts, Ballejos also was inspired by the interactions he had with other activists he met in the nation's capital. Ballejos primarily had been a problem solver that spring, such as procuring SCLC money for the New Mexico delegation's transportation back home and getting Corky Gonzales involved when SCLC looked like it might renege on providing resources to go to Washington. Yet it was his dealings with the much younger Brown Berets of East Los Angeles that motivated Ballejos to found a chapter of the organization in Albuquerque.[1]

In a sense, the unemployed schoolteacher and Alianza member some considered an heir apparent to Reies Tijerina was picking up where he had left off. In 1967 and early 1968, Ballejos and Los Duranes neighborhood activist Carlos Cansino led a series of protests calling for improvements at the local elementary school. While many of their demands focused on incorporating Spanish into the school's curriculum, hiring more bilingual teachers, and engaging more thoroughly in the school's Mexican American neighborhood by forming a Parent Teacher Association, the protesters also connected the school's deficiencies to the widespread poverty that affected African Americans, Indians, and whites throughout Albuquerque. In the short term, the demonstrations had little effect on the school but did lead to the two men's founding of *El Papel*, an underground Chicano newspaper that offered an alternative to the state's conservative dailies. Ballejos's vigorous activism and interest beyond just land rights raised his stature to the point that Tijerina tapped him as New Mexico's recruitment director for the Poor People's Campaign.[2]

After two months in Washington, Ballejos arrived in New Mexico ready to develop a dynamic local organization that would supplement, if not displace, the Alianza, its influence on the decline at least in Albuquerque. In August 1968, the Brown Berets of New Mexico mobilized hundreds to protest the police shooting death of a young Mexican American and to seek a civilian police review board with substantial minority representation. Despite membership fluctuations and internal leadership disputes, the Brown Berets remained a presence in Albuquerque, Santa Fe, and other parts of northern New Mexico during the next few years. Often joining forces with the Alianza and groups such as the Comancheros, a Tierra Amarilla youth organization also founded by veterans of the Poor People's Campaign, the Berets led direct action protests and called for stronger state minimum-wage laws, school community control boards, bilingual education, respectful welfare regulations, and reforms of New Mexico's corporation tax laws.[3]

Albuquerque's Brown Berets, at least initially, also fostered multiracial organizing, routinely cooperating with African Americans and American Indians in protest and political strategy. In October 1968, Brown Berets joined students in criticizing what they deemed to be race-based firings at a Santa Fe high school. Working with the Black Student Union and the United Mexican American Students at the University of New Mexico (UNM), the Berets later protested the school administration's whites-only definition of "community leaders" and its relationship with all-white Brigham Young University. Ballejos and the Berets helped organize a citizens grievance committee to assist university workers in fighting low wages and discrimination, an effort that foreshadowed the eventual collective bargaining agreements that UNM maintenance workers won in the early 1970s. In 1969, Ballejos ran on a school board reform ticket with Shirley Hill Witt, a Mohawk who had worked on the Poor People's Campaign and helped found the National Indian Youth Council. And the Tennessee-based Highlander Folk School tapped Ballejos as its primary partner in a new initiative called Highlander West.[4]

The pages of El Papel, edited by Ballejos, also encouraged multiracial organizing. The paper declared that the UNM demonstration over the Brigham Young affiliation was a "new day for black-brown cooperation."[5] Although perhaps overstating this "new day," Ballejos offered an insightful media critique, interestingly pointing out that mainstream news outlets characterized the demonstration as solely a black protest—a media tendency that he had noticed while in Washington and was determined to combat. The *Albuquerque Journal* "realized the significance of the Black-Chicano coalition and tried to suppress it through a process of selective omission," wrote Ballejos. "The contents of the accompanying article stated that Blacks and 'a few sympathizers' were present in the protest, thus omitting the significance of the new coalition between Blacks and Chicanos."[6] Similar coverage appeared in *El Grito del Norte*, a Chicano Press Association newspaper in nearby Española and edited by SNCC veteran Elizabeth "Betita" Martínez.[7]

But by 1970 the promise of vibrant multiracial activism in northern New Mexico had been put on hold, as it had across the Southwest. Ballejos was no longer affiliated with Albuquerque's Brown Berets, whose younger student members first aligned themselves more closely with the efforts of Corky Gonzales, José Angel Gutiérrez, and the race-based La Raza Unida party before the Berets chapter went defunct. Reies Tijerina, another proponent of black-brown cooperation, had questionable motives in the eyes of local African Americans and now was serving a prison term. The remaining members of the Alianza reverted to its bread-and-butter issue of land rights, nearly attaining the transfer of twenty thousand acres in northern New Mexico from the Presbyterian Church.[8] Groups such as the University of New Mexico's chapter of the United Mexican American Students (UMAS), as well as the founders of La Cooperativa Agricola, continued to address issues such as quality education, police brutality, and poverty in Albuquerque and northern New Mexico. But they routinely were framed in cultural and thus Chicano-based terms.[9]

Perhaps this had been inevitable. Racial pride and identity long had been a central motivating yet downplayed factor in African Americans' civil rights activism as well, long before the greatly publicized "black is beautiful" rhetoric of the 1970s. Such race-based politics was not incompatible with multiracial, class-oriented coalition, as the campaign and other efforts suggested. Many activists retained high hopes that thoroughly integrated black-brown cooperation was indeed the future of politics. But a belief also emerged among African Americans and Chicanos who had engaged in multiracial collaboration that to make it work in the long run required a strengthening of their own power bases. In a few isolated instances, activists continued to pursue cooperation—such as in local election campaigns in Texas and the feminist efforts of the Third World Women's Alliance.[10] But most people of Mexican descent and African Americans after 1969 shifted their emphasis toward organizing their own communities and, as a result, offered little beyond rhetorical support for each other. The work of Corky Gonzales and the Crusade for Justice in Denver and on the Chicano scene beyond Colorado epitomized this reality. Building local and regional power, in the short term, meant in the racially segregated barrio or school—not in the fifty-fifty black-brown neighborhood and certainly not in the multiracial city as a whole. Ironically, those who boldly pursued multiracial coalition just a year or two earlier stressed race-based identity politics as essential not just to meet their political needs of the moment but also to establish genuine coalition among the nation's politically weak and disempowered poor sometime in the not-so-distant future.

◆ ◆ ◆

For many participants, the dispiriting collapse of the Poor People's Campaign in Washington did not end their efforts at multiracial coalition building. Some attempted to continue the campaign through new Resurrection Cities and the Poor People's Embassy. Others turned to electoral politics, often as candidates themselves. Hank Adams took the fight for fishing rights and the War on Poverty to the Democratic congressional primary in Washington State, while Puerto Ricans Gilberto Gerena-Valentín and Grace Mora Newman ran for city council and Congress, respectively, in New York City. Welfare rights activist Peggy Terry of Chicago agreed to be vice president on the Peace and Freedom ticket. Even though the National Conference for New Politics had disintegrated by April, the California-based Peace and Freedom Party—founded in early 1968 by young antiwar activists—had created an alternative party structure for those on the left. Few had any illusions that they could beat a Democrat or Republican on the state and congressional levels, even though a black-Latino-labor-liberal coalition had had some success in blunting establishment power in places such as San Antonio. Rather, these activist candidates saw their efforts as a chance to publicize specific issues and build goodwill among disaffected constituencies, especially the poor of all colors.[11]

This was the thinking of Reies López Tijerina in mid-July. Although he had lost some luster in the eyes of Chicano activists from elsewhere, the land rights leader returned to Albuquerque seemingly a king. Arriving to much fanfare at the airport on July 20, 1968, Tijerina declared, "For me [the campaign] was the greatest experience of my life and I feel a great satisfaction for what we have done to advance the rights of the poor. . . . History is now on the side of the poor."[12] A week later, Tijerina's

Justice is His Creed

ELECT

The Poor is h. First Concern

TIJERINA

for

GOVERNOR Of New Mex.

He will Champion the Constitution of New Mexico
He will Speak and Fight for the Poor
**Like Robert Kennedy and Dr. King, He too will
Die for the Poor.** *Tijerina for Governor Committee.*

Vote Nov. 5 '68 On The People's Constitutional Party

After returning to New Mexico, Tijerina becomes one of several campaign participants to run for public office. He briefly ran for governor on the multiracial People's Constitutional Party ticket before officials ruled that his earlier legal issues disqualified him. (Karl Kernberger Pictorial Collection (PICT 2000-008-0001), Center for Southwest Research, University Libraries, University of New Mexico)

aides had persuaded him to maintain his perceived personal momentum from the campaign by announcing a run for governor on the People's Constitutional Party (PCP) ticket. Once rumored as a potential running mate to the Black Panthers' Eldridge Cleaver on the Peace and Freedom ticket in New Mexico, Tijerina saw a run for office as a logical next step. Tijerina and his inner circle in the Alianza believed a statewide campaign could capitalize on his heightened profile and continue to spread the word about land rights in New Mexico, not to mention "a good way of exposing bad elements in the state . . . raise issues to embarrass other candidates and shake up the legislature."[13]

But Tijerina's short-lived campaign also became a way to expand his message beyond the Treaty of Guadalupe Hidalgo, a calculation born out of his time in Washington. During the gubernatorial campaign, Tijerina routinely used the rhetoric of class politics. "If I am elected, the worker will be honored with a just wage and brakes will be put on the rich," he told delegates at the PCP's founding convention. Later, at the University of New Mexico, Tijerina joked, "The poor will have a good time watching the police chase the rich."[14] The PCP's platform mixed advocacy for land rights with policy prescriptions popular with urban Chicanos such as Gilberto Ballejos's Brown Berets and African Americans, including greater welfare rights, a civilian police review board, an end to racial discrimination on draft boards, and curriculum changes to include more Mexican history. In a bid for the youth vote, Tijerina called for lowering the voting age to eighteen years old and for the "protection of the rights of hippies and all those who want to maintain a particular lifestyle."[15] And while the majority of PCP candidates were of Mexican descent, the party also ran Preston Monongye, a Hopi silversmith, as attorney general and Roger Anderson, a white peace activist, for the state board of education. The new party attempted to be more than just a Chicano political party.[16]

Tijerina's campaign that summer and fall received considerable attention from those who believed they were left out of the system, from media observers, and especially from the mainstream parties. The latter focused on removing Tijerina and as many PCP candidates from the ballot as possible. State attorney general Boston Witt disqualified Tijerina, arguing that his conviction for trespassing on federal land disqualified him from state office, even though it was considered a misdemeanor in New Mexico. A state Supreme Court ruling upheld the decision and removed Tijerina, who was then replaced by activist José Alfredo Maestas. Other PCP candidates faced disqualifications on a range of technicalities. Despite Tijerina's disqualification and his successor's subsequent loss, few doubted the PCP's subtle influence on the governor's race, including siphoning enough Mexican American votes from Fabián Chávez Jr., a Democrat, to ensure the reelection of Republican governor David Cargo, a moderate and onetime Alianza sympathizer.[17]

Still fighting state and federal charges from the 1967 courthouse raid, Tijerina remained a prominent figure in New Mexico for years to come. After the election and his acquittal on Tierra Amarilla–related charges, he continued to pursue the issues from the governor's race well into 1969, making him a fixture at Albuquerque school board meetings and an advocate for welfare rights, income maintenance programs, and sanitation workers' collective bargaining rights. Yet he received fewer and fewer invitations to speak at regional and national Chicano events. By the time a jury convicted Tijerina for aiding and abetting the destruction of federal property in the Santa Fe National Forest in October 1969, Tijerina had seen his influence among the larger Chicano movement decline precipitously. And with him, an important alternative voice for the Chicano movement—one interested in legal documents and coalition building—

declined as well. His twenty-one-month imprisonment allowed younger Alianza members to reshape the organization's platform to include more explicit calls for cultural nationalism. Tijerina condemned this turn as unnecessarily separatist and counterproductive, a move that further marginalized the land-grant leader even after his release from federal prison in 1971. "My motto is justice," Tijerina argued, "but not independence from the government of the United States."[18]

Tijerina's forced departure from the scene also robbed the Poor People's Embassy of one of its most avid and high-profile champions. Although, even with an active Tijerina, the embassy may have been too radical for liberal foundations in retreat from much of their support of 1960s activism. Nita Jo Gonzales, eldest daughter of Corky, served as a representative of the Crusade for Justice and recalled both clarity of mission and finances as major challenges. "We weren't taken very seriously" by the media and foundations, and thus money remained a constant struggle. One cost-cutting measure moved the embassy to New York City, where it operated out of Puerto Rican organizer Anibal Solivan's house. In retrospect, Gonzales considered this decision a mistake because it moved the fledgling organization away from Washington. The move and Tijerina's departure sealed the embassy's irrelevance.[19]

The Poor People's Embassy accomplished little policywise, but at least for a time it fostered some multiracial dialogue among its young activists, mostly through periodic meetings and correspondence. Gonzales remained part of the staff for a year and a half before returning to Denver to work with her father at the Crusade for Justice. She considered the embassy experience invaluable to her leadership of the Crusade's new "freedom school" for Chicano youth, Escuela Tlatelolco. Others, such as Cornelius "Cornbread" Givens, used the embassy as a base to launch small nonprofit organizations, including the Poor People's Development Foundation in New Jersey. The organization, which featured a diverse board of activists, including Tijerina, Tillie Walker, and Black Panther Mark Comfort, worked on establishing farm cooperatives in the South and linking them to northern consumers, as well as supporting community control of urban renewal efforts in Chicago.[20]

The embassy—and the Poor People's Campaign by extension—also rejuvenated older activist institutions for social justice and civil rights such as the Highlander Folk School, based in Monteagle, Tennessee.[21] Despite his gripe that whites largely had been segregated within Resurrection City, school founder Myles Horton maintained a cautious optimism about the future of multiracial cooperation. "I have a good feeling about the Poor People's Embassy now and am anxious to get down to work on the educational and cultural aspects," Horton wrote Reies Tijerina in 1968. "Together we might be able to increase our effectiveness by exchanging experiences and developing new programs tailored to the various areas and groups."[22] The Washington campaign had made this possible, argued Highlander's Mike Clark, who lived in both Resurrection City and the Hawthorne School for several weeks. "It is this experience of living together," Clark said, "that will sow the seeds of change in the students of Resurrection City."[23]

Highlander pursued several opportunities based on connections first established in Washington. In addition to the Poor People's Embassy, Highlander emphasized building relationships in the Southwest beyond Tijerina. This took many forms, ranging from designing workshops and supporting a residential center for Chicanos in northern New Mexico to running cross-cultural programs for Navajo and Hopi Indians in the state's Gallup area. Many of these programs reflected Highlander's renewed efforts in Appalachia itself, especially "self-education programs" modeled after Highlander's citizenship schools from the 1950s and early 1960s. In Albuquerque, Highlander workshops provided valuable training and support for Gilberto Ballejos, the Brown Berets, and their allies. Ballejos, a former teacher, facilitated several workshops designed to strengthen their organizing before a disagreement over the proper use of Highlander funds ended their relationship. In the next few years, Highlander also provided programmatic support to Escuela Tlatelolco and sent activists to learn from a health clinic Maria Varela helped develop in Tierra Amarilla.[24]

Producing less-concrete results and illustrating the continued challenges to multiracial collaboration were several workshops hosted by Highlander staff in Tennessee. In 1970 and 1971, Highlander invited a variety of activists from across the country to participate in weeklong discussions of how to strengthen multiracial alliances among poor people. Participants included several Mexican Americans and Indians involved in Highlander West, such as the Alianza's Pedro Archuleta, *El Grito* writer and editor José Madril, and the National Indian Youth Council's Shirley Hill Witt. Also participating were African Americans from the Southwest Georgia Project in Albany and Black Panthers and Young Lords from Chicago. According to Mike Clark, conversations during the workshops touched on issues of common concern, such as the role of land in the movement, and more service-oriented efforts such as food programs and health clinics. Many participants forged friendships. But he lamented that interracial distrust remained an obstacle, particularly in dealing with Highlander's primarily white staff. "Many educational opportunities opened the first day were never adequately followed up," wrote Clark about the 1970 conference. "Time after time I saw opportunities to tie ideas or statements to earlier ones but felt I could not because I was white."[25] This anxiety, even hostility, was not imagined. At various times, non-whites accused Highlander staff of working for the Central Intelligence Agency or cooperating with liberal foundation officials to "find out what people were really doing" with their money. Years of federal surveillance and dirty tricks had taken its toll on many activists. The 1971 conference resulted in similar discomfort among participants.[26]

Yet, the workshops still prompted moments of clarity for those involved. For Arika Ducumus, a Filipina activist from San Francisco, the 1970 workshop paradoxically failed to provide "constructive data to bring back to my community" but still energized her and other activists she met. "The overall emotional effect that it had on us folks was tremendous," she wrote. She went on to explain how participants Patricia James, Jim Redcorn, and Eddie Brown, all close to burning out or pursuing other endeavors before the workshop, decided to devote themselves anew to their community projects in Georgia, Virginia, and New Mexico, respectively. "And me, after months of deliberation and avoidance of the issue, I've decided to return to school and set the S.F. Filipino community as my first priority," Ducumus continued. "For all of us, thank you."[27] Follow-ups by Mike Clark suggested other benefits, including Filipino visits to Indian communities in New Mexico and Mexican American help in forming a health clinic in Appalachia and in generating new writing styles for activist newspapers. But such links did not last. By early 1973, nearly all official correspondence between Highlander and western activists had stopped. Highlander had returned to its roots in Appalachia.[28]

◆ ◆ ◆

Mexican Americans of different stripes returned to their own roots after the Poor People's Campaign. Many recalled going home or seeing their friends come back from the campaign "a little more militant . . . a little more energetic," not to mention mindful of why they became activists in the first place.[29] José Angel Gutiérrez, who attended early planning meetings but did not make it to Washington because of work and family commitments, remembered the excitement of his fellow members of the Mexican American Youth Organization in Texas: "They came back euphoric. It was kind of like more medals from struggles. . . . Everybody had a story to tell, of how they got beat, or how they got Maced. . . . Everybody had war stories."[30] Such stories often became useful tools to recruit other Chicano youth, an appeal to male activists' masculinity and to everyone's outrage. Youth fresh from the campaign, such as Andres Valdez, attempted to emulate people and groups they encountered at the Hawthorne School or Resurrection City. For Valdez, the tough, nationalistic rhetoric of the San José-based Black Berets attracted him enough to found the organization's first Colorado chapter.[31]

For other organizers, the Poor People's Campaign both energized them and precipitated a new, more culturally and politically nationalist direction of activism. This was the experience of Miguel Barragan, a Roman Catholic priest hired as a field representative of the Bishop's Committee on the Spanish-Speaking in San Antonio. "I had to make a choice," he recalled. "I was given the choice of staying within the Catholic Church or (the) Poor People's Campaign. I called the PPC a moral issue. We all had to get involved and do our thing."[32] Barragan, praised by SCLC officials for organizing a contingent from central Texas to come to Washington with private money, had worked for the committee for less than a year when the campaign came to his attention. He believed that he would have left the church eventually, because of what he saw as a lack of commitment to ecumenical efforts and genuine programming to empower individuals. "It wasn't going anywhere, man. I'm not into services," he recalled, referring to the church's emphasis on paternalistic charity rather than more liberating empowerment. But the campaign was "my opportunity to grow, my opportunity to possible resources, my opportunity to make my voice heard as to the type of legislation we needed. . . . I had to grow. I'm not a social worker."[33] He resigned his church post, went to Washington, lived in the Hawthorne School, which he called "a blessing," and wrote songs, some of which became quasi anthems for the Chicano movement, including "Mujeres Valientes" about striking Chicana farm workers. Indeed, Barragan's most important cross-cultural exchanges were probably with a guitar in his hands. From sharing a stage with Guy Carawan and Pete Seeger in Resurrection City to smaller venues such as the Hawthorne School's common room, Barragan found a way to promote solidarity while he pursued his new calling.[34]

Like his Chicano brethren, Barragan also met a variety of people as part of the campaign. One of the most significant individuals he met, however, was actor Marlon Brando. The star of *On the Waterfront* supported the early fish-ins in Washington State and later had promised to devote his career to the civil rights cause. That commitment proved short-lived, but Brando did contribute to the campaign, appearing in New Mexico for the caravan and wowing fans such as campaign coordinator Shirley Hill Witt. Brando also donated $70,000 to the cause—$20,000 of which went to Barragan's efforts in Texas. With this seed money in the spring of 1968, Barragan and MAYO cofounder Ignacio "Nacho" Perez established an office in Laredo to organize conferences in preparation for the campaign, as well as to write proposals for larger foundation grants. These efforts initially produced several buses full of support for the campaign as well as the arresting image of hundreds of poor protesters marching around the "sacred" Alamo in San Antonio. Brando seed money also helped jump-start the fledgling Southwest Council of La Raza, according to Barragan, who became the council's first executive director. In turn, the council provided funding for Chicano organizations such as Chicanos Por La Causa, the Mexican American Legal Defense Fund, and the Southwest Voter Registration and Education Project into the 1970s.[35]

But of all the Mexican American activists who attended the Poor People's Campaign, Corky Gonzales became the most prominent individual to translate the Washington experience into an enthusiastically nationalist vision of the Chicano movement. Gonzales's orchestration of the Chicano Youth Liberation Conferences in 1969 and 1970 and his championing and leadership of the race-based La Raza Unida party demonstrated the ties between multiracial coalition building and the politics of identity. A new chapter in this relationship began to take shape most clearly near the end of the campaign, especially during the Solidarity Day rally, and accelerated when Gonzales returned to Denver.

The time in Washington did raise the nationalist consciousness of the Chicano movement, as Gonzales and other activists had hoped—but not through the national press, which largely ignored Chicanos.[36] Rather, Gonzales's high-profile pronouncements in Washington bolstered his credibility among Mexican Americans at home, by demonstrating his willingness and courage to take on some of the nation's most powerful officials. His angry but articulate tongue-lashing of Attorney General Ramsey Clark on criminal justice issues garnered some attention in the local press. So did *El Plan del Barrio*, a five-point program for the Chicano movement that he unveiled on Solidarity Day, and considered one of the most eloquent summations of the movement's policy objectives.[37]

Gonzales also could count many more high-profile friends from other movements, contacts that transformed the Crusade's new headquarters building into a mecca for radical organizers. "For me, more critically, was that SCLC knew about us now, that the Puerto Ricans knew about us now, and it allowed for those alliances at times on issues [that] . . . before we didn't have," said Nita Gonzales. Her brother, Rudy, added that, although the Crusade did not maintain close relations with SCLC, it did foster important connections with activists from non-Chicano organizations. His father regularly communicated with Stokely Carmichael, Father James Groppi, and Hank Adams, several of whom came to Denver to share their experiences. A Roman Catholic priest and former adviser to the NAACP Youth Council in Milwaukee, Groppi visited Denver a few times to discuss the marches he helped orchestrate, first for open housing and then for black and Latino welfare and labor rights. He even joined Gonzales for negotiations in a dispute with local school leaders. "Christ was a revolutionist," he reminded an audience in early 1969, "and was put to death because he dared to confront the system."[38] This message reflected Gonzales's own Roman Catholic interpretation. Suzette Bridges and Roxanne Allen, American Indian activists from Washington State, also visited that spring to discuss fishing rights. Other Indian activists soon followed, including Dennis Banks and Clyde Bellecourt, who founded the American Indian Movement (AIM) in Minneapolis in late 1968.[39]

But as Martin Luther King Jr. and campaign organizers were reminded when they struggled initially to put together the campaign, Gonzales recognized that impressive rhetoric and networks needed to be matched with genuine action. Therefore, upon returning to Denver, Crusade members again took a lead role in protesting discrimination, poverty, and police brutality in the city. Nearly a hundred people from the Crusade joined the picket line to support striking members of the National Florist Workers Organization. They led demonstrations against the city over a police officer's fatal shooting of a fifteen-year-old Mexican American and called for an independent investigation and the officer's firing. And the organization began to transition to a bigger headquarters building more centrally located in Denver's Mexican American community and large enough to house a variety of services, including Escuela Tlatelolco. Some of these efforts included fleeting partnerships with local African Americans and American Indians. Despite its differences with Lauren Watson and the local Panthers during the campaign, the Crusade demanded that the shooting of a nineteen-year-old African American also be investigated, and during Chicanos' school walkouts in March 1969 scores of black students and Panthers showed their solidarity by walking out as well. Moreover, members of the Crusade sought common ground with local American Indians, led by the Bordeaux family, which founded a local AIM chapter. Not coincidentally, Gonzales's embrace of the indigenous component of Chicano identity became more prominent in the organization's rhetoric and actions. Such interactions even produced a short-lived interracial marriage between two activists.[40]

Yet Corky Gonzales also recognized that, as important as such alliances were, it was essential to organize first as Chicanos. Ironically, this recognition was perhaps the most important lesson activists such as Gonzales drew from the Poor People's Campaign: that Chicano strength relied on ethnic and racial unity and that, although poverty and oppression were shared by many people, blacks, Mexican Americans, and Indians defined justice differently. Ethnically and racially driven culture, such as the importance of land symbolized by Aztlán, resulted in dissimilar and sometimes competing needs.

One example was quality education, an issue that normally might cross racial lines. Gonzales had been engaged with the challenges of Mexican American youth almost as long as he had been a public figure. But as the late 1960s arrived, the Crusade increasingly addressed these challenges—and education in particular—in strictly Chicano terms. The Crusade's demands at a late October 1968 school board meeting reflected this new focus. Surrounded by a small entourage that entered the boardroom singing "We Shall Overcome" in Spanish, Gonzales laid out eight demands, all related to "the preservation of our values, culture, and family life." These ranged from the inclusion of Mexican American history, culture, and contributions to the United States in all schools' curriculum and textbooks to making it mandatory that teachers be bilingual and live in the community they served. Other demands were payment for "the psychological destruction of our people, i.e. inferiority complexes, anglo superiority myth, rejection of our own identity and self-worth," and the end of counseling Mexican American children to join the military. Gonzales did not mention the plight of African Americans, even the similarly missing black historical and cultural contributions in Denver's school curriculum.[41]

Placing the Crusade at even greater odds with many—albeit not all—African Americans was the Chicano organization's opposition to school desegregation.[42] Calling it "a misleading proposition in regards to solving problems imposed upon the children of the Mexican-American segment of this society," Gonzales rejected presumptions by white and black liberals that the same sort of civil rights solutions applied equally to people of Mexican descent.[43] While vestiges of whiteness may have played a role in some Mexican Americans' decisions to pursue a different course, Gonzales had other reasons for opposing school desegregation plans proposed by both Denver's school board and black civil rights leaders.[44] Not only did they do little to address the absence of Mexican American culture, history, and language in the city's schools, but desegregation proposals also more alarmingly required busing Mexican American children out of the barrios to achieve racial balance. His vocal opposition to the plans' central tenets made Gonzales an unlikely ally of white busing opponents and an obstacle to the NAACP and local civil rights leaders. Despite being the numerically smaller minority, it was African American parents in the integrated Park Hill neighborhood—and not Mexican Americans—who took the lead in suing the school board in June 1969, after the Denver Public Schools denied the transfer of African American Wilfred Keyes's daughter to a predominantly white high school. One Mexican American family from the Westside joined the other seven in filing the lawsuit. The case, *Keyes v. Denver School District*, in 1973 eventually became the first Supreme Court ruling on school segregation outside the South and led to twenty years of court-ordered busing.[45]

Yet Chicanos' different vision did not mean markedly distinct rhetoric or tactics. Declaring that "our Selma is here," Chicanos compared the fight over educational equality to African Americans' struggle for voting rights. In March 1969, that fight erupted in the streets as more than two hundred students walked out of West High School in Denver's predominantly Mexican American Westside. As with the East Los Angeles "blowouts" of a year before, students had been protesting a school environment they deemed hostile to people of Mexican descent—in this case, white social science teacher Harry Shafer's racist remarks and the administration's unwillingness to discipline him. Coordinated by students Jeannie Perez, Priscilla Martinez, Auggie Botello, and Donald La-Forette, the boycott was definitely "the kids' thing," according to Corky Gonzales, yet the Crusade did provide assistance. As Gonzales began to speak to the crowd, police arrested him and several other students. While the local press blamed Gonzales for the whole affair, officers' rough tactics, including the liberal use of Mace and clubs, prompted a second day of protests. This time, more than one thousand demonstrators showed up outside West High School—mostly Mexican American students from West and neighboring junior and senior high schools and their parents, plus black students from East and Manual high schools, Black Panthers, and SDS members. More violence ensued. During the two days, at least three people were injured, one seriously, and twenty-eight arrested in what one journalist called "the first major outbreak of violence in the barrios of Denver's Westside, a neighborhood long smoldering but, until that day, never actually aflame."[46]

In the end, the walkouts produced positive results, as school administrators sought to avoid a potential multiracial school boycott. The violence subsided, and Harry Shafer, the teacher who admitted to racist slurs against both blacks and Mexican Americans to "stimulate debate," received a transfer. The administration granted students amnesty from the walkouts. It also promised new books, as well as smaller class sizes and teachers more sensitive to Chicano needs—some of which actually occurred. As a result, students called off plans for a district-wide boycott, but this did not end Chicano calls for quality education or their criticism of school desegregation plans. For its part, the Crusade opened Escuela Tlatelolco that summer to ensure that at least some Mexican American youth received what Gonzales saw as the proper cultural education. Ironically, the school's opening encouraged Chicanos to flee the public schools just like their white conservative counterparts in Denver and elsewhere.[47]

For Gonzales, the dynamic yet raw power of Chicano youth demonstrated by the West High boycott reaffirmed his call for the first annual Chicano Youth Liberation Conference, set to start a week later, on March 27 in Denver. The conference had been a dream of Gonzales's for a while, at least since his disappointing experience during the National Conference for New Politics convention in Chicago. He had delayed his plans in order to participate in the Poor People's Campaign and then again to move and settle into the Crusade's new building, the former Cavalry Baptist Church on Downing Street. But in January 1969, the Crusade put out a call for the national conference and then quietly began preparing for what organizers initially expected to be several hundred Chicano youth.[48]

Undoubtedly, the Crusade would have held a youth conference in 1969 whether or not Gonzales had attended the Poor People's Campaign. But Gonzales's decision to go had an important impact. Clearly, he raised his

profile among fellow Chicanos at the Solidarity Day rally when he unveiled *El Plan del Barrio*. But for some of the nearly fifteen hundred youth
who made the trip to Denver, the difference between going and not going
was their personal interactions with Corky Gonzales—and each other—
while in Washington. For participants such as Carlos Montes, Ralph
Ramirez, and Lorraine Escalante, spending a month or more with the
Chicano leader and his family in the Hawthorne School strongly disposed
them to respond to his call. "The fact that we knew Corky and Ernesto
Vigil real well, as soon as they told (us), we were there," Montes recalled.
"It was no question of that."[49] Escalante also found herself in Denver
with her welfare rights activist mother, Alicia, who had settled in Denver
for a time after meeting Gonzales in the nation's capital. So did Sal Candelaria, a Black Beret from San Jose who helped coordinate security during the conference—a duty he held during the campaign. Others, such as
Maria Varela and Gloria Arellanes, saw the youth conference as a natural
extension of relationships born in Washington. For "the young people,
there was a lot of impact," Varela said. "Again, many of them had never
traveled. Here they were in Washington, D.C. Here, they were meeting
people from other places. The kids from the Crusade hung with the guys
from New Mexico."[50] Thus, while the conference was a call to arms for
some, it also served as a reunion after these young activists' first big ad-
venture a year earlier.[51]

Overall, the first Youth Liberation Conference attracted a far larger
and more diverse group to Denver than organizers had expected. In addition to Brown Berets from several chapters, young Chicanos from a
geographically wide range mingled with each other at the Crusade's headquarters, including the United Mexican American Students (UMAS), the
Mexican American Youth Organization (MAYO), the Third World Liberation Front, Merritt College's Chicano Student Union, Arizona's Mexican-American Student Organization (MASO), and the Chicago-based
Latin American Defense Organization (LADO). Puerto Rican activists,
most notably the Young Lords Organization from Chicago's Near North
Side, also attended. Even a few people from Central America came, such
as Roberto "Beto" Vargas, a Nicaraguan who passed out posters of his
country's revolutionary hero, Augusto Sandino.[52]

With such a strong showing of solidarity, the conference became a
turning point in the rhetoric and direction of the student movement,
not to mention Corky Gonzales's role within that movement. In Denver, the participants embraced what one scholar calls a "foundational

blueprint for the Chicano movement."[53] *El Plan de Aztlán*, a document compiling the many resolutions passed during the five-day conference, trumpeted Chicano self-determination, racial pride and unity, and an emphasis on cultural values of "life, family, and home," in contrast to the larger society's alleged values of hyperindividualistic materialism and whiteness. Declaring themselves free of persistent feelings of inferiority, conference participants "publicly and proudly linked their political crusade to their cultural inheritance" by declaring, among other things, that "brown was beautiful."[54] In this vein, one of the youth conference's earliest chroniclers, Maria Varela, even questioned the moniker used for the event. In many ways, "'conference' is a poor word to describe those five days," wrote Varela in *El Grito del Norte*. "In reality it was a fiesta: days of celebrating what sings in the blood of people who, taught to believe they're ugly, discover the true beauty in their souls."[55] The plan, however, featured little policy beyond vague calls for community nationalization, organization, and self-defense. The most specific points were the declaration of a national Chicano boycott on Mexican Independence Day, September 16, and the creation of an independent political party.[56]

While endorsed overwhelmingly by the delegates, the masculine, Mexican-centric rhetoric was controversial as it called into question Chicanos' interest in multiracial alliances and their ability to recognize women's contributions and leadership. The Puerto Ricans from New York and Chicago, in particular, expressed concern over the statement's narrowness. Were other Spanish-speaking people included? Were poverty and class not the most important concepts around which to organize? "Culture isn't the whole answer," stated the Young Lords' newspaper. "The reason we are treated the way we are is usually because we are poor, not because of our race."[57] One Young Lord from Chicago also questioned "this intellectual talk . . . I'm used to street talk. . . . As far as I'm concerned we're the people that are really ready for the revolution."[58] A similar statement could have been made by Black Panthers or other African Americans at the time. And strikingly missing from *El Plan de Aztlán*—given the seeming solidarity demonstrated by blacks just days before in the streets of Denver—was any mention of mutual respect or support for their black brothers and sisters and how they defined their poverty and oppression.[59]

Chicanas also found their concerns, many of which were formalized during a woman's caucus, largely ignored or misrepresented by the majority of male delegates and antifeminist women. Enriqueta Vasquez, a columnist for *El Grito del Norte*, recalled her dismay when a representative of the caucus declared that the group determined that "the Chicana woman does not want to be liberated." "This was quite a blow," wrote Vasquez. "I could have cried. Surely we could have at least come up with something to add. . . . The woman must help liberate the man and the man must look upon this liberation with the woman at his side, not behind him, following."[60] Many Chicanas agreed. For instance, Gloria Arellanes, a Brown Berets minister and director of the Berets' free clinic in East Los Angeles, returned home and later found Las Adelitas de Aztlán in 1970, a short-lived Chicana feminist organization.[61]

Yet, despite being criticized as naïve, divisive, and sexist, this nationalist turn—best articulated during the first Denver conference—remained central to the Crusade and the Chicano movement into the mid-1970s. In the months that followed, the Crusade attempted to put the ideals of *El Plan de Aztlán* into action on a variety of local fronts. Immediately after the conference, Gonzales led several hundred people in support of farm worker legislation under consideration by the Colorado General Assembly. Later that summer, to protest city plans to close swimming facilities in the Eastside and Westside barrios, the Crusade hatched a "splash-in" at a suburban white pool. Tense at first, the demonstration won new white allies not interested in a repeat performance, which not only saved the barrio pools but also prompted the consideration of hiring Mexican American youth, not whites, there. Crusade members joined UMAS activists in protesting the local Roman Catholic diocese's decision not to fund a new UMAS-administered scholarship program for needy Mexican Americans. The Crusade provided counsel to any Mexican American youth who did not want to enter the military draft, and it supported the Chicano Moratorium Committee, which Carlos Montes, Ralph Ramirez, and other Brown Berets established after the youth liberation conference. The committee eventually sponsored a rally-turned-police riot in East Los Angeles in 1970 that scholars and activists often see as the climax of the Chicano movement.[62]

As promised in *El Plan de Aztlán*, Chicanos marched on September 16, 1969, Mexico's independence day. In preparation for massive school walkouts that day, the Crusade hosted a unity conference to coordinate demands for bilingual and bicultural education throughout the Southwest and then met with local educators to share their issues. Not surprisingly, school officials were unreceptive, affirming the students' plan, in Gonzales's words, to "recognize this day as a national holiday because we are related more to Pancho Villa then the so-called father of this country, George Washington."[63] At least three thousand people—with some estimates as high as six thousand—participated in the walkouts, representing thirty-one junior and senior high schools in Denver. One observer called it the largest civil rights march he had seen there. And while school administrators demonstrated little public sympathy, journalists reported several teachers walking alongside students.[64]

Most of the actions from the summer and fall were strictly Chicano affairs—although a few crossed racial lines. In early May 1969, Gonzales and supporters joined members of the Black Panther Party and Students for a Democratic Society to rally for the release of Huey Newton, a founder of the Panthers imprisoned in California for killing a police officer. There, Gonzales called for blacks and Mexican Americans to join forces against the common enemy. In November, Crusade members attended a multiracial antiwar rally and then a Black Panther Party–sponsored demonstration calling for an exchange of Panther political prisoners for American prisoners in Vietnam. Routinely, Lauren Watson of the local Panthers chapter showed up at Crusade marches, especially those protesting police brutality. Both Watson and Gonzales attributed this to mutual respect and a similar political outlook. FBI analysis also suggested that the local Panthers' sinking fortunes may have played a role. By 1970, police harassment, the questionable use of a federal Model Cities grant, and ensuing legal troubles had decimated Watson's organization. To FBI observers and journalists, Watson hoped to remain relevant by his proximity to the influential Gonzales. Even this tenuous alliance all but ended, however, when Gonzales announced the formation of the La Raza Unida Party of Colorado.[65]

Unveiled at the second annual Chicano Youth Liberation Conference in March 1970, La Raza Unida was the culmination of Gonzales's disgust with the two-party system he had once served. "The Democratic Party and the Republican Party are one animal with two heads eating out of the same trough," Gonzales told an interviewer in 1970. "Anything they deal in is in their vested interest because they both have money and shares in the same corporation." Rarely did this corporation have any interest in assisting, let alone empowering, people of Mexican descent in a substantial way. Therefore, "we decided that in order to create this independent party we had to build it on a program of real, gut issues, and the necessities of the people," he continued. "This will be one method of fighting on issues that are important to the people, which will create a stronger independent party, and stronger unity in the movement."[66]

Such a party already had strengthened Chicano activism in Texas. Organized by José Angel Gutiérrez and other founders of MAYO, La Raza Unida had built on the momentum of massive school walkouts in his hometown of Crystal City in late 1969 to run an organized slate of local candidates in several Mexican American–majority towns and counties in south Texas.[67] At first not taken seriously, the party eventually drew the fire of a coalition of whites and conservative Mexican Americans alarmed by the very real prospect of a Chicano takeover of government. But charges that the party was communist and under the despotic rule of Gutiérrez failed to resonate with voters, who instead heeded calls for community control of the public schools and other levers of local government. In April 1970, the three counties overwhelmingly voted for the party's candidates and, at least in the case of Crystal City, voter turnout surpassed that in the presidential year of 1968. There, the new majority quickly began to transform the town's government and school system. This included making full use of federal education grants and initiatives to improve student tutorial programs, teacher training and development, adult education, student retention, and college preparation. Reforms also embraced a bilingual and bicultural curriculum, one that incorporated Mexican and Chicano history, literature, and arts. City government made similar changes, greatly improving basic services such as trash pickup and street maintenance in poor neighborhoods. Recalled Gutiérrez, who chaired the school board for three years: "We were on a roll toward building a Chicano-controlled school and city."[68]

Corky Gonzales, perhaps fantastically, had hoped to repeat such success in Colorado, despite vastly different demographics than Texas.[69] After the unveiling of Colorado's newest political party with Gonzales as state chairman, several nominating conventions were held throughout the state to endorse a party platform and choose candidates from governor to local members of the General Assembly. The platform closely mirrored *El Plan de Aztlán*, including planks for an immediate withdrawal from Vietnam, communal style housing, and bilingual and bicultural programming in the schools. Some of the party's objectives, such as calls for agricultural reform and redistribution of wealth, were vague enough potentially to include other poor people, including African Americans and American Indians. But there was little indication that La Raza Unida of Colorado

actively sought the votes of non–Mexican Americans. The party, including Gonzales, remained exclusively focused on mobilizing people of
Mexican descent—and even more specifically, Chicanos. Those who most
identified with the middle class or strived for such status within the system, such as those affiliated with the more reformist Westside Coalition
in Denver, were not welcome.[70] But even if all Mexican Americans had
voted in lockstep in the fall 1970 elections, they would have won little.
The reality was even harsher, as the party garnered embarrassingly little
support at the ballot box, gaining no more than 3 percent of the vote in
any given race.[71]

These results did not dissuade Gonzales, however, who had aspirations
of making La Raza Unida not just a viable state party but a national one.
For him, the future was outside both the Democratic and Republican
party structures, and with his Chicano brothers and sisters exclusively.
High-profile efforts to accomplish just this occurred over the next two
years as José Angel Gutiérrez brought a message of Chicano party unity
to the third annual Chicano Youth Liberation Conference in Denver in
June 1971 and the following year during the first national convention of
La Raza Unida in El Paso. There, three of the so-called four horsemen
of the Chicano movement–Gutiérrez, Gonzales, and a recently released
Reies Tijerina—shared a stage to plan Chicano political strategy for the
1972 elections.[72] But such a historic show of unity proved quite shallow.
Cesar Chavez was conspicuously absent (and not invited) because of his
support for Democratic presidential nominee George McGovern. Tijerina was a shadow of his former self after prison, less confrontational but
also less connected to reality. Meanwhile, Gutiérrez and Gonzales sparred
over everything. Riddled with internal conflicts over direction and leadership, the convention demonstrated little ability to collaborate among
those who self-identified as Chicanos, let alone with African Americans.[73]

When asked if African Americans and Chicanos could work together,
Gonzales always remained optimistic. "There are issues which are important to black and Chicano and other minorities and to whites—the white
radicals, the whites who understand," he told an interviewer. "In those
areas, coalitions come about very easily. . . . Everyone knows who the
enemy is." But almost in the same breath, he then delineated the limits
of such an approach. No matter what, "you can't form coalitions unless
you have organization."[74] In a speech in 1970 at Arizona State University,
he crystallized this position in not just a domestic but also an international context. "The white radical says it is a class struggle, and we say,

that's fine!" Gonzales told the audience. But in characteristically color-ful—and sexist—language, he said it was different for Chicanos. "The Chicano comes along and tells me it's only a class struggle. I tell him no, it's just an ass struggle. You want to justify that you are with a radical white broad. . . . We want to say that it is a class struggle, but with the class struggle, the Black agrees that it is also a racist struggle. . . . As I told many young radicals five or six years ago, and I tell Blacks today, with whom we are friendly and have mutual respect, that until they are organized and they are doing their thing, and until we are organized, there will be no international coalition. There will be no international coalition until we have made Aztlán a reality and the Chicano has become a concentrated organized force."[75] Gonzales and much of his Chicano brethren had set a remarkably high bar for multiracial cooperation. It was a standard that was never achieved.

But Chicanos were not alone in this thinking. As the 1960s became the 1970s, African Americans drew similar conclusions. Multiracial collaboration to fight poverty remained a lofty goal but one realizable only if genuine black political power could be achieved. African Americans set out to do just that in the years after 1968.

8 ◆ Making the 1970s

Bobby Lee was about to leave an Uptown Chicago hall full of white Appalachian migrants in late 1968, when the Black Panther leader suddenly jumped on a chair. "Black power to black people," he declared to the stunned audience. And after a pause, he continued, "and white power to white people. Brown power to brown people, and red power to red people. And we say yellow power to yellow people, and all power to the people." After another pause, the crowed roared, and Lee pumped his fist and walked into a cool Chicago night knowing that he may have sealed the most unlikely of deals between the nation's best-known black power organization and poor native white southerners who called themselves the Young Patriots.[1]

Lee's words that night, remembered by filmmaker Mike Gray, were a variation of those used by Fred Hampton, the charismatic twenty-one-year-old chairman of the Illinois Panthers. Dubbed the Rainbow Coalition by Hampton, the new alliance brought together not just black and white, but also Latino groups, most prominently the Young Lords Organization. To Hampton, the Panthers' embrace of black nationalism and armed self-defense did not exclude revolutionary alliances with other oppressed people, even whites. "We say you put fire out best with water," Hampton said in 1969. "We say you don't fight racism with racism. We're gonna fight racism with solidarity." And for much of 1969, that is what the Rainbow Coalition did.[2]

Together, the diverse members of the Rainbow Coalition not only served their immediate communities but also envisioned a larger sea shift in Chicago politics from the conservative Democratic machine of Mayor Richard J. Daley to "all power to the people."[3] At the coalition's height in mid-1969, more than a dozen Panther sites on the West and South sides fed about four thousand children daily—solely through donations. The programming of the Young Patriots and Young Lords echoed that of the Panthers, from serving their own free breakfasts and running free health clinics to building "people's parks" and just being advocates for regular folks. In addition, all three groups, sometimes together, sometimes apart, intensified their critique of police harassment of poor people.

The Young Lords also made a name for themselves by successfully opposing urban renewal efforts in West Lincoln Park, where middle-class housing had begun to displace many poor Puerto Ricans, Mexican Americans, and whites. In one daring move, the Young Lords, under the auspices of the multiracial Poor People's Coalition of Lincoln Park, took over the administration building of the McCormick Theological Seminary to protest that institution's complicity in urban renewal. "When we talk about oppression—and it's the same for the Patriots, Panthers, and the Young Lords—we're talking about the essentials: food, decent housing, adequate clothing," said Art Turco, a white attorney who helped found a Young Patriots Party modeled on the Chicago organization in New York City. "In order to help solve the basic needs of the people, you have to go to the people, speak with them, live with them, become one of them."[4]

The coalition proved short-lived. Police officers working for the state's attorney's office killed Fred Hampton and fellow Panther Mark Clark in an early-morning raid on Hampton's apartment in December 1969. The coalition, already weakened by internal disputes and unending police harassment, did not survive long after the death of its most charismatic proponent. But this result was about more than just the brutal power of state violence. The Rainbow Coalition's demise also symbolized a larger change, as African Americans increasingly considered their own lessons from the multiracial experiments of the late 1960s. One of those lessons was that blackness, racial pride, and African Americans' unique place in the American psyche unified people in a way, at least in the short term, that disparate experiences of poverty often did not.

Freedom organizations committed to multiracial politics, such as the Southern Christian Leadership Conference, increasingly returned to more comfortable settings in the South. In Charleston, South Carolina, for example, SCLC helped re-create the labor–civil rights coalition of Memphis in support of black hospital workers. The same occurred in Chicago, as African American leaders such as Jesse Jackson interpreted Hampton's death as a call for blacks, specifically, to unite against an oppressive white state. Two years later and just months before the La Raza Unida convention, several thousand African Americans attended their own historical gathering at the National Black Political Convention in

Gary, Indiana, and flirted with starting a black political party. And while the delegates decided against a third party, black nationalism both had expanded its influence on black politics and hardened in a way that distanced—although did not sever—African American activism from the struggles of poor people of other races.

Just as Chicano activists claimed in the pursuit of La Raza Unida, African American activists viewed strengthened racial identity as essential to their own political development and inherent to eventual coalition. The spike in identity politics represented an important and powerful statement of racial pride and helped produce an impressive number of African American officeholders—a process that actually set the stage for more lasting urban electoral coalitions during the next decade. In the short term, however, it meant that multiracial coalitions to fight poverty, particularly among African Americans and Mexican Americans, received less attention—even amid the deindustrialization, oil shocks, and stagflation of the 1970s that had begun to marginalize the poor even more.

◆ ◆ ◆

Many of the seeds of this transformation toward identity had been planted long ago, but some emerged only in the immediate aftermath of the Poor People's Campaign. By mid-July 1968, most of the campaign's African American participants had gone home—with decidedly mixed feelings about the experience. Looking back years later, Bertha Johnson Luster of Marks, Mississippi, talked of deep disappointment with how the campaign turned out. "'Til this day a lot of folk won't talk about the Mule Train," she said. "We knew that we weren't going to get forty acres and a mule, but we did believe the part about being able to get better jobs and a better education for our children. . . . But most of us came back here to the same old same old." Yet, despite her disillusionment, Luster also recalled that, "I gained the courage to speak up for myself. . . . SCLC taught that there is no harm in speaking up."[5] Others from Marks, the impoverished town that helped inspire Martin Luther King Jr. to pursue the campaign, echoed Luster's thoughts. "I saw my government turn us down," said Dora Collins. "Lots of people around here were real disappointed because they thought things would change right away." Yet Collins added that going to Washington "lifted my spirits and changed the way I think forever. I got back here, and I don't say 'yes suh, boss' anymore." Soon after, the local antipoverty office of Head Start hired Collins.[6]

In fact, the narrative of gaining one's voice during the campaign became popular, particularly among African American women. Many said that the larger march experience empowered them. But rather than empower them to reach out to poor people of all races, the campaign created a space for them to speak up for African Americans. Gladys Givens, one of three women from central Seattle to work at Resurrection City's day-care center, believed the campaign ultimately "unified black people."[7] Flo Ware, also from Seattle, had her run-ins with people in the Hawthorne School and Resurrection City and concluded that the campaign had been part of the "most extravagant chess game ever played," one in which the poor were pawns. But while she swore that after the campaign she would not engage "in any civic activities at all . . . I was not permitted to give up." Within weeks of returning to Seattle, she joined a series of boards, including the King County Equal Opportunity Board and the local Model Cities program. She even ran for Congress.[8]

Arguably one of the largest beneficiaries of the campaign was the National Welfare Rights Organization. Despite their initial reluctance to join the SCLC venture, NWRO leaders such as George Wiley and Johnnie Tillmon ended up translating the march experience into greater access to the Johnson administration and the mass media. Starting with the much-praised Mother's Day march the day before Resurrection City broke ground and continuing through Solidarity Day, NWRO activists stayed focused on their own narrower set of issues even amid the campaign's chaos and drama. Wiley, Tillmon, and others, such as Etta Horn of the organization's D.C. chapter, spent much of their time lobbying and making contacts with members of Congress, federal Health, Education and Welfare Department officials, and journalists. Just as SCLC's Marian Wright Edelman built lasting ties to midlevel bureaucrats in several agencies, including HEW, welfare rights activists managed to maintain their own contacts. After it ended, HEW administrator Mary Switzer cited the "impetus of the Poor People's Campaign" when she expressed "the hope that some kind of a continuing channel could be established between the poor people and the Social and Rehabilitation Service."[9] Such channels indeed stayed open. Through a series of negotiations, NWRO officers persuaded bureaucrats to take on welfare abuse in the states and to institute several rule changes, including the provision of prior notice for benefits termination. The NWRO had emerged as a recognized and respected power broker on welfare policy.[10]

Another campaign by-product for the NWRO turned out to be the unflagging support of Ralph Abernathy and SCLC, especially during the ensuing fights over a guaranteed annual income. Both organizations viewed income maintenance as one solution to chronic poverty and unemployment in an age of automation, a position they shared during the Poor People's Campaign. Unable to persuade members of Congress or the major party conventions to endorse income maintenance over the summer, NWRO officials successfully championed an annual income of up to $5,500 during a White House Conference on Hunger and Malnutrition in October 1968. The conference-goers' nonbinding endorsement embarrassed the Johnson White House. But such influence convinced Daniel Patrick Moynihan, domestic policy adviser to the soon-to-be President Nixon, that the NWRO was a key player in any attempt to reform welfare—a primary domestic policy objective of Nixon's in his quest to build a lasting Republican majority. Therefore, in early 1969 Moynihan opened a dialogue with George Wiley and invited the NWRO leader and several representative welfare recipients to the White House.[11]

Welfare rights activists agreed with Nixon and his advisers that reform was necessary; however, they brought sharply different assumptions to the table. In August 1969, Nixon unveiled the Family Assistance Plan (FAP), which offered a guaranteed annual income of just $1,600, a figure less than current welfare benefits and far below the NWRO's own proposal. In hearings on welfare policy, Wiley, Beulah Sanders, and others argued that FAP was so low that if enacted, it would have encouraged women to seek dead-end, low-wage jobs or male partners with positions in the private sector. Many were particularly skeptical of the emphasis on traditional family structure. A proposal that "my ex-spouse, whose integrity is only to inflict cruelty on others as well as to himself, be returned to my household, should be folded up and buried," Eliza Williams told members of Congress.[12] Therefore, NWRO activists chose to defeat, or "zap," FAP and recruited civil rights allies in the fight. And despite FAP's attraction to SCLC's constituency of poor southern blacks to whom $1,600 was a lot of money, the civil rights organization remained steadfast in its support for the NWRO. A year later, Nixon changed his political calculus and all but abandoned FAP.[13]

SCLC's support probably did not impact Nixon's decision, but it did underscore the significance of race in the NWRO's identity. "We don't want to give the impression this is an all-black organization," Johnnie Tillmon told African Americans dressed in African garb at the organization's annual convention in 1969.[14] Yet the organization was mostly black. Despite the NWRO's multiracial rhetoric and the fact that people of all colors received welfare and benefited from NWRO advocacy, the organization was an estimated 85 percent African American and had been viewed as a "recognized and legitimate partner" in the black freedom struggle.[15] Its most prominent leaders—George Wiley, Johnnie Tillmon, Beulah Sanders, Hulbert James, and Catherine Jermany—were African American, and at least nationally the organization joined forces with the civil rights movement first and foremost.

The NWRO did have a small percentage of nonblack activists.[16] Several whites served as aides to Wiley or participated in local welfare rights groups, such as Peggy Terry of Chicago's JOIN. A few American Indians also worked with the national group, helping stop the reduction of welfare payments on North Dakota, Nebraska, Montana, and Utah reservations. And an estimated 5 percent of NWRO participants were Mexican American or Puerto Rican, including activists Clementina Castro in Wisconsin and Moiece Palladino in California. The NWRO also cooperated with the United Farm Workers to support Senator George McGovern for president in 1972.[17]

But more representative of the experience of Mexican American welfare rights activists was Alicia Escalante's. A single mother of five in East Los Angeles, Escalante entered activism in 1967 after learning that newly elected governor Ronald Reagan planned to slash the state's MediCal funding, which she depended upon for treatment for a daughter with chronic stomach problems. In protesting the funding cuts, she met welfare rights advocates, including Catherine Jermany and Johnnie Tillmon, both of Los Angeles. "I give them credit for opening up my eyes" about activism, Escalante recalled. But when it came to understanding how language and citizenship status affected Mexican Americans' ability to receive welfare, "it went in one ear and out the other."[18] As a result, she, Anna Nieto-Gómez, and others founded the Chicana Welfare Rights Organization, one of several local welfare groups that identified primarily with the Chicano movement. Thus, despite the NWRO's rhetoric as a "poor people's organization," its dominant racial identity reinforced the decision by Chicana activists—and subsequently undermined its legitimacy as a genuinely multiracial antipoverty organization.[19]

◆ ◆ ◆

For SCLC, the summer of 1968 began the long, slow—and perhaps inevitable—decline of an organization embodied by one man. Despite the many resources SCLC collected immediately after the death of Martin Luther

King Jr., the organization's surviving leadership could not translate them into the kind of victory that had propelled SCLC in Birmingham and Selma. Rather, it became clear that the organization's funds and goodwill largely had been depleted during the Washington phase of the Poor People's Campaign and that the organization's plan to follow it up with economic boycotts in forty cities would not materialize—all despite the energy of hundreds of diehard activists.[20] People would have to organize themselves without SCLC. Despite the campaign's modest but real accomplishments, its perceived disarray jeopardized much of the organization's continued support from both the public and liberal foundations, not to mention exposed the fissures among SCLC's top leadership without King to unite them. In an attempt to maintain pressure on politicians, but in a more manageable way, Ralph Abernathy turned his attention to smaller protests at the summer's two national party conventions. King earlier had hinted at such a choice if the campaign stumbled, because affecting the policy debate of the year's presidential race always had been a primary objective. Now that the Washington campaign was over, Abernathy vowed to bring the "51st state of hunger" to the conventions.[21]

For the convention protests, SCLC salvaged the Mule Train. It had been the campaign's most potent symbol of poverty, especially among the media. Nothing said wrenching poverty from another time more than mules slowly pulling a disheveled wagon down a modern main thoroughfare. But the Mule Train's even greater prominence during the conventions again signaled SCLC's willingness to highlight a particular face of poverty—that of the African American sharecropper in the rural South. Nowhere was the rhetoric or imagery of black, white, brown, and red. When the small antipoverty delegation reached Miami Beach, where Republicans prepared to anoint the reinvented Richard Nixon as their nominee, they portrayed poverty as black.

The convention protests had little impact. Abernathy spoke with the Republican Party Platform Committee, which politely listened to his request for jobs, welfare, health care, and income maintenance; he made no mention of land and treaty rights. Later, during the convention, he called for calm as civil disorder engulfed part of Miami's Liberty City neighborhood. But although at least one editor credited the Washington experience as "valuable to the campaign's leadership" because SCLC had reverted to standard channels of influence, journalists and delegates alike generally treated the poor as nothing more than a minor sideshow to the Republicans' nomination of Nixon.[22] The actual poor people who had traveled from Marks, Mississippi, stood in the shadows, while Nixon's acceptance speech focused on the Vietnam War, "law and order," and the emerging culture war. Federal prescriptions for poverty received nary a mention.[23]

SCLC-led antipoverty protests proved similarly ineffective in Chicago, where Democrats nominated Vice President Hubert Humphrey as the party's presidential nominee. But, unlike in Miami, a different kind of riot exploded in the streets, as Chicago police officers pummeled antiwar protesters on national television. Abernathy and the Mule Train unwittingly played a role as the marchers, who had been wandering aimlessly around Chicago's downtown loop, suddenly packed in behind the wagons on Michigan Avenue and prepared to descend on the convention hall together. Instead of providing cover to the protesters, however, the Mule Train was allowed to pass before police then attacked the crowd of protesters with a ferociousness rarely caught on camera. Journalist Norman Mailer captured the scene, especially the utter helplessness demonstrated by the mules—and, for that matter, Abernathy. "The mules had not moved through the entire fray," Mailer wrote. "Isolated from the battle, they had stood there in harness waiting to be told to go on. Only in a while did they turn their heads. Their role as actors in the Poor People's March was to wait and to serve. Finally they moved on. The night had come. It was dark. The intersection was empty. Shoes, ladies' handbags, and pieces of clothing lay on the street outside the hotel."[24] Abernathy joined a chorus of critics of the Chicago police's tactics. But, remarkably, such critics proved to be relatively few. As Mayor Richard Daley recognized in the next days, in his swift defense of the police, the majority of public opinion was on the side of the police, not the protesters. It would be the images of the Chicago streets—the jarring brutality of the police, the strange frivolity of the antiwar protesters, the irrelevance of the mules—that came to symbolize so powerfully the displacement of antipoverty politics with that of law and order at the national level.[25]

Despite the setbacks of the summer, Abernathy and SCLC returned to Atlanta as the most respected black civil rights leader and organization in the country. In a concerted effort to regain the organization's footing, delegates at SCLC's annual convention acknowledged the influence of black power, while Abernathy declared that SCLC would not be the nation's "babysitter" any longer, quelling uprisings as its officials tried to do in Miami Beach. "We are sick and tired of taking it easy," Abernathy said, before adding that, while nonviolence remained the group's philosophy, it would not prevent the organization from pursuing aggressive boycotts against stores and industries that discriminated. SCLC delegates also chose to continue the slogan of the Poor People's Campaign in support of economic justice in the South, particularly a series of successful labor strikes, and Operation Breadbasket. First in SCLC's hometown of Atlanta and then in Charleston, South Carolina, the organization threw its support behind workers and offered a compelling model for a black civil rights–labor coalition on the eve of the 1970s.[26]

The first effort at this new model came in mid-September in an Atlanta work stoppage in which nearly eight hundred black sanitation workers struck for better wages and conditions.[27] SCLC officials organized local ministers to show solidarity with union demonstrators and to help negotiate with the city, including threatening to lie in front of garbage trucks before they could leave a city vehicle depot. According to Andrew Young, however, outgoing Mayor Ivan Allen "did not want to see this escalate into a major confrontation. . . . Having presided over the 'City Too Busy to Hate,' I think he wanted to leave office with his progressive reputation intact."[28] The city soon offered a modest pay increase with no recriminations against striking workers. For Young, who did much of the negotiation, it cemented his reputation among city officials as "reasonable." And for Ralph Abernathy and the rest of the SCLC leadership, the Atlanta resolution suggested that the organization still could make a difference locally in the lives of poor people.[29]

In late 1968 and early 1969, SCLC reaffirmed its dedication to economic justice by descending on Charleston, South Carolina, where the civil rights organization harnessed its resources and allies to the cause of a mostly black female work force at the Medical College, later known as Medical University of South Carolina. An effort usually oversimplified or marginalized by movement scholars, the Charleston campaign represented not only another labor-civil rights coalition in which race and class were bound together but also the centrality of women to such organizing.[30] Tired of being underpaid, disrespected by their white colleagues, and at constant risk of arbitrarily losing their jobs, several black, female Medical College workers led by nurse's aide and Highlander School–trained Mary Moultrie began to discuss how to organize themselves better. Although the workers had not considered a union at first, Moultrie had asked for help from tobacco union official Isaiah Bennett and black power activist Bill Saunders after the Medical College fired five workers in February 1968 in a dispute over routine access to patients' medical records.[31] At the same time as longtime activists Septima Clark and Esau Jenkins led energetic and largely working-class protesters in local sympathy marches for the Poor People's Campaign that spring and summer, hospital workers endured more slights by their employers. The message of poor people's power percolated among increasingly frustrated black workers, and by the fall Mary Moultrie's gatherings attracted up to five hundred people each week—from nurse's aides and licensed practical nurses to orderlies and cafeteria workers, nearly all black and female.[32]

Initially viewing the situation as a way to rebuild fundraising networks, Abernathy and Young first committed SCLC to Charleston in October 1968. Workers had contacted New York City's Local 1199 of the Drug and Hospital Workers Union, an SCLC ally since the late 1950s. Local 1199 had been one of the few union supporters of the Poor People's Campaign and, after King's death, had retained connections to SCLC through Coretta Scott King and Stanley Levison. "The hospital workers . . . fit perfectly into our desire to combat fundamental economic inequities and was consistent with the long-term aims of the Poor People's Campaign," recalled Young. "In addition, in Septima Clark we had a staff person who knew intimately the personalities and tendencies of black and white leadership in Charleston."[33] Clark "felt exactly how we were feeling," said Moultrie. "We knew something had to be done, and Mrs. Clark told us . . . about getting the SCLC . . . and what they could do in terms of motivating the community."[34] SCLC quickly dispatched James Orange to Charleston, while workers organized picket lines outside the hospital and met with local legislators.[35]

Not until March, however, as SCLC prepared to announce another stage of its antipoverty campaign to mark the anniversary of King's assassination, did tensions push the hospital workers to drastic action—and SCLC into an ever-deeper commitment. After workers staged a sit-in protesting the Medical College president's refusal to meet with them, hospital authorities fired twelve workers including Moultrie. The next day, more than four hundred workers went on strike. Other than Local 1199, SCLC became the first prominent organization to signal its support and began to mobilize its civil rights, religious, and labor contacts. Promising "to sock it to Charleston," Abernathy and an entourage of aides arrived, tapped local ministers to hold mass rallies, inspired marches and protests in the city's historic business district, and helped spark "a conspicuous shift in focus as the strike became a social movement."[36] The campaign intensified in late April and early May as ten marches were held in six days, Abernathy called for a boycott by schoolchildren, and women conducted downtown "shop-ins" by crowding grocery store and cash register lines. Police arrested more than one thousand marchers during the 113-day strike, including Abernathy, jailed for the twenty-fourth time in his civil rights career. Similar to the welfare rights march of a year earlier, a Mother's Day March was a defining moment, drawing a crowd of twelve thousand. There, Coretta Scott King captivated a crowd that hoisted placards declaring "I Am Somebody," while Walter Reuther of the United Auto Workers publicly offered $10,000 to the cause. The NAACP, AFL-CIO, and UAW-Teamsters Alliance for Labor Action sent money and manpower, and forty-two sympathetic U.S. senators and House members called for federal mediation. Yet the hospital administration, backed by the city's white elites, refused to negotiate for two and a half months—despite the damage inflicted on the hospital's services and the tourist city's public image.[37]

Hospital officials agreed to negotiate in June 1969 only after a plea from the White House amid the threat of spreading labor activism to the Port of Charleston and the state's textile industry. Although the striking workers walked away with a partial victory—a healthy pay raise, their jobs back, and a formal grievance process, but no union recognition—the significance of the Charleston campaign went much further. News of the settlement motivated hospitals in Baltimore to negotiate with some seventy-five hundred employees, while hospital workers in Florida, Kansas, Ohio, Georgia, and Pennsylvania asked for Local 1199's assistance. In Charleston, the strike had strengthened the black community's resolve outside the workplace. Voter registration increased, and whites proved quicker to talk. They "respect blacks for having organized," said activist Bill Saunders. "They're a little scared now and will negotiate before they reach that same level of polarization."[38] This undermined more traditional assumptions about race relations, which in Charleston was no small feat, considering the city's immense pride in its southern heritage—even its historic role in the slave economy. In the following years, the election of African Americans to public office, the emergence of an Operation Breadbasket chapter, and other black activism among both middle and working-class African Americans, helped replace the white-dominated political oligarchy and its moderate black allies with a more diverse one.[39]

For SCLC, "phase two of the Poor People's Campaign," as Ralph Abernathy called Charleston, provided a certain level of redemption for the chaotic Washington experience of a year before, as well as a revamped

Coretta Scott King, Juanita Abernathy (wife of Ralph), and Mary Moultrie march in support of striking hospital workers in Charleston, South Carolina, in 1969. The mostly black labor strike gave new life to SCLC's work on economic justice and King a prominent, albeit brief, role in the organization. The Charleston strike also gave SCLC a chance to return to the more comfortable setting of black protest in the South. (AP Photo)

model for the civil rights organization's activism.[40] SCLC had emerged from Charleston in relative financial health and, at least in some quarters, out from under the shadow of Dr. King. Andrew Young remembered Charleston as the "singingest, preachingest, clappingest movement since our days in Albany and Selma."[41] Yet the campaign also distinguished itself by highlighting women's leadership. Ralph Abernathy spent more than a week in jail, fasting at times in solidarity with the hospital workers. But it was the actions of Coretta Scott King, Septima Clark, Mary Moultrie, and the striking women themselves that most galvanized community support and maintained pressure on white powerbrokers. In the wake of her husband's death, Mrs. King became a sought-after speaker for progressive causes and emerged as a leader in her own right, especially when issues of gender explicitly overlapped that of race and class. In a speech to a packed Emanuel AME Church in Charleston, King placed the workers' situation in a context that differed from Abernathy's approach and echoed her Solidarity Day speech from a year before. Calling herself a "sister 1199er," King told the mostly female audience: "Many of our hospital workers throughout the nation are women—black women, many of whom are the main supporters of their families. I feel that the black woman in our nation, the black working woman, is perhaps the most discriminated against."[42] King returned to Charleston several times during the strike and remained on the Local 1199 organizing committee for years. She continued to be a huge draw as she sought to link her husband's civil rights philosophy and her own gender analysis to the other movements of the day, from welfare rights and farm labor, to peace and women's liberation.[43]

Locally, Septima Clark and Mary Moultrie had, in different ways, set the stage for the strike and Coretta Scott King's influential appearances. Although semiretired from the citizenship schools that she had run for Highlander and SCLC since the 1950s, Clark remained one of the city's most influential grass-roots black leaders. "She was a woman everybody knew and really, really respected," recalled Moultrie.[44] The citizenship schools in South Carolina, in which many African Americans learned to read, write, and exercise their constitutional rights, provided her with a solid base to call upon blacks to act and complemented Moultrie's leadership well. As the striking workers' spokeswoman and leader of the fledgling Local 1199B, Moultrie in her light blue union hat became the face of the movement. A Charleston native, Moultrie had left Charleston "because there were no jobs of consequence to be had for blacks in the city," but not before she had worked with activists Esau Jenkins and Highlander's Guy Carawan on small community projects.[45] She returned in 1966 and became a nurse's aid—a lower position than she had held in New York because the Medical College denied her credentials. This experience and her previous activism emboldened her. In a speech to the AFL-CIO convention in 1969, she struck a modest tone, praising SCLC and the black community for doing their part. "They struggled with us and they suffered alongside us," Moultrie said. "Because like hospital workers, they, too, were sick and tired of being sick and tired. . . . And together we faced this armed strength with our bodies, with our souls, and with our hearts."[46] After the strike ended, the workers elected her president of 1199B.[47]

That what turned out to be SCLC's last prominent campaign was sparked, led, and dominated by black women should have given the organization pause when navigating its own leadership troubles. Perhaps women needed to play a larger public role in the next phases of SCLC's fight for economic justice, under the umbrella of the Poor People's Campaign or something else. Not only did women bring grass-roots organizing skills sometimes taken for granted by the charismatic leadership inherent to SCLC, but women also were more likely to be poor than men, yet were their families' sole breadwinners. An estimated 80 percent of the Charleston strikers were single mothers. Instead, SCLC paternalism in its relations with women—including Dr. King's widow—persisted, increasingly marginalizing the organization at the precise moment when the women's and Chicano movements were on the rise. The organization stuck with the tried and true—which meant Ralph Abernathy.[48]

Although on the surface Abernathy's leadership won several internal endorsements, observers and colleagues alike had deep doubts about his abilities and vision for the organization in the long term. SCLC conventions in Memphis and Charleston unanimously elected him president in 1968 and 1969. In addition to the strike resolutions, SCLC under Abernathy had spearheaded successful voter registration and school desegregation efforts, most spectacularly in Greene County, Alabama, where blacks won a majority on the local county council. Abernathy's ubiquitous overalls from the Poor People's Campaign even inspired a new fad called the "Reverend Ralph Look" in the fashion world.[49] Abernathy, thus, was an easy compromise choice, as much rewarded for being King's closest and most loyal friend in the organization as for the belief that his election would avoid a divisive fight over the presidency. "We knew that Ralph had weaknesses," said Andrew Young, "but there was a logic to his ascension on which we could all agree."[50] As both journalists and insiders had harped during the days of Resurrection City, however, those weaknesses stood in stark contrast to his predecessor's skills.[51]

This became most clear in Abernathy's failed attempts to capitalize on Charleston. Wanting to avoid a repeat of a Resurrection City-style encampment, SCLC returned to more conventional marches in the name of economic justice, such as ones led by longtime SCLC field organizers R. B. Cottonreader in Mississippi and Hosea Williams in Georgia. But these efforts attracted hundreds of people, not thousands, and almost no press. Echoing Solidarity Day themes from a year before, SCLC renewed its demands to "wipe out hunger" and added to a growing chorus for reform.[52] Considerable media and political pressure on hunger peaked in 1969, forcing President Nixon to promise in early May that he would "end hunger in America for all time."[53] That, of course, did not happen. Abernathy's private meeting with President Nixon generated little substantive dialogue on a range of issues, including hunger (through free food stamps), welfare reform, and a guaranteed national income and prompted the frustrated SCLC president to call it "the most disappointing and the most fruitless of all the meetings we have had up to this time."[54] Abernathy and his civil rights organization were just not that important to Nixon's domestic agenda, which shifted to the right as the 1970 elections approached. The president then compounded Abernathy's disappointment a few months later by unveiling the Family Assistance Plan, so low that it barely covered the amount of food recommended for a family of four. As one scholar concludes, "There were no new national victories" for SCLC.[55]

Instead, SCLC officials attempted to improve the organization's reputation by associating with others, with limited success. The NWRO's George Wiley and Johnnie Tillmon declined to participate in another Washington march and, officially, cited SCLC's inability to "adequately involve us in the planning of campaign demands and development of basic campaign strategy."[56] With its temporarily raised profile, the NWRO had little to gain from joining forces with Abernathy. SCLC correspondence with Reies Tijerina and Corky Gonzales produced similar responses. One exception was Abernathy's participation in the Coachella-to-Calexico march in California in support of striking farm workers in the spring of 1969. Joining a rainbow of local union and strike supporters, Abernathy told marchers that he, too, was a Mexican in spirit and that the "white man establishment's plan to divide Mexicans and blacks will not work because Negroes understand that 'su lucha es mi lucha.'"[57] He went on to lead the march for two miles before meeting with Cesar Chavez.

But despite the powerful gesture, Abernathy's appearance with Chavez produced more questions than answers. It was not clear who gained more from the meeting. In many ways, Abernathy needed to burnish his reputation by associating with Chavez, seen by many as a Mexican Martin Luther King Jr. SCLC leaders invited Chavez to their conventions for the next several years, but Chavez always turned them down. And there was no evidence that reciprocal invitations were forthcoming from the UFW. Such had become the reality for SCLC, which, one year after King's death, was still insistent on an organizing model reliant on a male charismatic presence—but without an individual at the top who could fill that role.[58]

The challenges to Abernathy's leadership and overall organizational inertia eventually exhausted many top SCLC officials. Both Bernard Lafayette and James Bevel left to pursue other interests, as did Andrew Young. Although often touted as a potentially more effective president than Abernathy, Young turned his attention instead to electoral politics. "I saw political office as a way of sustaining what we had done and needed to do again rather than as a deviation from our history of collective struggle," Young recalled. "My colleagues had a lukewarm reaction to my decision, though, and seemed to feel that I was running out on them."[59] And in some ways, he was, because he did not return to the organization even after losing a tight congressional race in 1970. Instead, he prepared for a rematch, which he won, launching a successful political career that culminated in his appointment as U.S. ambassador to the United Nations under President Jimmy Carter and then his election as Atlanta's mayor.[60]

Jesse Jackson also enjoyed a high-profile ascendancy after King's death and the Washington campaign. More than any other SCLC staffer, the director of Chicago's Operation Breadbasket emerged from the Poor People's Campaign with a stronger, more national image. Although Jackson had been "city manager" of Resurrection City for a while, Abernathy demoted him and unwittingly did the Chicago minister a huge favor. Avoiding journalists' blame for Resurrection City's problems, Jackson instead charmed the national press corps with his charisma and unique blend of capitalist solutions, black pride, and Christian moral authority. The result was an avalanche of positive publicity and the transformation of a mildly effective local leader in Chicago into a national civil rights star. That Jackson maintained his home base in Chicago—rather than relocating to Atlanta as Abernathy and other SCLC officials had urged—was significant. Not only could Jackson retain his independence there, but it also was in the Windy City where he could witness firsthand both the promise and difficulty of multiracial organizing in the late 1960s.[61]

◆ ◆ ◆

By the spring and summer of 1968, status quo politics in Chicago appeared imperiled. Riots had rocked the city after King's assassination in April and then again during the Democratic National Convention in August, and these were just the most dramatic events. The city had become a hotbed of activism that year through a series of labor strikes, economic boycotts, and welfare rights protests—the largest threat Mayor Richard J. Daley had faced since assuming the office in 1955. Even while SCLC's Washington campaign may have ground to a halt early that summer, a loose network of activists of different races and backgrounds—many of whom participated in the Poor People's Campaign—had begun to emerge in the city. Despite its universal reputation for hardball politics and expansive corruption, Chicago in the late 1960s offered a glimpse of what multiracial organizing could look like, as well as the forces that could stop it.[62]

In June 1968, Jesse Jackson returned to Chicago and Operation Breadbasket, determined to combat black poverty by expanding private-sector jobs. Jackson and the staff of Breadbasket, most prominently Calvin Morris, Gary Massoni, and Willie Barrow, recognized that, in a more conservative political climate, "building economic viability in the black community shifts our focus from economic security to economic independence. As this occurs we need to understand that BLACK COOPERATION IS THE MOST EFFECTIVE EXPRESSION OF RESPONSIBLE AND MEANINGFUL BLACK POWER that is POSSIBLE FOR BLACK PEOPLE AND BLACK ORGANIZATIONS."[63] In other words, Breadbasket tried to frame itself more vigorously in the emerging concept of black capitalism, championed by black power advocates such as CORE's Floyd McKissick. If anything, the Poor People's Campaign experience reinforced this direction. The hundreds of Chicagoans who participated in the campaign—the most from one city—witnessed firsthand how little Congress was willing to do. Thus, they returned to the city more open to the strategy offered by Breadbasket. People saw the Chicago operation as the embodiment of King's ideals, said Calvin Morris, Breadbasket's associate director for three years. "It unleashed a kind of new spirit of boldness here," he said, adding, "One of my regrets was our inability to really have the kind of apparatus to put those kind of people to work and hold them. We were just swamped with people. Breadbasket meetings, Saturday mornings, just exploded."[64] Attendance at the gatherings—part meeting, part worship service—had jumped from hundreds to more than three thousand in the months after King's death.

After a spring in which most staffers and many community participants devoted themselves to mobilizing people and raising funds for the Poor People's Campaign, Breadbasket officials planned to capitalize on this enthusiasm and launched a new series of negotiations with local retailers regarding jobs for blacks. In the previous twelve months, Breadbasket had negotiated a gain of nearly three thousand jobs worth $17 million from grocery chains and milk and soft drink companies represented in Chicago. Not all had complied with their Breadbasket agreements, and a review concluded that the A&P food chain had been one of the worst in meeting its goals and working in good faith with the community. In a coordinated effort on July 6, 1968, white and black Breadbasket supporters began picketing inner-city and suburban A&P stores. These efforts eventually brought company executives back to the table to negotiate "the most comprehensive covenant Operation Breadbasket had ever designed," including the hiring of black businessmen to oversee closely the company's training and employment programs from the inside.[65] It would be Breadbasket's most clear-cut success, as the company surpassed expectations. But negotiations with other stores proved more problematic. Many did not meet the negotiated job totals, while new talks stalled with both Walgreens drug store and Red Rooster food stores, the latter a particularly bad actor found only in the poorest neighborhoods and accused of painting meat and other offenses. Red Rooster went bankrupt before agreeing to anything.[66]

By the beginning of 1969, Breadbasket had expanded its programmatic scope, which had the potential to widen its opportunities to work with other advocates of the poor but also risked blurring the organization's focus. At the heart of this expansion was a paradoxical move that included somewhat contradictory tenets of cultural nationalism and "black socialism," the latter espoused by Ralph Abernathy and the national SCLC. In December 1968, Jackson spearheaded Black Christmas, a holiday spectacle with a ninety-float parade, a black Santa Claus–like figure from the South Pole, and strong encouragement to patronize only black-owned businesses. Breadbasket's ability to attract eighty thousand parade watchers and many more shoppers validated the concept, which was soon followed in 1969 by Black Easter—featuring a black lamb and passion play—and what became an annual trade fair called Black Expo. Materialism mingled freely amid the floats bedecked in the black, red, and green of the pan-African, or black liberation, flag. Yet the black Soul Saint also brought gifts, not of "toys or sugar plums but 'love, justice, peace, and power.'"[67]

Scholars often portray Jesse Jackson as a black capitalist, especially in contrast to the democratic socialism articulated by Martin Luther King Jr. and Ralph Abernathy.[68] Securing jobs for blacks remained the policy focus of Breadbasket, through negotiations with individuals and vigorous support for black labor in construction, the Chicago Transit Authority, and other industries. But the organization also lent its voice to the welfare debates of the era, complicating any label placed on Jackson. Building on relationships established during recruitment for the Poor People's

Campaign, Breadbasket representatives ratcheted up their welfare rights rhetoric in February 1969. Alongside activists from Uptown, the Latin American Defense Organization (LADO), and other groups, Breadbasket leaders warned city and county officials that "a dangerous climax would result from the crisis in welfare if 'county commissioners continue responding only to those with money and property, disregarding the poor and needy.'"[69]

Echoing the suddenly popular theme of hunger, Breadbasket in May and June led statewide protests and marches for a "human subsidy" bill "as an emergency measure to deal quickly and constructively with the problems of the poor and the hungry in this state."[70] Armed with hundreds of marchers, sharp-tongued rhetoric, and a two-hundred-voice choir and band, Breadbasket took its "Hunger is a Hurtin' Thing" tour throughout downstate Illinois. But in contrast with the earlier tepid response from Congress and the Nixon administration, thousands of Breadbasket-mobilized protesters on the steps of the Illinois Statehouse persuaded the governor and legislature to act. Legislators dropped consideration of millions of dollars in welfare cuts, while Breadbasket took credit for the state's creation of a free school lunch program. Even after setting its sights on expanding construction jobs for African Americans, as part of a larger effort by the Coalition for United Community Action later that year, Breadbasket remained engaged in issues of welfare and other government programs in the city.[71]

Although sponsoring "hunger hearings" in the city helped build Breadbasket's credibility among Chicago's poor, the greatest potential for multiracial cooperation and trust was for the United Farm Workers' national boycott against table grapes. On the surface, embracing the UFW's consumer boycotts seemed logical; many of the grocery stores targeted by Operation Breadbasket also sold non-union-label grapes. "We joined in the grape boycotts in the city and around the state," recalled Calvin Morris. "There was an identification . . . with what Mexicans were going through."[72] Not only did the farm workers' poverty strike a nerve among many blacks but so did the migrant experience. As late as the mid-1970s, migrant farm workers in the East remained predominantly African American, and in Chicago many blacks were recent migrants from the South or just a generation removed from such work. But, as Cesar Chavez's reluctance to participate in the Poor People's Campaign foreshadowed, the relationship between Breadbasket and the UFW proved far more complicated.[73]

Despite its endorsement of the grape boycott, as well as the UFW lettuce boycott in 1970, Breadbasket rarely offered more than rhetorical support, forcing Chicago UFW organizer Eliseo Medina to turn to other groups for more substantive assistance. When Medina arrived in 1967 as a green twenty-one-year-old organizer, the UFW had armed him with only the name of a postal worker loyal to the union cause, a bag of union buttons, and a few twenty-dollar bills. From there, Medina built such a successful boycott that Chicago routinely topped lists of cities that were "shut-down," and in 1969 he asked to be transferred to a more challenging area. Even Mayor Richard Daley eventually caved to community pressure, endorsed the boycott, and ordered city departments to not buy grapes. But to achieve such success, Medina called on the religious and labor communities to organize effective boycotts in a new town rather than tapping into existing civil rights circles. UFW records show that seemingly every major progressive-leaning white church in the city supported the boycott, as did the most prominent unions, including the autoworkers, steelworkers, meatpackers, and teachers, as well as the Central Trades and Labor Council and the Chicago Federation of Labor and Industrial Union Council. Grass-roots Chicano organizations such as the local Brown Berets did as well. Conspicuously missing were the city's black labor federation, large Southside churches, and Breadbasket itself. Overall, Breadbasket offered Medina supportive rhetoric and occasional radio time during the Saturday morning broadcasts, but longtime Breadbasket leader Gary Massoni stated, "I never thought we did enough."[74]

Yet, as logical and attractive as a black-brown coalition in Chicago might have seemed in the abstract to movement activists, there was actually little to nothing natural about it. Rather, Breadbasket ideology, practical politics, and paternalism dictated the situation and made any coalitional progress that much more remarkable. Although Jackson claimed that "Operation Breadbasket supports the grape strike as if it were our own project," in reality the organization's priority was to create black jobs and new buyers for black-made products.[75] Aiming to empower African Americans in Chicago specifically, Breadbasket sought mostly professional or service positions in the private sector—a modern version of "self-help," some critics claimed. In contrast, the UFW boycotts supported the collective bargaining of migrant agricultural workers—most of whom were Mexican American or Filipino—more than two thousand miles away, which had potentially less immediacy for consumers.[76]

More practically, new boycotts outside the realm of initial negotiation could have voided the carefully worded covenants that Breadbasket made with particular companies. This was usually not worth the risk, according to organizational leaders, because it drew the ire of black business benefactors who benefited the most from Breadbasket's negotiation and boycott program. Breadbasket also risked violating provisions of the Taft-Hartley Act of 1947 prohibiting secondary boycotts. While the UFW trained its activists to distinguish carefully between picketing the products inside a store and the establishment itself, Breadbasket supporters generally were not trained to make the distinction because of a protest model that targeted the store itself. It is not coincidental that in one of the rare instances in which Breadbasket arrived in force to boycott in the name of grapes, the target, Jewel Tea Stores, was suspected of backsliding on an earlier covenant to hire more blacks. Although Jewel had been a longtime UFW target, since at least July 1968, Breadbasket announced its support a year later when more than two hundred people picketed outside two stores on Chicago's South Side. That contrasted with the handful of Breadbasket protesters who joined UFW pickets more regularly and were usually white. That fact might help explain Breadbasket's decision making. Members of the white middle class were the primary consumers of table grapes.[77]

Paternalism also played a role in Breadbasket's uneven support for the UFW. As demonstrated during the preparation and execution of the Poor People's Campaign, many civil rights activists, especially within SCLC, viewed Mexican American antipoverty organizing as possible only because of earlier black efforts. Although worthy, the Chicano struggle owed African Americans a great debt for the trail they blazed, many activists believed. Cesar Chavez and others readily acknowledged some black influence, and in Chicago, Latino community leaders, including Medina, saw Jackson as an important potential ally. Yet they lamented that, time and time again, Jackson did not follow up on promises of coalition building. Granted, Breadbasket in general rarely followed up on its own projects, but some community leaders viewed this oversight as part of a larger problem. Obed Lopez, founder of the Latin American Defense Organization, recalled attending just one Saturday morning Breadbasket meeting and leaving after Jackson introduced him as "one of our little brown brothers."[78] Compounding this paternalism was what some called a tendency to show little enthusiasm for any idea or initiative that Breadbasket officials had not hatched or led. Not only did the UFW spearhead the grape boycott, but Breadbasket embraced the action only after the insistence of Ralph Abernathy and SCLC aides in Atlanta.[79] This, of course, was related to Jackson's own ambitions to be "black Chicago's great liberator," as one former colleague put it. "To Jesse that was his divinely ordained status in life," said Nate Clay, a former staff member of Breadbasket's successor, Operation PUSH. "As far as I'm concerned, that's not a point even open for discussion. It was too bad for anyone in Jesse's way."[80]

This style made Jackson extremely effective, however, in assisting African Americans in a city in which most black politicians remained under the thumb of Richard Daley's machine. "Many black critics of Jackson have denounced him until they became embroiled in trouble, looked around, and found that there was nobody else in sight to run to for help," writes one biographer. "Jackson, a nonbureaucrat, doesn't call a board meeting to study a problem or pass a resolution for him to act. He just runs out the door."[81] The examples were plentiful. When nobody else would, Jackson stood up for black students being intimidated at the formerly all-white Gage Park High School by appealing to one hundred young men to protect them. Breadbasket's Teacher Division provided a jolt to the student school boycotts in late 1968, as nearly seven hundred teachers walked out in solidarity. And after the assassination of Black Panther leader Fred Hampton, Breadbasket assisted Black Panther-in-hiding Bobby Rush as a liaison with the Afro-American Patrolmen's League to ensure Rush survived his police custody. Such efforts built goodwill but did not make Jackson a natural coalition builder between blacks and Mexican Americans—or even among blacks themselves.[82]

Although Breadbasket had support all over the city, its constituency remained predominantly from the more politically connected and less impoverished South Side. The West Side, in contrast, had far less political or economic clout. Neither working-class whites nor the increasingly southern-born and southern-raised blacks who replaced them there in the 1950s and 1960s held strategic importance to the Daley machine. Breadbasket had retained some West Side ties from SCLC's 1966 campaign and the ongoing Poor People's Campaign, particularly through community groups like the West Side Organization. But while South Side gangs such as the Blackstone Rangers allied with Breadbasket—working as marshals in Resurrection City, supporting direct action efforts in the construction trades, and providing security for Jackson and others—their counterparts on the West Side kept their distance. West Side activists in particular saw Breadbasket as too middle class, even accommodationist. One tenant union leader called Jackson "the Booker T. Washington of

Nathaniel Junior (center) of the Illinois Black Panthers and other members of the original Rainbow Coalition call for interracial unity on April 4, 1969, the first anniversary of Martin Luther King Jr.'s assassination. Also pictured are, standing left to right, Andy Keniston, Hi Thurman, Bill Fesperman, Bobby McGinnis, Mike James, Bud Paulin, Bobby Rush, Elisa McElroy, and Alfredo Matias. Seated are Junebug Boykin, Junior, and Luis Cuzo. James, a veteran of the JOIN community union, helped found Rising Up Angry. (Photo by Linn Ehrlich / Michael James Archive)

the late Sixties."[83] Instead, West-Siders founded their own independent organizations, including one of the nation's most vibrant Black Panther Party chapters under the dynamic leadership of Fred Hampton.[84]

◆ ◆ ◆

A charismatic orator and organizer, Fred Hampton had made the political journey from president of the NAACP Youth Council in the West Side suburb of Maywood in 1966 to cofounder and chairman of Illinois's Black Panthers two years later. In the wake of King's assassination and the Washington campaign, Hampton captivated a conference of black youth in Chicago including Bobby Rush, who was impressed by the young man's poised oration and artful dismissal of nonviolent strategy. Together with

Members of Chicago's Rainbow Coalition enjoyed the rich irony of wearing campaign buttons of the conservative law-and-order Nixon-Agnew ticket covered by a crudely painted rainbow. (Courtesy of Milo Pyne / gift of William "Preacherman" Fesperman in 1969)

young men from the East Garfield section of the West Side, Hampton, Rush, and former members of the city's defunct SNCC chapter founded a local Black Panthers organization. The Panthers established the traditional community survival programs for which they became known, such as free breakfasts. But they also embraced an openness to alliances with other oppressed peoples.[85]

Hampton quickly demonstrated that, to him, this was not just rhetoric. In what he called the Rainbow Coalition (a name Jesse Jackson borrowed years later), the Panthers found partners in two former street gangs, the Young Lords and the Young Patriots. The Young Lords, led by redheaded Jose "Cha-Cha" Jimenez, had started as a Puerto Rican street gang in West Lincoln Park and Humboldt Park on the Near West Side in 1959. Nine years later it had morphed into an explicitly political organization interested in protecting community "turf," not from other gangs but from the authorities. "We saw a common enemy and we used that to unite the community," Jimenez said. "The common enemy . . . was the urban renewal and the police that was attacking us everyday. So we got together, risen up angry."[86] While still predominantly Puerto Rican in 1969, the Young Lords also had a handful of Mexican American, black, and white members. The Young Patriots were poor white Appalachian migrants from Uptown and Lincoln Park on the Near North Side and had a loose affiliation with Peggy Terry's JOIN. Former JOIN members Doug Youngblood, who was Terry's son, and Junebug Boykin founded the Patriots. They too started off as a youth gang whose interest in protecting turf eventually translated into political activism over urban renewal, police brutality, and jobs. Facilitated by the Black Panthers' Robert E. Lee, better known as Bobby, the Patriots became a vocal partner in the Rainbow Coalition under the leadership of Bill "Preacherman" Fesperman, a charismatic local seminary student who had grown up poor in a North Carolina mill town. Coalition members wore old Nixon-Agnew political pins, crudely painted over with a rainbow.[87]

In addition, Hampton had at least come to a truce over territory with Jeff Fort and the Black P. Stone Nation, formerly the Blackstone Rangers, while his organizing inspired the founding of Rising Up Angry, a group of radical white working-class youths in Logan Square on the Northwest Side. P. Stone Nation, one of the fiercest South Side gangs, had provided protection for Jesse Jackson and Operation Breadbasket on occasion and served as marshals for Resurrection City during the Poor People's Campaign, before its members were sent home by SCLC officials. It also had flirted with coalitions with rival black gangs the Conservative Vice Lords and the Black Disciples. Less interested in the revolutionary socialism of the Black Panthers, P. Stone Nation and its magnetic but ruthless leader, Jeff Fort, still respected Hampton's efforts and acknowledgment of their gang. Rising Up Angry was a better ideological fit, emulating the Panthers' call for class unity in the working-class youth spaces of the predominantly white and Latino Near North Side. The organization also published a newspaper called *Rising Up Angry* that focused much of its reporting on the multiracial grass-roots activism bubbling up against police harassment and other state suppression. "Where are our people? We're everywhere," exclaimed the debut issue in July 1969. "We're guys and girls; greasers and hippies; white, black, Latin and Indian." The Panthers also had teamed up occasionally with LADO and Obed Lopez, a Mexican American, and the remnants of JOIN in Uptown in their efforts to reform welfare. LADO, based in Wicker Park on the Near Northwest Side, ran its own health clinic and provided food, welfare, and educational assistance to the community. Overall, the Rainbow Coalition was a loosely organized multiracial alliance of youth determined to empower the dispossessed: "We're straight on, we're about hard, low-down-dirty, straight-on Chicago," declared *Rising Up Angry*, "and what we're gonna have to do is take it back and make it ours."[88]

To at least some observers, the rhetoric of the Rainbow Coalition reminded them of the best of the Poor People's Campaign, especially the experience many had in the Hawthorne School. Charles Cheng, who worked for the Washington, D.C., teachers union, saw the Chicago alliance's roots squarely in the Washington campaign. "We do see Orientals, and Puerto Ricans, and blacks these days doing things together," Cheng said in 1969. "The Panthers are an example—what is it, the Patriots, a southern white group who had formed an alliance. If you carefully read the Poor People's Campaign you'll see that that's where a lot of this began."[89] Many such links were indirect at best, and just as many folks returned to their previous lives in Chicago as became activists in even a small way through Breadbasket, the Rainbow Coalition, or something else. Yet just as Highlander West in New Mexico had accomplished, the potential of Chicago captured the imagination of many, including Myles Horton and the staff of the Highlander Center. During the next several years after the Washington campaign, Highlander remained in constant touch with Chicago activists whom Horton had met at Resurrection City and subsequently ran workshops in Tennessee and Chicago. At various times, the Young Lords' Cha-Cha Jimenez and Omar Lopez, LADO's Obed Lopez, the Young Patriots' Bill Fesperman and Doug Youngblood, and the Uptown Coalition's Chuck Geary and Peggy Terry all attended Highlander events. Fesperman, Youngblood, and Terry all had gone to Washington in 1968. And the 1970 multiracial poor workshop featured black, white, and Puerto Rican members of Chicago's Rainbow Coalition, as well as activists from the Southwest and Deep South.[90]

Despite the promise and symbolism routinely emphasized by scholars, the Rainbow Coalition proved highly contingent.[91] One historian may have overstated it when he cited the "great man theory" to explain the coalition's existence, yet it was not clear who beyond a small cadre of leaders genuinely bought into the arrangement.[92] In fact, Bobby Lee, who had come to Chicago from the South a few years earlier as a War on Poverty organizer, may have been the Panthers' biggest proponent of multiracial collaboration. Recalling his approach with the Young Patriots, Lee said, "I didn't even tell Fred for the first three weeks of meeting with these cats. It wasn't easy to build an alliance. . . . I had to run with those cats, break bread with them, hang out at the pool hall. I had to lay down on their couch, in their neighborhood. Then I had to invite them into mine."[93] Lee's efforts in Uptown were captured in the gritty documentary "American Revolution II," which focused on the black-white portion of the coalition. While some of Lee's comments resonated with the crowd captured on film, others remained skeptical of this lone black man offering the Panthers' help. And it turned out that the Patriots proved less disciplined and committed to partnership than the Panthers had hoped. Panthers were welcome to come to Uptown and Lincoln Park to help Appalachian migrants fight for their dignity in housing and welfare, but going to the West Side was another story. In fact, by November 1969 many Patriots' rejection of the coalition persuaded Bill Fesperman to leave with his family and Black Panther attorney Art Turco for New York City, where they formed the short-lived national Young Patriots Party.[94]

The Young Lords witnessed their own limits to the coalition. Even while Jimenez traveled the city with Fesperman and Hampton touting their new alliance in mid-1969, the mostly Puerto Rican organization ran into considerable resistance. Community-police relations had been one issue that brought these disparate groups together initially, symbolized by the groups' response to the death of Manuel Ramos. Panthers, Patriots, and members of SDS and other organizations marched twice to demand a state's attorney investigation into Ramos's shooting by an off-duty police officer. The march produced a cursory inquiry, which concluded that the shooting was a "justifiable homicide." But when the Young Lords attempted to lead the march through the predominantly black Cabrini-Green public housing community on the Near North Side, recalled Omar Lopez, the marchers faced remarkable hostility from the Cobra Stones gang that ruled there. A "field marshal" had failed to make contact with the gang, said Lopez, a Mexican American leader in the Young Lords. "By the time we got to the police station to protest against the police we had a whole mess of Stones behind us. Yelling at us, throwing sticks." Then police in riot gear came out, temporarily trapping the marchers. Only after Cha-Cha Jimenez and Sal Rivero—not the Black Panthers present—explained to the Cobras' leadership why they were protesting did the tension abate. The Cobras understood police brutality well.[95]

What African Americans in Chicago—outside of the Nation of Islam—did not understand as well was the importance of land to their Latino counterparts. While Black Panther literature contained vague calls for land, such rhetoric did not translate into the same kind of substantive demands made by the Young Lords or the city's Chicano organizations, such as the Young Comancheros in Chicago Heights or Brown Berets in Pilsen. Resistance to the removal of Latinos from their communities had become a central organizing focus. The Young Lords' initial transformation into a political organization, the takeover of McCormick Theological Seminary, and their cofounding of the Poor People's Coalition all stemmed from their opposition to development plans for West Lincoln Park that would have displaced Puerto Ricans and other poor people. The Young Lords "found out that people were moving out because other people needed the land," Lopez recalled. "And that's why urban renewal was such an intricate part of the organizing."[96] While most kept their distance from Puerto Ricans, Mexican Americans in Chicago fiercely defended Pilsen and Little Village, on the city's Near West Side, from urban renewal threats. This was for good reason, since many Mexican Americans had been moved forcibly to construct the University of Illinois, Chicago, campus less than a decade before. Even the presence of poor white artists, sympathetic to the cause, drew suspicion because they routinely were the vanguard of gentrification.

In contrast, the Black Panthers and other African American groups like the West Side Organization and the Vice Lords faced little pressure from urban renewal. Developers and their allies in the Daley administration did not view the geographically and politically isolated West Side as fertile ground—just the opposite, in fact, reinforcing why SCLC had launched "ending the slums" there. Only Cabrini-Green, the one predominantly black neighborhood on the North Side, drew the interest of developers—and not until a decade later. Urban renewal simply did not loom as large for African Americans in Chicago, especially as police harassment intensified.[97]

Not surprisingly in a city called the "national capital of police repression," the white political establishment—and elements of the black establishment, for that matter—viewed even the possibility of a Rainbow Coalition as a grave threat.[98] And similar to the FBI's COINTELPRO, the Chicago police department reacted accordingly. The police's subversive unit, known colloquially as the Red Squad, long had targeted organizations on the left, especially quasi gangs such as the Black Panthers and Young Lords, as documented thoroughly by the city's underground press.[99] But activists became convinced that the coalition's existence made them that much more vulnerable. Throughout 1969, the Panthers and their allies withstood constant harassment, from questionable charges to unannounced raids in which Panther offices were ransacked, posters ripped down, food for the breakfast program ruined, and files and office equipment stolen. Several gun battles had broken out, and as a result two Panthers were killed. These actions had been prefaced by heavy surveillance, even infiltration, of the organizations by the Red Squad. And the Panthers were not alone. The Young Lords and Young Patriots—as well as the Chicago Peace Council, SDS, JOIN, LADO, and other notable organizations—had similar experiences. The harassment took a heavy toll. By the fall, the Panthers had spent much of their energy combating ever-greater police harassment and infiltration, including a November shootout that left three people, two of them officers, dead. The chapter, exhausted and isolated, entered December with only a few dozen active members.[100]

But as bad as such harassment was, none of it prepared the Panthers or their allies for the violent deaths of Fred Hampton and Mark Clark. In a predawn raid on December 4, officers with the state's attorney's office fired nearly one hundred rounds into the apartment where the men slept. Police informer William O'Neal had given law enforcement essential information on the apartment's layout and Hampton's daily routines, as well as drugged Hampton that night. Independent forensic investigations obliterated law enforcement claims that the officers acted in self-defense and sparked calls for a Justice Department investigation. A federal grand jury, despite documenting many inconsistencies in police accounts and in the physical evidence, did not bring charges. Although not political allies of Hampton, NAACP president Roy Wilkins and former U.S. attorney general Ramsey Clark chaired an independent inquiry into the deaths and concluded that the police shot early and often, with no provocation from the Panthers inside the apartment. "Systems of justice—federal, state, and local—failed to do their duty to protect the lives and rights of citizens," the commission wrote rather understatedly.[101] Others simply called it murder.[102]

At first, the ham-handed operation appeared to unify a rainbow of opposition to Mayor Daley and his machine. In the days after the killings, upward of a thousand people walked by the site patiently to pay their respects, and thousands more attended planned and impromptu memorial services across the city. "We had an all-night vigil" to protect the evidence, Cha-Cha Jimenez recalled, as the coalition partners tried to "pick up the torch."[103] Civil rights luminaries, including Ralph Abernathy and Jesse Jackson, joined more than four thousand people at Hampton's official funeral. And while most onlookers and attendees were African American, a significant number were white, Puerto Rican, and Mexican American. Many grieved over the death of yet another young man of color cut down in his prime. Many were outraged by authorities' gall to not just kill Hampton in cold blood but to create a ludicrous self-defense story to justify the force. Yet perhaps more than anything, those who recognized Hampton's passing mourned the loss of one of the city's most dynamic voices, black or otherwise. Hampton's survivors vowed to continue the Rainbow Coalition. Indeed, the pallbearers at his funeral represented the rainbow itself: Bobby Rush, the Panthers' second-in-command; Cha-Cha Jimenez of the Young Lords; Jeff Fort of the Blackstone Rangers; and Obed Lopez of LADO. And in the months afterward, perseverance looked possible. The Black Panthers opened up the Spurgeon Jake Winters People's Free Medical Care Center, named after another martyred Panther, and lent their know-how to their partners in the Rainbow Coalition. By the summer of 1970, the Young Lords, Young Patriots, LADO, and Rising Up Angry all had established free clinics to provide basic preventive health care to those in need in their communities.[104] Representatives of each group attended organizing workshops at Highlander. And greater efforts against police brutality emerged, most notably the Alliance to End Repression, a coalition of organizations started by a former priest that eventually organized lawsuits that exposed and shut down Chicago's subversive unit in 1975.[105]

But Hampton's murder, in the end, dampened the city's multiracial organizing by weakening the Rainbow Coalition's individual members and creating an atmosphere of fear and paranoia. Fearing for his life, Bobby Rush briefly went into hiding. Cha-Cha Jimenez went underground for twenty-seven months to avoid a trumped-up theft charge. Bobby Lee returned to his home state of Texas. The more traditional gangs, including Jeff Fort and the Blackstone Rangers, ended their flirtation with such coalitions. And Bill Fesperman, dogged by meritless charges, left for New York City in November 1969, returned to Chicago briefly in 1970, and then departed for good. Those left behind wondered if police or FBI plants were in their midst. Not all organizing ceased, of course, but nothing like Hampton's Rainbow Coalition emerged again until the electoral campaigns of Harold Washington and Jesse Jackson more than a decade later. Rather, those left behind were even more inclined to mistrust, to question each other's motivations and, as a result, to go their separate ways.[106]

◆ ◆ ◆

The devastation of key members of Chicago's grass-roots leadership allowed Jesse Jackson to emerge as the city's best-known black critic of the Daley machine. "When Fred was shot in Chicago, black people in particular, and decent people in general, bled everywhere," Jackson eulogized at the funeral.[107] Calling the death a "crucifixion" in a newspaper column the next week, Jackson implored the public not to let Hampton's "blood . . . be shed in vain."[108] But unlike Hampton's calls for multiracial activism through health, food, and other survival programs, Jackson proposed that African Americans direct their energy into buying from black establishments and registering voters in order to defeat State's Attorney Edward Hanrahan, who ordered the Hampton raid. While a worthy cause of potential interest to a multiracial audience, this action plan was far more traditional and typical of Jackson's approach. As Hampton himself said the year before, "Operation Breadbasket . . . programs are to benefit businessmen. It's not geared toward the masses."[109]

Jackson's proposal also proved self-serving as he openly considered challenging Daley for mayor in 1971. Daley's support among blacks, which had once been substantial through efficient machine politics, had declined every four years—even against weak primary and general election opponents. But Daley continued to win comfortably as he won more and more support among white ethnic voters who approved of his law-and-order stance against the black power and civil rights movements. Jackson, it turned out, was not a reliable candidate. While he and his media-savvy organization produced memorable rhetoric and managed to outmaneuver black rivals, he did not follow up on his calls for action—a critique Fred Hampton had made before he died. Telling was Jackson's failure to produce the seven thousand signatures needed for his independent candidacy or to challenge successfully such requirements. Jackson was disqualified from the race weeks later.[110]

His comfortable power base in Chicago also made it easier for Jackson to maintain his personal autonomy, whether or not he ran for office. Unlike Andrew Young, Jackson did not resign from SCLC when his flirtation with electoral politics became a serious endeavor. Instead, he maintained his control over Breadbasket and its resources and programming, while gathering signatures and fundraising promises for a campaign bid. By 1971, what Martin Luther King Jr. three years earlier had called Jackson's "little empire" simply had become too much for Ralph Abernathy and SCLC to tolerate.[111] "When we put Jesse in charge of the boycott operation," stated Andrew Young, "it was . . . so we could hit thirty or forty cities simultaneously. . . . But Jesse could never get out of Chicago to do it."[112] Breadbasket had some success in other cities, most notably New York, Cleveland, and Los Angeles, but that was not Jackson's priority. In late 1971, the feud between King's close friend and successor and the man who believed he was the true heir—and who persuaded the media of it—came to a head. After alleged financial improprieties from Black Expo 1971 gave Abernathy an excuse to order Breadbasket moved to Atlanta, Jackson resigned. For the Chicago minister, little changed other than the name of his organization, to the ambitious-sounding People United to Save Humanity, or PUSH.[113]

For SCLC and multiracial coalition, it was another blow. Cut off from its northern financial base in Chicago and rejected by its most charismatic if flawed spokesman, SCLC lost its voice in the early 1970s. While SCLC attempted to stay active in both local and national politics with Abernathy at the helm, the Charleston strike resolution was the organization's last high-profile victory. One could argue that if SCLC had embraced a different sort of organizing, represented by Coretta Scott King, the welfare rights mothers, the scattered activities that the Poor People's Campaign helped spawn among Mexican Americans, or a truly national form of Breadbasket, perhaps the organization born out of the Montgomery bus boycott could have built upon the coalition of the Poor People's Campaign and reinvented itself enough to remain relevant. Instead, its leaders pursued these new directions only halfheartedly, time and again returning to their old, paternalistic ways, and so became increasingly irrelevant.

Representative of this decline in influence, Ralph Abernathy did not make it to the National Black Political Convention in the spring of 1972. But most other black luminaries, including Jackson, did. Symbol of both postwar urban deindustrialization and decay and the rise of black political power, Gary, Indiana, and recently re-elected Mayor Richard Hatcher hosted more than three thousand African American delegates and four thousand more observers to this gritty steel industry city just beyond the South Side of Chicago. There, convention delegates flirted with the idea of a race-based political party, an alternative to the rapidly whitening Republican Party of President Richard Nixon and a tepid Democratic Party still beholden to conservatives uninterested in racial justice. In language similar to that of Corky Gonzales two years earlier, delegates repeatedly condemned the two parties, a sentiment that emerged in the final Gary Declaration. "Both parties have betrayed us whenever their interests conflicted with ours (which was most of the time)," it proclaimed. "By now, we must know that the American political system, like all other white institutions in America, was designed to operate for the benefit of the white race. . . . We begin here and now in Gary. We begin with an independent Black political movement, an independent Black Political Agenda, an independent Black spirit."[114]

In the end, the convention did not explicitly endorse a third party. The idea had the support of black power poet and activist Amiri Baraka, one of three key organizers of the convention, as well as a sizable percentage of the delegates in attendance, especially those from the urban North and West. Mainstream black newspapers such as New York's *Amsterdam News* called for a third party, as did Jackson. "Nationhood is the politics of multiple options," Jackson told a charged convention crowd. "One of those options must be a black political party."[115] Jackson eventually distanced himself from the idea, and in Gary, the power of sitting black politicians, especially in the Democratic Party, proved too great to make a third party a reality. Baraka's convention cohosts, Hatcher and Congressman Charles Diggs of Detroit, opposed the idea. Hatcher told the convention that he was "willing to give the two major political parties one more chance" in 1972 before he would "seriously probe the possibility of a third party movement in this country." Diggs's Michigan delegation, led by state senator and future Detroit Mayor Coleman Young, threatened to walk out if the convention endorsed a third party. Meanwhile, supporters of New York congresswoman Shirley Chisholm's presidential candidacy— the first by a black woman—lobbied for the convention's endorsement of her in the Democratic primary. And while eventually rebuffed, her backers were not interested in a third party either. The impractical nature of a minority race-based third party and blacks' slow but growing influence within the Democratic Party—more influence than Mexican Americans had—eventually won the day. Together, these forces combined with other major party members and even a few black Nixon administration officials to produce a declaration embracing a vague black independence short of a new party.[116]

Much like the La Raza Unida convention in El Paso five months later, mainstream media ignored the event or played up divisions to cast doubt on Gary's success. Headlines such as "Discord is the keynote" and "Blacks at parley divided on basic role in politics" dominated, while several newspapers—black and white—also condemned the passage of an antibusing resolution.[117] Yet what was remarkable was the level of unity. Other than a few old-guard officials from the NAACP, such as seventy-year-old Roy Wilkins, most African American political and civil rights leaders praised the gathering and stood side by side with representatives of the black masses on the convention floor. In addition to Jackson and the convention's prominent coordinators, Julian Bond, Coretta Scott King, the Urban League's Vernon Jordan, Bobby Seale, Betty Shabazz, CORE's Roy Innis, former King aides Walter Fauntroy and Albert Sampson, and Louis Farrakhan were in attendance. Upward of two thousand black officeholders, including former Cleveland mayor Carl Stokes and Congressmen John Conyers and Ronald Dellums, also participated.[118] Many observers concluded that, despite some negatives—one disgusted black journalist called for a "moratorium on partying"—the convention had been a worthwhile initial step toward greater black political power and influence.[119] It was a "lightweight miracle," declared Jesse Jackson.[120]

Historians have been equally positive, calling the Gary convention the "watershed" event linking 1960s and 1970s black activism, "the zenith . . . of the entire black movement," and the historic culmination of the "Modern Black Convention Movement."[121] Yet the convention also represented a different sort of milestone. It marked African Americans' most prominent departure from the recent regional and national efforts at multiracial cooperation. While the importance of economic justice remained constant—including the desire to combat poverty through a mix of state and local solutions—the language and rhetoric around African Americans' antipoverty organizing had changed since 1968. Talk of building rainbow coalitions and Third World alliances still occurred. But they were routinely linked to, even contingent on other calls for "unity without uniformity," not among all people of color, but specifically African Americans. Shirley Chisholm called for a "coalition of all colors" in her presidential campaign and, for many reasons, was roundly rejected.[122]

Instead, Jesse Jackson captured the delegates' imagination those few days in Gary. Even though the chairman of PUSH was not one of the convention organizers, his "It's Nation Time" speech stirred the delegates and became the unofficial theme of the convention. On the convention's last day, when the New York delegation unanimously adopted the official platform and resolutions, a seemingly spontaneous chant emerged from the crowd: "It's Nation Time. It's Nation Time. It's Nation Time." African Americans appeared poised to do what their Mexican American counterparts would do just a few months later.

Yet a black political party did not emerge. Jackson's advocacy—and the viability—of an alternative black party proved short-lived, as PUSH made little effort to support one. Instead, PUSH and other African American organizations orchestrated a different kind of change: the rejection of Mayor Richard Daley's handpicked delegates for the Democratic National Convention later that summer. And many of the more than a thousand black officeholders who went to Gary accomplished the same thing across the country. Their efforts, rooted in a mix of practical and black identity politics, represented a transformation of the Democratic Party that already had begun but took on new meaning in 1972. Although this change may have sped up the long-term decline in working-class white ethnic loyalty to the party, it also helped create the most diverse political assembly—race, class, gender, age, and religion—in major party history. By achieving this, African Americans ensured that a multiracial fight against poverty would not be abandoned completely in the years to come.[123]

Epilogue ◆ Poverty, Coalition, and Identity Politics

The Gary and El Paso conventions became potent symbols of what later would be called the era's "identity politics." First coined by black feminists in the Combahee River Collective in 1977, the term most often referred to the racial and cultural politics of African Americans. "Focusing on our own oppression is embodied in the concept of identity politics," they declared in the Combahee River Collective Statement. "We believe that the most profound and potentially the most radical politics comes directly out of our own identity, as opposed to working to end somebody else's oppression."[1] Yet such a statement could have been articulated by any number of the era's movements, from gay men to white working-class ethnics. And the term did come to define any politics rooted in the societal cleavages of ethnicity, religion, class, gender, region, age, and sexual orientation. Practitioners of such politics identified first and foremost with their subgroup and used it as a base to forward their specific policy agendas. This approach certainly embodied the beliefs that many African American and Mexican American activists had held for years, and that culminated in the political conventions of 1972. They declared that they can assist others only by empowering and seeking justice in their own communities first.

Not surprisingly, many social and political commentators—especially whites—found this perceived fragmentation in the body politic threatening. Critics left, right, and center demonized identity politics, characterizing it as destructive to both liberal democracy and the Marxist dream of class unity. Such criticism came to a head in the 1990s but pointed to the "rights revolution" of two decades before to explain the phenomenon. "The ethnic upsurge . . . began as a gesture of protest against the Anglocentric culture," wrote Arthur M. Schlesinger Jr., a liberal consensus historian and former aide to President Kennedy, in 1991. But epitomized by the 1974 passage of the Ethnic Heritage Studies Program Act, Schlesinger argued, the upsurge "became a cult, and today it threatens to become a counterrevolution against the original theory of America as 'one people,' a common culture, a single nation."[2] Schlesinger's protest sounded nearly identical to those of more traditional conservatives. "What is happening in this country," exclaimed William Simon, conservative foundation president and former Treasury Secretary under two Republican presidents, "is a fundamental assault on America's culture and its historic identity."[3] Some on the left, such as scholar and former SDS activist Todd Gitlin, offered a more nuanced yet still damning critique. "An imbalance has developed between the politics of group assertion and the politics of commonality," wrote Gitlin, drawing on his multiracial organizing experiences with Chicago's JOIN in the mid-1960s. "It is much too easy to lose sight of the . . . risk of narrowness, and of the gains that minorities have won when broad-based movements—in particular labor—have been strongest."[4] Many other commentators also lamented the decline of class-based politics in the 1970s.[5]

Although on the surface the era's identity politics may have seemed antithetical to multiracial antipoverty coalitions, the examples from Chicago, Denver, and the Southwest demonstrate a more complex, inextricably linked reality. And, therefore, the negative assessment of identity politics proves problematic in a number of ways. First, it suggests that whites had not employed their own version of identity politics throughout the American experience, in which they sought autonomous political, social, and economic influence over their communities—and eventually the nation—starting in seventeenth-century British North America. The "public and psychological wage" of being white, to quote W. E. B. Du Bois, remained one of the most valuable commodities one could have in the United States. Whites "were given public deference and titles of courtesy because they were white," Du Bois wrote in his seminal work on Reconstruction. "They were admitted freely with all classes of white people to public functions, public parks, and the best schools. The police were drawn from their ranks, and the courts, dependent upon their votes, treated them with such leniency as to encourage lawlessness. Their vote selected public officials, and while this had small effect upon the economic situations, it had great effect upon their personal treatment and the deference shown them."[6] In other words, whites—even those on the bottom of the economic order—enjoyed a system in which they had all of the legal, social, and economic advantages relative to blacks and pursued an aggressive and violent politics to perpetuate that hierarchy. And while Du Bois wrote specifically of the post-Reconstruction South, white privilege—or what could be called "white affirmative-action"—also has applied to the North and West, from the era of slavery to today.[7]

Second, in contrast to the racial politics of whites, oppressed people often employed identity politics in productive and affirming ways without the denigration and subjugation of others. For African Americans, the racial pride—or "black self-love," to quote one historian—that blossomed in the 1960s manifested itself in a variety of ways that went well beyond popular culture and proved just as significant as the legal destruction of the southern racial caste system.[8] The rise of black cultural identity and expression through the Black Panther Party, the US Organization, the black arts movement, CORE, SNCC, black campus groups, and even SCLC and Operation Breadbasket helped fuel both the establishment of black studies programs at universities and the radical black unions that broke the gentlemen's agreements of the auto, construction, and other industries. It offered a principled alternative to integrationist policies that did not necessarily benefit African Americans, especially black students. Overall, it further equipped African Americans with a powerful, prideful rhetoric and approach to their own communities, whether they were prisoners, poor residents of public housing, or candidates for public office. The result was considerable independent political power, both formal and informal, in black hands—the most since Reconstruction. So powerful, in fact, that such "future expressions of racial pride," according to one observer, "would achieve enough mainstream legitimacy to be co-opted by corporate entities and liberal politicians."[9]

Similarly, the Chicano cultural nationalism celebrated by the Crusade for Justice, Alianza, Brown Berets, and others made a difference. Not only did the movement identify structural inequalities and thus liberate Mexican Americans from solely blaming themselves for their poverty, but it also allowed them to become "comfortable in public in their own skins." By more fully embracing their brown-ness, people of Mexican descent rejected white supremacy and its deleterious influence on their understanding of Mexican immigration and their own history. Reies Tijerina, Corky Gonzales, and the Brown Berets, for instance, prioritized Mexican history—even if their understanding of *mestizaje* downplayed African descent. Moreover, cultural nationalism and Chicana feminism challenged gender roles by undermining traditional definitions of masculinity and creating space for women such as Gloria Arellanes and Alicia Escalante to pursue politics and other nontraditional avenues. "By providing an opening that permitted new ideas about culture, about race, and even about gender roles to emerge and flourish," concluded one Chicana scholar, "Chicano cultural nationalism promoted a sense of liberation among movement participants and served to heighten political awareness about Mexican Americans beyond the movement."[10]

In San Antonio, for instance, the movement produced lasting "second-generation" organizations in the Southwest Voter Registration Education Project (SVREP) and the Communities Organized for Public Service (COPS). While SVREP helped build lasting Mexican American voting power by registering thousands of voters around Texas, COPS created a grass-roots organization that empowered the Mexican barrios to challenge authorities on important yet seemingly "nonethnic" issues such as flooding and street lighting—a model that would be copied across the state and later the country. Combined with the opening up of universities to Mexican American students and the creation of Chicano studies programs, the development of a potent Mexican American political force made the movement—and the identity politics it spawned—a material success.[11]

Finally, but perhaps most importantly to the arguments this book makes, distinct identities were—and still are—inherent to the concept of coalition, antipoverty or otherwise. "Class," as one scholar suggests, "is lived through race and gender."[12] One cannot enter into an alliance without having some sense of oneself. Therefore, it would be out of these identity-based movements that more lasting multiracial coalitions, particularly electoral, would emerge in the late 1970s and 1980s. Cha-Cha Jimenez's 1975 run for Chicago alderman, while unsuccessful in making him the city's first Latino member of the City Council, offered a glimpse of the kind of coalition needed to elect someone mayor besides a protégé of Richard J. Daley. With Uptown and Lincoln Park at the heart of Ward 46, Jimenez's campaign was rooted squarely in the poor people's organizing of years earlier. Building upon the Young Lords' campaign against urban renewal, Jimenez proposed community control over zoning and security deposits by housing developers for repairs. More importantly, he promised an independent voice against the still-powerful Daley machine. "The campaign is not a reformist campaign," declared Jimenez at a unity rally. "It's not a revolutionary campaign. It's a campaign to organize the people."[13] Such rhetoric attracted a rainbow of support, including black and white activists such as future alderwoman Helen Schiller. Well before the election in late February 1975, the campaign declared victory simply because it "organized the people" by registering thousands of first-time voters. In the end, Jimenez came within one thousand votes (out of nearly twenty thousand) of winning the seat as an independent, surprising political observers and suggesting that a multiracial electoral coalition might work at least in parts of Chicago.[14]

Indeed, when black congressman Harold Washington won the 1983 mayoral race, supporters credited the coalitions of a decade before. "It was the coalition forged in the late '60s and early '70s that . . . brought Harold ultimately to power," argued Marilyn Katz, Washington's press manager.[15] Al Raby, Washington's campaign manager and veteran of the Chicago Freedom Movement, took it one step further by framing Washington's run as an echo of the Poor People's Campaign. Martin Luther King Jr. "brought together a coalition of diverse racial and ethnic groups which previously had wasted their energy and power fighting each other. He focused their efforts on the real opponent: a government which discriminates against minorities and women and which was bought and paid for by a small circle of wealth and influence. Dr. King gave his life for this dream, but not in vain. . . . Here in Chicago, Harold Washington is continuing that."[16] While independent black political power was central to Washington's rise, he would not have won without the growing political strength of Mexican American and Puerto Rican communities. More importantly, this coalition stayed together during Washington's often rocky tenure and reelected him in 1987. A similar coalition in Denver—albeit under different circumstances given that city's white majority—elected Federico Peña as Denver's first Latino mayor in 1983, much to the surprise of political observers.[17]

Of course, the electoral success of African American and Mexican American candidates was not a panacea. More than thirty-five hundred blacks held public office in 1975, mostly local posts in the urban North and the South's Black Belt; a few hundred Mexican Americans did so in California and the Southwest.[18] From Lowndes County, Alabama, to San Antonio to Chicago, black and Mexican American officials did not necessarily do what their constituents wanted them to do, especially in addressing poverty. Whether it was cutting lucrative personal deals with prominent white politicians or prioritizing the accumulation of personal power, many black and Mexican American politicians acted much like their white counterparts—sapping the energy from the larger freedom struggles that gave these individuals their start. The movement, if one existed beyond the mid-1970s, looked fundamentally different because many African Americans and Mexican Americans traded much of their street protest and grass-roots work for roles inside the system. This was an understandable change but one that did not produce the sea change that so many movement participants, broadly defined, had desired.[19]

This was particularly true in terms of economic justice. Poverty in the late 1970s remained intractable, with 32 percent of blacks and 26 percent of Mexican Americans living at or under the federal poverty rate, compared to a national rate of 12 percent. The War on Poverty to which Dr. Martin Luther King Jr. had demanded a rededication during the Poor People's Campaign had all but been abandoned. Certainly some antipoverty services had survived, and the freedom struggles had helped force an expansion of educational and job opportunities for upwardly mobile African Americans and Mexican Americans. But as deindustrialization, incarceration, and white (and black and brown) middle-class flight accelerated, millions were left behind in urban ghettos and barrios, as well as small towns across the country. Some scholars wrote controversially of an underclass, people hopelessly left behind in an increasingly segregated society along not just racial but also class lines. While this characterization robbed many people of their agency, it highlighted the freedom struggles' "unfinished business" and the need for new efforts at coalition.[20]

New coalitions did emerge in the 1980s in Chicago, Denver, and nationally, although many of the individuals who participated in the Poor People's Campaign, the Rainbow Coalition, and other alliances did not play prominent roles. Some faded from the scene. Blaming Ralph Abernathy for the organization's increasing irrelevance to the national civil rights conversation, SCLC officials in 1976 forced out King's successor and best friend. While his ouster did not restore SCLC to its former luster, Abernathy faced further ostracization in the following years after endorsing Ronald Reagan for president in 1980 despite the conservative Republican's use of states' rights rhetoric and policy favored by white supremacists. After serving federal and state jail terms stemming from Tierra Amarilla charges, Reies López Tijerina continued to pursue land rights for people of Mexican descent, as well as encourage multiracial unity through a series of "brotherhood conferences." But while he kept the Alianza going into the early 1980s, its grass-roots influence had waned long before, especially after Tijerina began issuing increasingly strange petitions to the newly crowned king of Spain on behalf of land rights. Corky Gonzales's influence also declined, although the Crusade for Justice survived as a nonprofit organization and sponsor of the flourishing Escuela Tlatelolco. Increasing federal and local police repression of the

Crusade's activities, including its ties to the American Indian Movement, exacerbated internal disputes over finances and organizational direction. By the late 1970s, the Crusade had become marginalized even in Denver's Mexican American community. The Brown Berets, also weakened by police suppression and charges of sexism, met a similar fate.

With the exceptions of two-time presidential candidate Jesse Jackson and future ambassador and Atlanta mayor Andrew Young, most other participants of the Poor People's Campaign found less high-profile ways to pursue justice and address poverty. Marian Wright Edelman remained an advocate for the poor, especially poor children, by starting the Children's Defense Fund. Carlos Montes returned to Los Angeles and became a labor organizer and later a peace activist against the Iraq War. Juanita Malouff-Dominguez, Craig Hart, Alicia Escalante, Miguel Barragan, Cornelius Givens, and Obed Lopez led or founded government antipoverty agencies and nonprofit groups. Maria Varela also helped start community development organizations, such as the land-grant-oriented La Cooperativa and Ganados Del Valle, and became a writer and lecturer. Ernesto Vigil also turned to research and writing, while Bernard Lafayette earned a doctorate and taught workshops on peace and nonviolent change. Leo Nieto and Willie Bolden continued to minister to the less fortunate. Vic Charlo founded a school on his reservation in Montana and wrote poetry. Gloria Arellanes reconnected with her Gabrielino-Tongva tribal roots in Los Angeles. And Bobby Lee became an influential organizer in Houston's historically black Fifth Ward.

Those who did pursue the burgeoning alliances of the 1980s and beyond discovered what their counterparts had a generation before and tried to learn from it: that despite similar histories of oppression, different people defined their poverty and justice in distinct ways. This reality did not preclude alliance. But it highlighted how difficult, uncomfortable, and closely linked to identity multiracial cooperation really was—and still is. Speaking to feminists in 1981, civil rights and Poor People's Campaign veteran Bernice Johnson Reagon captured the quandary activists of all stripes faced in the 1960s and 1970s when they sought cooperation with others. "Coalition work is not work done in your home," she said. "Coalition has to be done in the streets. And it is some of the most dangerous work you can do."[21]

Her statement still holds true today.

Notes

JG	Papers of James E. Groppi, Wisconsin State Historical Society, University of Wisconsin, Madison
LBJCP	Cabinet Papers, Lyndon Baines Johnson Presidential Library and Archives, University of Texas, Austin
LBJLB	Legislative Background Files, Lyndon Baines Johnson Presidential Library and Archives, University of Texas, Austin
LBJOH	Lyndon Baines Johnson Oral History Collection, Lyndon Baines Johnson Presidential Library and Archives, University of Texas, Austin
LP	Lincoln Park Neighborhood Collection, DePaul University Special Collections and Archives, Chicago
LWF	Lauren Watson File, Denver Public Library, Denver, Colorado
LWP	Papers of Lee Webb, Wisconsin State Historical Society, University of Wisconsin, Madison
MLK	Dr. Martin Luther King Jr. Papers, Martin Luther King Jr. Center for Peace and Nonviolent Change, Atlanta
MMSW	Records of Western Federation of Miners and the International Union of Mine, Mill and Smelter Workers, Norlin Library, University of Colorado, Boulder
NIYCR	Records of the National Indian Youth Council, Center for Southwest Research, University of New Mexico, Albuquerque
NK	Papers of Nick and Maryann Kotz, Wisconsin State Historical Society, University of Wisconsin, Madison
PNWRO	Papers of the National Welfare Rights Organization, Moorland-Spingarn Research Center, Howard University, Washington, D.C.
POCAM	Poor People's Campaign – Washington Headquarters File, Federal Bureau of Investigation, Washington, D.C.
PPC	Poor People's Campaign
PRC	Papers of Ramsey Clark, Lyndon Baines Johnson Presidential Library and Archives, University of Texas, Austin
PSNCC	Papers of Student Nonviolent Coordinating Committee Papers (microfilm), Walter R. Davis Library, University of North Carolina, Chapel Hill
PUFW	Papers of the United Farm Worker Organizing Committee, Walter P. Reuther Library, Wayne State University, Detroit, Michigan
RBOHC	Ralph Bunche Oral History Collection, Moorland-Spingarn Research Center, Howard University, Washington, D.C.
RCG	Papers of Rodolfo "Corky" Gonzales, Denver Public Library, Denver, Colorado
RLT	Papers of Reies López Tijerina, Center for Southwest Research, University of New Mexico, Albuquerque
RSCLC	Records of the Southern Christian Leadership Conference, Martin Luther King Jr. Center for Peace and Nonviolent Change, Atlanta, Georgia

SAC	Special Agent in Charge, Federal Bureau of Investigation, Washington, D.C.
SAC-WFO	Special Agent in Charge – Washington Field Office, Federal Bureau of Investigation, Washington, D.C.
SL	Stanley Levison File, Federal Bureau of Investigation, Washington, D.C.
UFWDC	UFW Documents Collection, http://farmworkermovement.com
WHA	Papers of White House Aides, Lyndon Baines Johnson Presidential Library and Archives, University of Texas, Austin
WHCF	White House Central Files, Lyndon Baines Johnson Presidential Library and Archives, University of Texas, Austin
YL	Young Lords Collection, DePaul University Special Collections and Archives, Chicago

Introduction

1. *People's World*, October 21, 1967.

2. U.S. Census Bureau, *1970 Census—Characteristics of the Population*, vol. I, part I, 963–68.

3. Blawis, *Tijerina and the Land Grants*, 99.

4. *Albuquerque Journal*, September 1 and 11, 1967, quoted in FBI memo, n.d., box 2, folder 20, RLT.

5. "Interview with Reies Tijerina," interview by Elsa Knight Thompson, n.d. [mid-April 1968?], in *Testimonio*, ed. F. Rosales, 309.

6. *People's World*, October 21, 1967; Garrow, *Bearing the Cross*, 719, n. 49; and Blawis, *Tijerina and the Land Grants*, 99–100.

7. By "class" I mean a more complicated culturally and racially infused version of the term than the more classical bread-and-butter interpretations that E. P. Thompson and others suggest. For alternatives, see for instance Du Bois, *Black Reconstruction*; and Gilroy, *The Black Atlantic*.

8. Popular, media, and scholarly narratives routinely depict the second half of the 1960s as negative, violent, and fractious, dominated by racial uprisings, black power, and white backlash, in contrast to the "good" early 1960s. And by the 1970s, much of the social change generated by the era's movements, these narratives further contend, had been replaced by deindustrialization and declining fortunes for most Americans. One even calls the decade the death of the (white) working class. Cowie, *Stayin' Alive*; Patterson, *Grand Expectations*; Matusow, *The Unraveling of America*; Fairclough, *Better Day Coming*; Roberts and Klibanoff, *The Race Beat*; Chafe, *The Unfinished Journey*; and Jenkins, *Decade of Nightmares*.

9. Quote by William Rutherford in *Voices of Freedom*, ed. Hampton and Fayer, 480. At least in 1876, the Sioux decisively "won" the Battle at Little Bighorn before losing the eventual war against federal soldiers. See also Fager, *Uncertain Resurrection*; McKnight, *The Last Crusade*; Chase, "Class Resurrection"; Gilbert et al., *Ten Blocks from the White House*; Ling, *Martin Luther King Jr.*; Fairclough, *Better Day Coming*; and Sitkoff, *The Struggle for Black Equality*.

By privileging King's life, award-winning biographers such as Taylor Branch and David Garrow disregard the campaign itself by discussing only the planning stages when King was still alive. Branch, *At Canaan's Edge*, 659, 661, 670–73, 679, 688–91, 707, 720–21, 754–55, 764–65; and Garrow, *Bearing the Cross*, 589–601, 606–9, 611–18, 622–23. See also Honey, *Going Down Jericho Road*, 173–90, 500–501; Ling, *Martin Luther King Jr.*, 297–301; Fairclough, *Better Day Coming*, 320–21; Sitkoff, *The Struggle for Black Equality*, 220–22, and *King*, 223–31; and Kotz, *Judgment Days*, 379–403.

A handful of scholars question the campaign's characterization as a "failure," yet only Ernesto Vigil and Jorge Mariscal delve into the participation of Mexican Americans. Vigil, *Crusade for Justice*; T. Jackson, *From Civil Rights to Human Rights*, 329–59; Mariscal, *Brown-Eyed Children of the Sun*, 178–99; and Wright, "The 1968 Poor People's Campaign, Marks, Mississippi, and the Mule Train," in *Civil Rights History From the Ground Up*, ed. Crosby.

10. These efforts have begun to receive attention only recently, with the Rainbow Coalition the most sustained. Ogbar, *Black Power*, chap. 6; Diamond, *Mean Streets*, 305–9; J. Williams, "Racial Coalition Politics in Chicago"; and Jon Rice, "The World of Illinois Panthers." On the farm workers, see Araiza, "'For Freedom of Other Men.'" On Tijerina, see Mariscal, *Brown-Eyed Children of the Sun*.

11. Poor whites, American Indians, and Puerto Ricans do show up here as they relate to African American and Mexican American efforts to fight poverty. But these other groups deserve in-depth analyses that are beyond the scope of this project. For more on their activism, see Kiffmeyer, *From Reformers to Radicals*; Cobb, *Native Activism*; Shreve, *Red Power Rising*; J. Sánchez, *Boricua Power*; and Torres, *Between Melting Pot and Mosaic*. During the Poor People's Campaign specifically, see Mantler, "Black, Brown, and Poor," chap. 4.

12. Most scholarly discussions on multiracial organizing are by social scientists interested in the urban coalitions of the past thirty-five years that elected black and/or Latino mayors in Chicago, Los Angeles, and elsewhere. Only Paula McClain and Joseph Stewart Jr., in their case study of Los Angeles, provide more than a few sentences on historical antecedents. McClain and Stewart, *Can We All Get Along?*; Teresa Córdova, "Harold Washington and the Rise of Latino Electoral Politics in Chicago, 1982–1987," in *Chicano Politics and Society in the Late Twentieth Century*, ed. Montejano, 31–57; Mindiola, Niemann, and Rodriguez, *Black-Brown Relations and Stereotypes*; Browning, Marshall, and Tabb, *Racial Politics in American Cities*; López, *Land Grants, Housing, and Political Power*; Betancur and Gills, *The Collaborative City*; Jennings, *Blacks, Latinos and Asians in Urban America*; and Dzidzienyo and Oboler, *Neither Enemies nor Friends*, chaps. 8–14.

13. Martínez, "Beyond Black/White: The Racisms of Our Time," 472.

14. Quote in Ogbar, *Black Power*, chap. 6. Also, Pulido, *Black, Brown, Yellow and Left*; Bernstein, *Bridges of Reform*; Araiza, "'For Freedom of Other Men'"; Mariscal, *Brown-Eyed Children of the Sun*, chaps. 5 and 6; Kevin Leonard, "'In the Interest of All Races': African Americans and Interracial Cooperation in Los Angeles during and after World War II," in *Seeking El Dorado*, ed. de Graaf, Mulroy, and Taylor, 309–41; Krochmal, "Labor, Civil Rights, and the Struggle for Democracy in

Texas"; and J. Williams, "Racial Coalition Politics in Chicago." Of course, Carey McWilliams' *Brothers under the Skin* remains the classic study in this vein.

15. Behnken, *Fighting Their Own Battles*; Foley, *Quest for Equality*, "Partly Colored or Other White," 123–44, "Straddling the Color Line," 341–54, and "Becoming Hispanic," 53–70; Clayson, *Freedom Is Not Enough*; Bauman, *Race and the War on Poverty*; Whitaker, *Race Work*, chap. 6; Vaca, *Presumed Alliance*; Luckingham, *Minorities in Phoenix*; and Skerry, *Mexican Americans*.

16. Brilliant, *The Color of America Has Changed*; Behnken, *The Struggle in Black and Brown*; and Alvarez, *The Power of the Zoot*.

17. Ransby, *Ella Baker and the Black Freedom Movement*; Kornbluh, *The Battle for Welfare Rights*, 101; Charron, *Freedom's Teacher*, 293–95, 342–43; Payne, *I've Got the Light of Freedom*, 76–77; T. Jackson, *From Civil Rights to Human Rights*, 146; and A. Young, *An Easy Burden*, 139, 479.

18. Garrow, *Bearing the Cross*, 607; and Obed Lopez Zacarías, interview by author.

19. On the power of whiteness on Mexican American identity, especially legal strategy, see Foley, *Quest for Equality*, "Partly Colored or Other White," "Straddling the Color Line," and "Becoming Hispanic"; and S. Wilson, "Brown over 'Other White.'" Carlos Blanton and Benjamin H. Johnson offer important correctives in the case of Texas. Blanton, "George I. Sánchez, Ideology, and Whiteness in the Making of the Mexican American Civil Rights Movement, 1930–1960"; and Johnson, "The Cosmic Race in Texas." For more on the broader whiteness debate, see Roediger, *The Wages of Whiteness: Race and the Making of the American Working Class*, and *Towards the Abolition of Whiteness*; Jacobson, *Whiteness of a Different Color*; Ignatiev, *How the Irish Became White*; and Arnesen, "Whiteness and Historians' Imagination."

20. "Interview with Reies Tijerina," interview by Elsa Knight Thompson, n.d. [mid-April 1968?], in *Testimonio*, ed. F. Rosales, 318.

21. On racial construction in Mexico and the newly expanded United States, see Menchaca, *Recovering History, Constructing Race*; Gómez, *Manifest Destinies*; Katzew, *Casta Painting*; Katzew and Deans-Smith, *Race and Classification*; Cuevas, *African Mexicans and the Discourse on Modern Nation*; and Vasquez, "The Long Durée of Africans in Mexico."

22. I also use "brown" to refer to Mexican Americans, but only in the context of black-brown relations or similar constructions. Puerto Ricans, however, were not "brown" in the 1960s in the manner that we consider them in the twenty-first century. To refer to them as such would be an anachronism. See Padilla, *Latino Ethnic Consciousness*.

23. See Omi and Winant, *Racial Formation in the United States*; Gómez, *Manifest Destinies*. For a brief but thoughtful discussion of Chicano nomenclature, see Bebout, *Mythohistorical Interventions*, 96–100.

24. McKnight, *The Last Crusade*; Donner, *Protectors of Privilege*; Vigil, *Crusade for Justice*; Austin, *Up Against the Wall*; Churchill and Vander Wall, *Agents of Repression*; and O'Reilly, *Racial Matters*.

25. J. Hall, "The Long Civil Rights Movement and the Political Uses of the Past." While Hall coined the term, many have embraced the concept, including broader periodization, region, and foci, to varying degrees. For instance, see Sugrue, *Sweet Land of Liberty*; MacLean, *Freedom Is Not Enough*; Theoharis and Woodard, *Freedom North*, and *Groundwork*; Jeffries, *Bloody Lowndes*; Countryman, *Up South*; Self, *American Babylon*; Payne, *I've Got the Light of Freedom*; and G. Gilmore, *Defying Dixie*.

26. Cha-Jua and Lang, "The 'Long Movement' as Vampire: Temporal and Spatial Fallacies in Recent Black Freedom Studies," 266. Others critique the concept of a long civil rights movement less convincingly, often by overstating the consensus of the traditional civil rights era in order to undercut an argument of continuity. Arnesen, "Reconsidering the 'Long Civil Rights Movement,'" and Chappell, "The Lost Decade of Civil Rights."

27. Most recent research in Chicano and Mexican American history continues to focus on Texas or California. Behnken, *Fighting Their Own Battles*; Brilliant, *The Color of America Has Changed*; Bernstein, *Bridges of Reform*; Foley, *Quest for Equality*; Montejano, *Quixote's Soldiers*; M. García, *Blowout!*; I. García, *White but Not Equal*; Zamora, *Claiming Rights and Righting Wrongs in Texas*; Orozco, *No Mexicans, Women or Dogs Allowed*; Araiza, "'For Freedom of Other Men'"; and Krochmal, "Labor, Civil Rights, and the Struggle for Democracy in Texas, 1935–1975." A few exceptions are Rodriguez, *The Tejano Diaspora*; and Fernández, "Of Immigrants and Migrants."

28. Ogbar, *Black Power*; and Pulido, *Black, Brown, Yellow and Left*.

29. Myles Horton letter to Andrew Young, April 5, 1968, box 177, folder 20, part 4, reel 26, frame 00614, RSCLC.

Chapter 1

1. Harrington, *The Other America*, 174.

2. Ibid., 3.

3. Quote in Isserman, *The Other American*, 175.

4. Quote in *Time*, June 8, 1998. James T. Patterson, Alice O'Connor, and Allen J. Matusow offer the classic interpretations of these elite origins of the War on Poverty. Patterson, *America's Struggle against Poverty in the Twentieth Century*, chaps. 6–8; O'Connor, *Poverty Knowledge*, chap. 6; and Matusow, *The Unraveling of America*, chap. 4. See also Gillette, *Launching the War on Poverty*, chap. 1; and Sugrue, *Sweet Land of Liberty*, chap. 11. Surprisingly, most of those who focus on the grass-roots implications, legacies, and contributions of the War on Poverty implicitly accept such a narrative as well. Ashmore, *Carry It On*; Germany, *New Orleans after the Promises*; Bauman, *Race and the War on Poverty*; Clayson, *Freedom Is Not Enough*; Kiffmeyer, *Reformers to Radicals*; and Orleck and Hazirjian, *The War on Poverty*. One exception is Robert Korstad and James Leloudis's study of the North Carolina Fund, a state-level antecedent to the federal War on Poverty. See *To Right These Wrongs*.

5. Quote in Harrington, *Fragments of the Century*, 93.

6. Isserman, *The Other American*, 183.

7. "Bigger than a Hamburger," *Southern Patriot*, June 1960.

8. *New York Amsterdam News*, March 2, 1963.

9. Blues musician J. B. Lenoir wrote "Eisenhower Blues" amid the three reces-sions that occurred between 1954 and 1960. Cities such as Detroit saw four between 1949 and 1960, impacting industries that employed a disproportionate number of African Americans and Mexican Americans. Sugrue, *The Origins of the Urban Crisis*, 126; and Matusow, *The Unraveling of America*, 23–24.

10. Michael Katz refers to the American welfare state as, at best, a "semiwelfare state." See *In The Shadow of the Poorhouse*, x. Also Galbraith, *The Affluent Society*; Harrington, *The Other America*, 179–82; *New Republic*, October 27, 1958; and Isser-man, *The Other American*, 177–80.

11. *Chicago Daily Defender*, February 12, 1962; *New York Times*, July 6 and August 29, 1960; Murrow, "Harvest of Shame"; Payne, *I've Got the Light of Freedom*, 17–18, 49; and Barbara Moffett, Mariana C. Alcock, and Mr. and Mrs. Pablo Barrera tes-timonies, U.S. Congress, *Migratory Labor*, parts 1 and 2, 604–10, 1344–48. See also Hahamovitch, *Fruits of Their Labor*; Rodriguez, *Tejano Diaspora*; and Galarza, *Farm Workers and Agribusiness*.

12. *Chicago Tribune*, November 25, 1962; *Chicago Daily Defender*, July 17, August 4 and 16, 1965; Chicago Urban League, "Housing and Race in Chicago"; Hirsch, *Making the Second Ghetto*; Washington, *Packing Them In*, chap. 6; and Diamond, *Mean Streets*.

13. Quotes in Theobald, *Free Men and Free Markets*, 20. Respected conservative economist Milton Friedman, an adviser to Republican presidential candidate Barry Goldwater in 1964, embraced a negative income tax in exchange for elimination of most federal social welfare measures. Friedman and Friedman, *Capitalism and Freedom*, chap. 12. See also Kornbluh, *The Battle for Welfare Rights*, 48–50.

14. Lewis, *La Vida*, xliii–xlix.

15. This occurred as early as 1965 with the release of the controversial Moyni-han report, which dubiously linked a culture of poverty among African Americans to slavery. By the 1970s, using Lewis's approach to blame the victim became the norm for conservative social commentators such as Charles Murray. Moynihan, *The Negro Family*, http://www.dol.gov/oasam/programs/history/webid-meynihan .htm; Rainwater, *The Moynihan Report and the Politics of Controversy*; and Murray, *Losing Ground*.

16. Katz, *The Undeserving Poor*, 16–20.

17. Charles Schultze, in Gillette, *Launching the War on Poverty*, 3.

18. *New York Times*, December 13, 1964.

19. Cloward and Ohlin, *Delinquency and Opportunity*, 211.

20. Patterson, *America's Struggle against Poverty in the Twentieth Century*, 97–111, 122–37; and Matusow, *The Unraveling of America*, 97–127, 262–65.

21. Patterson, *America's Struggle against Poverty*, 130.

22. Dudziak, *Cold War Civil Rights*, 179–87; Matusow, *The Unraveling of America*, 60–90; and Branch, *Parting the Waters*, chaps. 11, 12, 17, 21.

23. Korstad, *Civil Rights Unionism*; Brilliant, *The Color of America Has Changed*, 115–22, 129–31, 136–40; Sides, "The Civil Rights Congress in Los Angeles"; P. Sullivan, *Lift Every Voice*, chaps. 7–9; and Mantler, "Black, Brown and Poor," chap. 1.

24. Levenstein, *A Movement without Marches*.

25. Sides, "The Civil Rights Congress in Los Angeles"; Berg, *Ticket to Freedom*, 131–65; Biondi, *To Stand and Fight*, 165–71; Tyson, *Radio Free Dixie*, especially chaps. 5–6; and Payne, *I've Got the Light of Freedom*, 43–66.

26. M. García, *Mexican Americans*, 222.

27. *Progreso*, January–February 1951; Report of Alfonso Sena, National Board Member from Colorado, n.d.; Program for second annual ANMA convention, July 12–13, 1952; "Let's Work Together," ANMA flier, n.d., all in box 206, folder 11, MMSW; M. García, *Mexican Americans*, 200–203; and G. Sánchez, *Becoming Mexican American*, 209–26.

28. Pitti, *The Devil in Silicon Valley*, chap. 6; D. Gutiérrez, *Walls and Mirrors*, 155–68; Vargas, "In the Years of Darkness and Torment," 388–91; Acuña, *Occupied America*, 290–92, 304–6; and Galarza, *Farm Workers and Agri-business*.

29. Pitti, *The Devil in Silicon Valley*, 149.

30. Ibid., chap. 7; Vargas, "In the Years of Darkness and Torment," 398–99; D. Gutiérrez, *Walls and Mirrors*, 168–72; Bernstein, *Bridges of Reform*, chap. 5; Burt, "The Power of a Mobilized Citizenry and Coalition Politics"; and Ross, *Conquering Goliath*.

31. MacLean, *Freedom Is Not Enough*, 165–66; Gómez-Quiñones, *Mexican American Labor*, 168; I. García, *Hector P. García*, 254–58; Francisco "Pancho" Medrano and Albert Peña Jr., interviews by José Angel Gutiérrez.

32. M. García, *Memories*, 205.

33. Gómez-Quiñones, *Chicano Politics*, 67–69, and *Mexican American Labor*, 168; M. García, *Memories*, 198, 205; *Los Angeles Times*, March 10, 1963; and Sides, *L.A. City Limits*, 78.

34. M. García, *Memories*, 199–200.

35. E. Chávez, *!Mi Raza Primero!*, 34.

36. Quote in U.S. Commission on Civil Rights, *The 50 States Report*, 46. Also, Brilliant, *The Color of America Has Changed*, 172, 208; Oropeza, *¡Raza Si! ¡Guerra No!*, 51; E. Chávez, *!Mi Raza Primero!*, 33–34; *Los Angeles Sentinel*, September 3, 1964; *Los Angeles Times*, September 29, 1964; and G. Sánchez, *Becoming Mexican American*, 242–49.

37. Kells, *Hector P. García*, 116–18; I. García, *Hector P. García*, 260–61; Foley, *Quest for Equality*, 126–28; and Behnken, *Fighting Their Own Battles*, 32.

38. *New York Amsterdam News*, March 2, 1963.

39. Charron, *Freedom's Teacher*, 252. See also Payne, *I've Got the Light of Freedom*, 302–6.

40. MacLean, *Freedom Is Not Enough*, 53; T. Jackson, *From Civil Rights to Human Rights*, 158–66; and Branch, *Parting the Waters*, chap. 21. There were significant perils to portraying the movement as little more than a morality play. In Birmingham and later Selma, many complexities and ambiguities have remained largely absent from the public memory and, until recently, scholarship—including the earlier grass-

roots organizing built upon by SCLC, the role of local white elites in ending Jim Crow, and even the extent of violence by both blacks and whites. See Spratt, "When Police Dogs Attacked: Iconic News Photographs and Construction of History, Mythology, and Political Discourse"; Kelley, "'We Are Not What We Seem'"; Manis, *A Fire You Can't Put Out*; Eskew, *But for Birmingham*; Thornton, *Dividing Lines*; and J. Walker, "A Media-Made Movement," 41–66.

41. *New York Times*, August 15, 1963.

42. Sugrue, *Sweet Land of Liberty*, 290–91; Countryman, *Up South*, 120–51; Levenstein, *A Movement without Marches*; and L. Sullivan, *Build Brother Build*.

43. *Chicago Tribune*, May 24, 1963.

44. *Nation*, September 14, 1963.

45. *New York Times*, May 12 and June 1, 1963; *Chicago Tribune*, May 15, 1963; *Chicago Defender*, July 13, 27, and August 3, 10, 1963; *New Pittsburgh Courier*, June 29, 1963; Sugrue, *Sweet Land of Liberty*, 290–305; and T. Jackson, *From Civil Rights to Human Rights*, 166–68.

46. Quote in Vargas, *Labor Rights Are Civil Rights*. Also, Garrow, *Bearing the Cross*, 258; Branch, *Parting the Waters*, 788; T. Jackson, *From Civil Rights to Human Rights*, 87; Honey, *Going Down Jericho Road*, 26; and Horowitz, *Negro and White, Unite and Fight!*, 206–9.

47. Thompson, *Whose Detroit?*, 49.

48. Francisco "Pancho" Medrano, interview by José Angel Gutiérrez; Gomez-Quiñones, *Mexican American Labor*, 194–95, 228; Thompson, *Whose Detroit?*, 49–56; Sugrue, *The Origins of the Urban Crisis*, 162–63; Badillo, "From *La Lucha* to Latino," 38; Lichtenstein, *The Most Dangerous Man in Detroit*, 372–80; and Fink and Greenberg, *Upheaval in the Quiet Zone*.

49. Quote in Barnard, *American Vanguard*, 392. Also, Sugrue, *Sweet Land of Liberty*, 298–301; *Pittsburgh Courier*, July 3, 1963; *New York Times*, April 6, 1961, and June 24, 1963; and Angela D. Dillard, "Religion and Radicalism: The Reverend Albert B. Cleage Jr. and the Rise of Black Christian Nationalism in Detroit," in *Freedom North*, ed. Theoharis and Woodard, 166–68.

50. John F. Kennedy, "Civil Rights Address," June 11, 1963, http://www.american rhetoric.com/speeches/jfkcivilrights.htm, accessed September 1, 2011.

51. Sugrue, *Sweet Land of Liberty*, 294–97; and T. Jackson, *From Civil Rights to Human Rights*, 168–71.

52. "A Proposal to the Ford Foundation from the North Carolina Fund," August 12, 1963, 6–7, box 27, GE.

53. *New York Amsterdam News*, August 3, 1963; Kornbluh, *The Battle for Welfare Rights*, 24–26; Piven and Cloward, *Regulating the Poor*, 281, "The Great Society as a Political Strategy," 17–22, and "Reaffirming the Regulating of the Poor," 147–69; Korstad and Leloudis, *To Right These Wrongs*, 166; and King, "Why We Can't Wait," *Saturday Review*, May 30, 1964, and Alinsky, "Principles of Citizen Action," verbatim reprint, May 27, 1963, both in box 33, GE.

54. Branch, *Parting the Waters*, 216–18; D'Emilio, *Lost Prophet*, 262–64; and Kersten, *A. Philip Randolph*, 93–97.

55. D'Emilio, *Lost Prophet*, 335.

56. W. Jones, "The Unknown Origins of the March on Washington," 41–43; D'Emilio, *Lost Prophet*, 327–39; Branch, *Parting the Waters*, 816–17; and Kersten, *A. Philip Randolph*, 91–93, 97–98.

57. T. Jackson, *From Civil Rights to Human Rights*, 176.

58. Burke Marshall in *Voices of Freedom*, ed. Hampton and Fayer, 161.

59. *Washington Post*, July 18, 1963; and Barber, *Marching on Washington*.

60. Rustin and Robinson, "Final Plans for the March on Washington for Jobs and Freedom, Organizing Manual No. 2," 4; and T. Jackson, *From Civil Rights to Human Rights*, 177–80.

61. *New York Times*, July 26, 1963.

62. *New York Times*, August 25, 1963.

63. *Los Angeles Times*, August 27, 1963.

64. Quote in *New York Times*, July 18, 1963. Also, *Washington Post*, July 1, 3 and 18, and August 5 and 25, 1963; and *New York Times*, July 8, 15, 26, and 28, and August 4 and 26, 1963; *Los Angeles Times*, July 5, 15, 23, and 25, 1963; *Chicago Tribune*, July 6 and 10, and August 26, 1963; *Wall Street Journal*, August 28, 1963; and *U.S. News & World Report*, August 26, 1963.

65. Quotes in *New York Times*, August 29, 1963. See also *Washington Post*, August 29, 1963; *Wall Street Journal*, August 30, 1963; *Time*, September 6, 1963; and *Newsweek*, September 9, 1963.

66. John Lewis, "The Revolution Is at Hand" (1963), in *Let Nobody Turn Us Around*, ed. Marable and Mullings, 407–8.

67. Quotes from excerpted speeches, *New York Times*, August 29, 1963. Only the *Times* excerpted most of the speeches, and those appeared deep inside the news section. Also, Sugrue, *Sweet Land of Liberty*, 305–10.

68. *New York Times*, August 29, 1963, quotes; T. Jackson, *From Civil Rights to Human Rights*, 182; and W. Jones, "The Unknown Origins of the March on Washington."

69. B. F. McLaurin letter to Bayard Rustin, August 5, 1963, frame 0670, and Gladys Duppstadt of National Federation of Settlements and Neighborhood Centers, memo, August 12, 1963, frames 0745–0746, BR; Francisco "Pancho" Medrano, interview by José Angel Gutiérrez; Rustin, "Newsletter #2"; M. García, *Memories*, 216; and Behnken, *Fighting Their Own Battles*, 95.

70. Malcolm X, with Haley, *The Autobiography of Malcolm X*, 278; Marable, *Malcolm X*, 256; Branch, *Parting the Waters*, 889–96; and R. Romano, "Narratives of Redemption: The Birmingham Church Bombing Trials and the Construction of Civil Rights Memory," in *The Civil Rights Movement in American Memory*, ed. Romano and Raiford, 96–133.

71. Quote in *Washington Post*, January 9, 1964. Also, William Capron, William Cannon, Walter Heller, and Julie Sugarman, in *Launching the War on Poverty*, ed. Gillette, 8–21; and Matusow, *The Unraveling of America*, 119–24.

Chapter 2

1. King telegram to Cesar Chavez, September 19, 1966, box 21, folder 5, MLK.

2. Eleanor Eaton memo to Barbara Moffett, "Cesar Chavez," August 23, 1968, in

CRD folder 51910, "Economic Security and Rural Affairs 1968—Comms and Orgs: United Farm Workers Organizing Committee," AFSCA. Please note that AFSC uses folder numbers exclusively, not box numbers, in its archives.

3. *Los Angeles Times*, December 20, 1970; and *New York Times*, September 5, 1966, and February 1, 1970. Born in Arizona, Chavez had a hardscrabble childhood after his parents lost their land during the Depression and became migrant workers. His father was involved in farm labor unionization, and Chavez himself would join the National Farm Labor Union in California before becoming involved in the Community Service Organization. Chavez would apply the principles he learned there to his later labor organizing, although by the 1980s, he faced criticism for an increasingly autocratic leadership style. In contrast, King was born into Atlanta's black middle class, earned several college degrees, and had little to no training in such grass-roots work. Hammerback and Jensen, *The Rhetorical Career of Cesar Chavez*, 11–21; Griswold del Castillo and García, *César Chávez*, 3–33, 150, 173; Branch, *Parting the Waters*, 53–142; and Garrow, *Bearing the Cross*, 32–51. Jorge Mariscal also comments at length on this misconception. "Cesar and Martin, March '68," in *The Struggle in Black and Brown*, ed. Behnken, 148–78.

4. Honey, *Going Down Jericho Road*; and King, *All Labor Has Dignity*, ed. Honey.

5. Cesar Chavez, "An Organizer's Tale, July 1966," in C. Chavez, *An Organizer's Tale*, ed. Stavans, 22–24; and J. Levy, *Cesar Chavez*, chaps. 5–6.

6. NFWA merged with the Filipino-dominant AWOC to become the United Farm Workers Organizing Committee (UFWOC) in September 1966. The union later changed its name to the United Farm Workers of America (UFWA).

7. Dunne, *Delano*, xii.

8. J. Levy, *Cesar Chavez*, 537.

9. Chavez, "An Organizer's Tale," 18–20; Gómez-Quiñones, *Chicano Politics*, 54–56; Pitti, *The Devil in Silicon Valley*, chap. 7; and Ross, *Conquering Goliath*.

10. Griswold del Castillo and Garcia, *César Chávez*, quote 110, 100–115; and "Cesar Chavez on How It Began," in *Testimonio*, ed. F. Rosales, 282. On organizing as "slow and respectful work," see Payne, *I've Got the Light of Freedom*, especially chap. 8.

11. Araiza, "'For Freedom of Other Men,'" 28.

12. Quote in J. Levy, *Cesar Chavez*, 197. Dunne, *Delano*, 24, 120; Araiza, "'For Freedom of Other Men,'" 20–21; and Griswold del Castillo and García, *Cesar Chávez*, 48.

13. J. Levy, *Cesar Chavez*, 196.

14. *Movement*, August and October 1965; *El Malcriado*, no. 22 (October 1965), no. 24 (November 1965); Araiza, "'For Freedom of Other Men,'" 22, 24–26; Horne, *Fire This Time*, 182; James Farmer memo to CORE chapters, December 17, 1965, Wendy Brooks, "The Story of Wendy Goepel Brooks, Cesar Chavez and La Huelga," and SAC, Los Angeles to FBI director, March 28, 1966, UFWDC; and Meier and Rudwick, *CORE*, 358, 386–88.

While CORE's commitment to the farm workers declined in 1966, the Los Angeles chapter of CORE took on another union, the United Auto Workers, by organizing a Minority Protest Committee to challenge racial discrimination against blacks, Mexican Americans, and women in the area North American Aviation plant. Lewis-Colman, *Race against Liberalism*, 93–97.

15. Mike Miller letters to Karen Whitman, February 19 and April 13, 1966, reel 33, frames 0100, 0107, microfilm, PSNCC; Mike Miller letter to Cesar Chavez, March 8, 1966, UFWDC; Ganz, *Why David Sometimes Wins*, 113; Dunne, *Delano*, 123–24, and "Strike!" *Saturday Evening Post* 240, no. 9 (May 6, 1967): 44; and Araiza, "'For Freedom of Other Men,'" 28–29.

16. Mike Miller letter to Karen Whitman, April 13, 1966, reel 33, frame 0107, PSNCC.

17. *El Malcriado*, no. 32 (March 17, 1966), no. 33 (April 10, 1966); NFWA fund-raising letter, February 20, 1966, reel 33, frame 0101, PSNCC; Jim Drake memo to boycott staff, March 2, 1966, Jim Drake and Mike Miller, progress reports #1, 2 and 3, ca. March 1966,UFWDC; Araiza, "'For Freedom of Other Men,'" 32–36, 58–61; Ganz, *Why David Sometimes Wins*, chap. 5; Payne, *I've Got the Light of Freedom*, chap. 13; Carson, *In Struggle*, chaps. 14–15; Hogan, *Many Minds, One Heart*, chap. 8–10; and Evans, *Personal Politics*.

18. "The American Dream," July 4, 1965, in King, *A Knock at Midnight*, ed. Carson and Holloran, 94.

19. *Washington Post*, December 4, 1964.

20. Quote in L. D. Reddick letter to King, June 19, 1964, box 20, folder 5, MLK; T. Jackson, *From Civil Rights to Human Rights*, 231; Fink and Greenberg, *Upheaval in the Quiet Zone*, 103; and Hooper and Hooper, "The Scripto Strike," 13, 15–16, 23–26.

21. King, *Why We Can't Wait*, 176.

22. T. Jackson, *From Civil Rights to Human Rights*, 229–31; Dittmer, *Local People*, 364–65; P. Levy, *The New Left and Labor in the 1960s*, 134–35; and M. García, *Memories*, 215.

23. Horne, *Fire This Time*, 299.

24. T. Jackson, *From Civil Rights to Human Rights*, 230; *Los Angeles Times*, August 19–21, 1965; Horne, *Fire This Time*, 182–84, 298–99; E. Chávez, *¡Mi Raza Primero!*, 40; and Pulido, *Black, Brown, Yellow, and Left*, 69–73.

25. Quote in U.S. Commission on Civil Rights, *Report of the United States Commission on Civil Rights*, 365. Also, T. Jackson, *From Civil Rights to Human Rights*, 237–38, 279–81.

26. Quote in Jeanne Theoharis, "Introduction," in *Freedom North*, ed. Theoharis and Woodard, 4—a volume dedicated to critiquing this notion.

27. Most studies of the CFM argue it was a straightforward failure. A. Anderson and Pickering, *Confronting the Color Line*, 3; Garrow, *Bearing the Cross*, 569–70; Fairclough, *To Redeem the Soul*, 306–7; Ling, *Martin Luther King Jr.*, 239–40; and Kotz, *Judgment Days*, 362–67. Later scholarship generally argues that the CFM had some long-term benefits. Branch, *At Canaan's Edge*, 558; Ralph, *Northern Protest*, 220–35; and T. Jackson, *From Civil Rights to Human Rights*, 298–99. In addition, participants of a fortieth anniversary conference on the CFM in 2006, including Jesse Jackson, not surprisingly concluded that SCLC's campaign achieved some success.

28. Royko, *Boss*; Ralph, *Northern Protest*, 9–14; and A. Anderson and Pickering, *Confronting the Color Line*, 44–68. An influential black Republican operation had

emerged in the 1920s, headed by Oscar DePriest, who went to Congress in 1928—the first African American to do so since North Carolina's George White in 1902. Republicans began to lose their grip on the black vote in Chicago, as with the rest of the nation, because of the Great Depression and President Franklin D. Roosevelt's New Deal.

29. Chicago Urban League Research Department memo to director Edwin C. Berry, January 18, 1962, Hearings and Statements on Racial Segregation file, CPLG; Ralph, *Northern Protest*, 15–18; A. Anderson and Pickering, *Confronting the Color Line*, 84–102; Danns, *Something Better for Our Children*, 25–27; and Rury, "Race, Space, and the Politics of Chicago's Public Schools," 129–30.

30. Jobs Or Income Now (JOIN) Community Union, "Statement on Urban Progress Centers," February 12, 1965, 4, box 25, folder 1, GW. See also Frost, *An Interracial Movement of the Poor*, 54–57, 151–53.

31. Ralph, *Northern Protest*, 19–33, 70–71; A. Anderson and Pickering, *Confronting the Color Line*, 105–56, 178; Danns, *Something Better for Our Children*, 27–55; and Cohen and Taylor, *American Pharaoh*, 334–37.

32. Moyers, "Second Thoughts," 19–20.

33. *New York Times*, April 18, 1965; Mann, *Chicago's War on Poverty*, 16–26, 57–58; and Cohen and Taylor, *American Pharaoh*, 317–20, 343.

34. *Chicago Tribune*, April 14, 1965.

35. *Chicago Daily Defender*, April 27, 1966.

36. *Chicago Tribune*, April 14–15, October 13 and December 28, 1965, January 11, February 17, 19, 26, and March 24, 1966; *New York Times*, April 14, 1965; *Chicago Defender*, August 29, 1964; *Chicago Daily Defender*, December 7, 1965; *Time*, December 17, 1965; Cazenave, "Chicago Influences on the War on Poverty," 52–68; and Cohen and Taylor, *American Pharaoh*, 342, 345–46.

37. Cohen and Taylor, *American Pharaoh*, 319–20.

38. Quote in *Chicago Daily Defender*, December 7, 1965; *Chicago Tribune*, April 15, 1965; and Cohen and Taylor, *American Pharaoh*, 318, 340.

39. *Chicago Defender*, August 21, 1965.

40. Bernard Lafayette in *Voices of Freedom*, ed. Hampton and Fayer, 299.

41. Quote in *New York Times*, July 25, 1965. Also, Cohen and Taylor, *American Pharaoh*, 337–38, 347–48; and Branch, *At Canaan's Edge*, 321. For more on the great migration to Chicago, see Wilkerson, *The Warmth of Other Suns*; and Black, *Bridges of Memory*.

42. Garrow, *Bearing the Cross*, 455.

43. For the best narratives, see Ralph, *Northern Protest*; and A. Anderson and Pickering, *Confronting the Color Line*, 150–340. For early narratives by participants, see *Chicago 1966*, ed. Garrow.

44. *Jet*, August 25, 1966, quote; *New York Times*, January 16, 1967; A. Anderson and Pickering, *Confronting the Color Line*, 228; and Branch, *At Canaan's Edge*, 507–11.

45. Timuel D. Black letter to King, April 3, 1967, box 5, folder 32, MLK. Black was president of the Chicago chapter of the Negro American Labor Council.

46. Thomas G. Ayers, "The 'Summit Agreement': Report of the Subcommittee to the Conference on Fair Housing Convened by the Chicago Conference on Re-

ligion and Race," in *Chicago 1966*, ed. Garrow, 147–54; A. Anderson and Pickering, *Confronting the Color Line*, 273–74, 277; and Gray, "Cicero March."

47. T. Jackson, *From Civil Rights to Human Rights*, 287.

48. King, "I Need Victories," Chicago, July 12, 1966, box 11, Speeches, MLK.

49. Quote in *New York Amsterdam News*, July 30, 1966; *New York Times*, July 14, 1966; *Chicago Defender*, June 13, 1966, and July 14, 1967; Ralph, *Northern Protest*, 109–13, 220–35; A. Young, *An Easy Burden*, 410; McGraw, "An Interview with Andrew J. Young," 324–30; and Diamond, *Mean Streets*, 265–69.

50. Ralph, *Northern Protest*, 137.

51. Billy Hollins, interview by author.

52. Diamond, *Mean Streets*, 269–78; *Chicago Defender*, June 3 and October 24, 1967, and February 24, May 9 and 23, 1968; and Billy Hollins and Bernard Lafayette, interviews by author.

53. Diamond, *Mean Streets*, 91–97, 197–212; Arrendondo, *Mexican Chicago*; Fernández, "From the Near West Side to 18th Street," 162–83; Padilla, *Puerto Rican Chicago*, 125–44; Maura I. Toro-Morn, "Boricuas en Chicago: Gender and Class in the Migration and Settlement of Puerto Ricans," in *The Puerto Rican Diaspora*, ed. Whalen and Vázquez-Hernández, 128–50; Kerr, "Chicano Settlements in Chicago," 22–32, and "Mexican Chicago: Chicano Assimilation Aborted, 1939–1954," in *The Ethnic Frontier*, ed. Holli and Jones, 293–328.

54. James Bevel, "SCLC—Chicago Report," November 8, 1965, box 150, folder 22, "Addendum to Progress Report—Committee Reports at June 24, 1966, Meeting," box 149, folder 30, "Mobilization Plans," March 1966, and "The Lawndale Union to End Slums," n.d., box 46, folder 17, all in RSCLC; *Chicago Daily Defender*, June 13, 1966; and Obed Lopez Zacarías, interview by author.

Interestingly, SCLC did not deploy effectively its one high-ranking native Spanish speaker, Cirilo McSween, the organization's national treasurer. A prominent life insurance executive in Chicago, McSween was Afro-Panamanian but identified as African American after he became a college track star, businessman, and civil rights activist in the United States.

55. Obed Lopez Zacarías, in Méndez, "A Community Fights Back."

56. Méndez, "A Community Fights Back"; and Padilla, *Puerto Rican Chicago*, 144–79, and *Latino Ethnic Consciousness*, 48–54. Remarkably, none of the literature on the CFM even mentions the Division Street riot.

57. *Chicago Daily Defender*, June 16, 1966.

58. *Chicago Daily Defender*, June 20, 1966.

59. *Chicago Daily Defender*, June 27–29 and July 11, 1966; *Jet*, June 30, 1966; and Obed Lopez Zacarías, interview by author.

60. *Chicago Daily Defender*, January 10, 1966.

61. Gary Massoni, "Perspectives on Operation Breadbasket," in *Chicago 1966*, ed. Garrow, 192–95; L. Sullivan, *Build, Brother, Build*; Calvin Morris, interview by author; and *El Malcriado*, January 26, 1966. Morris remembers as a teenager in Philadelphia giving up Tastykake, his favorite snack, to honor Sullivan's boycott. For more on Sullivan's selective patronage organizing and its eventual transition into self-help, see Countryman, *Up South*, 83–86, 101–19.

62. Gary Massoni, interview by author.

63. Massoni, "Perspectives on Operation Breadbasket," in *Chicago 1966*, ed. Garrow, 192–93, 197–211; and Calvin Morris and Gary Massoni, interviews by author.

64. *El Malcriado*, March 17, 1966.

65. John Armendariz letter to Gene Boutilier, November 14, 1966, box 7, folder 1, United Farm Worker Organizing Committee papers, PUFW; *El Malcriado*, January 26, February 28, and March 17, 1966; Hooper and Hooper, "The Scripto Strike," 13–14; Bowman, "From Workers to Activists"; and Medina's monthly expense reports, May 10, June 28, November 11, and December 30, 1969, and February 25 and June 25, 1970, box 24, folder 11, PUFW Admin Dept., Pt. 1, PUFW.

66. Obed Lopez Zacarías, interview by author.

67. *Movement*, June 1967.

68. *Chicago Tribune*, August 3, 1967; *Chicago American*, July 1, 1967; *Worker*, September 3, 1967; *Chicago Daily Defender*, November 13, 1967; *Movement*, June 1967; LADO press releases, July 23 and September 23, 1967, courtesy of Obed Lopez; Obed Lopez Zacarías, interview by author; López, "LADO," 23, 25; Danns, *Something Better for Our Children*, 75, 78, 82, 88; and Donner, *Protectors of Privilege*, 90–154. See also Frost, *An Interracial Movement of the Poor*; Gitlin and Hollander, *Uptown*; and Sonnie and Tracy, *Hillbilly Nationalists*.

69. *New York Times*, July 5 and August 13, 1965; Ralph Abernathy, "Vietnam and the Negro Revolution," November 1, 1966, box 59, folder 19, RSCLC; Bernard S. Lee in *Voices of Freedom*, ed. Hampton and Fayer, 342–43; Fairclough, *To Redeem the Soul*, 334; and Garrow, *Bearing the Cross*, 543.

70. King's advisers, particularly Stanley Levison, were afraid that King would be seen walking side by side with known communists, anarchists, and other antiwar protesters at the "Spring Mobe," which was open to anyone who wanted to attend. The April 15 protest proved to be the largest antiwar rally to date, attracting nearly 250,000 people. While Stokely Carmichael and other activists carried Viet Cong flags, King joined more "respectable" participants Benjamin Spock, Harry Belafonte, and James Bevel, avoiding the worst of SCLC fears. *New York Times*, April 16, 1967; Fairclough, *To Redeem the Soul*, 340; and Garrow, *Bearing the Cross*, 556–57.

71. King, "A Time to Break Silence," in King, *A Testament of Hope*, ed. Washington, 233.

72. King, "The Casualties of the War in Vietnam," February 25, 1967, untitled address to peace march, March 25, 1967, and "Beyond Vietnam," April 4, 1967, all in box 12, Speeches, MLK; *New York Times*, February 11 and April 14, 1966, February 26 and March 26 and 31, 1967; *Los Angeles Times*, July 3 and August 22, 1965, and February 26, 1967; and *Chicago Tribune*, March 26, 1967.

73. John Roche memo to President Johnson, April 5, 1967, box 147, Confidential Name File "KI," WHCF.

74. *Washington Post*, April 6, 1967.

75. *New York Times*, April 14, 1967. Bunche privately told King later that he was in full agreement with the pastor's analysis of Vietnam, but that he could not say so in public. King dropped his criticism of Bunche, but expressed frustration to

Levison over Bunche's unwillingness to risk his standing on principle. King and Levison, telephone conversation, April 14, 1967, SL.

76. *New York Times*, April 6 and 14, 1967; *New York Amsterdam News*, April 15 and 22, 1967; *New Pittsburgh Courier*, April 15, 1967; and Carl Rowan, "Martin Luther King's Tragic Decision," *Reader's Digest*, September 1967.

77. *New York Times*, April 6, 1967.

78. Kwame Ture (Stokely Carmichael) in *Voices of Freedom*, ed. Hampton and Fayer, 340.

79. *Los Angeles Times*, April 23, 1967.

80. *New York Times*, April 24, 1967. Other examples of written support include Marian Wright letter to King, May 4, 1967, box 5, folder 35; Alfred Hassler (Fellowship of Reconciliation) letter to King, April 10, 1967, box 2, folder 14; and Robert Bird (AFSC) letter to King, April 21, 1967, box 2, folder 14, all in RSCLC.

81. Oropeza, *¡Raza Si! ¡Guerra No!*, 5.

82. J. Levy, *Cesar Chavez*, 197; and Jorge Mariscal, "Cesar and Martin, March '68," in *The Struggle in Black and Brown*, ed. Behnken, 148–78.

Chapter 3

1. S. Hall, "On the Tail of the Panther," 62.

2. In late 1966, the A. Philip Randolph Institute proposed the Freedom Budget, a detailed plan to wipe out poverty within ten years. Despite considerable support of its goals and spending strategies among the Left, the proposal went nowhere as antiwar activists charged Rustin and Randolph with implicitly endorsing current defense budgets, and therefore the Vietnam War. Randolph and Rustin, *A "Freedom Budget" for All Americans*; and D'Emilio, *Lost Prophet*, 429–39.

3. *National Guardian*, June 18, 1966; *People's World*, July 15 and 22, 1967; and William Pepper address to convention, August 31, 1967, box 3, folder 3, LWP.

4. Not only did King have little interest in running for office himself, he was skeptical of the NCNP—at least partly because senior adviser Stanley Levison believed King should not become involved in elements of a peace movement Levison deemed powerless. One historian suggests that King spoke at the convention because one of its founders, Martin Peretz, was the husband of SCLC's top donor, Ann Farnsworth. Garrow, *Bearing the Cross*, 719, n. 49.

5. Henry Wineberg letter to NCNP supporters, October 21, 1967, box 2, folder 36, LWP; *People's World*, September 9, 16, 1967; *New Yorker*, September 23, 1967; and S. Hall, "On the Tail of the Panther," 62–64.

6. The other demands included support for national liberation wars, such as those in Vietnam, Latin America, and South Africa; the reinstatement of New York congressman Adam Clayton Powell after charges of corruption; black control of African American political groups; rebuilding the ghettos; and the resolutions from the Newark black power conference in July 1967. Observers at the time noted that few of the delegates knew what these resolutions said because they were secret. *New Republic*, September 16, 1967.

7. *Nation*, September 25, 1967.

8. Quote in *Ramparts*, November 1967. Also, *New York Times*, September 5, 1967; and Sanford Gottlieb, "Report on National Conference for New Politics," 1967, box 11, folder 5, AOW.

9. One exception is S. Hall, "On the Tail of the Panther."

10. Vigil, *Crusade for Justice*, 39, 53; and *New Republic*, September 16, 1967.

11. Scholars once routinely viewed black power adherents as hostile to collaboration. While that may have been the case with most whites, a few historians now argue that black power facilitated some multiracial coalition building among ethnic minorities. See Ogbar, *Black Power*, chap. 6; Pulido, *Black, Brown, Yellow, and Left*; Murch, *Living for the City*; and Araiza, "'For Freedom of Other Men.'" The extent of this cooperation can be overstated, however, and virtually no one suggests that the antiwar movement had the same impact.

12. Quote in *Time*, July 1, 1966. For other representative samples, see *Newsweek*, July 11, 1966; and *Saturday Evening Post*, September 10, 1966.

13. Carmichael and Hamilton, *Black Power*; and Ogbar, *Black Power*, 124–25.

14. Tijerina, *They Called Me "King Tiger,"* 29 quote, chaps. 1–2; Oropeza, "The Heart of Chicano History," 52. One-third of U.S. territory, from the Northern Rockies and the Pacific Northwest to Texas and the Southwest, was once Mexico before the war. There is a rich literature on the conflicts over land grants in the Southwest, from the clashing of legal and economic cultures to the Mexican vigilante efforts of Las Gorras Blancas (the White Caps) and Mano Negra (Black Hand). More than 150 years after the signing of the Treaty of Guadalupe Hidalgo, such disputes continue to show up in courtrooms. Montoya, *Translating Property*; Ebright, *Land Grants and Lawsuits in Northern New Mexico*; Briggs and Van Ness, *Land, Water, and Culture*; Keleher, *Maxwell Land Grant*; G. Hall, *Four Leagues of Pecos*; Taylor, *O. P. McMains and the Maxwell Land Grant Conflict*; Rosenbaum, *Mexicano Resistance in the Southwest*; Schlesinger, "Las Blancas Gorras, 1889–1891," 87–143; and Griswold del Castillo, *The Treaty of Guadalupe Hidalgo*.

15. Notes on Alianza formation, February 2, 1963, and *Albuquerque North Valley News*, August 27, 1964, both in box 1, folder 1, RLT; and Busto, *King Tiger*, 35–58.

16. Quotes in Oropeza, "The Heart of Chicano History," 52; and Gardner, *!Grito!*, 131.

17. Tijerina, *They Called Me "King Tiger,"* xvi–xvii. See also Acuña, *Occupied America*, 14–15.

18. Quotes in Nabokov, *Tijerina and the Courthouse Raid*, 50–51; and Oropeza, "The Heart of Chicano History," 60. Also, Gardner, *Grito!*, chap. 9.

19. Busto, *King Tiger*, 59–61. For more detailed narratives of Tierra Amarilla, including the courtroom case to come later, see Gardner, *Grito!*; Nabokov, *Tijerina and the Courthouse Raid*; and Blawis, *Tijerina and the Land Grants*. Unhappy with these accounts, Tijerina provides his own retelling, first published in Spanish, and then in English. Tijerina, *Mi Lucha por La Tierra*, later translated into Tijerina, *They Called Me "King Tiger,"* trans. Gutiérrez.

20. *Santa Fe New Mexican*, December 29, 1967; and Nabokov, *Tijerina and the Courthouse Raid*, 217.

21. Nabokov, *Tijerina and the Courthouse Raid*, 157–58; and Lloyd, "Behind the

Mask of Middle-Class Decency." For an interesting discussion of the "bandido" trope in Chicano mythology, see Bebout, *Mythohistorical Interventions*, 84–92. While most contemporary coverage of Tijerina was quite negative in New Mexico's daily newspapers and the national press, scholars and biographers are often too sympathetic to Tijerina, glossing over his contradictions. See Mariscal, *Brown-Eyed Children of the Sun*; Busto, *King Tiger*; Nabokov, *Tijerina and the Courthouse Raid*; Blawis, *Tijerina and the Land Grants*; Acuña, *Occupied America*, 369; and Gómez-Quiñones, *Chicano Politics*, 115–18.

22. Gardner, *¡Grito!*, 256–57. For a more balanced treatment of Tijerina as a "memory entrepreneur," see Oropeza, "The Heart of Chicano History," 49–67.

23. *Movement*, August 1967.

24. Quote by Maria Varela, interview by author. Also, Blawis, *Tijerina and the Land Grants*, 97; Gardner, *¡Grito!*, 172–73, 204–6; Nabokov, *Tijerina and the Courthouse Raid*, 183–84; *Movement*, August 1967; and *New York Times*, July 16, 1967.

25. Gardner, *¡Grito!*, 208.

26. Quote in Blawis, *Tijerina and the Land Grants*, 99.

27. *Albuquerque Journal*, September 11, 1967, quoted in FBI memo, n.d., box 2, folder 20, RLT.

28. Reies Tijerina, interview by Elsa Knight Thompson, in *Testimonio*, ed. F. Rosales, 316.

29. Ibid., 311–13, 315–18; Tijerina, *They Called Me "King Tiger,"* 17–62; Nabokov, *Tijerina and the Courthouse Raid*, 217; and Gardner, *¡Grito!*, 203–4.

30. Quote in Tijerina letter to Varela, September 14, 1967, box 42, folder 1, RLT. Also, Maria Varela, interview by author; and Blawis, *Tijerina and the Land Grants*, 98–99. Sara Evans also argues that the convention was a turning point for women's liberation activists, whose Women's Caucus met considerable condescension from the NCNP's mostly male organizers. *Personal Politics*, 197–99.

31. Varela letter to Tijerina, September 7, 1967, box 42, folder 1, RLT; Maria Varela, interview by author; and Araiza, "'For Freedom of Other Men,'" 67.

32. Gardner, *¡Grito!*, 220.

33. Ibid., 221–23; Nabokov, *Tijerina and the Courthouse Raid*, 222–23; and Maria Varela, interview by author.

34. SAC, Albuquerque memo (AQ 100-2567), December 27, 1967, box 2, folder 23, RLT; Reies López Tijerina, interview by James Mosby, June 12, 1968, Washington, D.C., RBOHC; Nabokov, *Tijerina and the Courthouse Raid*, 222; Maria Varela and Ethel Minor, interviews by author; and Araiza, "'For Freedom of Other Men,'" 66.

35. Arthur Vasquez to Kenneth Smith memo, "The Federal Alliance: Sponsor of Convention," 12, n.d., box 3, folder 1, RLT.

36. Gardner, *¡Grito!*, 209, 222–25; Nabokov, *Tijerina and the Courthouse Raid*, 222–24; Ethel Minor, interview by author; and Karenga, "People of Color: We Shall Survive," October 21, 1967, box 34, folder 24, and FBI memo "Mexican American Militancy," n.d., box 3, folder 1, both in RLT.

37. Ethel Minor, Maria Varela, and Freddie Greene, interviews by author; and Payne, *I've Got the Light of Freedom*, 281–83.

38. "Treaty of Peace, Harmony, and Mutual Assistance at Albuquerque" (em-

phasis in original), in Karenga, "People of Color: We Shall Survive," October 21, 1967, box 34, folder 24, RLT; Ethel Minor and Maria Varela, interviews by author; Nabokov, *Tijerina and the Courthouse Raid*, 225.

39. Maria Varela, interview by author; and Lewels, *The Use of the Media by the Chicano Movement*, 64–66.

40. The decision not to invite so-called militant leaders to the conference backfired as other more mainstream organizations declined to attend in protest. For example, MAPA's board voted to boycott the conference, fifty-eight to five, as did the Latin American Civic Association. Cesar Chavez also chose not to go. *Carta Editorial*, October 24, 1967, box 42, folder 1, RLT; and *People's World*, November 11, 1967. See also Vigil, *Crusade for Justice*, 42–43; and Pycior, *LBJ & Mexican Americans*, 207–14.

41. "Youth Organizers Meet in New Mexico," *La Raza*, October 29, 1967, in *Testimonio*, ed. F. Rosales, 305; and FBI memo "Mexican American Militancy," n.d., box 3, folder 1, RLT.

42. Nabokov, *Tijerina and the Courthouse Raid*, 228–29; Karenga telegram to Governor David Cargo, January 9, 1968, Karenga letter to Tijerina, January 3, 1968, Karenga letter to Eduardo Chavez, January 17, 1968, box 34, folder 24, King telegrams to Tijerina, January 8 and March 5, 1968, folder 20, SNCC telegrams to Alianza, January 5, 7 and 9, 1968, SNCC telegram to Cargo, January 9, 1968, folder 36, and "Stokely Carmichael—Internal Security," February 26, 1968, and March 5, 1968, box 3, folders 4, 5, all in RLT; and *San Francisco Chronicle*, March 9, 1968.

43. *Rocky Mountain News*, September 29, 1965.

44. Vigil, *Crusade for Justice*, 8.

45. Romero, "Wearing the Red, White, and Blue Trunks of Aztlán," 94–99; Vigil, *Crusade for Justice*, 5, 8–10; Rudy Gonzales and Gerry Gonzales, interview by author; *Denver Post*, June 26, 1955; and *Rocky Mountain Life*, February 1948. The Viva Kennedy clubs influenced numerous Mexican American politicians from liberals such Albert Peña and Henry B. Gonzalez of San Antonio to future Chicano radicals like Corky Gonzales. I. García, *Viva Kennedy*, 175.

46. *Viva!*, May 20, 1964, courtesy of Ernesto Vigil.

47. Ibid.

48. Quote in *Rocky Mountain News*, September 29, 1965. See also Gerry and Rudy Gonzales, interview by author; *Viva!*, May 20, 1964; *Crusade for Justice Newsletter*, May 1966, box 3, "Prison info," RCG; Gonzales, *Message to Aztlán*, xxii–xxiv; and Vigil, *Crusade for Justice*, 19–26.

49. *Denver Post*, February 14, 1966.

50. *Rocky Mountain News*, February 14, April 21 and 23, and August 5, 1966; *Crusade for Justice Newsletter*, May 1966, box 3, "Prison Info," RCG; and Vigil, *Crusade for Justice*, 26–27.

51. *El Gallo*, June 23, 1967.

52. *Movement*, August 1967.

53. Vigil, *Crusade for Justice*, 26–27; and Marín, "Rodolfo 'Corky' Gonzales," 108–9.

54. Gonzales, "I Am Joaquin" and "The Revolutionist," in *Message to Aztlán*, ed. Esquibel, 16–29, 96–134.

55. Quote by Gonzales, "Address to 'Stop The War' Rally," August 6, 1966, RCG. Also, FBI memo, "Crusade for Justice," Denver field office no. 100-9365, May 10, 1968, CJ; Crusade timeline, n.d. [1971], both in RCG; and Oropeza, *¡Raza Sí! ¡Guerra No!*, 74–76.

56. *Movement*, August 1967.

57. Quote in Oropeza, *¡Raza Sí! ¡Guerra No!*, 75–76. Also, Jessica Bordeaux-Vigil, interview by author; *El Gallo*, 1967–68; and Gould, "The Life and Times of Richard Castro," 108–11.

58. Quote in *El Gallo*, July 28, 1967. Also, Lauren Watson, interview by author; Crusade timeline, n.d. [1971], RCG; Vigil, *Crusade for Justice*, 29–30, 33–35; and Oropeza, *¡Raza Sí! ¡Guerra No!*, 76.

59. "National Field Staff," July 20 and September 1, 1967, box 3, folder 18, LWP; *El Gallo*, October 1, 1967; Gitlin, *The Sixties*, 245; and Vigil, *Crusade for Justice*, 39.

60. *El Gallo*, October 1, 1967; and Vigil, *Crusade for Justice*, 39.

61. Ralph Ramirez, Gloria Arellanes, and Carlos Montes, interviews by author; E. Chávez, *¡Mi Raza Primero!*, 43–46; Pulido, *Black, Brown, Yellow, and Left*, 116–17; and Reyes, *Land of a Thousand Dances*.

62. *La Raza*, June 7, 1968; *Chicano Student News*, March 15, 1968; Ralph Ramirez, Gloria Arellanes, and Carlos Montes, interviews by author; E. Chávez, *¡Mi Raza Primero!*, 46–47; Oropeza, *¡Raza Sí! ¡Guerra No!*, 77; and M. García, *Blowout!*

63. José Angel Gutiérrez, interview by author; Behnken, *Fighting Their Own Battles*, 161–63; and Navarro, *Mexican American Youth Organization*, chap. 3.

64. J. Gutiérrez, *The Making of a Chicano Militant*, 93 quotes, 97, 114; José Angel Gutiérrez, interview by author; Behnken, *Fighting Their Own Battles*, 189; Montejano, *Quixote's Soldiers*, chaps. 3–5; and Oropeza, *¡Raza Sí! ¡Guerra No!*, 77–79.

65. *Movement*, August 1967.

66. *El Gallo*, 1967–1968; *Movement*, August 1967; and Vigil, *Crusade for Justice*, 31–33.

67. *People's World*, October 21, 28 and November 11, 1967; FBI memo, "Crusade for Justice," Denver field office no. 100-9365, May 10, 1968, CJ; Vigil, *Crusade for Justice*, 41–43; Pycior, *LBJ & Mexican Americans*, 207–14; Muñoz, *Youth, Identity and Power*, 99–100; and Kaplowitz, *LULAC*, 117–20.

Chapter 4

1. King, "Press conference transcript," December 4, 1967.

2. Although there had been extensive behind-the-scenes discussions among SCLC officials about the use of a central encampment to help dramatize poverty and coordinate action, King gave few such details during this press conference. In response to a reporter's question, he suggested that demonstrators might pitch tents in different parts of the city. King, "Press conference transcript," December 4, 1967; and *New York Times*, December 5, 1967.

3. Fager, *Uncertain Resurrection*, 141; Fairclough, *To Redeem the Soul*, 386–88; Ling, *Martin Luther King Jr.*, 298–301; T. Kahn, "Why the Poor People's Campaign

Failed," 50–55; and "Mini-city That Failed," 35. Newspaper accounts often drove this conclusion.

4. Fager *Uncertain Resurrection*, 13–17; Honey, *Going Down Jericho Road*, 184–85; Fairclough, *To Redeem the Soul*, 367–69; *Chicago Tribune*, August 17, 1967, and March 30, 1968; *Atlanta Constitution*, August 17, 1967, and March 29, 1968; *Time*, August 25, 1967; *Newsweek*, August 28, 1967; *U.S. News & World Report*, August 28, 1967, and April 8, 1968; *New York Times*, March 29–30, 1968; *Los Angeles Times*, March 29 and April 1, 1968; *Washington Post*, March 29 and April 3, 1968.

5. Fairclough, *To Redeem the Soul*, 49–50.

6. Sugrue, *The Origins of the Urban Crisis*, 259; and Mumford, *Newark*, 98.

7. Martin Luther King Jr. telegram to President Johnson, July 25, 1967, 3, box 122, folder 8, part 3, reel 4, frames 0002–0005, RSCLC. King had received private reports that worse violence could be expected in other cities, including two in which SCLC was active, Cleveland and Chicago. Garrow, *Bearing the Cross*, 570.

8. Officially the National Advisory Commission on Civil Disorders, the commission informally bore the name of chairman Otto Kerner, governor of Illinois. United States, *Report of the National Advisory Commission on Civil Disorders*; and New Jersey Governor's Commission on Civil Disorders, *Report for Action*.

9. Quote in *Washington Post*, August 14, 1967. A Lou Harris poll reported that substantial majorities of blacks and whites supported such programs, including 66 percent of whites backing large federal work projects and 59 percent agreeing with a federal program to exterminate rats.

10. "The Racial Crisis: A Consensus," *Newsweek*, August 21, 1967, 15–18; and Perlstein, *Nixonland*, 197–98.

11. Garrow, *Bearing the Cross*, 572.

12. Martin Luther King Jr., "The Crisis in America's Cities: Address at the [Eleventh] Annual Convention of the Southern Christian Leadership Conference," August 15, 1967, box 28, folder 37, RSCLC.

13. Wofford, *Of Kennedys and Kings*, 231.

14. Garrow, *Bearing the Cross*, 576–77.

15. *Atlanta Constitution*, *New York Times*, and *Chicago Tribune*, all August 17, 1967.

16. Hoover had tried for years to destroy King, gathering data on the SCLC leader's personal transgressions, his associations with former Communist Party members (Stanley Levison and Harry Wachtel), and his increasingly radical stances on the war and capitalism. Eventually, the Poor People's Campaign gave the bureau an opportunity to greatly expand COINTELPRO, first established in 1956, against the freedom struggle—including massive surveillance, informants, and dirty tricks. In fact, this aspect has emerged as a dominant historiographical theme in the limited scholarship of the campaign. See McKnight, *The Last Crusade*; and Vigil, *Crusade for Justice*, 54–63.

17. Tom Offenburger, interview by Kay Shannon, RBOHC; "The Poor People's March on Washington" and "Manual for Marchers," [1966], box 2101, Poor People's March on Washington folder, PNWRO; and Kornbluh, *The Battle for Welfare Rights*, 53. Offenburger recalled a frustrated King musing aloud after addressing a

group of "very cold and really uncomprehending" businessmen. "The only way to get the country to look at poverty was to get a large number of very poor people in the country to go to Washington, and possibly to some other large cities," Offenburger said. "I can remember him talking about it—he said, 'We ought to come in mule carts, in old trucks, any kind of transportation people can get their hands on. People ought to come to Washington, sit down if necessary in the middle of the street and say, "We are here; we are poor; we don't have any money; you have made us this way; you keep us down this way; and we've come to stay until you do something about it."'"

18. Marian Wright Edelman in *Voices of Freedom*, ed. Hampton and Fayer, 452.

19. Marian Wright Edelman quote in ibid., 453. See also Kotz, *Judgment Days*, 383; Dittmer, *Local People*, 373–74; Garrow, *Bearing the Cross*, 578; and U.S. Congress, *Examination of the War on Poverty, Part 2*, 642–58.

20. Tom Offenburger, interview by Kay Shannon, RBOHC.

21. Katherine Shannon, interview by Claudia Rawles; McGraw, "An Interview with Andrew J. Young," 327; and Barber, *Marching on Washington*, 89–106. See also Daniels, *The Bonus March*; and Lisio, *The President and Protest*.

22. McGraw, "An Interview with Andrew J. Young," 327.

23. Andrew Young, interview by Kay Shannon, RBOHC; William Rutherford and Stanley Levison, telephone conversation, June 2, 1968, SL; Garrow, *Bearing the Cross*, 578; and Fairclough, *To Redeem the Soul*, 358.

24. King, Levison, Young, and Abernathy, telephone conversation, January 19, 1967, SL; Tom Offenburger and Al Sampson, interviews by Kay Shannon, RBOHC; and Fairclough, *To Redeem the Soul*, 335. Gallup and Harris polls both suggested that a clear majority of Americans supported the war throughout 1967, ranging from a high of 71 percent in February to a low of 58 percent in late September. These numbers began to shift markedly, however, after the Tet Offensive, a massive attack by North Vietnamese troops and allies in January 1968. Fierce battles engulfed five of six major South Vietnamese cities, and a few were taken temporarily. Rather than a major military victory, Tet was a political coup, in that it demonstrated a large gap between reality and U.S. military-reported conditions. By March 1968, 49 percent of Americans believed the war was an "error." *New York Times*, February 27, May 17, August 29, October 3, November 11, and December 11 and 31, 1967, and March 10, 1968; and M. Young, *The Vietnam Wars*, 216–25.

25. Branch, *At Canaan's Edge*, 672.

26. Jackson's opposition turned out to be ironic, considering the often-positive publicity he received during the campaign itself and then his demotion by Abernathy before Resurrection City fell apart. For example, see "Emerging Rights Leader: Jesse Louis Jackson," *New York Times*, May 24, 1968; *Los Angeles Sentinel*, June 27, 1968; "Jesse Jackson Emerging as Poor Campaign's Hero," *Chicago Daily Defender*, June 1, 1968; and J. Jackson, "Resurrection City."

27. Bayard Rustin, "Memo on the Spring Protest in Washington, D.C.," in *Down the Line*, ed. Rustin, 204. See also Rustin, "From Protest to Politics," *Commentary*, February 1965, 25–31.

28. Quote in Marian Logan in *Voices of Freedom*, ed. Hampton and Fayer, 455.

Rustin, "The Lessons of the Long Hot Summer," "Minorities: The War Amidst Poverty," and "Memo on the Spring Protest in Washington, D.C.," in *Down the Line*, ed. Rustin, 187–99, 200–201, 202–5; Marian Logan memo to Martin Luther King Jr., March 8, 1968, box 40, folder 3, part 2, reel 6, frames 360–65, and executive committee meeting minutes, December 27, 1967, box 49, folder 11, part 2, reel 13, frames 0034–0043, both in RSCLC; Garrow, *Bearing the Cross*, 584–85; and A. Young, *An Easy Burden*, 444.

29. King, Statement to the National Advisory Commission on Civil Disorders, October 23, 1967, box 13, Speeches, MLK; and *New York Times, Los Angeles Times,* and *Washington Post*, October 24, 1967.

30. *Washington Post*, October 26, 1967.

31. *Washington Post*, December 5, 1967; *Chicago Tribune*, December 5, 1967; *Wall Street Journal*, December 5, 1967; *Atlanta Constitution*, December 5–6, 1967; *New York Times*, December 5, 1967, and March 5, 1968; *Los Angeles Times*, March 5, 1968; *New York Amsterdam News*, December 9 and 23, 1967; *Chicago Defender*, December 7, 12, and 14, 1967; and *Baltimore Afro-American*, December 9 and 23, 1967; José Yglesias, "Dr. King's March on Washington, Part II," *New York Times Magazine*, March 31, 1968; and *U.S. News & World Report*, March 18, 1968.

32. King, "Press conference transcript," December 4, 1967.

33. Bernard Lafayette, interview by author.

34. Published articles and surviving press conference transcripts suggest no interest in the multiracial angle—even to debunk King's claims. For instance, during the December 4 press conference, no one asked for elaboration on the campaign's nonblack participation. The next day, only the *Los Angeles Times* and *Atlanta Constitution* mentioned Mexican Americans or American Indians, the *Times* adding—with no evidence—that "there is little indication that such assistance from those quarters is forthcoming." *Los Angeles Times*, December 5, 1967; and King, "Press conference transcript," December 4, 1967.

35. Press release, January 9, 1968, box 122, folder 9, RSCLC; and T. Jackson, *From Civil Rights to Human Rights*, 341.

36. Tijerina letter to King, September 7, 1967, box 34, folder 20, RLT; *El Gallo*, August 31, 1967; and Vigil, *Crusade for Justice*, 39–40.

37. SCLC press release, December 13, 1967, box 122, folder 8, and Bill Rutherford letter to King, September 21, 1967, box 5, folder 15, both in RSCLC; *New York Times*, December 5 and 14, 1967; and Garrow, *Bearing the Cross*, 583–87. Rutherford was successful in making SCLC staff more accountable for expenditures—and therefore made the organization more efficient—but not without stepping on some toes. Rutherford memos to SCLC Steering Committee, December 8 and 11, 1967, box 48, folder 3, and Hosea Williams memo to Rutherford, December 15, 1967, box 57, folder 2, all in RSCLC.

38. Lafayette went to Selma in 1963 as a field secretary with SNCC—two years before James Bevel convinced King and SCLC to go there. Bernard Lafayette, interview by author; and Carson, *In Struggle*, 157.

39. King letter to Lafayette, 1967, box 4, folder 26, and SCLC press release, December 13, 1967, box 122, folder 8, both in RSCLC; Bernard Lafayette, interview by

author; Tom Houck, interview by Kay Shannon, RBOHC; *New York Times*, December 14, 1967; and Carson, *In Struggle*, 21, 157. For more on Lafayette's activism, see Arsenault, *Freedom Riders*; and Halberstam, *The Children*.

40. "Why We Need to Go to Washington" press conference transcript, January 16, 1968, 6, box 14, Speeches, MLK.

41. Bernard Lafayette memo to SCLC staff, January 20, 1968, box 34, folder 19, RSCLC; Bernard Lafayette, interview by author; Tom Houck, interview by Kay Shannon, RBOHC; and *Washington Post*, January 17, 1968.

42. AFSC had a twenty-year relationship with American Indian activists in the Pacific Northwest fighting relocation and termination of federal tribal recognition and became the first prominent non-Indian organization to support tribal fights with local authorities over fishing rights in ancestral waters. Starting in 1965, AFSC staff and volunteers began to compile material on the fishing rights struggle to help inform the organization's stance, resulting in the book *Uncommon Controversy*. Although the editors ensured readers that the book did "not speak for any of the Indians, Indian groups, public agencies or private agencies or groups" involved in the fishing rights struggle, the report did help legitimate the fight in white peace and civil rights circles. "Resumé of Pacific Northwest Regional Indian Program for Fundraising Purposes," in Pacific Northwest Regional Office box, "Indian Program—General" folder, AFSCA; AFSC, *Uncommon Controversy*; and C. Wilkinson, *Messages from Frank's Landing*, 46.

43. Quote by Tom Houck, interview by Kay Shannon, RBOHC. Also, Bernard Lafayette, interview by author; Ernie Austin, interview by Kay Shannon, RBOHC; Barbara Moffett memo to Warren Witte, February 23, 1968, CRD Administration folder 32557, "Poor People's Campaign: General, Planning Materials—Regional, 1968," Steve Cary memo, February 9, 1968, and Eleanor Eaton memo to Barbara Moffett, February 26, 1968, CRD Administration folder 32556, "Poor People's Campaign: General, Planning Materials," and Eleanor Eaton memo to National Community Relations Committee, CRD Administration folder 49038, "Housing and Urban Affairs 1970—United Farm Workers Organizing Committee," all in AFSCA; Pam Coe, of AFSC's American Indian Program, letter to Tom Houck, March 1, 1968, box 177, folder 18, RSCLC; and Branch, *At Canaan's Edge*, 716. For criticism of SCLC's exploitation of existing grass-roots work, see Carson, *In Struggle*, 62–63, 153–64; Payne, *I've Got the Light of Freedom*, 92–93, 99; Branch, *Parting the Waters*, 558, 578–79; Carmichael with Thelwell, *Ready for Revolution*, 305, 445–46; and Ransby, *Ella Baker and the Black Freedom Movement*, 282–83, 345–46.

44. Tom Houck, interview by Kay Shannon, RBOHC.

45. Tillie Walker, director of United Scholarship Service, interview by Kay Shannon, RBOHC; and Cobb, *Native Activism*, 150, 171–72. Other prominent women organizers included Geraldine Smith of the NWRO and Carol Williams of the Southern Consumer Cooperative. Honey, *Going Down Jericho Road*, 184.

46. "Action Committee Meeting" transcript, February 11, 1968, box 34, folder 15, MLK.

47. *Los Angeles Times* and *Atlanta Constitution*, both December 6, 1967.

48. T. Jackson, *From Civil Rights to Human Rights*, 341–45; Fairclough, *To Redeem the Soul*, 358–59, 362; and Garrow, *Bearing the Cross*, 590–93, 600–604.

49. Executive staff meeting transcript, December 27, 1967, box 49, folder 11, RSCLC; Tom Offenburger, interview by Kay Shannon, RBOHC; Garrow, *Bearing the Cross*, 590–91; and "Action Committee Meeting" transcript, February 11, 1968, box 34, folder 15, MLK.

50. Bill Rutherford letter to Harry Wachtel, January 25, 1968, box 56, folder 10, RSCLC. See also King telegram to Colin Bell, December 6, 1967, CRD Administration folder 32556, "Poor People's Campaign: General, Planning Materials," AFSCA.

51. For instance, the AFSC Family Aid Fund helped black families, such as the Carters of Sunflower County, Mississippi, withstand financial and physical intimidation in order to send their children to white schools. And in Florida, the local Friends society in St. Petersburg played a key supporting role by offering not only funds but also literacy classes and meeting space to striking sanitation workers. Curry, *Silver Rights*, xxiii, 59, 132–33, 138, 140, 143–45, 208–9; and Paulson and Stiff, "An Empty Victory: The St. Petersburg Sanitation Strike, 1968," 421–33. Remarkably, there is no full study devoted to AFSC's activities in civil rights. In fact, most scholars give AFSC only passing mention.

52. *Quaker Service: Bulletin of American Friends Service Committee*, Summer 1968.

53. Marjorie Penney letter to Andrew Young, December 19, 1967, box 39, folder 23, part 2, reel 6, frame 0011, RSCLC. Penney knew King from his seminary days in Chester, Pennsylvania, and encouraged King to make Philadelphia his foray into the North. Countryman, *Up South*, 175–77.

54. Maria Pappalardo and Eleanor Eaton, "Some Rough Notes on AFSC Staff Discussion," January 5, 1968; Barbara Moffett letter to Bernard Lafayette, January 9, 1968; Stewart Meacham memo to Moffett, January 12, 1968; Charlotte Meacham memo to Lafayette and Bill Rutherford, January 24, 1968; Pappalardo memo to Lafayette and Rutherford, January 24, 1968; Steve Cary memo, February 9, 1968; Eleanor Eaton memo to Barbara Moffett, February 26, 1968; and Eleanor Eaton letter to Tom Houck, February 26, 1968, all in CRD Administration folder 32556, "Poor People's Campaign: General, Planning Materials," AFSCA.

55. Barbara Moffett memo to Martin Luther King Jr. and Harry Wachtel, February 22, 1968, box 39, folder 23, part 2, reel 6, frames 0238–0242, RSCLC; and Eleanor Eaton memo to Barbara Moffett, February 21, 1968, "SCLC's Second Draft 'Manifesto,'" CRD Administration folder 32556, "Poor People's Campaign: General, Planning Materials," AFSCA.

56. I use the term "welfare" as shorthand for the original federal program Aid for Families with Dependent Children (AFDC), established under the New Deal in 1935, and the corresponding system of local and state programs. For more on the grass-roots nature of the NWRO and its treatment of "poor women and men as thinkers as well as actors," see Kornbluh, *The Battle for Welfare Rights*, 9, "To Fulfill Their 'Rightly Needs,'" 76–113, and "Black Buying Power: Welfare Rights, Consumerism, and Northern Protest," in *Freedom North*, ed. Theoharis and Woodard, 199–222; and Nadasen, *Welfare Warriors*. Although touching on the NWRO's grass-

roots nature, older studies privilege the national organization and executive director George Wiley. See Kotz and Kotz, *A Passion for Equality*; West, *The National Welfare Rights Movement*; and Piven and Cloward, *Poor People's Movements*, 264–361.

57. "The Poor People's March on Washington" and "Manual for Marchers," both n.d., and George Wiley and Ed Day, telephone transcript, September 15, 1966, Poor People's March folder, box 2101, PNWRO; and *New York Times*, August 12, 1966. King discussed the "guaranteed income" in his last book, written in early 1967, but only began to highlight it in his speeches for the campaign in the fall. *Where Do We Go from Here*, 162–65, 189.

58. Designed in response to a perceived "welfare crisis," the Social Security Amendments of 1967 were designed to reduce the welfare rolls. The legislation required most adult welfare recipients to work for wages or enroll in a training program or risk losing their benefits; capped the percentage of a state's population that could receive federal public assistance; and mandated states to raise their standards of need, the all-important measure used by governments to judge the adequacy of their grants. Despite fierce opposition from the NWRO and its allies, Congress passed the package of somewhat contradictory amendments. Kornbluh, *The Battle for Welfare Rights*, 96–100.

59. Tim Sampson, interview by Nick Kotz, box 25, NK.

60. Ibid.

61. George Wiley letter to Andrew Young, March 25, 1968, box 40, folder 3, part 2, reel 6, frames 354–55, RSCLC.

62. Tim Sampson, interview by Nick Kotz, box 25, NK.

63. George Wiley letter to Andrew Young, March 25, 1968, box 40, folder 3, part 2, reel 6, frames 354–55, RSCLC; *Washington Post*, February 6, 1968; West, *The National Welfare Rights Movement*, 214–15; Nadasen, *Welfare Warriors*, 71–72; and *NOW!*, February 23, 1968, in "Tim Sampson set—newsletters," box 8, NK. Demonstrating their independence, the NWRO's February and March newsletters trumpet King's support for welfare legislation, yet make no mention of the campaign.

64. King, "Pre-Washington Campaign," February 16, 1968, Selma, Alabama, box 14, Speeches, MLK. In speech after speech, whether it was a press conference or a church-based address in SCLC's "people-to-people" campaign recruitment tours, King used similarly gendered language. Jobs in the most traditional sense of the word were front and center.

65. Nadasen, *Welfare Warriors*, 166.

66. Also, U.S. Congress, House, Subcommittee on Fiscal Policy of the Joint Economic Committee, *Income Maintenance Programs*, 58–86; and Kornbluh, *The Battle for Welfare Rights*, 37–38, 48, 50–51, 60–61, 96, 99, 112.

67. Finding King's position on Vietnam untenable, Meany reaffirmed support for the war. We "in the AFL-CIO are neither 'hawk' nor 'dove—nor 'chicken,'" declared Meany. "We believe in human freedom and in democracy—not just for ourselves but for everyone who prefers to live under such a system." *American Federationist*, January 1968. Such sentiment certainly reflected the war positions of many predominantly white and male craft unions. See Koscielski, *Divided Loyalties*, 17–54; and Wehrle, *Between a River and a Mountain*.

68. Chase, "Class Resurrection," 11–13; and Honey, *Going Down Jericho Road*, 185–86. Kevin Boyle argues Reuther did not commit the UAW because of the Johnson administration's general opposition to the march. *The UAW*, 242.

69. Certain "old left" unions, such as the United Electrical, Radio and Machine Workers (UE) and Mine-Mill, had called for an end to the war in 1965. In the next few years, other unions turned against the war, including the UPWA and UAW, the latter of which split from the AFL-CIO in the summer of 1968 over major policy differences. Organizations such as the Labor Leadership Assembly for Peace and the heavily working-class Vietnam Veterans against the War emerged. The latter reflected the polls from early 1968 that showed that nearly half of rank-and-file union members considered the war a "mistake." P. Levy, *The New Left and Labor in the 1960s*, 48, 52–58; Koscielski, *Divided Loyalties*, 55–87; Boyle, *The UAW*, 255; Lannon and Rogoff, "We Shall Not Remain Silent," 536–44; *Packinghouse Worker*, May 1968; *New York Times*, January 3 and 5, 1968; and *Washington Post*, January 3, 1968.

70. *New York Times*, May 28, 1968.

71. *UAW Solidarity*, August 1968; *Steel Labor*, June and July 1968; *United Mine Workers Journal*, July 1, 1968; *Wall Street Journal*, May 14, 1968; *Packinghouse Worker*, March, April, May, and July 1968; and *Daily Worker*, March 19, 1968.

72. Chavez to Marcos Muñoz, April 3, 1968, box 5, folder 6, PUFW; *El Malcriado*, March 15 and April 1, 1968; Billy Hollins memo to Andrew Young, n.d., box 49, folder 3, part 2, reel 12, frame 0767, RSCLC; and Levison and Rutherford, telephone conversations, May 8 and 10, 1968, SL.

73. Garrow, *Bearing the Cross*, 607.

74. José Angel Gutiérrez, interview by author.

75. Yglesias, "Dr. King's March on Washington, Part II," 60.

76. Ibid., 60. King specifically cited the Selma campaign of 1965 as an example. Although told by President Johnson and others that a voting rights act could not be passed, King led a large militant demonstration that forced government officials to find a solution.

77. Yglesias, "Dr. King's March on Washington, Part II," March 31, 1968; and Fairclough, *To Redeem the Soul*, 363.

78. Tom Houck, interview by Kay Shannon, RBOHC; and J. Jackson, "Resurrection City."

79. Journalists all but ignored the conference. King's press conference after the gathering received little attention. Of prominent newspapers, only the *New York Times*, *Atlanta Constitution*, *Chicago Defender*, and *Pittsburgh Courier* mention the Minority Group Conference—the *Times* on page 36, the *Constitution* within a larger article on King's presidential preferences, and the *Defender* as a barely rewritten press release. Only the *Courier* recognized the conference as "a historic meeting of American minority group leaders." *New York Times*, March 15, 1968; *Atlanta Constitution*, March 15, 1968; *Chicago Daily Defender*, March 23–29, 1968; and *Pittsburgh Courier*, March 30, 1968. Not even Atlanta's local black newspaper, the *Atlanta Daily World*, mentions the gathering. Taylor Branch and Thomas Jackson do not dismiss the conference outright, but both gloss over its historic significance. Branch, *At Canaan's Edge*, 715–17; and Jackson, *From Civil Rights to Human Rights*, 348–49.

80. Eleanor Eaton memo to Barbara Moffett, April 2, 1968, CRD Administration folder 32556, AFSCA; "American Indians, Poor Whites, Spanish-Americans Join Poor People's Washington Campaign," SCLC release, March 15, 1968, Poor People's Campaign folder, box 2101, PNWRO; "Participants of Minority Group Conference," March 14, 1968, box 179, folder 11, part 4, reel 27, frames 01009–01016, RSCLC; and Tom Houck, interview by Kay Shannon, RBOHC.

81. Eleanor Eaton memo to Barbara Moffett, April 2, 1968, CRD Administration folder 32556, AFSCA; "American Indians, Poor Whites, Spanish-Americans Join Poor People's Washington Campaign," SCLC release, March 15, 1968, Poor People's Campaign folder, box 2101, PNWRO; and "Participants of Minority Group Conference," March 14, 1968, box 179, folder 11, part 4, reel 27, frames 01009–01016, RSCLC.

82. Quotes in Eleanor Eaton memo to Barbara Moffett, April 2, 1968, CRD Administration folder 32556, AFSCA. Also, Tom Houck, interview by Kay Shannon, RBOHC; and Bernard Lafayette, interview by author.

83. Quotes in Eleanor Eaton memo to Barbara Moffett, April 2, 1968, CRD Administration folder 32556, AFSCA. Also, José Angel Gutiérrez, interview by author; and Tom Houck and Ernie Austin, interviews by Kay Shannon, RBOHC.

84. Quote in "American Indians, Poor Whites, Spanish-Americans Join Poor People's Washington Campaign," SCLC release, March 15, 1968, Poor People's Campaign folder, box 2101, PNWRO. Also, Eleanor Eaton memo to Barbara Moffett, April 2, 1968, CRD Administration folder 32556, AFSCA.

85. M. García, *Memories*, 216.

86. Quotes in *San Antonio Inferno*, April 1968, and Nabokov, *Tijerina and the Courthouse Raid*, 242. As became clear in the months to come, Tijerina believed King had promised to create a black demand for a return of southern land, parallel to Mexican Americans' land demands—something Abernathy and SCLC never pursued. Nabokov, *Tijerina and the Courthouse Raid*, 248–49.

87. This, of course, was before activists such as Gutiérrez knew the extent of FBI surveillance of them and their activities. He apparently had been on an FBI and Texas Ranger watchdog list because of a so-called inflammatory speech for MAYO in 1967. José Angel Gutiérrez, interview by author. For more on the exceptional journey of Chicago activist Peggy Terry, see Sonnie and Tracy, *Hillbilly Nationalists*, chap. 1.

88. Tom Houck, interview by Kay Shannon, RBOHC; and *Jet*, May 16, 1968.

89. José Angel Gutiérrez, Bernard Lafayette, and Leo Nieto, interviews by author; Tom Houck, interview by Kay Shannon, RBOHC; "Mexican American to Join Rev. Martin Luther King March on Washington," Alianza press release, n.d., box 31, folder 28, and Della Rossa interview with Reies Tijerina, April 15, 1968, 1, box 52, folder 5, both in RLT; Tijerina, *They Called Me "King Tiger*," 103; and Doug Otto, "The Use of Converging Caravans in the Poor People's Campaign: An Historical and Descriptive View," November 17, 1968, in "PPC—Caravans" folder, no box number, AG.

90. Baldemar Velásquez, interview by author.

91. José Angel Gutiérrez, interview by author. He was joined by five other MAYO activists, including Mario Compean and Nacho Perez.

92. Despite their opposition to King's tactics, CORE and the Black Panther Party took a similar stance. Carmichael's decision stemmed from his friendship with King and his perception that they were on the same side politically, if not strategically.

93. Myles Horton letter to Andrew Young, April 5, 1968, box 177, folder 20, part 4, reel 26, frame 00614, RSCLC. Horton dictated the letter immediately after the conference, originally written to King, but did not mail the letter, readdressed to Young, until after his friend's death. His optimism had turned to despair temporarily: "I am too numbed by Martin's death to think clearly and I am sending it as dictated in the hopes that you who are his heirs may still find these ideas of some value. . . . The lights are dim in my world today."

94. The support of these religious organizations particularly alarmed FBI officials. "Both Protestant and Catholic leadership in Washington give clear signs of being almost totally unaware of the lawlessness and the violence-prone elements who will be involved in this march," wrote William Sullivan to Cartha DeLoach. "I would like to sow the idea that as eminent church leaders they have an enormous responsibility relative to assisting and maintaining law and order." Sullivan memo to DeLoach, March 20, 1968, POCAM.

95. *Evening Star*, March 13, 1968, and *Washington Daily News*, March 13 and 18, 1968, all in FBI newspaper clippings. Individual NAACP officials remained critical of the campaign, however, including the organization's treasurer, Alfred Baker Lewis. Wilkins later called for the campaign's cancellation. *Grenada (Miss.) Daily Sentinel*, March 20, 1968, FBI clipping file, POCAM .

96. Levison and Young, telephone conversation, March 4, 1968, SL.

97. *Birmingham News*, February 25, 1968, *Clarksdale Press Register*, *Laurel Leader Call*, and *Hattiesburg American*, March 20, 1968, all in FBI clipping file; SAC, Mobile to FBI director, March 12 and 19, 1968; SAC, Jackson to FBI director, March 11 and 19, 1968; SAC, Boston to FBI director, March 20, 1968; and "WSP Racial Matters," Chicago, March 19, 1968, and New York, March 26, 1968, all in POCAM; *New York Times*, March 27, 1968, and April 1, 1968; and Curry, *Silver Rights*, 164–66. Such successes were not universal, however. FBI reports from Richmond, Los Angeles, and Milwaukee, for instance, suggested that recruitment had been challenging or nonexistent. Although it appears that the FBI may not have had the best informants in Los Angeles, given the amount of activity surrounding King's March 16 visit and subsequent organizing by both Mexican American and African American activists in preparation for the campaign. SAC, Los Angeles to FBI director, March 12, 1968; "WSP Racial Matter," Los Angeles, March 19 and 26, 1968; SAC, Milwaukee to FBI director, March 28, 1968; and FBI memo, Richmond, March 12, 1968, all in POCAM.

98. United States, *Report of the National Advisory Commission on Civil Disorders*, 1–2. Of course, the explanation for the timing, location, and manifestation of the disorders was more complicated, including "relative deprivation" and "unmet promises of postwar liberalism." Sugrue, *Sweet Land of Liberty*, 348–49.

99. Other than a passing mention to making "good the promises of American democracy to all citizens—urban and rural, white and black, Spanish-surname, American Indian, and every minority group" in the report's introduction, the commission only addresses the black-white divide. United States, *Report of the National Advisory Commission*, 2. Missing among the growing list of burning cities was the June 1966 Division Street disorder in Chicago. It was an omission that reinforced the stereotype that nonblacks were somehow more passive than their black counterparts, a common claim made after Mexican Americans remained on the sidelines during the Watts uprising in 1965. Acuña, *Occupied America*, 334.

100. SCLC press release, March 4, 1968, 2, box 122, folder 10, RSCLC.

101. Lares Tresjan and Sandra Green, minutes of Committee of 100 meeting, n.d. [March 21, 1968?], 1–2, 4, "PPC Steering Committee," box 2101, PNWRO, emphasis in original.

102. Tresjan and Green, minutes of Committee of 100 meeting, n.d. [March 21, 1968?], 2, PNWRO.

103. Ibid., 1–2.

104. Ibid., 2–3, 5–6; and Leo Nieto, interview by author.

105. Marian Logan memo to Martin Luther King Jr., March 8, 1968, box 40, folder 3, part 2, reel 6, frames 360–65, RSCLC; and *Washington Post*, March 5, 1968.

106. Green, *Battling the Plantation Mentality*, 282.

107. Memphis has earned extensive scholarly attention because of King's death, as well as the prominence of labor activism and gendered rhetoric in the city's postwar freedom struggle. See Green, *Battling the Plantation Mentality*; and Honey, *Southern Labor and Black Civil Rights*, and *Black Workers Remember*. Honey and Joan Turner Beifuss offer the best narratives of the strike itself. Honey, *Going Down Jericho Road*; and Beifuss, *At the River I Stand*. See also Estes, *I Am a Man!*, 131–52; and McKnight, "The 1968 Memphis Sanitation Strike and the FBI," 138–56.

108. See T. Jackson, *From Civil Rights to Human Rights*; 349–52; Beifuss, *At the River I Stand*; and Honey, *Going Down Jericho Road*, and *Black Workers Remember*, 286–321.

109. A. Young, *An Easy Burden*, 449.

110. Ibid., 458.

111. "Dr. King Touring Nation in Poor People's Campaign," SCLC press release, March 17, 1968, box 122, folder 10, RSCLC; *Washington Post*, March 5, 1968; *Los Angeles Times*, March 12, 1968; *Columbia (S.C.) State*, March 23, 1968; A. Young, *An Easy Burden*, 451; and Branch, *At Canaan's Edge*, 718.

112. Quote in King, "Address at Mason Temple," box 14, Speeches, MLK. Also, Honey, *Going Down Jericho Road*, 296–304.

113. *Los Angeles Times*, April 1, 1968.

114. Cartoon in *Commercial-Appeal*, March 31, 1968. Also, *Memphis Commercial-Appeal* and *Memphis Press-Scimitar*, March 29, 30, 31, and April 1, 2, 1968; and Garrow, *Bearing the Cross*, 605–6, 610–11. For more detailed accounts of the March 28 violence and the fatal police shooting of suspected looter Larry Payne, unarmed and sixteen years old, see McKnight, *The Last Crusade*, 53–63; and Honey, *Going Down Jericho Road*, 343–61.

115. N. P. Callahan memo to FBI director, April 1, 1968, POCAM.

116. For more on Stennis's approach to civil rights opposition, especially in contrast to Eastland, see Crespino, *In Search of Another Country.*

117. *Washington Evening Star*, March 29, 1968; *New York Times*, March 30, 1968; *U.S. News & World Report*, April 8, 1968; *Washington Daily News*, April 3, 1968; N. P. Callahan memo to director, April 1, 1968, POCAM; and Kotz, *Judgment Days*, 403–4.

118. Abernathy, *And the Walls Came Tumbling Down*, 420.

119. SAC, New York to FBI director, March 29, 1968, POCAM; *New York Times*, March 30, 1968; and Garrow, *Bearing the Cross*, 612.

120. Organizing its own march became an important point to SCLC because the Invaders said they fueled the riots after their exclusion by James Lawson and local organizers in Memphis. King had trusted Lawson that such disunity would not be a problem; his disappointment with Lawson caused at least some of King's consternation. Garrow, *Bearing the Cross*, 617.

121. Quote in A. Young, *An Easy Burden*, 457. Also, Levison and Alice Loewi, telephone conversation, March 31, 1968, and Levison and Adele Kanter, telephone conversation, April 1, 1968, both in SL; and Garrow, *Bearing the Cross*, 611–12.

122. *New York Times*, April 1, 1968.

123. *Washington Post*, April 1, 1968; *Washington Evening Star*, April 1, 1968; and Tom Offenburger, interview by Kay Shannon, RBOHC.

Chapter 5

1. Katherine Shannon, interview by Claudia Rawles, RBOHC.

2. Government officials and elite journalists believed that such uprisings could not happen in the nation's capital. Gilbert et al., *Ten Blocks from the White House*, 1. Police estimated that thirty-eight people—almost all black—died during the uprisings following the assassination. *New York Times*, April 10, 1968.

3. Indeed, King scholars generally end the story with his death, perhaps including an epilogue that the campaign went forward and failed miserably, all because King was not present to keep the various factions in line. In turn, campaign scholars blame the campaign's ineffectiveness indirectly on the death of King, because of the leadership vacuum his absence created. See Branch, *At Canaan's Edge*; Garrow, *Bearing the Cross*; Ling, *Martin Luther King Jr.*; Fager, *Uncertain Resurrection*; McKnight, *The Last Crusade*; Chase, "Class Resurrection"; and Honey, *Going Down Jericho Road.* Other scholars of the period, even if their periodizations differ slightly, offer a similar perspective regarding King and the campaign's potential. Fairclough, *To Redeem the Soul* and *Better Day Coming*; Sitkoff, *The Black Struggle for Equality*; Matusow, *The Unraveling of America*; Chafe, *The Unfinished Journey*; and T. Anderson, *The Movement and the Sixties.*

4. *Washington Post*, April 23, 1968.

5. *U.S. News & World Report*, May 6, 1968.

6. Quote in *Los Angeles Times*, April 5, 1968. Abernathy reiterated the decision six days later. *New York Times*, April 11, 1968.

7. James Edward Peterson, administrative assistant to the campaign's national

deputy coordinator, interview by Kay Shannon, RBOHC. SCLC headquarters was at the corner of 14th and U streets, where the urban disorders started the night of King's death. Gilbert et al., *Ten Blocks from the White House*, 13–14.

8. Quote by Katherine Shannon, interview by Claudia Rawles, RBOHC.

9. Quote by James Edward Peterson, interview by Kay Shannon, RBOHC. Also, Lois Gray, "Black Community Report and Notes," box 10, AG; Interreligious Committee on Race Relations, "A Message to the Religious Community in Greater Washington," box 2101, PNWRO; *Washington Post*, February 24, 1968; *Evening Star*, March 13, 14, 16, and 20, 1968; *Washington Daily News*, February 21, 1968, all in FBI clipping file, POCAM; *New York Times*, May 17, 1968; and *Washington Post*, April 6, 1968.

10. A. Young, *An Easy Burden*, 476.

11. Lauren Watson, interview by author.

12. Quote by Lauren Watson, interview by author. Also, *New York Times*, April 28, 1968; Ernesto Vigil, interview by author, and Rudy and Gerry Gonzales, interview by author; "Lauren Watson bio sheet," folder 1, LWF; *Denver Post*, April 30, 1968; and Vigil, *Crusade for Justice*, 29–30, 33–35.

13. Organizations like SNCC were skeptical of the campaign's success, but remained neutral in order for members to participate if they desired. "We believe that those Black People who have accepted the non-violent technique and those who believe in demonstrations should participate in the Poor People's Campaign.... We hope that the Poor People's Campaign accomplishes its goals, because it will make our work unnecessary," said Lester McKinnie, director of the Washington, D.C., office of SNCC. "Black Newsletter" press release, n.d. [May–June 1968], reel 58, frame 0343, PSNCC.

14. SAC, Portland memo to FBI director, May 20, 1968; SAC, Milwaukee memo to FBI director, April 9, 1968; FBI memos, Milwaukee, Wisconsin, April 23 and 30, 1968, and Louisville, Kentucky, May 14, 1968; and FBI director memo to the President, May 12, 1968, all in POCAM; *Milwaukee Journal*, April 28, 1968; and John Rutherford and Tom Houck, interviews by Kay Shannon; Katherine Shannon, interview by Claudia Rawles; and Mark Comfort, interview by Robert Wright, all in RBOHC.

15. *Atlanta Constitution*, April 10, 1968. See also *Constitution* editorial pages on April 6 and 11, 1968.

16. *Washington Daily News*, April 3, 1968, FBI clipping file, POCAM; *Los Angeles Times*, May 27, 1968; *New York Times*, April 9, 1968; and *New Amsterdam News*, April 20, 1968.

17. James Hargett, interview by author; *Los Angeles Sentinel*, June 20, 1968; *Los Angeles Times*, May 17, 1968; Minutes of the Entertainment and Information Committee of the Hollywood SCLC, May 22, 1968, box 177, folder 40, RSCLC; FBI memo, Los Angeles, Calif., May 14, 1968; and FBI director J. Edgar Hoover to SAC, Albany, April 5, 1968, all in POCAM. Several celebrities, including producer Edward Lewis, director Robert Wise, and actors Carl Reiner, Gene Kelly, Rod Steiger, and Shirley MacLaine, spearheaded the committee.

18. *La Raza*, May 11, 1968.

19. Quotes in "The Prince of Peace Is Dead—Unidos Venceremos," April 1968, and "A Luther King Por Magali Chain Palavicini," *El Gallo*, May 1968. Also, "En Memoria de Martin Luther King," May 1968, *El Gallo*; Alba Sanchez, "In Memoriam: Dr. Martin Luther King," *LADO*, May–June 1968; Guadalupe Saavedra, untitled, *Chicano Student*, April 25, 1968; and Cesar Chavez telegram to Coretta Scott King, republished in *El Grito del Norte*, Spring 1968.

20. Leo Nieto, "The Poor People's Campaign, 1968," unpublished chapter, in author's possession; and Nieto, interview by author.

21. "Interview with Reies Tijerina," interview by Elsa Knight Thompson, n.d. [mid-April 1968?], in *Testimonio*, ed. F. Rosales, 320.

22. Quote by Reies Tijerina, interview by Della Rossa, April 15, 1968, box 52, folder 5, RLT. See also A. Young, *An Easy Burden*, 476; and *Atlanta Constitution*, April 10, 1968.

23. Baldemar Velásquez, interview by author.

24. Eleanor Eaton memo to Barbara Moffett, "Cesar Chavez," August 23, 1968, CRD folder 51910, "Economic Security and Rural Affairs 1968—Comms and Orgs: United Farm Workers Organizing Committee," AFSCA.

25. Chavez and Larry Itliong telegram to SCLC, April 29, 1968, and Abernathy, Young, and Lafayette telegram to Chavez, June 4, 1968, both in box 69, folder 11; and Leo Nieto telegram to Chavez, May 2, 1968, box 70, folder 1, all in Office of the President Files, part I, PUFW. Lauren Araiza also argues that Chavez did not always approve of King's tactics. See "'For Freedom of Other Men.'"

26. *Atlanta Constitution*, April 8, 1968; *Washington Post*, April 26–27, and May 3, 1968; and *New York Times*, May 3, 7 and 8, 1968; and C. D. DeLoach memos to Clyde Tolson, May 8 and 10, 1968, POCAM.

27. Quote in Matt Nimetz memo to Joe Califano, April 25, 1968, "Death of Martin Luther King & Subsequent Riots" folder, box 1, LBJLB.

28. Quote by Ramsey Clark, attorney general, interview V by Harri Baker, LBJOH.

29. Quote in Matt Nimetz memo to Joe Califano, May 16, 1968, "Death of Martin Luther King & Subsequent Riots" folder, box 1, LBJLB. Nimetz passed around a nine-page excerpt to his colleagues. Schlesinger, *The Age of Roosevelt*, 257–65. See also *Washington Post*, April 12, 1968; U.S. Congress, *Conference on Problems Involved in the Poor Peoples' March on Washington, D.C.*, 1–77; and Nimetz memo to Califano, April 25, 1968, "Death of Martin Luther King & Subsequent Riots" folder, box 1, LBJLB.

30. The agreement allowed up to three thousand people to camp out in the Mall's West Potomac Park, the construction of up to six Mississippi sharecropper shacks in front of the Smithsonian Institution, and the campaign's use of the Lincoln Memorial for mass meetings. The park permit, however, could be revoked "at any time" in the interests of security or if there were violations of the permit's language. National Park Service Regional Director Nash Castro letter to Bernard Lafayette, May 10, 1968, in "Death of Martin Luther King and Subsequent Riots," box 1, LBJLB; and *New York Times*, April 26 and May 3, 7, 8, and 11, 1968.

31. Victor Charlo, interview by author. Charlo's great-grandfather was Salish

Chief Charlo, who won notoriety in the late nineteenth century for leading a twenty-year resistance movement against federal efforts to move the Salish from Montana's Bitterroot Valley to the Flathead reservation. *Weekly Missoulian*, April 26, 1876; and *Missoulian*, October 21, 2006.

32. "Poor People's Campaign, 1968," n.d., box 177, folder 8, RSCLC.

33. "Statements of Demands for Rights of the Poor Presented to Agencies of the U.S. Government by the Poor People's Campaign and Its Committee of 100," April 29–30 and May 1, 1968, 1–2, box 177, folder 24, RSCLC.

34. Quotes in ibid.

35. Quote in A. Young, *An Easy Burden*, 480. Also, "Statements of Demands for Rights of the Poor Presented to Agencies of the U.S. Government by the Poor People's Campaign and Its Committee of 100," April 29–30 and May 1, 1968, 50–56, box 177, folder 24, RSCLC.

36. SCLC leaders protested and called the arrest a clear attempt at hampering the march. Tijerina was bonded out only after the initial Washington action. William Rutherford telegram to New Mexico governor David Cargo, April 28, 1968, box 179, folder 5, RSCLC.

37. Rodolfo Gonzales and Lares Tresjan testimonies, U.S. Congress, Senate, Subcommittee on Employment, Manpower, and Poverty, *Employment Training Legislation—1968*, March 13, April 1, 3, 5, 30, May 7, 9, 10, 13–15, 24, 1968, 294–95, 301–8.

38. Quote in "Statements of Demands for Rights of the Poor Presented to Agencies of the U.S. Government by the Poor People's Campaign and Its Committee of 100," May 1, 1968, box 177, folder 24, RSCLC. Also, *Washington Post*, April 29–30, 1968; and Cobb, *Native Activism*, 163–70.

39. Quotes in Martha Grass testimony, U.S. Congress, Senate, *Employment Training Legislation—1968*, 293–94, and *Washington Post*, April 30, 1968. Also, *Jet*, May 16, 1968; and Cobb, *Native Activism*, 165–66.

40. Robert Fulcher testimony, U.S. Congress, Senate, *Employment Training Legislation—1968*, March 13, April 1, 3, 5, 30, May 7, 9, 10, 13–15, 24, 1968, 298–99.

41. *Atlanta Constitution*, April 30, 1968.

42. *Washington Post*, April 30, 1968.

43. Quote in *New York Times*, April 30, 1968. Also, Robert Fulcher, José Ortiz, Alberta Scott, Lilly Brooks, Phyllis Robinson, and Ray Robinson testimony, U.S. Congress, Senate, *Employment Training Legislation—1968*, 297–301, 309–13; *Washington Post*, April 30–May 1, 1968; and *Jet*, May 16, 1968.

44. Quote in *Washington Post*, May 6, 1968. Also, President's Cabinet meeting minutes, May 1, 1968, box 13, LBJCP.

45. *New York Times*, April 30, 1968; *Chicago Tribune*, April 29–30 and May 1–2, 1968; *Wall Street Journal*, May 1, 1968; *Time*, May 10, 1968; *U.S. News & World Report*, May 13, 1968; and *Newsweek*, May 13, 1968.

46. *Los Angeles Times*, April 30, 1968.

47. *New York Times*, May 3 and 5, 1968.

48. Indeed, sympathy rallies and marches continued throughout the campaign's Washington phase, including its climactic rally called Solidarity Day. The most prominent marches occurred in Chicago's Uptown, Sacramento, and New York's

Central Park; in the New York rally, thousands of Puerto Ricans gathered. *Chicago Tribune*, May 19, 1968; *People's World*, June 29, 1968; and *Worker*, May 28, 1968.

49. While designated caravan marshals called into headquarters with daily progress reports on their caravan's mileage, location, planned evening activities, and numbers of people and buses (or mules), many caravans faced setbacks caused by illnesses, delays, vehicle breakdowns, and logistical snags. According to marcher-analyst Doug Otto, many participants on the Eastern Caravan were so exhausted by the trip, they returned home immediately. This convinced him that the caravans were ultimately more destructive than constructive. Tom Offenburger, interview by Kay Shannon, RBOHC; *New York Times*, May 10, 1968; and Otto, "The Use of Converging Caravans in the Poor People's Campaign: An Historical and Descriptive View," in "PPC—Caravans" folder, 29, 36, 39–40, AG.

50. *Time*, May 17, 1968; *Washington Post*, May 8–10, 12, 1968; *Newsweek*, May 13, 20, 1968; *U.S. News & World Report*, May 13, 1968; *Christian Science Monitor*, May 6, 1968; and Fager, *Uncertain Resurrection*, 29.

51. Journalists and historians inordinately focus on the Mule Train. It inspired at least two books and receives disproportionate attention in several others. See Freeman, *The Mule Train*; Lackey, *Marks, Martin, and the Mule Train*; McKnight, *The Last Crusade*, 94–97; Chase, "Class Resurrection"; and T. Jackson, *From Civil Rights to Human Rights*, 355.

52. *Washington Post*, May 7–10, 12, 1968; *Los Angeles Times*, May 3–4, 6–7, 1968; *New York Times*, May 6–10, 1968; *Pittsburgh Courier* and *New York Amsterdam News*, both May 11 and 18, 1968; *Chicago Defender*, May 4–10, 1968; *Christian Science Monitor*, May 9, 1968; Abernathy, *And the Walls Came Tumbling Down*, 506–8; and Willie Bolden, interview by author.

53. *New York Times*, May 11, 1968; *Los Angeles Times*, May 11 and 14–15, 1968; *Washington Post*, May 17–23, 1968; *Chicago Tribune*, May 12–14, 17–25, 1968; *Atlanta Constitution*, May 12–24, 1968; *Pittsburgh Courier* and *New York Amsterdam News*, both May 11, 18 and 25, 1968; *Chicago Defender*, May 11–17 and 18–24, 1968; G. C. Moore memos to W. C. Sullivan, May 15 and 18, 1968, POCAM; Otto, "The Use of Converging Caravans in the Poor People's Campaign," in "PPC—Caravans" folder, 1–45, AG; and "Poor People's Campaign 1968—Caravan Chronicle," box 177, folder 8, RSCLC.

54. *Washington Post*, May 13, 1968.

55. Ibid.; and Kornbluh, *The Battle for Welfare Rights*, 102–3.

56. Brinkley, *Washington Goes to War*, 119; *New York Times*, May 10, 1968; *Washington Post*, May 13–14, 1968; Wiebenson, "Planning and Using Resurrection City," 405–11; and Resurrection City sketch, n.d., box 177, folder 19, RSCLC.

57. Tony Henry, interview by Kay Shannon, RBOHC.

58. Fager, *Uncertain Resurrection*, 59–60; *True Unity News*, June 8, box 2101, "PPC" folder, PNWRO; and *Washington Post*, June 9, 1968.

59. Quote in *Washington Post*, May 19, 1968. Also, *Washington Post*, May 18, 1968; and Fager, *Uncertain Resurrection*, 42–48.

60. Fager, *Uncertain Resurrection*, 42.

61. Fairclough, *To Redeem the Soul*, 2.

62. Quote by Tom Offenburger, interview by Kay Shannon, RBOHC. For a fuller analysis of media coverage of the campaign, see Mantler, "'The Press Did You In': The Poor People's Campaign and the Mass Media," 33–54.

63. King confidant Stanley Levison was particularly concerned with Abernathy's impact on long-term fundraising. He told Bill Rutherford that Abernathy's personality was as "ill-suited to the donors as you can possibly find." FBI memo, New York, April 23, 1968, SL.

64. Quote in *Chicago Defender*, May 14, 1968. Also, Paul Good, "'No Man Can Fill Dr. King's Shoes'—But Abernathy Tries," *New York Times Magazine*, May 26, 1968; *Los Angeles Times*, May 7, 1968; *Houston Post*, May 19, 1968; *Washington Post*, May 26, 1968; *Time*, May 31, 1968; Katherine Shannon, interview by Claudia Rawles, and Tom Offenburger, interview by Kay Shannon, both in RBOHC; and Fager, *Uncertain Resurrection*, 21–29. For a rare sympathetic piece on Abernathy, see Simeon Booker's profile. "Rev. Abernathy 'To Get Moving' on 'Job Left Behind by Martin,'" *Jet*, April 25, 1968.

65. *Time*, May 31, 1968.

66. Quote in Berry, "The Anger and Problems and Sickness." *Washington Post*, May 14–15, 18–20, 24, and 28, 1968; *New York Times*, May 18–19 and 24, 1968; *Time*, May 24, 1968; *Worker*, May 26, 1968; *Los Angeles Sentinel*, June 20, 1968; Stoney Cooks, Tom Offenburger, and Ernie Austin, interviews by Kay Shannon, RBOHC; *True Unity News*, June 1968, box 180, folder 14, RSCLC; and Linda Avena, "PPC—Participants Observe," June 7, 1968, folder 1, AG.

67. "Cultural Activities of the Poor People's Campaign," June 3, 1968, box 178, folder 23, frames 0494–0495, RSCLC.

68. Myles Horton, "Poor People's Cultural Workshop," June 29, 1968, box 109, folder 10, Pt. 2, HFS.

69. Quote in Chase, "Class Resurrection," 23. Mike Clark, interview by Robert Chase; Myles Horton letters to Bernard Lafayette, May 1, 1968, and Haskell Wexler, May 2, 1968, and Horton, "Poor People's Cultural Workshop," June 29, 1968, all in box 109, folder 10, Pt. 2, HFS.

70. Quote by Ernie Austin, interview by Kay Shannon, RBOHC.

71. Michael Harrington in *Voices of Freedom,* ed. Hampton and Fayer, 478.

72. Quote by Charles Cheng, interview by Malika Lumumba, RBOHC. Also, "Newsletters for PPU," May 30–31, 1968, box 159-10, folder 30, CRDPVF; Linda Wilson Avena, "PPC—Participants Observer," June 6–7, 1968, AG; Mike Clark, interview by Robert Chase; and Stoney Cooks and Ernie Austin, interviews by Kay Shannon, RBOHC. A partial list of classes offered through the Poor People's University included Power and How It Can Be Used Effectively; Urban Planning; Planning Education; Effects of Poverty on Growth and Development; The Negro in Literature; and Biblical Bases for Social Action and Human Dignity.

73. Quotes in *Washington Post*, May 24, 1968.

74. Quote in Berry, "The Anger and Problems and Sickness." Also, Simeon Booker, "D.C. 'Resurrection City' Is Model Community Run by Poor," *Jet*, June 6, 1968.

75. The only detailed media accounts of the Western Caravan come from two

known communists—Patricia Bell Blawis, an activist with the Alianza in New Mexico, and Sam Kushner, editor of the San Francisco-based weekly *People's World*. Blawis's account is most extensive but suffers analytically because of a close allegiance to Tijerina. Blawis, *Tijerina and the Land Grants*, 116–25; and *People's World*, May 25, 1968, and June 1 and 8, 1968. The journalists' affiliations interested the federal government, which used the FBI and Community Relations Service to shadow the caravan. FBI memo, Albuquerque, New Mexico, May 20, 1968; and FBI director J. Edgar Hoover memo to President Johnson, May 16, 1968, POCAM; and Daily Summary, May 15–23, 1968, "Poor People's Campaign—CRS—Daily Log" folder, box 73, PRC. See also Harrison Fletcher, "Seeing Red," *Westword* (a Denver weekly), February 19, 1998.

76. See Vigil, *Crusade for Justice*; Mariscal, *Brown-Eyed Children of the Sun*; Tijerina, *They Called Me "King Tiger"*; and Blawis, *Tijerina and the Land Grants*.

77. Quote in Tijerina, *They Called Me "King Tiger*," 102, 104. This certainly seems true, as Bob Brown, editor of the *Albuquerque Journal* and longtime nemesis of Tijerina's, called him the "wrong choice" who was "almost certain to lessen the prospects that the march will be a nonviolent one." The local archbishop and LULAC chapter also criticized the choice of Tijerina, although both supported the campaign's "intent." *Albuquerque Journal*, April 26, 1968; and *Albuquerque Tribune*, May 11, 1968, box 61, folder 7, RLT. Also, *Washington Post*, June 4, 1968; and Roque Garcia, interview by author.

78. Quote in Vigil, *Crusade for Justice*, 56.

79. Nita Jo Gonzales, Ernesto Vigil, Gerry Gonzales, and Rudy Gonzales, interviews by author; and Vigil, *Crusade for Justice*, 56, 63.

80. Leo Nieto, interview by author; and Nieto letter to Ralph Abernathy, April 23, 1968, box 49, folder 3, RSCLC.

81. Quote in *Worker*, May 28, 1968. Also, *Washington Post*, May 28, 1968; and Cobb, *Native Activism*, 160–61.

82. Roque Garcia, interview by author.

83. Quote by Alicia Escalante, interview by author. Roque Garcia, interview by author; *Washington Post*, May 24, 1968; *People's World*, May 18, 25 and June 1, 1968; and *Worker*, June 2, 1968. Chicano activists in Wisconsin's United Migrant Opportunity Services also went to Washington and sought to connect farm worker rights with those of urban Chicanos and the War on Poverty. Rodriguez, *Tejano Diaspora*, 113.

84. Ernesto Vigil, interview by author.

85. Carlos Montes, interview by author.

86. Carlos Montes and Alicia Escalante, interviews by author; *Los Angeles Sentinel*, May 16, 1968; and *Los Angeles Times*, May 16, 1968.

87. According to James Hargett, PPC coordinator in Los Angeles, the cost for transportation, food, and accommodations was about $125 per person. *Los Angeles Times*, May 9, 1968.

88. Maria Varela, interview by author.

89. *Los Angeles Sentinel*, May 9 and 16, 1968; *Albuquerque Journal*, May 19, 1968, box 61, folder 8, RLT; and J. Gutiérrez, *The Making of a Chicano Militant*, 221–22. An

earlier dispute over who would be the figurehead of the campaign's southwestern contingent—Tijerina or Corky Gonzales—prompted Tijerina to threaten to pull out. Organizers asked Black Panther Lauren Watson to mediate, considering his geographic proximity and ideological ties to the two men. Watson and another Panther traveled to Tierra Amarilla, where Tijerina and company "were shocked to see us," Watson recalled. "There's no telling what they thought when these two big black guys showed up. Because they had it laid out like a Western movie. Everybody had guns, were wearing bandoleros . . . but they were gracious." The parties resolved the dispute after a day, reaffirming Tijerina's position in the campaign but forcing him to make a key concession to top SCLC officials: leave the guns at home. Lauren Watson, interview by author.

90. Gloria Arellanes, interview by author.

91. *People's World*, June 1, 1968.

92. FBI director J. Edgar Hoover memo to President Lyndon Johnson, May 15, 1968; SAC, El Paso to FBI director, May 17, 1968; and FBI memo, El Paso, May 15, 1968, all in POCAM; *Los Angeles Times*, May 16, 1968; *People's World*, June 1, 1968; "SCLC PPC: Caravan Chronicle," n.d., box 177, folder 8, RSCLC; and Carlos Montes, Ralph Ramirez, and Gloria Arellanes, interviews by author.

93. *People's World*, May 25, 1968.

94. *Albuquerque Tribune*, May 11, 1968, box 61, folder 7, RLT.

95. *Albuquerque Journal*, May 16 and 18–19, 1968, box 61, folders 7–8, and Katherine Hattenbach and Shirley Hill Witt form letter to New Mexico hosts, May 29, 1968, box 31, folder 21, both in RLT; *Denver Post*, May 15, 1968; *People's World*, May 25, 1968; Tom Houck, interview by Kay Shannon, RBOHC; SAC, Albuquerque to FBI director, May 18, 1968, POCAM; and Blawis, *Tijerina and the Land Grants*, 116–17.

96. According to SCLC, the caravan coming from the Bay Area had forty Mexican Americans, sixty blacks, ten whites, ten Asian Americans, and thirty-six American Indians. "SCLC PPC: Caravan Chronicle," 10, n.d., box 177, folder 8, RSCLC.

97. Ernesto Vigil, interview by author.

98. *People's World*, June 1, 1968.

99. Quote in *Rocky Mountain News*, May 20, 1968. Also *Denver Post*, May 20, 1968; and Blawis, *Tijerina and the Land Grants*, 117–18.

100. Ralph Ramirez, interview by author.

101. *Denver Post*, May 19, 1968; *Rocky Mountain News*, May 19, 1968; Tom Houck, interview by Kay Shannon, RBOHC; and Alicia Escalante, Carlos Montes, Ralph Ramirez, Maria Varela, and Gloria Arellanes, interviews by author.

102. *People's World*, June 1, 1968.

103. Craig Hart, interview by author.

104. Quote by Juanita Malouff-Dominguez, interview by author. Also, Craig Hart and Gloria Arellanes, interviews by author; and *People's World*, June 1, 1968.

105. *Denver Post*, May 20, 1968.

106. Tom Houck, interview by Kay Shannon, RBOHC; and Blawis, *Tijerina and the Land Grants*, 120.

107. Craig Hart, interview by author.

108. FBI memo, May 20, 1968, Denver, Colo., POCAM; *St. Louis Post-Dispatch*, May 20–21, 1968; *Denver Post*, May 20, 1968; Ralph Ramirez, interview by author; Vigil, *Crusade for Justice*, 57; Tijerina, *They Called Me "King Tiger"* 103, 106–7; and Blawis, *Tijerina and the Land Grants*, 120–22.

109. Ralph Ramirez, interview by author.

110. Tom Houck, interview by Kay Shannon, RBOHC.

111. Ralph Ramirez, interview by author.

112. *Louisville Courier-Journal*, May 23, 1968; FBI memo, Louisville, Ky., May 23, 1968, POCAM; Ralph Ramirez, Carlos Montes, and Lauren Watson, interviews by author; Tom Houck, interview by Kay Shannon, and Mark Comfort, interview by Robert Wright, both in RBOHC.

113. Lauren Watson, interview by author.

114. Quote in Ridlon, *A Black Physician's Struggle for Civil Rights*, 275. Also, Health Services Coordinating Committee memos, May 28, 1968, and n.d., "Health Services," folder 21, box 159–10, CRDPVF; *Washington Post*, May 29–31; Matt Nimetz memo to Joe Califano, May 29, 1968, box 36, Aides—Gaither, WHA; and Fager, *Uncertain Resurrection*, 66. Campaign official Tony Henry attempted to find something positive amid the rain and boasted to a reporter that Resurrection City did not have roaches. *Worker*, June 16, 1968.

115. William H. Moyer, interview by Kay Shannon, RBOHC.

116. "PPC—SCLC Coordinating Cmte," April 11 and 26, 1968, box 5, AG; and "Fact Sheet: General Services Administration," and "Information System," n.d., box 178, folder 26, frames 0517–0520, 0523–0524, RSCLC.

117. A. Young, *An Easy Burden*, 485.

118. Maria Varela, interview by author.

119. Ridlon, *A Black Physician's Struggle for Civil Rights*, 275.

120. Ernesto Vigil, interview by author.

121. Estimates of how many Mexican Americans participated range widely. Overly optimistic SCLC reports suggested as many as one thousand Mexican Americans, while more skeptical press accounts and a detailed demographic study by Al Gollin concluded the total was much lower. Gollin, *The Demography of Protest*, 2–3; *New York Times*, May 26 and 28, 1968, and March 31, 1999; Tom Houck memo to William Rutherford, April 20, 1968, box 177, folder 20, RSCLC; *Albuquerque Journal*, May 10 and June 3, 1968; *Denver Post*, May 16 and 20, 1968; *Washington Post*, May 27, 1968; and FBI memo, Albuquerque, May 14, 1968.

122. Quote in Mike Clark letter to Chuck Fager, "Resurrection City comments," 5, box 105, folder 12, HFS.

Chapter 6

1. *Washington Post*, May 30–31, 1968; *El Grito del Norte*, October 31, 1968; Ernesto Vigil, Rudy Gonzales, Maria Varela, and Gloria Arellanes, interviews by author.

2. Gloria Arellanes, interview by author.

3. Ibid.

4. Ibid.

5. Ibid. On Chicana feminism, see Espinoza, "'Revolutionary Sisters'"; Blackwell, *¡Chicana Power!*; and Vasquez, *Enriqueta Vasquez and the Chicano Movement*.

6. Acuña, *Occupied America*, 370–71; Oropeza, *¡Raza Si! ¡Guerra No!*, 73–74; M. García, *Memories*, 216; Gómez-Quiñones, *Chicano Politics*, 114–15; J. Gutiérrez, *The Making of a Chicano Militant*, 221; Muñoz, *Youth, Identity, Power*, 66; and Navarro, *Mexican American Youth Organization*, 26, 39–40, 153. Exceptions are Ernesto Vigil's book on the Crusade for Justice and George Mariscal's study of the Chicano movement's "lessons." Vigil, *Crusade for Justice*, 54–63; and Mariscal, *Brown-Eyed Children of the Sun*, 196–200.

7. Lorena Oropeza argues that "his greatest contribution was not as a gun-wielding militant," but as someone who "constructed and popularized narratives of Chicana/o history that remain foundational today: themes of land, conquest, and mestizaje, or racial mixing." "The Heart of Chicano History," 50–51.

8. *New York Times*, May 26, 1968; Eric L. Metzner, "Partial Report on the Trip to Washington," June 3, 1968, and "Report on Second Trip to Washington," June 28, 1968, both in box 40, folder 15, AV; and Pittsburgh SAC memos to FBI director, June 11 and 17, 1968, POCAM.

9. *New York Times*, May 26, 1968; *Washington Post*, May 28, 1968; "Reies Lopez Tijerina: Internal Security—Spanish American," June 6, 1968, and SAC-WFO to director, May 30, 1968, box 3, folder 6, RLT; and Tijerina, *They Called Me "King Tiger,"* 107–12.

10. Nita Jo Gonzales, interview by author.

11. *El Gallo*, May 1968; Vigil, interview by author; *Washington Daily News*, July 10, 1968; *Washington Post*, October 30, 2008; Hoyt, "A Free-Wheeling School with High Marks," and Blawis, *Tijerina and the Land Grants*, 124–25. Hawthorne founder Eleanor Orr's book, *Twice as Less*, details her teaching philosophy.

12. Journalists made little effort to explore Hawthorne and its deeper significance; not only was Resurrection City more centrally located and easier to access, but the shantytown offered a more straightforward setting for a troubled campaign. Nor did the FBI or government officials seem to pay Hawthorne much heed. Daily reports to FBI director J. Edgar Hoover and Attorney General Ramsey Clark gave blow-by-blow accounts of the activities inside Resurrection City but never the Hawthorne School.

13. Ernesto Vigil, interview by author. SCLC provided the food, hauling provisions from the organization's warehouse to the school and then letting Crusade and Alianza activists handle preparation. No matter how independent the folks in Hawthorne believed they were, SCLC still financed most things. Ernie Austin, interview by Kay Shannon, RBOHC.

14. Ernie Austin, interview by Kay Shannon, RBOHC; and Gerry Gonzales, Nita Jo Gonzales, Ralph Ramirez, Ernesto Vigil, Gloria Arellanes, Alicia Escalante, and Juanita Malouff-Dominguez, interviews by author. In discussing Resurrection City in his demographic study of the campaign, Albert Gollin suggests, "Any such concentration of young people, strangers to each other, free of parental or neighborhood constraints, and with sketchily-defined roles in the situation, is quite likely to make the task of creating community organization a difficult one." It seems

logical that the opposite may have occurred in Hawthorne, something confirmed by its residents. Gollin, *The Demography of Protest*, 9–10.

15. Quote in Linda Avena, "Participants Observe," June 21, 1968, folder 2, AG. Also, "Reies Lopez Tijerina: Internal Security—Spanish American," June 6, 1968, and SAC-WFO to director, May 30, 1968, box 3, folder 6, RLT.

16. Ernesto Vigil, interview by author.

17. Rudy Gonzales, interview by author.

18. *Santa Fe New Mexican*, June 4, 1968, box 61, folder 9, RLT; and Roque Garcia, interview by author.

19. Carlos Montes, Rudy and Gerry Gonzales, Ernesto Vigil, and Nita Jo Gonzales, interviews by author.

20. Ralph Ramirez, interview by author.

21. Carlos Montes, interview by author.

22. Carlos Montes, Rudy and Gerry Gonzales, and Nita Jo Gonzales, interviews by author.

23. Carlos Montes, interview by author.

24. Rudy Gonzales, Gerry Gonzales, Ernesto Vigil, Alicia Escalante, Nita Jo Gonzales, Carlos Montes, Ralph Ramirez, and Gilberto Ballejos, interviews by author; and 1969 and 1970 appointment calendars, box 14, folder 11, JG.

25. *Akwesasne Notes*, January 1975.

26. Ibid.; Hank Adams, interview notes by Oliver Stone, n.d. [1966], Pacific Northwest Regional Office box, "Indian Program—Fishing Rights Controversy, 1966" folder, AFSCA; *National Observer*, March 9, 1964, box 19, folder 4, NIYCR; Steiner, *The New Indians*, 57–64; C. Wilkinson, *Messages from Frank's Landing*, 44–46, and *Blood Struggle*, 122–23; Smith and Warrior, *Like a Hurricane*, 44–45, 59; and Cobb, *Native Activism*, 178. For more on the American Indian fishing rights movement, see Shreve, "'From Time Immemorial'"; American Friends Service Committee, *Uncommon Controversy*; and Deloria, *Indians of the Pacific Northwest*.

27. Hank Adams note to Reies Tijerina, May 28, 1968, box 47, folder 4, RLT.

28. Abernathy, *And the Walls Came Tumbling Down*, 520.

29. Tijerina, *They Called Me "King Tiger,"* 107–12; Poor People's Campaign New Mexico delegation press release, May 29, 1968, box 31, folder 21, FBI memo, "Reies Lopez Tijerina: Internal Security—Spanish American," June 6, 1968, and SAC-WFO to director, May 30, 1968, box 3, folder 6, all in RLT; *New York Times*, May 26, 1968; Fager, *Uncertain Resurrection*, 108; Abernathy, *And the Walls Came Tumbling Down*, 518–21; *Los Angeles Times*, June 23, 1968; Brigadier General Thomas J. Camp "ticker tape" memo to White House, May 30, 1968, box 57, HU4 confidential, WHCF; and Robert Taylor (of secret service) memo to Jim Jones and Joe Califano, May 29, 1968, "Riot Control—Poor People's March," Aides—Gaither, box 36, WHA.

30. *Washington Post*, May 30, 1968; *New York Times*, May 30, 1968; and *Los Angeles Times*, May 30, 1968. On public support of the court, see Caldiera and Gibson, "The Etiology of Public Support for the Supreme Court," 635–64.

31. *Washington Post*, May 31, 1968; *Time*, June 7, 1968; and *New York Times*, May 30, 1968.

32. *Washington Post*, May 31, 1968.

33. *Washington Post*, May 30, 1968.

34. *New York Times*, May 30, 1968; *Los Angeles Times*, May 30–31 and June 2, 1968; *Time*, June 7, 1968; *U.S. News & World Report*, June 10, 1968; and *People's World*, June 15, 1968.

35. See Fager, *Uncertain Resurrection*, 55; McKnight, *The Last Crusade*, 131; and Mariscal, *Brown-Eyed Children of the Sun*, 189–200. The protest goes unmentioned in T. Jackson, *From Civil Rights to Human Rights*; and Fairclough, *To Redeem the Soul*. The work of Robert Chase and Daniel Cobb are exceptions. Chase, "Class Resurrection"; and Cobb, *Native Activism*, chap. 8, and "Talking the Language of the Larger World," in *Beyond Red Power*, ed. Cobb and Fowler, 161–77.

36. Tijerina, *They Called Me "King Tiger,"* 112.

37. *Washington Post*, May 30–31, 1968; *El Grito del Norte*, October 31, 1968; and Ernesto Vigil, Rudy Gonzales, Maria Varela, and Gloria Arellanes, interviews by author.

38. Ernesto Vigil, interview by author.

39. Ernesto Vigil, Craig Hart, and Lauren Watson, interviews by author; and *Washington Post*, May 30, 1968.

40. *New York Times*, June 2, 1968.

41. *Washington Post*, June 5, 1968.

42. *Washington Post*, June 4, 1968; *New York Times*, May 25 and June 3, 1968; *Atlanta Constitution*, June 1, 3, and 7, 1968; *Time*, May 31 and June 7, 1968; *Wall Street Journal*, June 10, 1968; *Pittsburgh Courier*, June 8, 1968; *New York Amsterdam News*, June 1, 1968; and *Jet*, June 6, 1968.

43. *Washington Post*, June 7, 1968.

44. *People's World*, June 15, 1968; *Worker*, June 11, 1968; *Atlanta Constitution*, June 11, 1968; and *Chicago Tribune*, June 8, 1968.

45. *New York Times*, June 8, 1968.

46. Quote in *Washington Post*, June 8, 1968. Other press reports used even harsher language, calling the campaign a "nightmare," where "squabbles replace mud," and several national newspapers, including the *Constitution*, *Los Angeles Times*, and *Wall Street Journal*, reduced their coverage substantially. Also, Fager, *Uncertain Resurrection*, 62–63.

47. Quote in *Chicago Daily Defender*, June 11, 1968. The *Amsterdam News*, for which Rustin was a columnist, also suggested a leadership breakdown. Yet the newspaper still endorsed Solidarity Day, as did its less vocal colleagues at the *Courier*, *Afro-American*, and *Jet*. *New York Amsterdam News*, June 15, 1968; *Los Angeles Sentinel*, June 13, 1968; and *Jet*, June 13, 1968.

48. Luís Diaz de León, interview by José Angel Gutiérrez.

49. Ibid.

50. *People's World*, June 29, 1968.

51. Mike Clark, interview by Robert Chase.

52. *Southern Patriot*, June 1968, emphasis in original.

53. Buck Maggard, interview by Robert Chase; Joseph Mulloy, interview by James Mosby, Anne Braden, interview by James Mosby, and Tom Houck, interview by Kay Shannon, all in RBOHC; "American Indians, Poor Whites, Spanish-Americans Join Poor People's Washington Campaign," SCLC release, March 15,

1968, Poor People's Campaign folder, box 2101, PNWRO; Eleanor Eaton memo to Barbara Moffett, April 2, 1968, CRD Administration folder 32556, "Minority Leaders Conference Washington's Poor People's Campaign," AFSCA; Montrie, *To Save the Land and People*, 86–96; and Kiffmeyer, *From Reformers to Radicals*.

54. *Southern Patriot*, June 1968.

55. L. Wilson Avena, "Participants Observer," June 1, 1968, AG.

56. Quote in *Southern Patriot*, June 1968. Also, *Washington Post*, June 2, 1968.

57. Maria Varela, interview by author.

58. Carlos Montes and Maria Varela, interviews by author; *Washington Post*, May 29, June 4–5, 7, 10, 13, and 14, 1968; *Jet*, June 20, 1968; and Blawis, *Tijerina and the Land Grants*, 135.

59. *Washington Post*, June 9, 1968.

60. Faith Berry, "The Anger and Problems and Sickness," 22.

61. "Statement to National and International Press," June 11, 1968, box 32, folder 2, RLT.

62. *Washington Post*, June 4, 1968.

63. Ibid.; *People's World*, June 22, 1968; and *New York Times*, June 4–5, 1968.

64. Eric L. Metzner, "Partial Report on the Trip to Washington," June 3, 1968, and "Report on Second Trip to Washington," June 28, 1968, both in box 40, folder 15, AV; SAC, Pittsburgh memos to FBI director, June 11 and 17, 1968, POCAM; and Juanita Malouff-Dominguez, interview by author.

65. Torres, "Political Radicalism in the Diaspora: The Puerto Rican Experience," in *Puerto Rican Movement*, ed. Torres and Velázquez, 5.

66. Quote in *LADO*, August 1968. Also, *Washington Post*, June 16, 1968; "Position Paper: Puerto Ricans March to Washington," June 15, 1968, box 32, folder 1, RLT; *New York Times*, June 16, 1968; *Worker*, May 28, 1968; and Blawis, *Tijerina and the Land Grants*, 138–39.

67. Poor People's Campaign National Mobilization press release and Solidarity Day program June 10, 1968, box 31, folder 23, and Alianza press release, June 3, 1968, box 31, folder 21, both in RLT; Blawis, *Tijerina and the Land Grants*, 140–41; and *Los Angeles Sentinel*, June 20, 1968.

68. Quote by Gonzales, "El Plan del Barrio," in *Message to Aztlán*, ed. Esquibel, 32. Also *Washington Post*, May 29, June 4–5 and 13–14, 1968; and Gonzales, "Sons of Chiefs and Kings and Bloody Revolutionists" press release, box 179, folder 10, RSCLC.

69. Juanita Malouff-Dominguez, interview by author.

70. *Chicago Defender*, June 22–28, 1968. In contrast, the 1963 march had zero women speakers.

71. Fager, *Uncertain Resurrection*, 78–80.

72. Quote in *Baltimore Afro-American*, June 22, 1968. Also, *Washington Post*, June 20, 1968; *Worker*, June 23, 1968; *Chicago Daily Defender*, June 22, 1968; and Cobb, *Native Activism*, 187.

73. *New York Times*, June 20, 1968.

74. Quote in *Newsweek*, July 1, 1968. Also, Fager, *Uncertain Resurrection*, 77; *Time*, June 28, 1968; *Washington Post*, June 20, 1968; and *Atlanta Constitution*, June 20, 1968.

75. Quote in *Washington Post*, June 21, 1968. Also, *Washington Post*, June 7, 1968; *Los Angeles Times*, June 10 and 19, 1968; *Chicago Tribune*, June 11 and 22, 1968; *New York Times*, June 16, 1968; Berry, "The Anger and Problems and Sickness"; Juneau Wilkinson, "Response to Resurrection City," unpublished manuscript, 1968, POCAM; and Fager, *Uncertain Resurrection*, 86–95.

76. *Washington Post*, June 21, 1968.

77. Berry, "The Anger and Problems and Sickness," 22.

78. Tillie Walker, interview by Kay Shannon, RBOHC.

79. James Orange and John C. Rutherford, interviews by Kay Shannon and Katherine Shannon, interview by Claudia Rawles, all in RBOHC; and Berry, "The Anger and Problems and Sickness." False accusations of black-on-white sexual violence long had been used to justify violence within the racial caste system of the South. McGuire, *At the Dark End of the Street*, 21–24.

80. Quote in *Washington Post*, June 22, 1968. Fager, *Uncertain Resurrection*, 86–95, 101, 111–12.

81. *Washington Post*, June 23 and 25, 1968; *Los Angeles Times*, June 23, 1968; Cobb, *Native Activism*, 189–92; and Fager, *Uncertain Resurrection*, 108, 112–17.

82. *Washington Post*, June 25, 1968.

83. Ibid.; *Chicago Daily Defender*, July 1, 1968; and Fager, *Uncertain Resurrection*, 118.

84. Berry, "The Anger and Problems and Sickness," 19.

85. *I. F. Stone's Weekly*, July 8, 1968.

86. Al McSurely, "What Have We Done and What Should We Do?" n.d. [July 1968?], box 32, folder 5, RLT.

87. Minutes of the Poor People's Organizing Convention, June 25 and 27, 1968, box 20, folder 31, RLT. Others listed as participating included Raymond Etheridge, Ted Wulpert, Manuel Holloway, and Dionice Paden.

88. Ibid.

89. Minutes of the Poor People's Organizing Convention, June 25 and 27, 1968, box 20, folder 31, RLT; Andrew Young, interview by Nick Kotz, n.d., NK; and *Washington Post*, July 2, 1968.

90. McSurely, "What Have We Done and What Should We Do?" n.d. [July 1968?], box 32, folder 5, RLT.

91. "Proposal Draft for Developing National Cooperation and Communication among Minority Group Leadership," undated [September 1968?], box 31, folder 20, RLT.

92. According to Reies Tijerina, the Poor People's Embassy planning committee had already received an initial $20,000 in grant money. Alianza press release, July 20, 1968, box 31, folder 28, RLT. Also, minutes of Poor People's Coalition, July 17, 1968, box 31, folder 24, RLT; and Roger Wilkins memo to Ramsey Clark, undated [late 1968?], box 73, "Poor People's Campaign—Arrest Statistics" folder, PRC.

93. See Mariscal, *Brown-Eyed Children of the Sun*; Busto, *King Tiger*; Nabokov, *Tijerina and the Courthouse Raid*; Gardner, *¡Grito!*; Acuña, *Occupied America*, 369; and Gómez-Quiñones, *Chicano Politics*, 115–18.

94. Maria Varela, interview by author.

95. Nabokov, *Tijerina and the Courthouse Raid*, 15–18; and *Washington Post*, June 4, 1968.

96. Miguel Barragan, interview by author.

97. *Denver Post*, June 10, 1968.

98. Quote by Rudy Gonzales, interview by author. Also Gerry Gonzales, interview by author; Katherine Shannon, interview by Claudia Rawles, RBOHC; SAC, Atlanta to director, May 24, 1968, box 3, folder 6, RLT; and Oropeza, "The Heart of Chicano History," 49–67.

99. Maria Varela, interview by author.

100. Rudy and Gerry Gonzales, Craig Hart, and Gloria Arellanes, interviews by author.

101. Tijerina also received several supportive telegrams in early 1968 from militant black leaders he had courted, including Ron Karenga and H. Rap Brown. Karenga to Tijerina, January 3, 1968, box 34, folder 24, and SNCC to Alianza, January 5 and 9, 1968, box 34, folder 26, both in RLT. Such support would continue sporadically throughout his legal troubles into the 1970s.

102. *El Gallo*, August 31, 1967.

103. Maria Varela and Rudy Gonzales, interviews by author; Chavez and Gonzales telegrams to Tijerina, June 1967, box 34, folders 1–3, RLT; *El Gallo*, June 23, July 28, and August 31, 1967; *Rocky Mountain News*, June 8, 11–12, 1967; Nabokov, *Tijerina and the Courthouse Raid*, 150–51, 183, 192, 229, 241; Gonzales, *Message to Aztlán*, 254; and Vigil, *Crusade for Justice*, 31–33, 50–52.

104. Ernesto Vigil, interview by author.

105. *Commonweal*, July 12, 1968.

106. *Washington Post*, June 25, 1968.

107. Quote in *Chicago Defender*, June 26, 1968. Also, *Washington Post*, June 25–26 and 28, 1968; *New York Times*, June 27 and 30, 1968; and Berry, "The Anger and Problems and Sickness."

108. Quote in "History of Refugees of Resurrection City, U.S.A. for Human Rights," box 33, folder 1, GW. Also, *Washington Post*, June 27–30 and July 1, 3–8, 1968; *Chicago Daily Defender*, August 17, 1968; and FBI memos, Richmond, Virginia, July 19, 1968, and St. Louis, July 31, 1968, both in POCAM.

109. *People's World*, June 29, 1968; *Daily World*, July 14, August 17, September 10 and 17, and October 29, 1968; and press release, June 20, 1968, box 47, folder 4, RLT.

110. *Washington Post*, July 17, 1968.

111. Vigil, *Crusade for Justice*, 56.

112. Quote in David Wham, "The Politics and Dramatism of Conflict in the Poor People's Campaign: A Case Study," January 1969, box 10, "Wham 4th," AG. Also, J. Jackson, "Resurrection City," 65–74; Bill Hayden memo to Eleanor Eaton, August 12, 1968, CRD 32556, "PPC: General," AFSCA; *Soul Force*, June 19, July 15, and August 15, 1968; *Los Angeles Sentinel*, July 27, 1968; *Chicago Daily Defender*, June 25, July 2, 13, and December 4, 1968; *Evening Star*, June 7, 1968; *Washington Post*, June 30, 1968; *New York Times*, June 30, 1968; *Denver Post*, July 27, 1968; and Kotz, *Let Them Eat Promises*, 171–92. Kotz notes that Johnson continued to oppose massive expansion of such hunger programs and concluded, "There is little doubt that Con-

gress would have taken major steps forward on the hunger issue in 1968 if Lyndon Johnson had only lent his support" (*Promises*, 190).

113. James Gaither memo to Harry McPherson, June 21, 1968, box 1, "Death of Martin Luther King and Subsequent Riots—Poor People's Campaign," LBJLB.

114. Ralph K. Huitt, interview by Helen Hall, RBOHC.

115. Cabinet meeting minutes, March 13, April 3, May 1, 14, and 29, 1968, box 13, and June 12, 1968, box 14, LBJCP; Roger Wilkins daily summary memos to Ramsey Clark, May 15–28, 1968, box 73, "Poor People's Campaign—CRS Daily Log," PRC; Andrew Young interview by Thomas H. Baker, June 18, 1970, LBJOH; Wilbur Cohen letter to Richard Weil, assistant to Marian E. Wright, January 17, 1969, box 15, folder 16, NK; Cohen letter to Ralph Abernathy, June 18, 1968, CRD 32554, AFSCA; *New York Times*, June 30, 1968; and Marian Wright Edelman, interview by Blackside.

Chapter 7

1. Gilberto Ballejos and Shirley Hill Witt, interviews by author; *Albuquerque Journal*, August 20, 1968; and Carlos Cansino, "A Barrio Organizer during the Chicano Movement," 18, box 1, folder 1, CEC.

2. *Albuquerque Tribune*, June 2–6, 1967, and *Albuquerque Journal*, June 6, 1967, and Cansino, "A Barrio Organizer during the Chicano Movement," all in box 1, folder 1, CEC; and Gilberto Ballejos and Shirley Hill Witt, interviews by author.

3. SAC, Albuquerque to FBI director, August 21, 1968; SAC-WFO to FBI director, September 13, 1968, BBNM; *Albuquerque Tribune*, August 20 and October 22, 1968; *El Grito del Norte*, August 24, September 15, and December 18, 1968, all in box 68, RLT; *Albuquerque Journal*, November 18, 1968; and Gilberto Ballejos, interviews by author.

4. *El Grito del Norte*, September 15, 1968, January 11 and 29, and May 19, 1969; *El Papel*, March 1969; Gilberto Ballejos and Shirley Hill Witt, interview by author; and Gilberto Ballejos, "Introduction to Highlander West," October 18, 1969, "Ballejos report," box 50, HFS.

5. *El Papel*, March 1969.

6. Ibid.

7. SAC, Albuquerque confidential memo, April 30, 1969, including copy of *Albuquerque News*, March 6, 1969, BBNM; *Albuquerque Journal*, August 29, 1968; *El Grito del Norte*, September 15, 1968, January 11 and 29, and May 19, 1969; *El Papel*, March 1969 and October–November 1969; and Martínez, "A View from New Mexico: Recollections of the Movimiento Left."

8. In 1969 Presbyterian Church delegates initially voted to transfer this acreage in the Piedra Lumbre grant in Rio Arriba County to the Alianza, along with a sizable development grant. Known as Ghost Ranch because of its nonexistent land title, the land never changed hands after the church balked at Alianza claims to represent the original landowners. Tijerina and his allies claimed that Bob Brown, editor of the *Albuquerque Journal*, a Presbyterian, and longtime nemesis of the Alianza, used his

influence to scuttle the deal. Blawis, *Tijerina and the Land Grants*, 172–74; and Busto, *King Tiger*, 63–64.

9. Maria Varela, "Time to Get Ready," in *Hands on the Freedom Plow*, 570–71; Maria Varela and Gilberto Ballejos, interviews by author; SAC, Albuquerque memos to FBI director, April 30, 1969, and January 19, 1970, BBNM; and Busto, *King Tiger*, 65–69.

10. R. Rosales, *The Illusion of Inclusion*, 62–77; Krochmal, "Labor, Civil Rights, and the Struggle for Democracy in Texas"; and Stephen Ward, "The Third World Women's Alliance: Black Feminist Radicalisms and Black Power Politics," in *The Black Power Movement*, ed. Joseph, 119–144.

11. *People's World*, August 24, September 14, and November 9, 1968; *Los Angeles Times*, November 3 and 22, 1968; *Daily World*, July 31, 1968, and June 11, 1969; Elden and Schweitzer, "New Third Party Radicalism," 761–74; J. Wilson, "'Free Huey'"; and R. Rosales, *The Illusion of Inclusion*, 62–77. All used their candidacies to enhance their activism, with Hank Adams the most prominent. Acknowledging that they had failed to persuade officials to embrace sympathetic Indian policies proposed in Congress, Hank Adams said that the campaign instead had sparked a "responsible revolution" among U.S. tribes, a foundation on which to build Indian pressure for reform in the next Congress. Part of that process included participation in the Poor People's Embassy, his congressional candidacy, and a newly formed organization called the Coalition of Indian Citizens. In the fall, Adams and others prompted a new wave of fishing rights protests for more than three months, sparking arrests and publicity before reaching a compromise with state officials. Eventually, the federal courts recognized the tribes' right to fish in their traditional waters. *Daily World*, July 14, August 17, September 10 and 17, and October 29, 1968; C. Wilkinson, *Messages from Frank's Landing*, 49–56; and Cobb, *Native Activism*, 199–200.

12. Reies López Tijerina, statement to the press, July 20, 1968, box 31, folder 28, RLT.

13. Quote in Nabokov, *Tijerina and the Courthouse Raid*, 249. Also, *Albuquerque Journal*, March 19, 22, 1968, box 61, folder 5, RLT; *People's World*, April 6, 1968; *Denver Post*, July 28, 1968; and Blawis, *Tijerina and the Land Grants*, 146–47.

14. Quotes in Blawis, *Tijerina and the Land Grants*, 146–47.

15. *El Grito del Norte*, September 15, 1968.

16. *El Grito del Norte*, August 24, September 15, and October 5, 1968; Tijerina for Governor campaign material, "People's Constitutional Party General File," 1968, box 32, folders 6–7, RLT; and Blawis, *Tijerina and the Land Grants*, 147–49.

17. *New York Times*, October 26, 1968; *El Grito del Norte*, October 5 and 31, 1968; *Daily World*, October 16, 1968; *Albuquerque Journal*, November 7, 1968; Blawis, *Tijerina and the Land Grants*, 148–51; Gardner, *¡Grito!*, 262–64; and Wolf, "The 1968 Elections in New Mexico," 510–16. PCP had several smaller constitutional impacts, including a change allowing candidates to run in a House district in which they did not reside. The PCP effort also prompted Democrats and Republicans to join in making conditions even stricter for third parties to make the ballot in New Mexico.

18. Busto, *King Tiger*, quote in 66, 64–66; *Albuquerque Journal*, January 7–8, 18,

and February 1, 1969, and *New Mexico Lobo*, March 5, 1969, all in box 42, folder 7; and FBI reports, SD 157-815, February 3, 1969, San Diego, Calif., and AQ 100-2567, "Internal Security—Spanish American," March 13, 1969, both in box 3, folder 13, all in RLT.

19. Nita Jo Gonzales, interview by author; Mark Comfort, interview by Robert Wright, RBOHC; Nina Ryan, administrative assistant to Marian Wright, letter to Anibal Solivan, October 9, 1968, box 31, folder 24, RLT.

20. Poor People's Embassy staff letter to "Board members and friends," April 22, 1969, and Poor People's Development Foundation (PPDF) brochure, 1973, both in box 31, folder 24, and PPDF inaugural report, 1974, box 31, folder 25, all in RLT; and William Waters, "Statement on Behalf of Seven Members of the Conservation Community Council of Lincoln Park before the Urban Renewal Board Meeting," February 11, 1970, and *Lerner Booster*, February 25, 1970, in "Poor People's Coalition" folder, LP, http://digicol.lib.depaul.edu/u?/lpnc6,1113 accessed October 25, 2010.

21. In their histories of Highlander, scholar John M. Glen and former executive director Frank Adams focus on the school's heyday in the labor and civil rights movements from the 1930s to the mid-1960s. As a result, they give Highlander's efforts in the campaign and beyond only brief consideration. Yet it was this critical period in which the school transitioned successfully to the smaller-scale organizing and training work it continues today. Glen, *Highlander*, 215–17; and Adams, with Horton, *Unearthing the Fire*, 180.

22. Myles Horton letter to Reies Tijerina, September 18, 1968, box 49, folder 20, RLT.

23. Quote by Mike Clark, "Resurrection City comments," December 13, 1968, box 105, folder 12, HFS. Executive director C. Conrad Browne echoed similar sentiments in the months to come. "It is good that you got there and participated in the activities," Browne wrote one participant. "That experience was one of the best of the last several years. I have never seen education on such a mass scale as was taking place in Resurrection City." C. Conrad Browne letter to F. R. Rowe, July 12, 1968, box 98, folder 16; Browne letter to Charles G. Gomillion, April 1, 1970, box 95, folder 18; and Browne letter to Ernest Austin, February 17, 1969, box 98, folder 5, all in HFS.

24. "Highlander Self-Education Project," in Myles Horton letter to Carl Rowan, May 16, 1969, box 105, folder 13, and box 100, folder 10, HFS; Myles Horton letter to Rodolfo "Corky" Gonzales, November 10, 1972, Mike Clark letter to Ricardo Romero, November 14, 1972, and Jim Branscome letter to José Gonzales, December 14, 1972, all in "Escuela," box 28, Gilberto Ballejos, "Introduction to Highlander West," October 18, 1969, "Ballejos report," box 50, Ron Short letter to Maria Varela, October 29, 1975, "Tierra Amarilla," box 36, and "Accounting of Indian and Chicago programs," April 24, 1971, box 26, all in unprocessed HFS; and *Southern Patriot*, April 1969.

25. Mike Clark, "Multi-Racial Workshop Notes," May 2, 1970, box 109, folder 21, HFS.

26. On the 1970 workshop, see "Multi-Racial Workshop for American Poor,"

n.d., Mike Clark, "Multi-Racial Workshop Notes," May 2, 1970, and Conrad Browne letter to Shirley Witt, May 8, 1970, all in box 109, folder 21, HFS. For the 1971 workshop, see "The Social Movement Workshop," n.d. [May 1971?], and directory of participants, April 26, 1971, both in box 109, folder 25, HFS.

27. Arika Ducumus letter to "the Folks at Highlander," June 15, 1970, box 109, folder 21, HFS. Ducumus also lamented the fact that participants' suspicions prevented photography during the workshop, which she argued may have assisted in publicizing such programming. The White Citizens Council's doctoring of a Martin Luther King Jr. photo at Highlander with the label "Communist Training School" for publicity may have prompted organizers' caution.

28. The last Myles Horton letter to Reies Tijerina found was dated March 9, 1973, box 49, folder 20, RLT. See also Mike Clark, "Multi-Poor Workshop April 1970 excerpts and follow ups," [summer 1970?], box 109, folder 21, and Ed and Pat Lynch letter, July 15, 1970, box 102, folder 3, both in HFS; and Glen, *Highlander*, 218.

29. Roque Garcia, interview by author.

30. José Angel Gutíerrez, interview by author.

31. Vigil, *Crusade for Justice*, 71.

32. Miguel Barragan, interview by author.

33. Ibid.

34. Ibid.; *San Antonio Express/News*, May 14 and 19, 1968; *Alamo Messenger*, May 10, 1968; and *National Register*, May 12, 1968; Luís Diaz de León, interview by José Angel Gutiérrez; SAC, San Antonio to FBI director, May 16 and 21, 1968, POCAM; and Sepulveda, *The Life and Times of Willie Velasquez*, 66–67.

35. Miguel Barragan, interview by author; *Jet*, May 16, 1968; *San Antonio Express/ News*, May 19, 1968; and SAC, San Antonio to FBI director, May 16 and 18, 1968, POCAM. In the first of many grants, the Ford Foundation provided the Southwest Council of La Raza with $630,000 in June 1968. Although smeared as a communist front, the council was a community development organization designed to provide funding and training support for local projects in Mexican American communities. In Phoenix, it helped fund Chicanos Por La Causa, made up of Arizona State University students and other activists interested in "obtaining resources to confront the educational, economic, youth, and housing problems of the Chicano community." Most notable was the council's support for the Mexican American Legal Defense Fund, founded in 1967, as well as the Southwest Voter Registration and Education Project in 1974, both of which provided Mexican Americans with valuable legal and electoral tools to expand their influence under the Civil Rights Act of 1964. By the 1980s, the council—renamed the National Council of La Raza— had become "the premier civil rights advocacy organization for Chicanos and other Latinos" in the country, according to José Angel Gutiérrez. J. Gutiérrez, *The Making of a Chicano Militant*, quote in 274, 118–19; Miguel Barragan, interview by author; *New York Times*, June 17, 1968, and April 20, 1969; Southwest Council of La Raza (SWCLR) brochure, undated, and SWCLR minutes, June 15, 1968, both in box 65, folder 16, PUFW; Gómez-Quiñones, *Chicano Politics*, 110–11; and Sepulveda, *The Life and Times of Willie Velasquez*, 64–65.

36. Mantler, "'The Press Did You In': The Poor People's Campaign and the Mass

Media." Scholars who do acknowledge the campaign routinely argue that it raised the movement's profile. See Vigil, *Crusade for Justice*, 63; Navarro, *Mexican American Youth Organization*, 40; and Mariscal, *Brown-Eyed Children of the Sun*, 178.

37. *Denver Post* and *Rocky Mountain News,* June 4 and 20, 1968; *La Raza,* July 10, 1968; *Washington Post,* June 4, 1968; Gonzales, "El Plan del Barrio," in *Message to Aztlán,* ed. Esquibel, 32–34; Gómez-Quiñones, *Chicano Politics,* 114; and Navarro, *Mexican American Youth Organization,* 39–40.

38. *El Gallo,* March 1969.

39. Ibid.; *Denver Post,* March 20, 1969; Gerry Gonzales, Rudy Gonzales, Nita Gonzales, Ernesto Vigil, and Craig Hart, interviews by author; 1969 and 1970 travel planners, box 14, folder 11, JG; P. Jones, *The Selma of the North,* 243–48; and Vigil, *Crusade for Justice,* 202.

40. *El Gallo,* July 1968, December 1968, and June 1970; *Daily World,* March 28, 1969; *Denver Post,* March 21–25, 1969; *El Grito del Norte,* October 5, 1968; Nita Jo Gonzales, Lauren Watson, Ernesto Vigil, and Jessica Bordeaux-Vigil, interviews by author; Vigil, *Crusade for Justice,* 68; and Acuña, *Occupied America,* 356.

41. Marín, "Rodolfo 'Corky' Gonzales," 110.

42. Despite the dominant narrative of unqualified black support for school desegregation of any kind, African Americans across the country were wary of school board implementation, especially the disproportionate burden carried by black communities and children through busing and the closure of historically black schools. Cecelski, *Along Freedom Road;* and Mantler, "'I'm against the Way It Is Being Done.'"

43. Marín, "Rodolfo 'Corky' Gonzales," 110.

44. Whiteness played a substantial role in Mexican American desegregation efforts in Texas. Neil Foley, "Partly Colored or Other White: Mexican Americans and Their Problem with the Color Line," 123–44, "Straddling the Color Line: The Legal Construction of Hispanic Identity in Texas," 341–54, and "Becoming Hispanic: Mexican Americans and the Faustian Pact with Whiteness," 53–70.

45. Romero, "Our Selma Is Here," 73–74, 90–97; *Denver Post,* June 19–20, 1969; and *Keyes et. al. v. School District, No. 1, Denver,* 413 U.S. 189 (June 21, 1973).

46. Quote in Lieberman, "No More Mañana," 181. SAC, Denver to FBI director, "Crusade for Justice—Internal Security," March 21, 22, 26, 1969, CJ; *El Gallo,* April 1969; *Denver Post,* March 20–22, 1969; Romero, "Our Selma Is Here," 90–97; and Vigil, *Crusade for Justice,* 82–86.

47. *Denver Post,* March 21–24, 1969; Lieberman, "No More Mañana," 181–90; Romero, "Our Selma Is Here," 90–97; Nita Jo Gonzales, interview by author; and Vigil, *Crusade for Justice,* 87, 117.

48. *El Gallo,* March 1969; Vigil, *Crusade for Justice,* 68, 95–96; and *El Grito del Norte,* May 19, 1969.

49. Carlos Montes, interview by author.

50. Maria Varela, interview by author.

51. Maria Varela, Alicia Escalante, Carlos Montes, Ralph Ramirez, Ernesto Vigil, and Gloria Arellanes, interviews by author; and Vigil, *Crusade for Justice,* 96.

52. *El Grito del Norte*, April 14, 1969, box 68, RLT; *Los Angeles Times*, March 30 and April 1, 1969; and Vigil, *Crusade for Justice*, 96.

53. Oropeza, *¡Raza Si! ¡Guerra No!*, 86.

54. Ibid., 87.

55. Quote in *El Grito del Norte*, April 14, 1969, box 68, RLT.

56. "El Plan Espiritual de Aztlán," 1969, in *Testimonio*, ed. F. Rosales, 361–63; *El Grito del Norte*, April 14 and May 19, 1969, box 68, RLT; Muñoz, *Youth, Identity, Power*, 75–78; Oropeza, *¡Raza Si! ¡Guerra No!*, 85–88; Gómez-Quiñones, *Chicano Politics*, 123–24; and Vigil, *Crusade for Justice*, 95–100. El Plan Espiritual de Aztlán is technically Alurista's opening poem to El Plan de Aztlán, but *Testimonio* mislabels it.

57. *Y.L.O.*, May 1969, YL, http://eres.lib.depaul.edu/eres/coursepage.aspx?cid= 4075&page=docs, accessed December 5, 2010.

58. *People's World*, May 3, 1969.

59. "El Plan Espiritual de Aztlán," 1969, in *Testimonio*, ed. F. Rosales, 361–63; *El Grito del Norte*, April 14 and May 19, 1969, box 68, RLT; *Militant*, May 9, 1969; and *Y.L.O.*, May 1969, YL.

60. Vasquez, "The Woman of La Raza, Part I," July 6, 1969, in *Enriqueta Vasquez and the Chicano Movement*, ed. Oropeza and Espinoza, 116–21.

61. "El Plan Espiritual de Aztlán," 1969, in *Testimonio*, ed. F. Rosales, 361–63; *Militant*, May 9, 1969; Gloria Arellanes, interview by author; Espinoza, "'Revolutionary Sisters,'" 17–58; and Blackwell, *¡Chicana Power!*, 138–41.

62. SAC, Denver, "Internal Security—Spanish American," July 30 and November 28, 1969, CJ; *Denver Post*, March 26, 1969; *Rocky Mountain News*, October 28, 1969; Vigil, *Crusade for Justice*, 103–6; and Carlos Montes, interview by author. The antiwar march and rally attracted approximately twenty thousand Chicano activists and their supporters. Police responded to a small dispute near Laguna Park, which erupted into a full-blown riot. Three died, including *Los Angeles Times* columnist Ruben Salazar. See E. Chávez, *¡Mi Raza Primero!*, chap. 3.

63. FBI memo, "Chicano Independence Day: September 16, 1969," Denver, September 19, 1969, 2, CJ.

64. *Denver Post*, September 19, 1969; Marín, "Rodolfo 'Corky' Gonzales," 111–12; and Vigil, *Crusade for Justice*, 106–9.

65. SAC, Denver, "Internal Security—Spanish American," July 30 and November 28, 1969, CJ; and Lauren Watson, and Rudy and Gerry Gonzales, interviews by author.

66. Corky Gonzales, interview by Karen Wald. This interview of Gonzales and Cha-Cha Jimenez of Chicago's Young Lords originally appeared as "Chicanos: Identity Recovered," *Tricontinental*, July–October 1970.

67. Zavala County, home to Crystal City or Cristal, was roughly 80 percent Spanish-speaking or Spanish-surnamed, with a poverty rate of 55.6 percent. U.S. Census Bureau, *1970 Census, Vol. 1—Characteristics of the Population, Part 45—Texas, Section 1*, tables 130 and 119, pp. 1117 and 927.

68. J. Gutiérrez, *The Making of a Chicano Militant*, quote 214, 202–14. Also, Navarro, *La Raza Unida Party*, 31–38; and I. García, *United We Win*, 48–50.

69. Unlike in Texas, in which Mexican Americans made up 18 percent of the state's population and a majority in several counties, they were a distinct minority in Denver (roughly 20 percent) and Colorado (12.5 percent). *The 1970 Census, Vol. 1—Characteristics of the Population, Part 45—Texas, Section 1*, table 17, p. 103, and *Vol. 1—Characteristics of the Population, Part 7—Colorado*, tables 17, 124, 129, and 130, pp. 41, 291, 300, 303–5.

70. Led by Waldo Benavidez, a former Crusade member, and Rich Castro, the Westside Coalition emerged in November 1969 in opposition to a massive urban renewal project to build a new education complex on the Westside. Made up of more reform-minded organizations such as the local chapters of the American GI Forum, the coalition attempted to carve out more Mexican American control in the depressed Westside while maintaining ties to the Democratic Party and white business leaders. The coalition advocated for the community on land use, police-civilian relations, and other issues until 1975. Corky Gonzales saw the Westside Coalition as a rival for Mexican American support, but as one scholar suggests, "Without the existence . . . of a more moderate group advocating gradual reform, the swiftly moving wave of militants would have quickly been isolated." Quote in Gould, *The Life and Times of Richard Castro*, 6. Also, George Rivera, Aileen F. Lucero, and Richard Castro, "Internal Colonialism in Colorado: The Westside Coalition and Barrio Control," in *La Gente*, ed. de Baca, 203–21.

71. "Colorado Platform—La Raza Unida Party," in *Testimonio*, ed. F. Rosales, 389–90; Marín, "Rodolfo 'Corky' Gonzales," 112–13; Navarro, *La Raza Unida Party*, 92–94; and *Denver Post,* November 4, 1970.

72. In their 1972 text, *The Chicanos: A History of Mexican Americans*, Matt S. Meier and Feliciano Rivera coined this apocalyptic—and now rather outdated—moniker for these four high-profile leaders of the Chicano movement.

73. Navarro, *La Raza Unida Party*, 231–43; Marín, "Rodolfo 'Corky' Gonzales," 114–19; and Busto, *King Tiger*, 68–69.

74. *Militant*, May 9, 1969.

75. Rodolfo "Corky" Gonzales, "Arizona State University Speech," October 14, 1970, in *Message to Aztlán*, ed. Esquibel, 36–37, 55. The use of "international" suggests several influences on Gonzales's thinking, including the internationalist rhetoric of the Black Panthers and his identification with those suffering during the Vietnam War and under the brutal U.S. government-backed military dictatorship in Mexico. The Crusade's "freedom school," Escuela Tlatelolco, was named after the October 2, 1968, massacre in which soldiers killed hundreds of protesting Mexican students in preparation to host the Summer Olympics. Poniatowska, *Massacre in Mexico*. See also Ogbar, *Black Power*, chap. 6.

Chapter 8

1. Quote by Mike Gray, interview by author.

2. Quote in Fred Hampton, "The People Have to Have the Power," in *Let Nobody Turn Us Around*, ed. Marable and Mullings, 480. Also, Gray, *The Murder of Fred Hampton*; and Jon Rice, "The World of Illinois Panthers," 50–51, 54.

3. *Rising Up Angry*, July 1969.

4. Quote in *People's World*, November 29, 1969. Also, *People's World*, June 7, 1969; *Chicago Sun-Times*, March 11, 18, 1969; *Chicago Today*, May 15, 1969; Obed Lopez Zacarías, interview by author; Jon Rice, "The World of the Illinois Panthers," 58; *Rising Up Angry*, July and August 1969; *Chicago Seed* 6, nos. 11, 13 [May, July 1971?]; Johanna Fernandez, "Between Social Service Reform and Revolutionary Politics: The Young Lords, Late Sixties Radicalism, and Community Organizing in New York City," in *Freedom North*, ed. Theoharis and Woodard, 258–60; and Frost, *An Interracial Movement of the Poor*, 170.

5. Freeman, *The Mule Train*, 114.

6. Ibid., 117.

7. *Daily World*, August 10, 1968. See also Roland Freeman's interview with Lee Dora Collins in *The Mule Train*, 115–17.

8. Flo Ware, "Check Mate: The Poor People's Campaign," unpublished essay, 1974, box 1, folder 37, FW.

9. Mary Switzer letter to Johnnie Tillmon, NWRO executive director, July 17, 1968, box 2024, "NCC" folder, PNWRO.

10. Marian Wright Edelman and Etta Horn, interviews by Nick Kotz, November 20, 1974, NK; Marian Wright Edelman, interview by Blackside; West, *The National Welfare Rights Movement*, 215; and Kotz and Kotz, *A Passion for Equality*, 258.

11. West, *The National Welfare Rights Movement*, 216–17; Kotz and Kotz, *A Passion for Equality*, 260; and Piven and Cloward, *Poor People's Movements*, 325.

12. Kornbluh, *The Battle for Welfare Rights*, 157.

13. Nixon aides reintroduced FAP to Congress several times and the president himself maintained his verbal support. But behind the scenes, FAP advocates such as Moynihan and HEW Secretary Robert Finch had lost much of their influence. The nation's "social fracturing" in 1970, to quote Felicia Kornbluh, led to the rise of a harder-edged rhetoric by Vice President Spiro Agnew and speechwriter Patrick Buchanan. The notion that any kind of guaranteed income—even in the guise of welfare reform—would attract working-class white and southern voters seemed increasingly farfetched. NWRO statement in *Social Security and Welfare Proposals*, 1013–43; Kornbluh, *The Battle for Welfare Rights*, 137–60; and Perlstein, *Nixonland*, 396.

14. Kotz and Kotz, *A Passion for Equality*, 284.

15. West, *The National Welfare Rights Movement*, 45, 215.

16. Premilla Nadasen makes a case for interracialism in the NWRO, but she speaks mainly of blacks and whites, as do most other welfare rights scholars. "Welfare's a Green Problem: Cross-Race Coalitions in Welfare Rights Organizing," in *Feminist Coalitions*, ed. S. Gilmore, 178–95. See West, *The National Welfare Rights Movement*; Kornbluh, *The Battle for Welfare Rights*; Williams, *The Politics of Public Housing*, chap. 6; and Orleck, *Storming Caesar's Palace*.

17. West, *The National Welfare Rights Movement*, 44–45, 216–17; Kotz and Kotz, *A Passion for Equality*, 287; Kornbluh, *The Battle for Welfare Rights*, 169, 171; Ruiz, *From Out of the Shadows*, 112–13; and Nadasen, "Welfare's a Green Problem," 183–84, 190–92.

18. Alicia Escalante, interview by author.

19. F. Gonzales, *Chicano!*, 259; Adelaida R. Del Castillo, "La Visión Chicana," in *Chicana Feminist Thought*, ed. A. García, 44–48; and Alicia Escalante, interview by author.

20. It remains striking that, despite the strain the campaign placed on staffers, most of those interviewed for the Civil Rights Documentation Project in the summer of 1968 remained quite enthusiastic about the ongoing struggle. For example, see Tom Houck and Cornelius Givens, interviews by Kay Shannon, and Katherine Shannon, interview by Claudia Rawles, all in RBOHC.

21. Quote in *New York Times*, July 17, 1968. Yglesias, "It May Be a Long, Hot Spring in the Capital"; and *New York Times*, July 15, 1968.

22. *New York Times*, July 24, 1968.

23. *New York Times*, August 1, 7–9, 1968; *Los Angeles Times*, August 6–8 and 11, 1968; Mailer, *Miami and the Siege of Chicago*, 51, 54–55; and Perlstein, *Nixonland*, 304–7.

24. Mailer, *Miami and the Siege of Chicago*, 173–74.

25. *Chicago Tribune*, August 31 and September 8, 1968; Royko, *Boss*, 193–94; *New York Times*, August 27, 1968; *Los Angeles Times*, August 30, 1968; *Chicago Defender*, August 31–September 6, 1968; Mailer, *Miami and the Siege of Chicago*, 51, 54–55, 168–69, 173; Wills, *Nixon Agonistes*, 319–34; and Patterson, *Grand Expectations*, 694–97. See also Farber, *Chicago '68*.

26. *New York Times*, August 16 and September 3, 1968; *Washington Post*, August 15, 1968; and *Southern Patriot*, October 1968.

27. The strike added to the list of high-profile work stoppages by sanitation workers that year. Most involved predominantly African American sanitation forces, striking for better wages and benefits and union recognition, similar to their Memphis counterparts. Those cities included St. Petersburg, Florida; Baltimore; New Orleans; Gary, Indiana; Chicago; and Cleveland. Other cities, such as Scranton, Pennsylvania; Oklahoma City; Evansville, Indiana; Miami Beach; and Boca Raton, Florida, also saw garbage strikes. In New York City a strike left mounds of garbage for nine days in February 1968, but rather than highlight racial discrimination, the strike was a demonstration of white ethnic working-class power in a period of declining unionization. *New York Times*, March 1 and 22, and September 10 and 14, 1968.

28. A. Young, *An Easy Burden*, 494.

29. *New York Times*, September 3, 6, 9, and 11, 1968; *Atlanta Daily World*, September 8, 11–15, 1968, and March 20, 1970; *Atlanta Constitution*, September 10–14, 1968; and A. Young, *An Easy Burden*, 493–95. Two years later, workers joined a larger municipal strike of almost twenty-five hundred people, and SCLC became involved again in support of the workers. Abernathy and Hosea Williams found themselves leading marches, protests, and rallies for most of the thirty-seven days, as many others in the religious, labor, and civil rights communities joined the fight, including the national AFL-CIO. The strike ended with workers winning substantial pay concessions. *New York Times*, March 25 and April 23, 1970; and *Atlanta Daily World*, March 29 and April 1–5, 7, 17, 22, 24, 1970.

30. Unlike Memphis, Charleston has received relatively little attention—particularly the intersection of gender, class, race, labor, and civil rights. Those scholars who have studied the strike have focused on the longtime failure of the labor–civil rights coalition and the strike's watershed effect on race relations in Charleston. See Fink, "Union Power and Soul Power," 9–20; Fink and Greenberg, *Upheaval in the Quiet Zone*; and O'Neill, "From the Shadow of Slavery," 248–87, and "The Struggle for Black Equality Comes to Charleston," 82–91.

31. At the beginning of each shift, registered nurses provided medical records to white nursing assistants and licensed practical nurses to ensure better medical care but not always to black aides. In this instance, the five fired workers had walked off the job, angry over being denied basic information about their patients. Fink, "Union Power and Soul Power," 11; and Mary Moultrie, interview by Jean-Claude Bouffard.

32. O'Neill, "From the Shadow of Slavery," 251–52; Fink, "Union Power and Soul Power," 11; Abernathy, *And the Walls Came Tumbling Down*, 546; and Mary Moultrie, interview by Jean-Claude Bouffard.

33. A. Young, *An Easy Burden*, 497.

34. Mary Moultrie, interview by Jean-Claude Bouffard.

35. O'Neill, "From the Shadow of Slavery," 266–67; Fink, "Union Power and Soul Power," 9, 13; A. Young, *An Easy Burden*, 497; and Abernathy, *And the Walls Came Tumbling Down*, 544. For a more holistic examination of the forty-thousand-plus-member union, see Fink and Greenberg, *Upheaval in the Quiet Zone*.

36. Quotes in *New York Times*, April 23, 1969, and Fink, "Union Power and Soul Power," 14.

37. *New York Times*, April 1, 5, 8, 11, 21, 23, 27, 29, and May 4, 1969; *Wall Street Journal*, May 27, 1969; Fink, "Union Power and Soul Power," 12–13, 15–16; and O'Neill, "From the Shadow of Slavery," 267–68.

38. Fink and Greenberg, *Upheaval in the Quiet Zone*, 155.

39. *Jet*, May 5, 1969, and *1199 Drug and Hospital News*, July 1969, both in part 3, reel 10, frames 0843–0853, RSCLC; *Time*, July 4, 1969; *New York Times*, June 26 and 28, 1969, and March 22 and May 30, 1970; *Wall Street Journal*, March 3, 1970; Fink and Greenberg, *Upheaval in the Quiet Zone*, 159–67; O'Neill, "From the Shadow of Slavery," 285–87; Mary Moultrie, interview by Jean-Claude Bouffard; and *Charleston Post and Courier*, February 23, 2007.

40. Quote in *Los Angeles Times*, May 12, 1969.

41. A. Young, *An Easy Burden*, 501.

42. Coretta Scott King, in M. Anderson, *I Am Somebody*, a union-produced film on the strike.

43. *Jet*, April 10, May 15 and 22, and October 30, 1969; *Los Angeles Times*, August 15, 17, 1969; *People's World*, November 29, 1969; *Atlanta Journal-Constitution*, February 1, 2006; *Newsweek*, March 24, 1969; Sanders, "Finally, I've Begun to Live Again," 172–81; Alice Walker, "Growing Strength of Coretta King," *Redbook* 137 (September 1971): 96–97; and Vivian, *Coretta*, 113, 129–34. Remarkably, other than her advocacy for a King holiday and a "living memorial" to her husband, Coretta Scott King's activism largely has been ignored by historians. See Crawford, "Coretta Scott King."

44. O'Neill, "From the Shadow of Slavery," 273.

45. *Jet*, June 5, 1969.

46. *People's World*, November 29, 1969.

47. *Jet*, June 5, 1969; *People's World*, November 29, 1969; Fink, "Union Power and Soul Power," 11; O'Neill, "From the Shadow of Slavery," 248–52, 258–59; Esau Jenkins, interview by Jim Leeson, RBOHC; and A. Young, *An Easy Burden*, 496. See also Payne, *I've Got the Light of Freedom*, 68–77; Clark, *Ready from Within*; and Charron, *Freedom's Teacher*, and "We've Come a Long Way: Septima Clark, the Warings and the Changing Civil Rights Movement," in *Groundwork*, ed. Theoharis and Woodard, 116–39.

48. King had wanted to involve herself more in the organization's executive leadership, but her husband's aides (as he himself had before) resisted the idea. Jesse Jackson's dismissive tone, speaking to his staff about King, was typical: "We'll take care of our business and then Mrs. King can do her woman-power thing." Despite calling Abernathy "hopeless and unbelievable," an exasperated Stanley Levison also did not view King as capable of proper leadership. Perhaps still stung by her earlier criticism of their decision making during the Washington campaign, Young and Rutherford agreed at the time and joined Levison and others within SCLC in encouraging her to focus on a book about her life with Dr. King, which many saw as a certain moneymaker. "Ralph and the board wanted to use Coretta to raise money for SCLC, but they didn't want her to play any kind of policy role in the organization," Young recalled. "The men in SCLC were incapable of dealing with a strong woman like Coretta." Sanders, "Finally, I've Begun to Live Again," 174, 180–81; Lieferman, "Profession: Concert Singer, Freedom Movement Lecturer," ; SAC, New York to FBI director J. Edgar Hoover, June 7, 1968, SL; *Chicago Defender*, June 29–July 5, 1968; A. Young, *An Easy Burden*, 479; and Fairclough, *To Redeem the Soul*, 392. Coretta Scott King's book, *My Life with Dr. Martin Luther King Jr.*, ends not surprisingly with her husband's funeral—before her troubles with the organization he once led came to a head.

49. Fashion designers saw little bits of denim as part of a big trend the following spring. *Washington Post*, October 4, 1968.

50. A. Young, *An Easy Burden*, 502.

51. *Jet*, September 19, 1968, and August 14, 1969.

52. *New York Times*, May 17, 1969.

53. Quote in Kotz, *Let Them Eat Promises*, 224. Hunger policy became a small cottage industry between 1967 and 1970, with several new studies, a documentary, and the creation of the Senate Select Committee on Nutrition and Human Needs. In addition to journalist Nick Kotz's *Let Them Eat Promises*, see Coles, *Still Hungry in America*; Hollings, *The Case against Hunger*; Citizens' Board of Inquiry into Hunger and Malnutrition in the United States, *Hunger U.S.A.*; and Committee on School Lunch Participation, *Their Daily Bread*.

54. *New York Times*, May 14, 1969.

55. Quote in Fairclough, *To Redeem the Soul*, 396. Other scholars concur. See Patterson, *Grand Expectations*, 688–89; Sitkoff, *The Black Struggle for Equality*, 222–25; and Branch, *At Canaan's Edge*. In his brief epilogue, Branch does not discuss SCLC

after King's death. Kotz, *Let Them Eat Promises*, 193–223; G. C. Moore memo to W. C. Sullivan, April 24, 1969; SAC, Washington to FBI director, May 1, 1969; Washington FBI memo, May 19, 1969; SAC, Jackson memo to FBI director, May 26, June 6, 9–10, 12–13 and 15, and July 11, 1969; SAC, Mobile memo to FBI director, June 22, 1969, all in POCAM; *New York Times*, May 11, 13–14, 17, 1969; and Walter Fauntroy memo to SCLC staff, April 29, 1969, box 13, folder 13, NK.

56. George Wiley and Johnnie Tillmon letter to Abernathy, May 6, 1969, box 15, folder 16, NK.

57. *New York Times*, May 18, 1969.

58. George Wiley and Johnnie Tillmon letter to Abernathy, May 6, 1969, box 15, folder 16, NK; Abernathy telegrams to Reies Tijerina, March 31 and December 22, 1969, and Abernathy telegrams to Patsy Tijerina, April 27 and May 17, 1971, all in box 34, folder 20, RLT; Rudy Gonzales, interview by author; SAC, Washington memo to FBI director, May 12, 1969, POCAM; *New York Times*, May 18, 1969; *People's World*, May 24, 1969; Abernathy letter to Dolores Huerta, July 29, 1969, Abernathy letter to Chavez, July 25, 1970, and Hosea Williams letters to Chavez, March 12 and April 21, 1971, all in box 5, folder 38, Administrative Department Papers, PUFW.

59. A. Young, *An Easy Burden*, 508.

60. Ibid., 508–13; Fairclough, *To Redeem the Soul*, 391; and Billy Hollins and Bernard Lafayette, interviews by author.

61. Calvin Morris and Billy Hollins, interviews by author; Levine, "Jesse Jackson"; "Emerging Rights Leader: Jesse Louis Jackson," *New York Times*, May 24, 1968; "Jesse Jackson Emerging as Poor Campaign's Hero," *Chicago Daily Defender*, June 1, 1968; and Reynolds, *Jesse Jackson*, 316.

62. Rivlin, *Fire on the Prairie*, 4–18; A. Anderson and Pickering, *Confronting the Color Line*, 326; Mailer, *Miami and the Siege of Chicago*, 103–4, 156; and Royko, *Boss*, 171–98. See also Grimshaw, *Black Politics and the Chicago Machine*.

63. Jesse L. Jackson memo to staff and fellow ministers, September 1968, in *Chicago 1966*, ed. Garrow, 306, emphasis in original.

64. Calvin Morris, interview by author.

65. Gary Massoni, "Perspectives on Operation Breadbasket," in *Chicago 1966*, ed. Garrow, 220–21.

66. *Jet*, August 8 and October 24, 1968; *Southern Patriot*, October 1968; Massoni, "Perspectives," 218–21, 232–34; and Reynolds, *Jesse Jackson*, 133, 141–43.

67. *Jet*, January 23, October 23, and December 25, 1969, and January 1, 1970; *New York Times*, April 7, 1969; Levine, "Jesse Jackson," 69–70; Reynolds, *Jesse Jackson*, 164–68; and Landess and Quinn, *Jesse Jackson and the Politics of Race*, 48–49.

68. T. Jackson, *From Civil Rights to Human Rights*, 303–4; Fairclough, *To Redeem the Soul*, 394; and Garrow, *Bearing the Cross*, 585.

69. Quote in *Chicago Daily Defender*, February 13, 1969. Also, Gary Massoni, interview by author; and Brooks, "Black Upsurge in the Unions," 130–33.

70. *Chicago Daily Defender*, May 8, 1969.

71. *Chicago Daily Defender*, June 12, July 14, and August 21, 1969; *New York Times*, June 2 and August 16, 1969; *Jet*, July 3, September 4, and October 2 and 9, 1969,

and January 22, 1970; *People's World*, October 4, 1969; and Reynolds, *Jesse Jackson*, 191–93, 195–96. In addition to participating in the Chicago Coalition for United Community Action, led by SCLC veteran C. T. Vivian, Breadbasket also founded Black Labor Leaders of Chicago.

72. Calvin Morris, interview by author.

73. *Chicago Daily Defender*, November 14, 1968; *Chicago Tribune*, March 26, 1970; Reynolds, *Jesse Jackson*, 202–4; and Hahamovitch, *The Fruits of Their Labor*, 200–201.

74. Quote by Gary Massoni, interview by author. "Farmworkers-Breadbasket in Historic Alliance," [1970], SCLC West, box 5, folder 34; Eliseo Medina letter to Cesar Chavez, May 10, 1969, and Medina, Chicago boycott monthly expense reports, May 10, June 28, November 29, and December 30, 1969, and February 25 and June 25, 1970, box 24, folder 11, all in PUFW Administrative Department, part I, and John Armendariz letter to Gene Boutilier, November 14, 1966, box 7, folder 1, United Farm Worker Organizing Committee papers, PUFW; *Los Angeles Times*, November 23, 1969, and January 11, 2006; *Daily World*, October 29, 1968, and December 17, 1969; and Pawel, *The Union of Their Dreams*, 32–33, 50–51, 53, 61.

75. Jesse Jackson, interview in *Playboy*, November 1969, http://www.geocities .com/Heartland/9766/jackson.htm, accessed March 3, 2007.

76. Reynolds, *Jesse Jackson*, 150, 172; *New York Times*, July 9, 1972; Mooney and Majka, *Farmers' and Farmworkers' Movements*, 162; and Gary Massoni, interview by author.

77. *Chicago Daily Defender*, July 26, 1968, and July 16 and August 4, 1969; *Roosevelt Torch*, November 4, 1968; *Lincoln Park Press*, November 20, 1968; *New York Times*, July 9, 1972; Reynolds, *Jesse Jackson*, 150, 172; Mooney and Majka, *Farmers' and Farm-workers' Movements*, 162; and Gary Massoni, interview by author.

78. Obed Lopez Zacarías, interview by author.

79. Jackson took similar issue with SCLC's endorsement of Hubert Humphrey in the 1968 presidential election. Levine, "Jesse Jackson," 67.

80. Quote in Rivlin, *Fire on the Prairie*, 83. Also, Cesar Chavez, "Martin Luther King Jr.: He Showed Us the Way, April 1978," in *The Words of Cesar Chavez*, ed. Jensen and Hammerback, 96–97; M. García, *Memories*, 216; Rivlin, *Fire on the Prairie*, 88–94; and Landess and Quinn, *Jesse Jackson and the Politics of Race*, 57–58.

81. Reynolds, *Jesse Jackson*, 285.

82. Calvin Morris, interview by author; Reynolds, *Jesse Jackson*, 285; and Danns, *Something Better for Our Children*, 85–86.

83. Levine, "Jesse Jackson," 64.

84. *New York Times*, August 3, 1968, and June 2, 1969; *Chicago Daily Defender*, May 22, 1969; Calvin Morris, interview by author; FBI memo, Chicago, May 10, 1968, POCAM; A. Anderson and Pickering, *Confronting the Color Line*, 210–13; and Seligman, *Block by Block*, 59–98.

85. Gray, *The Murder of Fred Hampton*; and Jon Rice, "The World of Illinois Panthers," 50–51, 54.

86. Jose "Cha-Cha" Jimenez, interview by Mervin Méndez.

87. *Rising Up Angry*, July and August 1969; Bobby Rush in *Voices of Freedom*, ed. Hampton and Fayer, 528; Darlene Jesse, interview by author; Jose "Cha-Cha"

Jimenez, interview by Mervin Méndez; Omar Lopez, interview by Miguel Morales; and Sonnie and Tracy, *Hillbilly Nationalists*, 72–76.

88. Quotes in *Rising Up Angry*, July 1969. *Rising Up Angry*, August 1969; *Chicago Defender*, July 29–31, 1969; Jon Rice, "The World of the Illinois Panthers," in *Freedom North*, ed. Theoharis and Woodard, 50–52, 54–56; Diamond, *Mean Streets*, 306; C. López, "LADO," 22–27; Obed Lopez Zacarías, interview by author; and Omar Lopez, interview by Miguel Morales.

89. Charles Cheng, interview by Malika Lumumba, RBOHC.

90. Myles Horton, report, February 1970, and Horton letter to Kay Boyle, February 16, 1970, folder 15; Horton letter to Rev. Jack Mendelsohn, May 6, 1971, and Horton, Chicago report, September 15–28, 1969, and October 23–28, 1970, folder 11; Horton, Chicago report, February 21–22, 1971, and Conrad Browne letter to Charles Geary, January 19, 1971, folder 18, all in box 101; and Horton, Chicago Field Report, August 3, 1969, Horton letters to William Fesperman, October 7, 1969, and to Cha-Cha Jimenez, October 9, 1969, folder 19; Horton letter to Rev. Harold Smith, January 29, 1970, folder 21, all in box 109, all in HFS; and Darlene Jesse, interview by author.

91. Ogbar, *Black Power*, 178–80, and *"Puerto Rico en mi corazón"*; Jon Rice, "The World of the Illinois Panthers," 55–56; and Williams, "Rainbow Coalition Politics."

92. Diamond, *Mean Streets*, 309.

93. James Tracy, "The (Original) Rainbow Coalition," *Solidarities* (Chicago: AREA, September 30, 2006), http://www.areachicago.net/p/issues/solidarities/original-rainbow-coalition/, accessed May 13, 2009.

94. Gray and Alk, "American Revolution 2"; *New York Times*, November 9, 1969; *People's World*, November 29, 1969; and Darlene Jesse, interview by author.

95. *Rising Up Angry*, July 1969; *Chicago Daily Defender*, May 15, 1969; Omar Lopez, interview by Miguel Morales; and Darlene Jesse, interview by author.

96. Omar Lopez, interview by Miguel Morales.

97. Jose "Cha-Cha" Jimenez, interview by Ralph Cintron and Erika Rodriguez; Omar Lopez, interview by Miguel Morales; F. Browning, "From Rumble to Revolution," 19–25; "Black Panther Party Platform and Program: What We Want, What We Believe," October 1966, in *Let Nobody Turn Us Around*, ed. Marable and Mullings; 469–70; *Rising Up Angry*, July 1969; *Chicago Daily Defender*, August 23, 1969; Kerr, "Chicano Experience in Chicago, 1920–1970," 183; and Fernández, "From the Near West Side to 18th Street," 162–83.

98. Donner, *Protectors of Privilege*, 90.

99. While the city's primary daily newspapers, the *Tribune, Sun-Times*, and *Daily News*, covered only the most egregious police actions, if that, the city's underground press could fill its pages with coverage of police department malfeasance. See copies of *Chicago Seed, Rising Up Angry, LADO, Chicago Journalism Review*, and *Roosevelt Torch* in the microfilm series *Underground Newspaper Collection, 1963–1985*. The *Chicago Reader* is another source. Also see Donner, *Protectors of Privilege*, 90–154; and the Chicago Police Department's Red Squad files at the Chicago Historical Society, with written permission only.

100. *Black Panther*, May 19, 1969; *Rising Up Angry*, July and August 1969; Don-

ner, *Protectors of Privilege*, 90–154; Obed Lopez Zacarías, interview by author; Jose "Cha-Cha" Jimenez, interviews by author, and Ralph Cintron and Erika Rodriguez; Jon Rice, *Up on Madison, Down on 75th*, 74; and Commission of Inquiry, *Search and Destroy*, 26–27.

101. Commission of Inquiry, *Search and Destroy*, quote in ix, vii–xii, 3–13; and William O'Neal in *Voices of Freedom*, ed. Hampton and Fayer, 531–32.

102. Gray, *Murder of Fred Hampton; New York Times*, December 7, 1969; *Chicago Defender*, December 13, 1969; and Haas, *The Assassination of Fred Hampton*.

103. Cha-Cha Jimenez, interview by author.

104. With donated equipment and more than 150 volunteers from the medical community, the Panther clinic featured a level of professionalism unusual for such clinics. Five nights a week, medical professionals provided first aid, physical exams, prenatal care, and other services. Ron Satchel, severely injured in the Hampton raid, was the Panthers' Minister of Health and a former premed student. He recalled that the clinic took a real leadership role on sickle cell anemia—a blood condition that struck African Americans—by testing some fifty thousand students. This service prompted the Chicago Board of Health to step up both its testing and public awareness efforts of the disease. Overall, for the next two years, the clinic became a more convenient and less chaotic alternative to the only nearby hospital willing to take indigent patients, Cook County General. The Young Lords' Dr. Emeterio Betances Health Center organized screening efforts for tuberculosis and lead poisoning in Lincoln Park. LADO launched a clinic in Humboldt Park, and in white working-class Logan Square, Rising Up Angry helped operate the Fritzi Englestein Free People's Health Center. It pioneered the use of patient advocates, who could accompany patients needing more extensive treatment to local hospitals, making sure they received good care and were not overcharged for services. Volunteers also circulated through the surrounding neighborhoods in a van, testing children of all races for lead poisoning. By the mid-1970s, the clinic sponsored an annual health fair. *Rising Up Angry*, Summer 1970, 16, January 30–February 20, 1972, 15, June 25–July 9, 1972, 12, July 16–August 6, 1972, September 17, 1972, 7–8, 10, April 14–May 5, 1973, May 6–27, 1973, 6; Obed Lopez Zacarías, interview by author. In 1971, Abbie Hoffman listed all of these clinics in his survival guide to Chicago, called "Fuck Chicago." *Steal This Book*, 255–64.

105. *Jet*, December 18 and 25, 1969; *Chicago Defender*, December 11, 1969, and April 25, 1970; *Chicago Tribune*, December 10, 1969; and *The Patriot: Peoples News Service,* March 21 and July 21, 1970. Historians interested in black unity after Hampton's and Clark's deaths focus on the 1972 electoral defeat of State's Attorney Edward Hanrahan, who ordered the raid. Bucking Mayor Daley's machine in large numbers, African Americans did what one scholar called "the unthinkable, i.e. vote for a Republican," rather than Hanrahan. However, replacing one law-and-order state's attorney with another arguably proved less influential than the work of a handful of grass-roots organizations fighting for greater police accountability. Kleppner, *Chicago Divided*, 78; *Chicago Tribune*, April 13, 1975; and John Hill, in "A Notable Reversal," in *The Price of Dissent*, ed. Schultz and Schultz, 402–34.

106. *Rising Up Angry*, Mid-Winter, Early Spring, and Summer 1970; *Jet*, December 18 and 25, 1969; Commission of Inquiry, *Search and Destroy*; Rivlin, *Fire on the Prairie*, 19; Austin, *Up Against the Wall*, 209–22; Diamond, *Mean Streets*, 308–10; and Darlene Jesse, interview by author.

107. *Chicago Daily News*, December 10, 1969.

108. *Chicago Daily Defender*, December 13, 1969.

109. *Chicago Sun-Times*, May 25, 1969.

110. *New York Times*, December 11, 1969; Calvin Morris, interview by author; *Jet*, December 25, 1969; *Chicago Daily Defender*, August 23 and December 13, 1969, and February 2 and 20, 1971; Reynolds, *Jesse Jackson*, 15, 221–28; Kleppner, *Chicago Divided*, 74–78; and Rivlin, *Fire on the Prairie*, 91–92.

111. A. Young, *An Easy Burden*, 444.

112. Reynolds, *Jesse Jackson*, 139.

113. *Chicago Daily Defender*, May 31, 1969; *Jet*, December 4, 1969, and March 26 and May 7, 1970; Reynolds, *Jesse Jackson*, 140, 324–25, 347–55; Rivlin, *Fire on the Prairie*, 89; and Fairclough, *To Redeem the Soul*, 396–97.

114. "The Gary Declaration: Black Politics at the Convention," in *Let Nobody Turn Us Around*, ed. Marable and Mullings, 494–95.

115. *New York Times*, March 12, 1972.

116. *Amsterdam News*, March 4, 1972; *New York Times*, March 12, 1972; *Chicago Daily Defender*, March 8 and 13, 1972; *Los Angeles Sentinel*, March 16, 1972; Woodard, *A Nation within a Nation*, 205–17; and Ben Chavis and Ivanhoe Donaldson in *Voices of Freedom*, ed. Hampton and Fayer, 581–82. The debates over a third party echoed those on the local level in Lowndes County, Alabama, in 1966, when activists argued over the formation of the Lowndes County Freedom Organization and its symbol, the Black Panther. Jeffries, *Bloody Lowndes*, 146–49.

117. *Washington Post*, March 11 and 19, 1972; *New York Times*, March 12 and 16, 1972; *Chicago Daily Defender*, March 16, 1972; and Richard Hatcher in *Voices of Freedom*, ed. Hampton and Fayer, 583.

118. *Chicago Daily Defender,* March 13, 1972; *Baltimore Afro-American*, March 18, 1972; Woodard, *A Nation within a Nation*, 203, 205; and Richard Hatcher, in *Voices of Freedom*, ed. Hampton and Fayer, 570.

119. Quote in *Los Angeles Sentinel*, March 16, 1972. *Chicago Daily Defender*, March 13, 15, 1972; *Atlanta Daily World*, March 16, 1972; *Baltimore Afro-American*, March 18, 1972; and *Ebony*, June 1972.

120. *Baltimore Afro-American*, March 18, 1972.

121. Harding, *The Other American Revolution*, 216; Marable, *Race, Reform and Rebellion*, 123; and Woodard, *A Nation within a Nation*, 160.

122. Other factors included her gender and her unwillingness to seek permission from New York's black powerbrokers to run. *Amsterdam News*, March 11, 1972; Chisholm, *The Good Fight*; and Joshua Guild, "To Make That Someday Come: Shirley Chisholm's Radical Politics of Possibility," in *Want to Start a Revolution?*, ed. Gore, Theoharis and Woodard, 248–70.

123. *Washington Post*, March 16, 1972; Ben Chavis, Mary Hightower, and Ivanhoe

Donaldson in *Voices of Freedom*, ed. Hampton and Fayer, 584–86; Cohen and Taylor, *American Pharaoh*, 521–23; Rivlin, *Fire on the Prairie*, 90; and Cowie, *Stayin' Alive*, 105–13.

Epilogue

1. Barbara Smith with Demita Frazier and Beverly Smith, "Combahee River Collective Statement, 1977," in *Let Nobody Turn Us Around*, ed. Marable and Mullings, 526.

2. Schlesinger, *The Disuniting of America*, 17.

3. Gitlin, *The Twilight of Common Dreams*, 183.

4. Gitlin, "Organizing across Boundaries," 38.

5. They include Eric Hobsbawm, Ralph Nader, Michael Tomasky, and Betty Friedan. Martin Duberman, "The Divided Left: Identity Politics versus Class," in *Left Out*, 415. Also see Cowie, *Stayin' Alive*.

6. Du Bois, *Black Reconstruction in America*, 700–701.

7. Quote in Rubio, *A History of Affirmative Action*, xiv. See also Roediger, *The Wages of Whiteness*, *How Race Survived U.S. History*, and *Working toward Whiteness*; Ignatiev, *How the Irish Became White*; and Katznelson, *When Affirmative Action Was White*.

8. Ogbar, *Black Power*, 191.

9. Quote in Joseph, *Waiting 'Til the Midnight Hour*, 303. Also, Murch, *Living for the City*; Goldberg and Griffey, *Black Power at Work*; Biondi, *The Black Revolution on Campus*; Williams, *The Politics of Public Housing*; and Van Deburg, *New Day in Babylon*.

10. Oropeza, *¡Raza Si! ¡Guerra No!*, quotes 196, 191–95. See also Blackwell, *¡Chicana Power!*, chap. 6; and Bebout, *Mythohistorical Interventions*, chap. 4.

11. Montejano, *Quixote's Soldiers*, 209, 237–61.

12. Kelley, *Yo Mama's Disfunktional!*, 11.

13. *BPINS*, October 19, 1974, folder 15, YL.

14. Jose "Cha-Cha" Jimenez, "Statement of Candidacy," June 20, 1974, folder 12, *Rising Up Angry*, January 5–26, 1975, and *Lincoln Park–Lake View Booster*, December 18, 1974, folder 15, and *New City*, April 6, 1975, folder 11, all in YL; *Chicago Tribune*, January 7 and February 20, 1975; Jose "Cha-Cha" Jimenez, interview by author; and Fremon, *Chicago Politics*, 303–9.

15. Frost, *An Interracial Movement of the Poor*, 170.

16. Al Raby, "The Meaning of Harold Washington's Campaign: A Conversation with Al Raby," n.d. [1983], box 4, folder 6, HW.

17. Robert T. Starks and Michael B. Preston, "Harold Washington and the Politics of Reform in Chicago: 1983–1987," and Carlos Muñoz Jr. and Charles Henry, "Coalition Politics in San Antonio and Denver: The Cisneros and Peña Mayoral Campaigns," in *Racial Politics in American Cities*, ed. Browning, Marshall, and Tabb, 88–107, 179–90; and Kleppner, *Chicago Divided*.

18. Lawson, *Running for Freedom*, 260; and Juan Gómez-Quiñones, *Chicano Politics*, 162–74.

19. Jeffries, *Bloody Lowndes*, 207–45; Manning, *William L. Dawson and the Limits of Black Electoral Leadership*; Montejano, *Quixote's Soldiers*, 228–34; and Payne, *I've Got the Light of Freedom*, 409.

20. U.S. Census Bureau, "Table 689: People Below Poverty Level and Below 125 Percent of Poverty Level by Race and Hispanic Origin: 1980 to 2005," in *The 2008 Statistical Abstract: The National Data Book*, http://www.census.gov/compendia/ statab/2008/cats/income_expenditures_poverty_wealth.html; MacLean, *Freedom Is Not Enough*; Thompson, "Why Mass Incarceration Matters," 703–34; K. Jackson, *Crabgrass Frontier*; W. Wilson, *The Truly Disadvantaged*; and Klarman, *Unfinished Business*.

21. Bernice Johnson Reagon, "Coalition Politics: Turning the Century," in *Home Girls*, ed. Smith, 346.

Bibliography

Manuscript Collections

American Friends Service Committee Archives, Philadelphia
Center for Southwest Research, University of New Mexico, Albuquerque
    Carlos E. Cansino Papers
    Records of the National Indian Youth Council
    Papers of Reies López Tijerina
Chicago Historical Society, Chicago
    Chicago Police Department Red Squad Records
Walter R. Davis Library, University of North Carolina, Chapel Hill
    Papers of Student Nonviolent Coordinating Committee, microfilm
Denver Public Library, Denver, Colorado
    Papers of Rodolfo "Corky" Gonzales
    Lauren Watson File
DePaul University Special Collections and Archives, Chicago
    Lincoln Park Neighborhood Collection
    Young Lords Collection
Lyndon Baines Johnson Presidential Library and Archives, University of Texas,
    Austin Cabinet Papers
    Papers of Ramsey Clark
    Legislative Background Files
    Lyndon Baines Johnson Oral History Collection
    Papers of White House Aides
    White House Central Files
Martin Luther King Jr. Center for Peace and Nonviolent Change, Atlanta,
    Georgia
    Dr. Martin Luther King Jr. Papers
    Records of the Southern Christian Leadership Conference
Moorland-Spingarn Research Center, Howard University, Washington, D.C.
    Ralph Bunche Oral History Collection
    Civil Rights Documentation Project Vertical File
    Papers of the National Welfare Rights Organization, unprocessed
Norlin Library, University of Colorado, Boulder
    Records of Western Federation of Miners and the International Union
        of Mine, Mill and Smelter Workers

William R. Perkins Library, Duke University, Durham, North Carolina
   Bayard Rustin Papers, microfilm
   Papers of the Southern Christian Leadership Conference, microfilm
Walter P. Reuther Library, Wayne State University, Detroit, Michigan
   Papers of Cesar Chavez, Office of the President, United Farm Workers
      Collection
   Papers of the United Farm Worker Organizing Committee
Schomburg Center for Research in Black Culture, New York Public Library,
      New York
   Papers of Albert E. Gollin, unprocessed
Southern Appalachian Archives, Berea College, Berea, Kentucky
   Appalachian Volunteers Papers
Southern Historical Collection, Wilson Library, University of North Carolina,
      Chapel Hill
   George H. Esser Papers
University of Washington Libraries, Seattle
   Flo Ware Papers
Harold Washington Library Center, Chicago Public Library, Chicago
   Government Publications
   Mayoral Campaign Records, Harold Washington Archives and Collections
Wisconsin State Historical Society, University of Wisconsin, Madison
   Papers of James E. Groppi
   Papers of the Highlander Folk School and Center for Education and Research,
      processed and unprocessed
   Papers of Nick and Maryann Kotz
   Papers of Arthur Ocean Waskow
   Papers of Lee Webb
   Papers of George A. Wiley

Government Documents

Gollin, Albert. *The Demography of Protest: A Statistical Profile of Participants in the Poor
   People Campaign.* Washington, D.C.: Bureau of Social Science Research, 1968.
Keyes et al. v. School District, No. 1, Denver, 413 U.S. 189 (June 21, 1973).
New Jersey Governor's Commission on Civil Disorders. *Report for Action.* State of
   New Jersey, 1968.
United States. *Report of the National Advisory Commission on Civil Disorders.*
   Washington, D.C.: U.S. Government Printing Office, 1968.
U.S. Census Bureau. *1970 Census—Characteristics of the Population,* vol. I, part
   I—U.S. Summary, Section 2. Washington, D.C.: U.S. Government Printing
   Office, 1971.
———. *1970 Census—Characteristics of the Population,* vol. 1, part 45—Texas,
   Section 1. Washington, D.C.: U.S. Government Printing Office, 1971.
U.S. Commission on Civil Rights. *The 50 States Report.* Washington, D.C.: U.S.
   Government Printing Office, 1961.

————. *Report of the United States Commission on Civil Rights*. Washington, D.C.: U.S. Government Printing Office, 1959.

U.S. Congress. House. Committee on Ways and Means. *Social Security and Welfare Proposals: Hearings of the Committee on Ways and Means, Part 3*. Washington, D.C.: U.S. Government Printing Office, 1970.

————. Subcommittee on Fiscal Policy of the Joint Economic Committee. *Income Maintenance Programs: Hearings before the Subcommittee on Fiscal Policy of the Joint Economic Committee*. 90th Cong., 2nd sess., 1968.

U.S. Congress. Permanent Subcommittee on Investigations of the Committee on Government Operations. *Conference on Problems Involved in the Poor Peoples' March on Washington, D.C.* 90th Cong., 2nd sess., 1968.

U.S. Congress. Senate. Subcommittee on Employment, Manpower, and Poverty. *Employment Training Legislation—1968: Hearings before the Subcommittee on Employment, Manpower, and Poverty*. 90th Cong., 2nd sess., 1968.

————. Subcommittee on Employment, Manpower, and Poverty. *Examination of the War on Poverty, Part 2: Jackson, Miss.: Hearings before the Subcommittee on Employment, Manpower, and Poverty*. 90th Cong., 1st sess., 1967.

————. Subcommittee on Migratory Labor of the Committee on Labor and Public Welfare. *Migratory Labor—Hearings before the Subcommittee on Migratory Labor of the Committee on Labor and Public Welfare*. 86th Cong., 1st sess., 1959.

————. Subcommittee on Migratory Labor of the Committee on Labor and Public Welfare. *Migratory Labor—Hearings before the Subcommittee on Migratory Labor of the Committee on Labor and Public Welfare*. 86th Cong., 2nd sess., 1960.

U.S. Federal Bureau of Investigation. Brown Berets of New Mexico File (100-450812). Washington, D.C., 1968–70.

————. Crusade for Justice File (105-178283). Washington, D.C., 1967–75.

————. Stanley D. Levison File (100-392452). Washington, D.C., 1965–69.

————. Poor People's Campaign File (157-8428). Washington, D.C., 1967–69.

Internet-Accessed Documents

Kennedy, John F. "Civil Rights Address." June 11, 1963. http://www.american rhetoric.com/speeches/jfkcivilrights.htm, accessed September 1, 2011

King, Martin Luther, Jr. "Press conference transcript announcing Poor People's Campaign." December 4, 1967. Martin Luther King Jr. Papers Project. http://www.stanford.edu/group/King/publications/papers/ unpub/671204–003_Announcing_Poor_Peoples_campaign.htm, accessed September 9, 2005

Rustin, Bayard. "Newsletter #2." August 1963. http://www.crmvet.org/docs/ mownews2.pdf, accessed September 3, 2011

Rustin, Bayard, and Cleveland Robinson. "Final Plans for the March on Washington for Jobs and Freedom, Organizing Manual No. 2." 1963. http:// www.crmvet.org/docs/moworg2.pdf, accessed September 3, 2011

United Farm Workers Documents Collection. http://farmworkermovement.com, accessed June 23, 2011

Newspapers and Magazines

Akwesasne Notes (Rooseveltown, N.Y.)
Alamo Messenger (San Antonio, Tex.)
Albuquerque Journal
Albuquerque Tribune
American Federationist
Atlanta Constitution
Atlanta Daily World
Baltimore Afro-American
Black Panther (Oakland, Calif.)
Chicago American
Chicago Defender and Daily Defender
Chicago Reader
Chicago Seed
Chicago Sun-Times
Chicago Today
Chicago Tribune
Chicano Student and Chicano
   Student News (Los Angeles)
Christian Science Monitor (Boston)
Christianity Today
Commentary
Commercial Appeal (Memphis)
Commonweal
Daily World (San Francisco)
Denver Post
Ebony (Chicago)
Evening Star (Washington, D.C.)
El Gallo (Denver)
El Grito del Norte (Española, N.M.)
Harper's
Houston Post
I. F. Stone's Weekly
Inferno (San Antonio)
Jet (Chicago)
LADO (Chicago)
Lincoln Park Press (Chicago)
Los Angeles Sentinel
Los Angeles Times
Louisville Courier-Journal
El Malcriado (Delano, Calif.)
Militant
Missoulian (Missoula, Mont.)
Movement (San Francisco)

Nation
National Guardian
National Register
New Republic
New York Amsterdam News
New York Times
New York Times Magazine
New Yorker
Newsweek
Packinghouse Worker
El Papel (Albuquerque, N.M.)
Parade
People's World (San Francisco)
Pittsburgh Courier
Playboy
Press-Scimitar (Memphis)
La Raza (Los Angeles)
Readers Digest
Redbook
Rising Up Angry (Chicago)
Rocky Mountain Life
Rocky Mountain News (Denver)
Roosevelt Torch (Chicago)
Quaker Service
St. Louis Post-Dispatch
San Antonio Express/News
San Francisco Chronicle
Saturday Review
Soul Force (Atlanta)
Southern Patriot (Louisville, Ky.)
Steel Labor
Time
UAW Solidarity
United Mine Workers Journal
U.S. News & World Report
Wall Street Journal
Washington Daily News
Washington Post
Weekly Missoulian (Missoula,
   Montana Territory)
Westword (Denver)
Worker and Daily Worker
   (New York)

Oral Histories by Author (in Author's Possession)

Gloria Arellanes, November 9, 2006, El Monte, Calif.
Gilberto Ballejos, December 6, 2007, Albuquerque, N.M.
Miguel Barragan, October 27, 2006, by telephone
Willie Bolden, November 4, 2005, Atlanta, Ga.
Jessica Bordeaux-Vigil, September 9, 2007, by telephone
Joan Browning, March 2, 2008, by telephone
Victor Charlo, February 23, 2007, by telephone
Alicia Escalante, September 19, 2005, by telephone
Roque Garcia, August 17, 2005, by telephone
Gerry Gonzales, June 26, 2005, Denver, Colo.
Nita Jo Gonzales, June 27, 2005, Denver, Colo.
Rudy Gonzales, June 26, 2005, Denver, Colo.
Mike Gray, May 11 and 27, 2011, by telephone
Freddie Greene, June 14, 2010, by telephone
José Angel Gutiérrez, January 8, 2006, by telephone
James Hargett, August 6, 2005, Carlsbad, Calif.
Louilyn F. Hargett, August 6, 2005, Carlsbad, Calif.
Craig Hart, November 29, 2007, Denver, Colo.
Billy Hollins, October 9, 2006, Atlanta, Ga.
Darlene Jesse, March 9, 2011, Greenville, N.C.
Jose "Cha-Cha" Jimenez, December 19, 2011, by telephone
Bernard Lafayette, June 13, 2005, and January 23, 2006, by telephone
Obed Lopez Zacarías, July 11, 2006, by telephone
Juanita Malouff-Dominguez, December 12, 2007, Taos, N.M.
Gary Massoni, September 5, 2007, by telephone
Al McSurely, June 10, 2005, Chapel Hill, N.C.
Ethel Minor, June 7, 2010, by telephone
Carlos Montes, August 8, 2005, Los Angeles, Calif.
Calvin Morris, July 24, 2006, Chicago
Leo Nieto, March 9, 2006, by telephone
Ralph Ramirez, September 11, 2005, by telephone
Bert Ransome, September 11, 2006, by telephone
Maria Varela, June 18, 2005, Albuquerque, N.M.
Maria Varela, August 30, 2005, and July 29, 2010, by telephone
Baldemar Velásquez, August 2 and 8, 2007, by telephone
Ernesto Vigil, December 10, 2005, by telephone
Lauren Watson, June 27, 2005, Denver, Colo.
Shirley Hill Witt, December 6, 2007, Albuquerque, N.M.

Other Oral Histories (All in Ralph Bunche Oral History Collection, Moorland-Spingarn Research Center, unless Otherwise Noted)

Ernie Austin, interview by Kay Shannon, July 6, 1968, Washington, D.C.

Anne and Carl Braden, interview by James Mosby, September 18–19, 1968, Louisville, Ky.

Charles Cheng, interview by Malika Lumumba, June 6, 1970, Washington, D.C.

Mike Clark, interview by Robert Chase, November 26, 1997, by telephone

Ramsey Clark, interview by Harri Baker, June 3, 1969, Falls Church, Va., LBJ Library Oral History Collection

Mark Comfort, interview by Robert Wright, November 16, 1968, Oakland, Calif.

Stoney Cooks, interview by Kay Shannon, July 12, 1968, Washington, D.C.

Luís Diaz de León, interview by José Angel Gutiérrez, September 23, 1999, Tejano Voices, University of Texas at Arlington Center for Mexican American Studies Oral History Project

Marian Wright Edelman, interview by Blackside, Inc., December 21, 1988, for *Eyes on the Prize II: America at the Racial Crossroads 1965 to 1985*, Washington University Libraries, Film and Media Archive, Henry Hampton Collection

Cornelius Givens, interview by Kay Shannon, July 7, 1968, Washington, D.C.

Tom Houck, interview by Kay Shannon, July 10, 1968, Washington, D.C.

Ralph K. Huitt, interview by Helen Hall, September 17, 1969, Washington, D.C.

Esau Jenkins, interview by Jim Leeson, May 1968, Charleston, S.C.

Jose "Cha-Cha" Jimenez, interview by Mervin Méndez, December 6, 1993, Chicago, Young Lords Collection

Jose "Cha-Cha" Jimenez, interview by Ralph Cintron and Erika Rodriguez, June 2002, Chicago. http://www.gangresearchnet/ChicagoGangs/younglords/ chacha.htm, accessed November 15, 2009

Jose "Cha-Cha" Jimenez and Corky Gonzales, interview by Karen Wald. October 1970. http://www.walterlippmann.com/klw-1970.html

Omar Lopez, interview by Miguel Morales, February 10, 1995, Chicago, Young Lords Collection

Buck Maggard, interview by Robert Chase, December 10, 1997, by telephone

Francisco "Pancho" Medrano, interview by José Angel Gutiérrez, July 16, 1997, CMAS 37, Special Collections, University of Texas at Arlington Libraries

Mary Moultrie, interview by Jean-Claude Bouffard, July 28, 1982, MN-500.009.005, Jean-Claude Bouffard Civil Rights Interviews, Charleston, S.C., Avery Research Center

William H. Moyer, interview by Kay Shannon, July 7, 1968, Washington, D.C.

Joseph Mulloy, interview by James Mosby, May 26, 1970, New Orleans

Tom Offenburger, interview by Kay Shannon, July 2, 1968, Washington, D.C.

James Orange, interview by Kay Shannon, July 17, 1968, Washington, D.C.

Albert Peña, Jr., interview by José Angel Gutiérrez, July 2, 1996, CMAS 15, Special Collections, University of Texas at Arlington Libraries

James Edward Peterson, interview by Kay Shannon, July 3, 1968, Washington, D.C.

John Rutherford, interview by Kay Shannon, June 4, 1968, Washington, D.C.

Al Sampson, interview by Kay Shannon, July 8, 1968, Washington, D.C.

Tim Sampson, interview by Nick Kotz, December 8, 1974, Papers of Nick and
    Maryann Kotz

Katherine Shannon, interview by Claudia Rawles, August 12, 1968, Washington,
    D.C.

Frieda Wagner, interview by Kay Shannon, July 1968, Washington, D.C.

Tillie Walker, interview by Kay Shannon, July 1968, Washington, D.C.

Andrew Young, interview by Thomas H. Baker, June 18, 1970, Lyndon Baines
    Johnson Presidential Library Oral History Collection

Andrew Young, interview by Kay Shannon, July 16, 1968, Washington, D.C.

Films

Anderson, Madeline. *I Am Somebody*. 1970; reissue, New York: First Run/Icarus
    Films, 1999.

Birnbaum, Bernard, and Edward R. Murrow. *Harvest of Shame*. 1960; reissue,
    New York: Ambrose Video, 1991.

Gray, Mike. *Cicero March*. 1966; reissue, Chicago: Facets Video, 2007.

———. *The Murder of Fred Hampton*. 1970; reissue, Chicago: Facets Video, 2007.

Gray, Mike, and Howard Alk. *American Revolution 2*. 1969; reissue, Chicago:
    Facets Video, 2007.

Published Articles and Books

Abernathy, Ralph. *And the Walls Came Tumbling Down: An Autobiography*. New
    York: Harper & Row, 1989.

Acuña, Rodolfo. *Occupied America: A History of Chicanos*. New York: Longman,
    2000.

Adams, Frank, with Myles Horton. *Unearthing the Fire: The Idea of Highlander*.
    Winston-Salem, N.C.: John F. Blair, 1975.

Alvarez, Luis. *The Power of the Zoot: Youth Culture and Resistance during World War
    II*. Berkeley: University of California Press, 2008.

American Friends Service Committee. *Uncommon Controversy: Fishing Rights of the
    Muckelshoot, Puyallup and Nisqually Indians*. 1967; reprint, Seattle: University of
    Washington Press, 1970.

Anderson, Alan B., and George W. Pickering. *Confronting the Color Line: The
    Broken Promise of the Civil Rights Movement in Chicago*. Athens: University of
    Georgia Press, 1986.

Anderson, Terry H. *The Movement and the Sixties: Protest in America from Greensboro
    to Wounded Knee*. New York: Oxford University Press, 1995.

Arnesen, Eric. "Reconsidering the 'Long Civil Rights Movement.'" *Historically
    Speaking* 10, no. 2 (April 2009): 31–34.

———. "Whiteness and Historians' Imagination." *International Labor and Working
    Class History* 60 (2001): 3–32.

Arrendondo, Gabriela F. *Mexican Chicago: Race, Identity and Nation, 1916–1939.* Urbana-Champaign: University of Illinois Press, 2008.

Arsenault, Raymond. *Freedom Riders: 1961 and the Struggle for Racial Justice.* New York: Oxford University Press, 2006.

Ashmore, Susan Youngblood. *Carry It On: The War on Poverty and the Civil Rights Movement in Alabama, 1964–1972.* Athens: University of Georgia, 2008.

Austin, Curtis J. *Up Against the Wall: Violence in the Making and Unmaking of the Black Panther Party.* Fayetteville: University of Arkansas Press, 2006.

Badillo, David A. "From La Lucha to Latino: Ethnic Change, Political Identity, and Civil Rights in Chicago." In *La Causa: Civil Rights, Social Justice and the Struggle for Equality in the Midwest*, ed. Gilberto Cárdenas. 37–54. Houston: Arte Público Press, 2004.

Barber, Lucy. *Marching on Washington: The Forging of an American Political Tradition.* Berkeley: University of California Press, 2002.

Barnard, John. *American Vanguard: The United Auto Workers during the Reuther Years, 1935–1970.* Detroit: Wayne State University Press, 2004.

Bauman, Robert. *Race and the War on Poverty: From Watts to East L.A.* Norman: University of Oklahoma, 2008.

Bebout, Lee. *Mythohistorical Interventions: The Chicano Movement and Its Legacies.* Minneapolis: University of Minnesota Press, 2011.

Behnken, Brian D. *Fighting Their Own Battles: Mexican Americans, African Americans, and the Struggle for Civil Rights in Texas.* Chapel Hill: University of North Carolina Press, 2011.

———, ed. *The Struggle in Black and Brown: African American and Mexican American Relations during the Civil Rights Era.* Lincoln: University of Nebraska Press, 2011.

Beifuss, Joan Turner. *At the River I Stand: Memphis, the 1968 Strike, and Martin Luther King.* 1985; reprint, Brooklyn, N.Y.: Carlson, 1989.

Bernstein, Shana. *Bridges of Reform: Interracial Civil Rights Activism in Twentieth-Century Los Angeles.* New York: Oxford University Press, 2010.

Berry, Faith. "The Anger and Problems and Sickness of the Poor of the Whole Nation Were in This One Shantytown." *New York Times Magazine*, July 7, 1968.

Betancur, John J., and Douglas C. Gills, eds. *The Collaborative City: Opportunities and Struggles for Blacks and Latinos in U.S. Cities.* New York: Garland, 2000.

Biondi, Martha. *The Black Revolution on Campus.* Berkeley: University of California Press, 2012.

———. *To Stand and Fight: The Struggle for Civil Rights in Postwar New York City.* Cambridge, Mass.: Harvard University Press, 2003.

Black, Timuel. *Bridges of Memory: Chicago's Second Generation of Black Migration.* Evanston, Ill.: Northwestern University Press; DuSable Museum of African American History, 2007.

Blackwell, Maylei. *¡Chicana Power! Contested Histories of Feminism in the Chicano Movement.* Austin: University of Texas Press, 2011.

Blanton, Carlos. "George I. Sánchez, Ideology, and Whiteness in the Making of the Mexican American Civil Rights Movement, 1930–1960." *Journal of Southern History* 72 (August 2006): 569–604.

Blawis, Patricia Bell. *Tijerina and the Land Grants: Mexican Americans in Struggle for Their Heritage*. New York: International Publishers, 1971.

Bowman, Timothy Paul. "From Workers to Activists the UFW in Texas' Lower Rio Grande Valley." *Journal of the West* 47, no. 3 (Summer 2008): 87–94.

Boyle, Kevin. *The UAW and the Heyday of American Liberalism*. Ithaca, N.Y.: Cornell University Press, 1995.

Branch, Taylor. *At Canaan's Edge: America in the King Years, 1965–1968*. New York: Simon & Schuster, 2006.

———. *Parting the Waters: America in the King Years, 1954–1963*. New York: Simon & Schuster, 1988.

Briggs, Charles L., and John R. Van Ness, eds. *Land, Water, and Culture: New Perspectives on Hispanic Land Grants*. Albuquerque: University of New Mexico, 1987.

Brilliant, Mark. *The Color of America Has Changed: How Racial Diversity Shaped Civil Rights Reform*. New York: Oxford University Press, 2010.

Brinkley, David. *Washington Goes to War*. New York: Ballantine Books, 1988.

Brooks, Thomas R. "Black Upsurge in the Unions." *Dissent* 17 (1970): 130–33.

Browning, Frank. "From Rumble to Revolution: The Young Lords." *Ramparts* 9 (1970–71): 19–25.

Browning, Rufus P., Dale Rogers Marshall, and David H. Tabb, eds. *Racial Politics in American Cities*. 3rd ed. New York: Longman, 2003.

Burt, Kenneth C. "The Power of a Mobilized Citizenry and Coalition Politics: The 1949 Election of Edward R. Roybal to the Los Angeles City Council." *Southern California Quarterly* 85 (2003): 413–38.

Busto, Rudy V. *King Tiger: The Religious Vision of Reies López Tijerina*. Albuquerque: University of New Mexico Press, 2005.

Caldiera, Gregory A., and James L. Gibson. "The Etiology of Public Support for the Supreme Court." *American Journal of Political Science* 36 (1992): 635–64.

Carmichael, Stokely, and Charles V. Hamilton. *Black Power: The Politics of Liberation in America*. London: Cape, 1968.

Carmichael, Stokely, with Ekwueme Michael Thelwell. *Ready for Revolution: The Life and Struggles of Stokely Carmichael (Kwame Ture)*. New York: Scribner, 2003.

Carson, Clayborne. *In Struggle: SNCC and the Black Awakening of the 1960s*. Cambridge, Mass.: Harvard University Press, 1981.

Cazenave, Noel. "Chicago Influences on the War on Poverty." *Journal of Policy History* 5, no. 1 (January 1993): 52–68.

Cecelski, David S. *Along Freedom Road: Hyde County, North Carolina and the Fate of Black Schools in the South*. Chapel Hill: University of North Carolina Press, 1994.

Chafe, William H. *The Unfinished Journey: America since World War II*. New York: Oxford University Press, 1999.

Cha-Jua, Sundiata Keita, and Clarence Lang. "The 'Long Movement' as Vampire: Temporal and Spatial Fallacies in Recent Black Freedom Studies." *Journal of African American History* 92, no. 2 (Spring 2007): 265–88.

Chappell, David L. "The Lost Decade of Civil Rights." *Historically Speaking* 10, no. 2 (April 2009): 37–41.

Charron, Katherine Mellen. *Freedom's Teacher: The Life of Septima Clark*. Chapel Hill: University of North Carolina Press, 2009.

Chase, Robert T. "Class Resurrection: The Poor People's Campaign of 1968 and Resurrection City." *Essays in History* 40 (1998). http://etext.virginia.edu/journals/EH/EH40/chase40.html.

Chavez, Cesar. *An Organizer's Tale: Speeches*. Edited by Ilan Stavans. New York: Penguin, 2008.

Chávez, Ernesto. ¡*Mi Raza Primero! Nationalism, Identity, and Insurgency in the Chicano Movement in Los Angeles, 1966–1978*. Berkeley: University of California Press, 2002.

Chicago Urban League. *Housing and Race in Chicago: A Preliminary Analysis of 1960 Census Data*. Chicago, 1963.

Chisholm, Shirley. *The Good Fight*. New York: Harper & Row, 1973.

Churchill, Ward, and Jim Vander Wall. *Agents of Repression: The FBI's Secret War against the Black Panther Party and the American Indian Movement*. Boston: South End Press, 2002.

Citizens' Board of Inquiry into Hunger and Malnutrition in the United States. *Hunger U.S.A.: A Report*. Boston: Beacon Press, 1968.

Clark, Septima Poinsette. *Ready from Within: Septima Clark and the Civil Rights Movement*. Trenton, N.J.: Africa World Press, 1990.

Clayson, William. *Freedom Is Not Enough: The Civil Rights Movement and the War on Poverty in Texas*. Austin: University of Texas Press, 2010.

Cloward, Richard, and Lloyd Ohlin. *Delinquency and Opportunity: A Theory of Delinquent Gangs*. Glencoe, Ill.: Free Press, 1960.

Cobb, Daniel M. *Native Activism in Cold War America: The Struggle for Sovereignty*. Lawrence: University of Kansas Press, 2008.

Cobb, Daniel M., and Loretta Fowler, eds. *Beyond Red Power: American Indian Politics and Activism since 1900*. Sante Fe, N.M.: School for Advanced Research, 2007.

Cohen, Adam, and Elizabeth Taylor. *American Pharaoh: Mayor Richard J. Daley, His Battle for Chicago and the Nation*. New York: Little Brown, 2000.

Cole, Stephanie, and Alison M. Parker, eds. *Beyond Black and White: Race, Ethnicity and Gender in the U.S. South and Southwest*. College Station: Texas A&M University Press, 2004.

Coles, Robert. *Still Hungry in America*. New York: World Publishing, 1969.

Commission of Inquiry into the Black Panthers and the Police, chairmen Roy Wilkins and Ramsey Clark. *Search and Destroy: A Report*. New York: Metropolitan Applied Research Center, 1973.

Committee on School Lunch Participation. *Their Daily Bread*. Atlanta: McNelley-Rudd Print. Service, 1968.

Córdova, Teresa. "Harold Washington and the Rise of Latino Electoral Politics in Chicago, 1982–1987." In *Chicano Politics and Society in the Late Twentieth Century*, ed. David Montejano, 31–57. Austin: University of Texas, 1999.

Countryman, Matthew J. *Up South: Civil Rights and Black Power in Philadelphia*. Philadelphia: University of Pennsylvania Press, 2006.

Cowie, Jefferson. *Stayin' Alive: The 1970s and the Last Days of the Working Class*. New York: New Press, 2010.

Crawford, Vicki. "Coretta Scott King and the Struggle for Civil and Human Rights." *Journal of African American History* 92, no. 1 (Winter 2007): 106–17.

Crespino, Joseph. *In Search of Another Country: Mississippi and the Conservative Counterrevolution*. Princeton, N.J.: Princeton University Press, 2007.

Curry, Constance. *Silver Rights*. San Diego: Harcourt, 1995.

Daniels, Roger. *The Bonus March: An Episode of the Great Depression*. Westport, Conn.: Greenwood, 1971.

Danns, Dionne. *Something Better for Our Children: Black Organizing in Chicago Public Schools, 1963–1971*. New York: Routledge, 2003.

de Baca, Vincent, ed. *La Gente: Hispano History and Life in Colorado*. Denver: Colorado Historical Society, 1998.

De Graaf, Lawrence, Kevin Mulroy, and Quintard Taylor, eds. *Seeking El Dorado: African Americans in California*. Seattle: University of Washington Press, 2001.

De Jong, Greta. *A Different Day: African American Struggles for Justice in Rural Louisiana, 1900–1970*. Chapel Hill: University of North Carolina Press, 2002.

Deloria, Vine, Jr. *Indians of the Pacific Northwest: From the Coming of the White Man to the Present Day*. New York: Doubleday, 1977.

D'Emilio, John. *Lost Prophet: The Life and Times of Bayard Rustin*. Chicago: University of Chicago Press, 2003.

Diamond, Andrew. *Mean Streets: Chicago Youths and the Everyday Struggle for Empowerment in the Multiracial City, 1908–1969*. Berkeley: University of California Press, 2009.

Dittmer, John. *Local People: The Struggle for Civil Rights in Mississippi*. Urbana: University of Illinois Press, 1994.

Donner, Frank J. *Protectors of Privilege: Red Squads and Police Repression in Urban America*. Berkeley: University of California Press, 1990.

Duberman, Martin. *Left Out: The Politics of Exclusion, Essays, 1964–1999*. New York: Basic Books, 1999.

Du Bois, W. E. B. *Black Reconstruction in America, 1860–1880*. 1935; reprint, New York: Free Press, 1992.

Dudziak, Mary L. *Cold War Civil Rights: Race and the Image of American Democracy*. Princeton, N.J.: Princeton University Press, 2000.

Dunne, John Gregory. *Delano: The Story of the California Grape Strike*. New York: Farrar, Straus and Giroux, 1967.

———. *Delano: The Story of the California Grape Strike*. Foreword by Ilan Stavans. 1967; reprint, New York: Oxford University Press, 2007.

Dzidzienyo, Anani, and Suzanne Oboler, eds. *Neither Enemies nor Friends: Latinos, Blacks, Afro-Latinos*. New York: Palgrave Macmillan, 2005.

Ebright, Malcolm. *Land Grants and Lawsuits in Northern New Mexico*. Albuquerque: University of New Mexico, 1994.

Elden, James M., and David R. Schweitzer. "New Third Party Radicalism: The Case of the California Peace and Freedom Party." *Western Political Quarterly* 24 (1971): 761–74.

Eskew, Glenn T. *But for Birmingham: The Local and National Movements in the Civil Rights Struggle*. Chapel Hill: University of North Carolina Press, 1997.

Espinoza, Dionne. "'Revolutionary Sisters': Women's Solidarity and Collective Identification among Chicana Brown Berets in East Los Angeles, 1967–1970." *Aztlán* 26 (2001): 17–58.

Estes, Steve. *I Am a Man! Race, Manhood, and the Civil Rights Movement*. Chapel Hill: University of North Carolina Press, 2005.

Evans, Sara. *Personal Politics: The Roots of Women's Liberation in the Civil Rights Movement and the New Left*. New York: Vintage Books, 1979.

Fager, Charles. *Uncertain Resurrection: The Poor People's Washington Campaign*. Grand Rapids, Mich.: William B. Eerdmans, 1969.

Fairclough, Adam. *Better Day Coming: Blacks and Equality, 1890–2000*. New York: Viking, 2001.

———. *To Redeem the Soul of America: The Southern Christian Leadership Conference and Martin Luther King Jr*. Athens: University of Georgia Press, 1987.

Farber, David. *Chicago '68*. Chicago: University of Chicago Press, 1988.

Fernández, Lilia. "From the Near West Side to 18th Street: Mexican Community Formation and Activism in Mid-twentieth Century Chicago." *Journal of the Illinois State Historical Society* 98, no. 3 (Autumn 2005): 162–83.

———. "Of Immigrants and Migrants: Mexican and Puerto Rican Labor Migration in Comparative Perspective, 1942–1964." *Journal of American Ethnic History* 29, no. 3 (Spring 2010): 6–39.

Fink, Leon. "Union Power and Soul Power: The Story of 1199B and Labor's Search for a Southern Strategy." *Southern Changes* 5 (March–April 1983): 9–20.

Fink, Leon, and Brian Greenberg. *Upheaval in the Quiet Zone: A History of Hospital Workers' Union, Local 1199*. Urbana: University of Illinois Press, 1989.

Foley, Neil. "Becoming Hispanic: Mexican Americans and the Faustian Pact with Whiteness." In *Reflexiones: New Directions in Mexican American Studies*, ed. Neil Foley, 53–70. Austin: CMAS Books, 1997.

———. "Partly Colored or Other White: Mexican Americans and Their Problem with the Color Line." In *Beyond Black and White: Race, Ethnicity and Gender in the U.S. South and Southwest*, ed. Stephanie Cole and Alison M. Parker, 123–44. College Station: Texas A&M University Press, 2004.

———. *Quest for Equality: The Failed Promise of Black-Brown Solidarity*. Cambridge, Mass.: Harvard University Press, 2010.

———. "Straddling the Color Line: The Legal Construction of Hispanic Identity in Texas." In *Not Just Black and White: Historical and Contemporary Perspectives on Immigration, Race and Ethnicity in the United States*, ed. Nancy Foner and George M. Fredrickson, 341–54. New York: Russell Sage Foundation, 2004.

Foner, Nancy, and George Fredrickson, eds. *Not Just Black and White: Historical and Contemporary Perspectives on Immigration, Race and Ethnicity in the United States*. New York: Russell Sage Foundation, 2004.

Freeman, Roland L. *The Mule Train: A Journey of Hope Remembered*. Nashville, Tenn.: Rutledge Hill Press, 1998.

Fremon, David K. *Chicago Politics: Ward by Ward*. Bloomington: Indiana University Press, 1988.

Friedman, Milton, with Rose Friedman. *Capitalism and Freedom*. Chicago: University of Chicago Press, 1962.

Frost, Jennifer. *"An Interracial Movement of the Poor": Community Organizing and the New Left in the 1960s*. New York: New York University Press, 2001.

Galarza, Ernesto. *Farm Workers and Agri-business in California, 1947–1960*. South Bend, Ind.: University of Notre Dame Press, 1977.

Galbraith, John Kenneth. *The Affluent Society*. Boston: Houghton Mifflin, 1958.

Ganz, Marshall. *Why David Sometimes Wins: Leadership, Organization, and Strategy in the California Farm Worker Movement*. New York: Oxford University Press, 2009.

García, Alma M., ed. *Chicana Feminist Thought: The Basic Historical Writings*. New York: Routledge, 1997.

García, Ignacio M. *Hector P. García: In Relentless Pursuit of Justice*. Houston: Arte Público Press, 2002.

———. *United We Win: The Rise and Fall of La Raza Unida Party*. Tucson: MASRC, 1989.

———. *Viva Kennedy: Mexican Americans in Search of Camelot*. College Station: Texas A&M University Press, 2000.

———. *White but Not Equal: Mexican Americans, Jury Discrimination and the Supreme Court*. Tucson: University of Arizona Press, 2009.

García, Mario T. *Blowout! Sal Castro and the Chicano Struggle for Educational Justice*. Chapel Hill: University of North Carolina Press, 2011.

———. *Mexican Americans: Leadership, Ideology, and Identity, 1930–1960*. New Haven: Yale University Press, 1989.

García, Mario T., with Bert Corona. *Memories of Chicano History: The Life and Narrative of Bert Corona*. Berkeley: University of California Press, 1994.

Gardner, Richard. *¡Grito! Reies Tijerina and the New Mexico Land Grant War of 1967*. Indianapolis, Ind.: Bobbs-Merrill, 1970.

Garrow, David J. *Bearing the Cross: Martin Luther King Jr. and the Southern Christian Leadership Conference*. New York: William Morrow, 1986.

———, ed. *Chicago 1966: Open Housing Marches, Summit Negotiations, and Operation Breadbasket*. Brooklyn, N.Y.: Carlson, 1989.

Germany, Kent B. *New Orleans after the Promises: Poverty, Citizenship, and the Search for the Great Society*. Athens: University of Georgia Press, 2007.

Gilbert, Ben W., and the staff of the Washington Post. *Ten Blocks from the White House: Anatomy of the Washington Riots of 1968*. London: Pall Mall Press, 1968.

Gillette, Michael L. *Launching the War on Poverty: An Oral History, Second Edition*. New York: Oxford University Press, 2010.

Gilmore, Glenda Elizabeth. *Defying Dixie: The Radical Roots of Civil Rights, 1919–1950*. New York: W. W. Norton, 2008.

Gilroy, Paul. *The Black Atlantic: Modernity and Double Consciousness*. Cambridge, Mass.: Harvard University Press, 1993.

Gitlin, Todd. "Organizing across Boundaries: Beyond Identity Politics." *Dissent* 44, no. 4 (Fall 1997): 38.

———. *The Sixties: Years of Hope, Days of Rage.* New York: Bantam Books, 1987.

———. *The Twilight of Common Dreams: Why America Is Wracked by Culture Wars.* New York: Metropolitan Books, 1997.

Gitlin, Todd, and Nanci Hollander. *Uptown: Poor Whites in Chicago.* New York: Harper & Row, 1970.

Glen, John M. *Highlander: No Ordinary School, 1932–1962.* Lexington: University Press of Kentucky, 1998.

Goffman, Erving. *Frame Analysis: An Essay on the Organization of Experience.* Cambridge, Mass.: Harvard University Press, 1974.

Goldberg, David, and Trevor Griffey, eds. *Black Power at Work: Community Control, Affirmative Action, and the Construction Industry.* Ithaca, N.Y.: Cornell University Press, 2010.

Gómez, Laura E. *Manifest Destinies: The Making of the Mexican American Race.* New York: New York University Press, 2007.

Gómez-Quiñones, Juan. *Chicano Politics: Reality and Promise, 1940–1990.* Albuquerque: University of New Mexico Press, 1990.

———. *Mexican American Labor, 1790–1990.* Albuquerque: University of New Mexico Press, 1994.

Gonzales, Francisco A. *Chicano! The History of the Mexican American Civil Rights Movement.* Houston: Arte Público Press, 1996.

Gonzales, Rodolfo "Corky." *Message to Aztlán: Selected Writings of Rodolfo "Corky" Gonzales.* Edited by Antonio Esquibel. Houston: Arte Público Press, 2001.

Good, Paul. "'No Man Can Fill Dr. King's Shoes'—But Abernathy Tries." *New York Times Magazine,* May 26, 1968.

Gore, Dayo F., Jeanne Theoharis, and Komozi Woodard. *Want to Start a Revolution? Radical Women in the Black Freedom Struggle.* New York: New York University, 2009.

Gould, Richard. *The Life and Times of Richard Castro: Bridging a Cultural Divide.* Denver: The Colorado Historical Society, 2007.

Green, Laurie B. *Battling the Plantation Mentality: Memphis and the Black Freedom Struggle.* Chapel Hill: University of North Carolina Press, 2007.

Grimshaw, William J. *Black Politics and the Chicago Machine, 1931–1991.* Chicago: University of Chicago Press, 1992.

Griswold del Castillo, Richard. *The Treaty of Guadalupe Hidalgo: A Legacy of Conflict.* Norman: University of Oklahoma Press, 1990.

Griswold del Castillo, Richard, and Richard A. Garcia. *César Chávez: A Triumph of the Spirit.* Norman: University of Oklahoma Press, 1995.

Gutiérrez, David G. *Walls and Mirrors: Mexican Americans, Mexican Immigrants, and the Politics of Ethnicity.* Berkeley: University of California Press, 1995.

Gutiérrez, José Angel. *The Making of a Chicano Militant: Lessons from Cristal.* Madison: University of Wisconsin Press, 1998.

Haas, Jeffrey. *The Assassination of Fred Hampton: How the FBI and the Chicago Police Murdered a Black Panther.* Chicago: Lawrence Hill Books, 2011.

Hahamovitch, Cindy. *The Fruits of Their Labor: Atlantic Coast Farmworkers and the Making of Poverty, 1870–1945*. Chapel Hill: University of North Carolina Press, 1997.

Halberstam, David. *The Children*. New York: Random House, 1998.

Hall, G. Emlen. *Four Leagues of Pecos: A Legal History of the Pecos Grant, 1800–1933*. Albuquerque: University of New Mexico, 1984.

Hall, Jacquelyn Dowd. "The Long Civil Rights Movement and the Political Uses of the Past." *Journal of American History* 91 (2005): 1233–63.

Hall, Simon. "On the Tail of the Panther: Black Power and the 1967 Convention of the National Conference for New Politics." *Journal of American Studies* 37 (2003): 59–78.

Hammerback, John C., and Richard J. Jensen. *The Rhetorical Career of César Chávez*. College Station: Texas A&M University, 1998.

———. *The Words of Cesar Chavez*. College Station: Texas A&M University Press, 2002.

Hampton, Henry, and Steve Fayer, eds. *Voices of Freedom: An Oral History of the Civil Rights Movement from the 1950s through the 1980s*. New York: Bantam Books, 1990.

Harding, Vincent. *The Other American Revolution*. Los Angeles: Center for Afro-American Studies, UCLA, 1980.

Harrington, Michael. *The Other America: Poverty in the United States*. New York: Macmillan, 1962.

Hernández Cuevas, Marco Polo. *African Mexicans and the Discourse on Modern Nation*. Dallas: University Press of America, 2004.

Hirsch, Arnold. *Making the Second Ghetto: Race and Housing in Chicago, 1940–1960*. New York: Cambridge University Press, 1983.

Hoffman, Abbie. *Steal This Book*. 1971; reprint, New York: Four Walls, Eight Windows, 1996.

Hogan, Wesley C. *Many Minds, One Heart: SNCC's Dream for a New America*. Chapel Hill: University of North Carolina Press, 2007.

Holli, Melvin G., and Peter d'Alroy Jones, eds. *The Ethnic Frontier: Essays in the History of Group Survival in Chicago and the Midwest*. Grand Rapid, Mich.: William B. Eerdmans, 1977.

Hollings, Ernest F. *The Case against Hunger: A Demand for a National Policy*. New York: Cowles Book Company, 1970.

Honey, Michael K. *Black Workers Remember: An Oral History of Segregation, Unionism and the Freedom Struggle*. Berkeley: University of California Press, 1999.

———. *Going Down Jericho Road: The Memphis Strike, Martin Luther King's Last Campaign*. New York: W. W. Norton, 2007.

———. *Southern Labor and Black Civil Rights: Organizing Memphis Workers*. Urbana: University of Illinois Press, 1993.

Hooper, Hartwell, and Susan Hooper. "The Scripto Strike: Martin Luther King's 'Valley of Problems': Atlanta, 1964–1965." *Atlanta History* 43, no. 3 (Fall 1999): 5–34.

Horne, Gerald. *Fire This Time: The Watts Uprising and the 1960s.* Charlottesville: University of Virginia Press, 1995.

Horowitz, Roger. *Negro and White, Unite and Fight: A Social History of Industrial Unionism in Meatpacking, 1930–1990.* Urbana: University of Illinois Press, 1997.

Hoyt, Mary Finch. "A Free-Wheeling School with High Marks." *Parade,* January 18, 1970.

Ignatiev, Noel. *How the Irish Became White.* 1995; reprint, New York: Routledge, 2009.

Isserman, Maurice. *The Other American: The Life of Michael Harrington.* New York: PublicAffairs, 2000.

Jackson, Jesse. "Resurrection City: The Dream, the Accomplishments." *Ebony* 23 (October 1968): 65–74.

Jackson, Kenneth T. *Crabgrass Frontier: The Suburbanization of the United States.* New York: Oxford University Press, 1985.

Jackson, Thomas F. *From Civil Rights to Human Rights: Martin Luther King Jr. and the Struggle for Economic Justice.* Philadelphia: University of Pennsylvania Press, 2006.

Jacobson, Matthew Frye. *Whiteness of a Different Color: European Immigrants and the Alchemy of Race.* Cambridge, Mass.: Harvard University Press, 1998.

Jeffries, Hasan Kwame. *Bloody Lowndes: Civil Rights and Black Power in Alabama's Black Belt.* New York: New York University Press, 2009.

Jenkins, Philip. *Decade of Nightmares: The End of the Sixties and the Making of Eighties America.* New York: Oxford University Press, 2006.

Jennings, James, ed. *Blacks, Latinos and Asians in Urban America: Status and Prospects for Politics and Activism.* Westport, Conn.: Praeger, 1994.

Jensen, Richard J., and John C. Hammerback, eds. *The Words of César Chávez.* College Station: Texas A&M University Press, 2002.

Johnson, Benjamin H. "The Cosmic Race in Texas: Racial Fusion, White Supremacy, and Civil Rights Politics." *Journal of American History* 98, no. 2 (September 2011): 404–19.

Jones, Patrick D. *The Selma of the North: Civil Rights Insurgency in Milwaukee.* Cambridge, Mass.: Harvard University Press, 2009.

Jones, William P. "The Unknown Origins of the March on Washington: Civil Rights Politics and the Black Working Class." *Labor: Studies in Working-Class History in the Americas* 7, no. 3 (2010): 33–52.

Joseph, Peniel. *Waiting 'til the Midnight Hour: A Narrative History of Black Power in America.* New York: Henry Holt, 2006.

———, ed. *The Black Power Movement: Rethinking the Civil Rights–Black Power Era.* New York: Routledge, 2006.

Kahn, T. "Why the Poor People's Campaign Failed." *Commentary* 46 (September 1968): 50–55.

Kaplowitz, Craig A. *LULAC, Mexican Americans, and National Policy.* College Station: Texas A&M University Press, 2005.

Katz, Michael B. *In the Shadow of the Poorhouse: A Social History of Welfare in America.* Rev. ed. New York: Basic Books, 1996.

Katzew, Ilona. *Casta Painting: Images of Race in Eighteenth-Century Mexico*. New Haven: Yale University Press, 2004.

Katzew, Ilona, and Susan Deans-Smith, eds. *Race and Classification: The Case of Mexican America*. Stanford, Calif.: Stanford University Press, 2009.

Katznelson, Ira. *When Affirmative Action Was White: An Untold History of Racial Inequality in Twentieth-Century America*. New York: W. W. Norton, 2005.

Keleher, William. *Maxwell Land Grant: A New Mexico Item*. Albuquerque: University of New Mexico Press, 1984.

Kelley, Robin D. G. "'We Are Not What We Seem': Rethinking Black Working-Class Opposition in the Jim Crow South." *Journal of American History* 80 (1993): 75–112.

———. *Yo Mama's Disfunktional: Fighting the Culture Wars in Urban America*. Boston: Beacon Press, 1997.

Kells, Michelle Hall. *Hector P. García: Everyday Rhetoric and Mexican American Civil Rights*. Carbondale: Southern Illinois University Press, 2006.

Kerr, Louise Año Nuevo. "Chicano Settlements in Chicago: A Brief History." *Journal of Ethnic Studies* 2 (1975): 22–32.

Kersten, Andrew E. *A. Philip Randolph: A Life in the Vanguard*. Lanham, Md.: Rowman and Littlefield, 2007.

Kiffmeyer, Thomas. "From Self-Help to Sedition: The Appalachian Volunteers in Eastern Kentucky, 1964–1970." *Journal of Southern History* 64 (1998): 65–94.

———. *Reformers to Radicals: The Appalachian Volunteers and the War on Poverty*. Lexington: University Press of Kentucky, 2008.

King, Coretta Scott. *My Life with Dr. Martin Luther King Jr.* New York: Holt, Rinehart and Winston, 1969.

King, Martin Luther, Jr. *"All Labor Has Dignity."* Edited by Michael K. Honey. Boston: Beacon Press, 2011.

———. *A Knock at Midnight: Inspiration from the Great Sermons of Reverend Martin Luther King Jr.* Edited by Clayborne Carson and Peter Holloran. New York: Intellectual Properties Management, 1998.

———. *A Testament of Hope: The Essential Writings and Speeches of Martin Luther King Jr.* Edited by James M. Washington. San Francisco: HarperCollins, 1986.

———. *Where Do We Go from Here: Chaos or Community?* New York: Harper & Row, 1967.

———. *Why We Can't Wait*. New York: Harper & Row, 1964.

Klarman, Michael. *Unfinished Business: Racial Equality in American History*. New York: Oxford University Press, 2007.

Kleppner, Paul. *Chicago Divided: The Making of a Black Mayor*. DeKalb: Northern Illinois University Press, 1985.

Kornbluh, Felicia. *The Battle for Welfare Rights: Poverty and Politics in Modern America*. Philadelphia: University of Pennsylvania Press, 2007.

———. "To Fulfill Their 'Rightly Needs': Consumerism and the National Welfare Rights Movement." *Radical History Review* 69 (1997): 76–113.

Korstad, Robert R., and James L. Leloudis. *To Right These Wrongs: The North*

Carolina Fund and the Battle to End Poverty and Inequality in 1960s America. Chapel Hill: University of North Carolina Press, 2010.

Koscielski, Frank. *Divided Loyalties: American Unions and the Vietnam War.* New York: Garland, 1999.

Kotz, Nick. *Judgment Days: Lyndon Baines Johnson, Martin Luther King Jr., and the Laws that Changed America.* Boston: Houghton Mifflin, 2005.

———. *Let Them Eat Promises: The Politics of Hunger in America.* Englewood Cliffs, N.J.: Prentice-Hall, 1969.

Kotz, Nick, and Mary Lynn Kotz. *A Passion for Equality: George A. Wiley and the Movement.* New York: W. W. Norton, 1977.

Lackey, Hilliard. *Marks, Martin, and the Mule Train.* Jackson, Miss.: Town Square Books, 1998.

Landess, Thomas H., and Richard M. Quinn. *Jesse Jackson and the Politics of Race.* Ottawa, Ill.: Jameson Books, 1985.

Lannon, Albert Vetere, and Marvin Rogoff. "We Shall Not Remain Silent: Building the Anti-Vietnam War Movement in the House of Labor." *Science and Society* 66 (Winter 2002–3): 536–44.

Lassiter, Matthew J. *The Silent Majority: Suburban Politics in the Sunbelt South.* Princeton, N.J.: Princeton University Press, 2006.

Lawson, Steven F. *Running for Freedom: Civil Rights and Black Politics in America since 1941.* New York: McGraw-Hill, 1991.

Lentz, Richard. *Symbols, the Newsmagazines, and Martin Luther King.* Baton Rouge: Louisiana State University Press, 1990.

Leonard, Kevin Allen. *The Battle for Los Angeles: Racial Ideology and World War II.* Albuquerque: University of New Mexico Press, 2006.

Levenstein, Lisa. *A Movement without Marches: African American Women and the Politics of Poverty in Postwar Philadelphia.* Chapel Hill: University of North Carolina Press, 2009.

Levine, Richard. "Jesse Jackson: Heir to Dr. King?" *Harper's* (March 1969): 58–70.

Lewels, Francisco J., Jr. *The Use of the Media by the Chicano Movement: A Study in Minority Access.* New York: Praeger, 1974.

Lewis, Oscar. *La Vida: A Puerto Rican Family in the Culture of Poverty—San Juan and New York.* New York: Random House, 1966.

Lewis-Colman, David M. *Race against Liberalism: Black Workers and the UAW in Detroit.* Urbana: University of Illinois Press, 2008.

Levy, Jacques E. *Cesar Chavez: Autobiography of La Causa.* New York: W. W. Norton, 1975.

Levy, Peter B. *The New Left and Labor in the 1960s.* Urbana: University of Illinois Press, 1994.

Lichtenstein, Nelson. *The Most Dangerous Man in Detroit: Walter Reuther and the Fate of American Labor.* New York: Basic Books, 1995.

Lieberman, Mark. "No More Mañana." *Colorado Quarterly* 18, no. 2 (Autumn 1969): 181–90.

Lieferman, Henry P. "Profession: Concert Singer, Freedom Movement Lecturer." *New York Times Magazine,* November 26, 1972.

Ling, Peter. *Martin Luther King Jr.* New York: Routledge, 2002.

Lisio, Donald. *The President and Protest: Hoover, MacArthur, and the Bonus Riot.* New York: Fordham University Press, 1994.

Lloyd, Rees. "Behind the Mask of Middle-Class Decency: Inside the Albuquerque Journal." *New Mexico Review and Legislative Journal* 2, no. 2 (February 1970): 1–2, 20–24.

López, Antoinette Sedillo. *Land Grants, Housing, and Political Power.* New York: Garland, 1995.

López, Clara. "LADO: Latin American Defense Organization." *Diálogo* 1, no. 2 (1998): 22–27.

Luckingham, Bradford. *Minorities in Phoenix: A Profile of Mexican American, Chinese American, and African American Communities, 1860–1992.* Tucson: University of Arizona Press, 1994.

MacLean, Nancy. *Freedom Is Not Enough: The Opening of the American Workplace.* New York: Russell Sage Foundation; Cambridge, Mass.: Harvard University Press, 2006.

Mailer, Norman. *Miami and the Siege of Chicago.* New York: Primus, 1968.

Malcolm X, with Alex Haley. *The Autobiography of Malcolm X.* New York: Random House, 1965.

Manis, Andrew M. *A Fire You Can't Put Out: The Civil Rights Life of Birmingham's Reverend Fred Shuttlesworth.* Tuscaloosa: University of Alabama, 1999.

Mann, Seymour Z. *Chicago's War on Poverty.* Chicago: Center for Research in Urban Government, 1966.

Manning, Christopher. *William L. Dawson and the Limits of Black Electoral Leadership.* DeKalb: Northern Illinois University Press, 2009.

Mantler, Gordon. "'The Press Did You In': The Poor People's Campaign and the Mass Media." *The Sixties: A Journal of History, Politics, and Culture* 3, no. 1 (June 2010): 33–54.

Marable, Manning. *Malcolm X: A Life of Reinvention.* New York: Viking, 2011.

———. *Race, Reform and Rebellion: The Second Reconstruction in Black America, 1945–1990.* Jackson: University Press of Mississippi, 1991.

Marable, Manning, and Leith Mullings, eds. *Let Nobody Turn Us Around: Voices of Resistance, Reform, and Renewal, an African American Anthology.* Lanham, Md.: Rowman and Littlefield, 2000.

Marín, Christine. "Rodolfo 'Corky' Gonzales: The Mexican-American Movement Spokesman." *Journal of the West* 14, no. 4 (October 1975): 107–20.

Mariscal, George. *Brown-Eyed Children of the Sun: Lessons from the Chicano Movement, 1965–1975.* Albuquerque: University of New Mexico Press, 2005.

Martínez, Elizabeth "Betita." "Beyond Black/White: The Racisms of Our Time." In *The Latino/a Condition: A Critical Reader,* ed. Richard Delgado and Jean Stefancic, 466–77. New York: New York University Press, 1998.

———. "A View from New Mexico: Recollections of the Movimiento Left." *Monthly Review* 54 (July–August 2002): 79–86. http://www.monthlyreview.org/0702martinez.htm, accessed July 23, 2007.

Matusow, Allen. *The Unraveling of America: A History of Liberalism in the 1960s.* New York: Harper TorchBooks, 1984.

McClain, Paula D., and Joseph Stewart. *"Can We All Get Along?" Racial and Ethnic Minorities in American Politics.* 5th ed. New York: Westview Press, 2010.

McGraw, James. "An Interview with Andrew J. Young." *Christianity and Crisis* 27 (January 1968): 324–30.

McGuire, Danielle L. *At the Dark End of the Street: Black Women, Rape, and Resistance—A New History of the Civil Rights Movement from Rosa Parks to the Rise of Black Power.* New York: Alfred A. Knopf, 2011.

McKnight, Gerald D. *The Last Crusade: Martin Luther King Jr., the FBI, and the Poor People's Campaign.* Boulder, Colo.: Westview Press, 1998.

———. "The 1968 Memphis Sanitation Strike and the FBI: A Case Study in Urban Surveillance." *South Atlantic Quarterly* 83, no. 2 (1984): 138–56.

McWilliams, Carey. *Brothers under the Skin.* Boston: Little, Brown, 1951.

Meier, August, and Elliott Rudwick. *CORE: A Study in the Civil Rights Movement, 1942–1968.* New York: Oxford University Press, 1973.

Meier, Matt S., and Feliciano Rivera. *The Chicanos: A History of Mexican Americans.* New York: Hill and Wang, 1972.

Menchaca, Martha. *Recovering History, Constructing Race: The Indian, Black, and White Roots of Mexican Americans.* Austin: University of Texas Press, 2001.

Méndez, Mervin. "A Community Fights Back: Recollections of the 1966 Division Street Riot." *Diálogo* 2 (1998). http://condor.depaul.edu/~dialogo/back_issues/issue_2/issue_2_index.htm, accessed August 29, 2005.

Mindiola, Tatcho, Jr., Yolando Flores Niemann, and Nestor Rodriguez. *Black-Brown Relations and Stereotypes.* Austin: University of Texas, 2002.

"Mini-city That Failed," *Christianity Today* 12 (July 19, 1968): 35.

Montejano, David. *Quixote's Soldiers: A Local History of the Chicano Movement, 1966–1981.* Austin: University of Texas, 2010.

Montoya, María E. *Translating Property: The Maxwell Land Grant and the Conflict over Land in the American West, 1840–1900.* Berkeley: University of California Press, 2002.

Montrie, Chad. *To Save the Land and People: A History of Opposition to Surface Coal Mining in Appalachia.* Chapel Hill: University of North Carolina Press, 2003.

Mooney, Patrick H., and Theo J. Majka. *Farmers' and Farmworkers' Movements: Social Protest in Agriculture.* New York: Twayne Publishers, 1995.

Moyers, Bill. "Second Thoughts: Reflections on the Great Society." *New Perspectives Quarterly* 4, no. 1 (Winter 1987).

Moynihan, Daniel Patrick. *The Negro Family: The Case for National Action.* Washington, D.C.: Department of Labor, 1965.

Mumford, Kevin. *Newark: A History of Race, Rights, and Riots in America.* New York: New York University, 2007.

Muñoz, Carlos, Jr. *Youth, Identity, Power: The Chicano Movement.* New York: Verso, 1989.

Murch, Donna. *Living for the City: Migration, Education, and the Rise of the Black*

Panther Party in Oakland, California. Chapel Hill: University of North Carolina Press, 2010.

Murray, Charles. *Losing Ground: American Social Policy, 1950–1980.* New York: Basic Books, 1984.

Nabokov, Peter. *Tijerina and the Courthouse Raid.* Albuquerque: University of New Mexico Press, 1969.

Nadasen, Premilla. "'Welfare's a Green Problem': Cross-Race Coalitions in Welfare Organizing." In *Feminist Coalitions: Historical Perspectives on Second-Wave Feminism in the United States,* ed. Stephanie Gilmore, 178–95. Urbana: University of Illinois Press, 2008.

———. *Welfare Warriors: The Welfare Rights Movement in the United States.* New York: Routledge, 2005.

Navarro, Armando. *La Raza Unida Party: A Chicano Challenge to the U.S. Two-Party Dictatorship.* Philadelphia: Temple University Press, 2000.

———. *Mexican American Youth Organization: Avant-Garde of the Chicano Movement in Texas.* Austin: University of Texas Press, 1995.

Nieto, Leo D. "The Chicano Movement and the Churches in the United States." *Perkins Journal* 29 (Fall 1975): 32–41.

O'Connor, Alice. *Poverty Knowledge: Social Science, Social Policy, and the Poor in Twentieth-Century U.S. History.* Princeton, N.J.: Princeton University Press, 2001.

Ogbar, Jeffrey O. G. *Black Power: Radical Politics and African American Identity.* Baltimore: Johns Hopkins University Press, 2004.

———. "*Puerto Rico en mi corazón*: The Young Lords, Black Power, and Puerto Rican Nationalism in the U.S." *Centro: Journal of the Center for Puerto Rican Studies* 18 (2006): 148–69.

Omi, Michael, and Howard Winant. *Racial Formation in the United States: From the 1960s to the 1980s.* New York: Routledge & Kegan Paul, 1986.

O'Neill, Stephen. "The Struggle for Black Equality Comes to Charleston: The Hospital Strike of 1969." *Proceedings of the South Carolina Historical Association* 60 (1986): 82–91.

O'Reilly, Kevin. *Racial Matters: The FBI's Secret File on Black America, 1960–1972.* New York: Free Press, 1989.

Orleck, Annelise. *Storming Caesar's Palace: How Black Mothers Fought Their Own War on Poverty.* Boston: Beacon Press, 2005.

Orleck, Annelise, and Lisa Gayle Hazirjian, eds. *The War on Poverty: A New Grassroots History, 1964–1980.* Athens: University of Georgia Press, 2011.

Oropeza, Lorena. "The Heart of Chicano History: Reies López Tijerina as a Memory Entrepreneur." *The Sixties: A Journal of History, Politics and Culture* 1, no. 1 (June 2008): 49–67.

———. *¡Raza Si! ¡Guerra No!: Chicano Protest and Patriotism during the Viet Nam War Era.* Berkeley: University of California Press, 2005.

Orozco, Cynthia. *No Mexicans, Women, or Dogs Allowed: The Rise of the Mexican American Civil Rights Movement.* Austin: University of Texas Press, 2009.

Orr, Eleanor. *Twice as Less: Black English and the Performance of Black Students in Mathematics and Science*. New York: Norton, 1987.

Padilla, Felix M. *Latino Ethnic Consciousness: The Case of Mexican Americans and Puerto Ricans in Chicago*. South Bend, Ind.: University of Notre Dame Press, 1985.

———. *Puerto Rican Chicago*. South Bend, Ind.: University of Notre Dame Press, 1987.

Patterson, James T. *America's Struggle against Poverty in the Twentieth Century*. Rev. ed. Cambridge, Mass.: Harvard University Press, 2000.

———. *Grand Expectations: The United States, 1945–1974*. New York: Oxford University Press, 1996.

Paulson, Daryl, and Janet Stiff. "An Empty Victory: The St. Petersburg Sanitation Strike, 1968." *Florida Historical Quarterly* 57 (1979): 421–33.

Pawel, Miriam. *The Union of Their Dreams: Power, Hope, and Struggle in Cesar Chavez's Farm Worker Movement*. New York: Bloomsbury Press, 2009.

Payne, Charles M. *I've Got the Light of Freedom: The Organizing Tradition and the Mississippi Freedom Struggle*. Berkeley: University of California Press, 1995.

Perlstein, Rick. *Nixonland: The Rise of a President and the Fracturing of America*. New York: Scribner, 2008.

Pitti, Steven. *The Devil in Silicon Valley: Northern California, Race and Mexican Americans*. Princeton, N.J.: Princeton University Press, 2003.

Piven, Frances Fox, and Richard A. Cloward. "The Great Society as a Political Strategy." *Columbia Forum* 13 (Summer 1970): 17–22.

———. *Poor People's Movements: Why They Succeed, How They Fail*. New York: Random House, 1977.

———. "Reaffirming the Regulating of the Poor." *Social Service Review* 48 (June 1974): 147–69.

———. *Regulating the Poor: The Functions of Public Welfare*. 1971; reprint, New York: Vintage Books, 1993.

Poniatowska, Elena. *Massacre in Mexico*. New York: Viking Press, 1975.

Pulido, Laura. *Black, Brown, Yellow, and Left: Radical Activism in Los Angeles*. Berkeley: University of California Press, 2006.

Pycior, Julie Leininger. *LBJ & Mexican Americans: The Paradox of Power*. Austin: University of Texas Press, 1997.

Rainwater, Lee. *The Moynihan Report and the Politics of Controversy: A Trans-action Social Science and Public Policy Report*. Cambridge, Mass.: MIT Press, 1967.

Ralph, James R., Jr. *Northern Protest: Martin Luther King Jr., Chicago, and the Civil Rights Movement*. Cambridge, Mass.: Harvard University Press, 1993.

Randolph, A. Philip, and Bayard Rustin. *A "Freedom Budget" for All Americans: A Summary*. New York: A. Philip Randolph Institute, 1967.

Ransby, Barbara. *Ella Baker and the Black Freedom Movement: A Radical Democratic Vision*. Chapel Hill: University of North Carolina Press, 2003.

Reyes, David. *Land of a Thousand Dances: Chicano Rock 'n' Roll from Southern California*. Albuquerque: University of New Mexico Press, 1998.

Reynolds, Barbara. *Jesse Jackson: America's David*. Washington, D.C.: JFJ Associates, 1975; 1985.

Rice, J. F. *Up on Madison, Down on 75th, Part I: A History of the Illinois Black Panther Party*. Evanston, Ill.: The Committee, 1983.

Rice, Jon. "The World of Illinois Panthers." In *Freedom North: Black Freedom Struggles Outside the South, 1940–1980*, ed. Jeanne Theoharis and Komozi Woodard, 55–56. New York: Palgrave Macmillan, 2003.

Ridlon, Florence. *A Black Physician's Struggle for Civil Rights: Edward C. Madzique, M.D.* Albuquerque: University of New Mexico, 2005.

Rivlin, Gary. *Fire on the Prairie: Chicago's Harold Washington and the Politics of Race*. New York: Henry Holt, 1992.

Roberts, Gene, and Hank Klibanoff. *The Race Beat: The Press, the Civil Rights Struggle, and the Awakening of a Nation*. New York: Alfred A. Knopf, 2006.

Rodriguez, Marc S. *The Tejano Diaspora: Mexican Americanism and Ethnic Politics in Texas and Wisconsin*. Chapel Hill: In Association with the William P. Clements Center for Southwest Studies, Southern Methodist University, University of North Carolina Press, 2011.

Roediger, David. *How Race Survived U.S. History: From Settlement and Slavery to the Obama Phenomenon*. London: Verso, 2010.

———. *Towards the Abolition of Whiteness: Essays on Race, Politics, and Working Class History*. London: Verso, 1994.

———. *The Wages of Whiteness: Race and the Making of the American Working Class*. London: Verso, 1991.

———. *Working toward Whiteness: How America's Immigrants Became White: The Strange Journey from Ellis Island to the Suburbs*. New York: Basic Books, 2005.

Romano, Renee C., and Leigh Raiford, eds. *The Civil Rights Movement in American Memory*. Athens: University of Georgia Press, 2006.

Romero, Tom I. "Our Selma Is Here: The Political and Legal Struggle for Educational Equality in Denver, Colorado, and Multiracial Conundrums in American Jurisprudence." *Seattle Journal for Social Justice* 3, no. 1 (2004): 73–142.

———. "Wearing the Red, White, and Blue Trunks of Aztlán: Rodolfo 'Corky' Gonzales and the Convergence of American and Chicano Nationalism." *Aztlán* 29, no. 1 (Spring 2004): 83–117.

Rosales, F. Arturo, ed. *Testimonio: A Documentary History of the Mexican American Struggle for Civil Rights*. Houston: Arte Público Press, 2000.

Rosales, Rodolfo. *The Illusion of Inclusion: The Untold Political Story of San Antonio*. Austin: University of Texas, 2000.

Rosenbaum, Robert. *Mexicano Resistance in the Southwest: The Sacred Right of Self-Preservation*. Austin: University of Texas Press, 1981.

Ross, Fred. *Conquering Goliath: Cesar Chavez at the Beginning*. Keene, Calif.: El Taller Grafico Press, 1989.

Royko, Mike. *Boss: Richard J. Daley of Chicago*. New York: Plume, 1971.

Rubio, Philip F. *A History of Affirmative Action, 1619–2000*. Jackson: University Press of Mississippi, 2001.

Ruiz, Vicki L. *From Out of the Shadows: Mexican Women in Twentieth-Century America*. New York: Oxford University Press, 1998.

Rury, John L. "Race, Space, and the Politics of Chicago's Public Schools: Benjamin Willis and the Tragedy of Urban Education." *History of Education Quarterly* 39, no. 2 (Summer 1999): 117–42.

Rustin, Bayard, ed. *Down the Line: The Collected Writings of Bayard Rustin*. Chicago: Quadrangle Books, 1971.

Sánchez, George. *Becoming Mexican-American: Ethnicity, Culture and Identity in Chicano Los Angeles, 1900–1945*. New York: Oxford University Press, 1993.

Sánchez, José Ramón. *Boricua Power: A Political History of Puerto Ricans in the United States*. New York: New York University Press, 2007.

Sanders, C. L. "Finally, I've Begun to Live Again." *Ebony* 26 (November 1970): 172–81.

Schlesinger, Andrew B. "Las Blancas Gorras, 1889–1891." *Journal of Mexican American History* 1, no. 2 (1971): 87–143.

Schlesinger, Arthur M., Jr. *The Age of Roosevelt*. Boston: Houghton Mifflin, 1957.

———. *The Disuniting of America*. Knoxville, Tenn.: Whittle Direct Books, 1991.

Schultz, Bud, and Ruth Schultz. *The Price of Dissent: Testimonies to Political Repression in America*. Berkeley: University of California Press, 2001.

Self, Robert O. *American Babylon: Race and the Struggle for Postwar Oakland*. Princeton, N.J.: Princeton University Press, 2003.

Seligman, Amanda I. *Block by Block: Neighborhoods and Public Policy on Chicago's West Side*. Chicago: University of Chicago Press, 2005.

Sepúlveda, Juan A., Jr. *The Life and Times of Willie Velásquez: Su Voto es Su Voz*. Houston: Arte Público Press, 2003.

Shreve, Bradley G. "'From Time Immemorial': The Fish-In Movement and the Rise of Intertribal Activism." *Pacific Historical Review* 78, no. 3 (2009): 403–34.

———. *Red Power Rising: The National Indian Youth Council and the Origins of Native Activism*. Norman: University of Oklahoma Press, 2011.

Sides, Josh. *L.A. City Limits: African American Los Angeles from the Great Depression to the Present*. Berkeley: University of California Press, 2003.

———. "'You Understand My Condition': The Civil Rights Congress in Los Angeles." *Pacific Historical Review* 67, no. 2 (May 1998): 233–57.

Singh, Nikhil. *Black Is a Country: Race and the Unfinished Struggle for Democracy*. Cambridge, Mass.: Harvard University Press, 2004.

Sitkoff, Harvard. *The Black Struggle for Equality, 1954–1980*. New York: Hill & Wang, 1981.

———. *King: Pilgrimage to the Mountaintop*. New York: Hill & Wang, 2008.

Skerry, Peter. *Mexican Americans: The Ambivalent Minority*. New York: Free Press, 1993.

Smith, Barbara, ed. *Home Girls: A Black Feminist Anthology*. New Brunswick, N.J.: Rutgers University Press, 2000.

Smith, Paul Chaat, and Robert Warrior. *Like a Hurricane: The Indian Movement from Alcatraz to Wounded Knee*. New York: New Press, 1996.

Sonnie, Amy, and James Tracy. *Hillbilly Nationalists, Urban Race Rebels and Black Power: Community Organizing in Radical Times.* Brooklyn, N.Y.: Melville House, 2011.

Spratt, Meg. "When Police Dogs Attacked: Iconic News Photographs and Construction of History, Mythology, and Political Discourse." *American Journalism* 25 (2008): 85–105.

Steiner, Stan. *The New Indians.* New York: Harper & Row Publishers, 1968.

Sugrue, Thomas. *Origins of the Urban Crisis: Race and Inequality in Postwar Detroit.* Princeton, N.J.: Princeton University Press, 1996.

———. *Sweet Land of Liberty: The Forgotten Struggle for Civil Rights in the North.* New York: Random House, 2008.

Sullivan, Leon. *Build, Brother, Build.* Philadelphia: Macrae Smith, 1969.

Sullivan, Patricia. *Lift Every Voice: The NAACP and the Making of the Civil Rights Movement.* New York: New Press, 2009.

Taylor, Morris F. *O. P. McMains and the Maxwell Land Grant Conflict.* Tucson: University of Arizona Press, 1979.

Theobald, Robert. *Free Men and Free Markets.* New York: C. N. Potter, 1963.

Theoharis, Jeanne, and Komozi Woodard, eds. *Freedom North: Black Freedom Struggles Outside the South, 1940–1980.* New York: Palgrave Macmillan, 2003.

———, eds. *Groundwork: Local Black Freedom Movements in America.* New York: New York University, 2005.

Thompson, Heather Ann. *Whose Detroit? Politics, Labor and Race in a Modern American City.* Ithaca, N.Y.: Cornell University Press, 2001.

———. "Why Mass Incarceration Matters: Rethinking Crisis, Decline, and Transformation in Postwar American History." *Journal of American History* 97, no. 3 (December 2010): 703–34.

Thornton, J. Mills. *Dividing Lines: Municipal Politics and the Struggle for Civil Rights in Montgomery, Birmingham and Selma.* Tuscaloosa: University of Alabama Press, 2002.

Tijerina, Reies López. *Mi Lucha por La Tierra.* Mexico City: Fondo de Cultura Economica, 1978.

———. *They Called Me "King Tiger": My Struggle for the Land and Our Rights.* Translated by José Angel Gutiérrez. Houston: Arte Público Press, 2000.

Torres, Andrés. *Between Melting Pot and Mosaic: African Americans and Puerto Ricans in the New York Political Economy.* Philadelphia: Temple University Press, 1995.

Torres, Andrés, and José Velázquez, eds. *The Puerto Rican Movement: Voices from the Diaspora.* Philadelphia: Temple University Press, 1998.

Vaca, Nicolás C. *Presumed Alliance: The Unspoken Conflict between Latinos and Blacks and What It Means for America.* New York: HarperCollins, 2004.

Van Deburg, William L. *New Day in Babylon: The Black Power Movement and American Culture.* Chicago: University of Chicago Press, 1992.

Varela, Maria, "Time to Get Ready." In *Hands on the Freedom Plow: Personal Accounts by Women in SNCC.* Edited by Faith S. Holsaert, Martha Prescod Norman Noonan, Judy Richardson, Betty Garman Robinson, Jean Smith Young, and Dorothy M. Zellner, 570–71. Urbana: University of Illinois Press, 2010.

Vargas, Zaragosa. "In the Years of Darkness and Torment: The Early Mexican American Struggle for Civil Rights, 1945–1963." *New Mexico Historical Review* 76:4 (Summer 2001): 382–413.

———. *Labor Rights Are Civil Rights: Mexican American Workers in Twentieth-Century America*. Princeton, N.J.: Princeton University Press, 2005.

Vasquez, Enriqueta. *Enriqueta Vasquez and the Chicano Movement: Writing from El Grito del Norte*. Edited by Lorena Oropeza and Dionne Espinoza. Houston: Arte Público Press, 2006.

Vasquez, Irene A. "The Long Durée of Africans in Mexico: The Historiography of Racialization, Acculturation, and Afro-Mexican Subjectivity." *Journal of African American History* 95, no. 2 (Spring 2010): 183–201.

Vigil, Ernesto B. *The Crusade for Justice: Chicano Militancy and the Government's War on Dissent*. Madison: University of Wisconsin Press, 1999.

Vivian, Octavia. *Coretta: The Story of Coretta Scott King*. Minneapolis: Fortress Press, 1970; 2006.

Walker, Jenny. "A Media-Made Movement? Black Violence and Nonviolence in the Historiography of the Civil Rights Movement." In *Media, Culture and the Modern African American Freedom Struggle*, ed. Brian Ward. Gainesville: University Press of Florida, 2001.

Washington, Sylvia Hood. *Packing Them In: An Archaeology of Environmental Racism in Chicago, 1865–1954*. Lanham, Md.: Lexington Books, 2005.

Wehrle, Edmund F. *Between a River and a Mountain: The AFL-CIO and the Vietnam War*. Ann Arbor: University of Michigan Press, 2005.

West, Guida. *The National Welfare Rights Movement: The Social Protest of Poor Women*. New York: Praeger, 1981.

Whalen, Carmen Teresa, and Víctor Vázquez-Hernández, eds. *The Puerto Rican Diaspora: Historical Perspectives*. Philadelphia: Temple University Press, 2005.

Whitaker, Matthew C. *Race Work: The Rise of Civil Rights in the Urban West*. Lincoln: University of Nebraska Press, 2005.

Wiebenson, John. "Planning and Using Resurrection City." *Journal of the American Institute Planners* 35 (November 1969): 405–11.

Wilkerson, Isabel. *The Warmth of Other Suns: The Epic Story of America's Great Migration*. New York: Random House, 2010.

Wilkinson, Charles. *Blood Struggle: The Rise of Modern Indian Nations*. New York: W. W. Norton, 2005.

———. *Messages from Frank's Landing: A Story of Salmon, Treaties and the Indian Way*. Seattle: University of Washington Press, 2000.

Williams, Rhonda Y. *The Politics of Public Housing: Black Women's Struggles against Urban Inequality*. New York: Oxford University Press, 2004.

Wills, Garry. *Nixon Agonistes: The Crisis of the Self-Made Man*. Boston: Houghton Mifflin, 1969.

Wilson, Steven H. "Brown over 'Other White': Mexican-Americans' Legal Arguments and Litigation Strategy in School Desegregation Lawsuits." *Law and History Review* (Spring 2003). http://www.historycooperative.org/journals/lhr/21.1/forum_ wilson.html, accessed March 3, 2004.

Wilson, William Julius. *The Truly Disadvantaged: The Inner City, the Underclass, and Public Policy*. Chicago: University of Chicago Press, 1987.

Wofford, Harris. *Of Kennedys and Kings: Making Sense of the Sixties*. New York: Farrar, Straus, Giroux, 1980.

Wolf, T. Phillip. "The 1968 Elections in New Mexico." *Western Political Quarterly* 22 (September 1969): 510–16.

Woodard, Komozi. *A Nation within a Nation: Amiri Baraka (LeRoi Jones) and Black Power Politics*. Chapel Hill: University of North Carolina Press, 1999.

Wright, Amy Nathan. "The 1968 Poor People's Campaign, Marks, Mississippi, and the Mule Train." In *Civil Rights History from the Ground Up: Local Struggles, a National Movement*, ed. Emilye Crosby, 109–43. Athens: University of Georgia, 2011.

Yglesias, José. "It May Be a Long, Hot Spring in the Capital." *New York Times Magazine*, March 31, 1968.

Young, Andrew. *An Easy Burden: The Civil Rights Movement and the Transformation of America*. New York: Harper Collins, 1996.

Young, Marilyn B. *The Vietnam Wars, 1945–1990*. New York: HarperCollins, 1991.

Zamora, Emilio. *Claiming Rights and Righting Wrongs in Texas: Mexican Workers and Job Politics during World War II*. College Station: Texas A&M University, 2009.

Unpublished Sources

Araiza, Lauren. "'For Freedom of Other Men': Civil Rights, Black Power and the United Farm Workers, 1965–1973." Ph.D. diss., University of California, Berkeley, 2007.

Krochmal, Max. "Labor, Civil Rights, and the Struggle for Democracy in Texas, 1935–1975." Ph.D. diss., Duke University, 2011.

Mantler, Gordon K. "Black, Brown, and Poor: Martin Luther King Jr., the Poor People's Campaign and Its Legacies." Ph.D. diss., Duke University, 2008.

———. "'I'm against the Way It Is Being Done': Civility and School Desegregation in Pinellas County, Florida." M.A. thesis, University of South Florida, 2002.

Nieto, Leo. "The Poor People's Campaign, 1968." Unpublished chapter, in author's possession.

Nuevo de Kerr, Louise Año. "The Chicano Experience in Chicago, 1920–1970." Ph.D. diss., University of Illinois, Chicago Circle, 1976.

O'Neill, Stephen. "From the Shadow of Slavery: The Civil Rights Years in Charleston." Ph.D. diss., University of Virginia, 1994.

Williams, Jakobi. "Racial Coalition Politics in Chicago: A Case Study of Fred Hampton, the Illinois Black Panther Party and the Origin of the Rainbow Coalition." Ph.D. diss., University of California Los Angeles, 2008.

Wilson, Joel R. "'Free Huey': The Black Panther Party, the Peace and Freedom Party, and the Politics of Race in 1968." Ph.D. diss., University of California, Santa Cruz, 2002.

Acknowledgments

As a onetime journalist, I know a project often starts with a seemingly innocuous question about the world around us. The genesis of this one came as I wondered why the attempts at interracial and multiracial coalition building that I first witnessed and then joined in my current hometown of Durham, North Carolina, played out the ways they did. Why did African Americans, Latinos, and white liberals disagree vehemently about how to pursue and achieve justice for the neediest among us? Why was poverty so often addressed separately? Was there anything natural about the coalitions activists sought but rarely could achieve? Obviously, these turned out to be remarkably complex questions—questions that set me on a path that resulted in this book. While not exactly a community study itself, this book was born in a community, and it took a community to write it.

First, I want to acknowledge those men and women who shared with me their stories, experiences, and memorabilia from more than forty years ago. They did not have to return a stranger's phone calls or invite me into their homes and offices, but they did. I am honored that they would trust me enough to attempt to relate their stories, and I hope I did them justice. A few folks that deserve particular mention are Gloria Arellanes, Gilberto Ballejos, Carlos Montes, Maria Varela, and Ernesto Vigil, all of whom went above and beyond in helping me make sense of this era through their personal experiences. Also deserving mention are the movement icons that I corresponded with but did not formally interview, including Andrew Young, Jesse Jackson, Tim Black, Reies Tijerina, William "Preacherman" Fesperman, and Corky Gonzales (the last just weeks before he died in 2005).

I am grateful to those who read all or part of this book in the making, including Lauren Araiza, Rob Chase, Erik Gellman, Bryan Gilmer, Tom Jackson, Max Krochmal, Orion Teal, Justice, Power, and Politics series editors Heather Thompson and Rhonda Williams, and my not-so-anonymous readers Lorena Oropeza and Paul Ortiz. A special thanks goes to my editor, Mark Simpson-Vos—who patiently fielded many an anxious email or phone call throughout the long process—and to Zach Read, Paul Betz, David Perry, and the other good folks at the University of North Carolina Press (despite their unfortunate basketball loyalties). And I deeply appreciate the work of copy editor Brian MacDonald for cleaning up my notes in particular. Any errors that remain in this book are mine alone.

In addition, I want to thank the world-class scholars at Duke University, the University of South Florida, Guilford College, and beyond who helped shape my thinking and writing about U.S. social movement history. I am particularly grateful to my mentors who trained me as a historian: Charles Payne, Sally Deutsch, Bill Chafe, Felicia Kornbluh, Gunther Peck, Christina Greene, Ray Arsenault, John French, Bob Korstad, Gary Mormino, Bob Ingalls, Ray Gavins, Thavolia Glymph, and Peter Wood. More than anybody, Gunther helped me figure out what this book was really about. The extensive support of my current academic home, the Thompson Writing Program at Duke, made this project possible— especially thanks to the leadership of Joe Harris, Kristen Neuschel, and Denise Comer. Also of great assistance was funding from several other Duke entities, as well as the American Council of Learned Societies, the Andrew W. Mellon Foundation, and the Johnson Presidential Library.

My gratitude also goes out to a larger community of scholars, writers, teachers, and activists who, through conversations, conferences, writing groups, and more than a beer or two, made a difference: Anne-Marie Angelo, Brian Behnken, Dan Berger, Jim Berkey, Tressa Berman, Michael Berryhill, Tim Black, Tamar Carroll, David Carter, Kat Charron, Ernie Chávez, David Cline, Daniel Cobb, Caitlin Crowell, John Dittmer, Seth Dowland, Jon Dueck, Kathleen DuVal, Erica Edwards, Kate Ellis, Mike Ennis, Dionne Espinoza, Michael Foley, Kathy Roberts Forde, Mitch Fraas, Katharine French-Fuller, Julia Gaffield, Alisha Gaines, Mario García, Kent Germany, Kelly Gilmer, Reena Goldthree, Anne Gollin, Neill Goslin, Trevor Griffey, Sarah Hallenbeck, Alisa Harrison, Lisa Hazirjian, Steve Inrig, Walter Jackson, Michael James, Amy Johnson, Rhonda Jones, Tara Kelly, Jonah and Caty Kendall, Kelly Kennington, Tom Kiffmeyer, Nick Kotz, Pam Lach, Ian Lekus, Adrienne Lentz-Smith, Sebastian Lukasik, Sarah Malino, Aimee Mapes, John Mckiernan-González, Chuck McKinney, Jerry McKnight, John McMillian, Kathleen Millar, Nan Mullenneaux, Brian Murray, Jimmy Patiño, Kennetta Perry, Milo Pyne,

Jim Ralph, Lisa Ramos, Jacob Remes, Marc Rodriguez, Phil Rubio, Ami Shah, Liz Shesko, Lindsey Smith, Marty Smith, Henry Sommerville, Scott Tang, Kerry Taylor, John Thompson, James Tracy, Tim Tyson, LaNitra Walker, Brian Watkins, Michael Weisel, Matt Whitaker, Kale Williams, and David Zonderman.

As the son of two librarians, I would be remiss if I did not thank the many archivists who demonstrated a deep knowledge of their collections and patiently helped me sift through finding aides, photocopy request slips, and permission to publish forms. They include Ann Massmann, Rose Diaz, and Eileen Hogan at the University of New Mexico's Center for Southwest Research; Joellen ElBashir and Ida Jones at Howard's Moorland-Spingarn Research Center; Elaine Hall and Cynthia Lewis at the King Center; Lesley Martin of the Chicago Historical Society; Allen Fisher of the Johnson Presidential Library; Don Davis of the American Friends Service Committee; Morgen MacIntosh Hodgetts of DePaul University; Wendel Cox and Coi Drummond-Gehrig at Denver Public Library; Nurah-Rosalie Jeter of the Schomburg Center for Research in Black Culture; William LeFevre and Elizabeth Clemens of Wayne State's Walter Reuther Library; Leah Richardson of George Mason University; and Lee Sorensen and Kelley Lawton at Duke.

Lastly, I want to express my deep gratitude to family for all of their support and belief that, yes, I could do this. As my extended family, Lucille Headrick, Amanda and Brendan O'Brien, Carmen and Nick Phifer, and Mary Kay Louder were not obligated to ask about this project or show any interest in it. But they did anyway and listened patiently as I prattled on. My parents, Ed and Judy Mantler, instilled in me a deep love and respect for the past, equality, and fair play. While other families went to Disney World on summer vacation, we went to Gettysburg. My daughter, Zella Mantler, was born in the midst of this project and keeps me grounded. I hope she reads this book one day and understands why I was such a grouch at times. Finally, my wife, Christina Headrick, has cheered me on all these many years and has shown remarkable generosity and love, as well as her trademark sense of humor. And, as she keeps reminding me, "I fed you!" That she did, in more ways than she could know.

Index

Abernathy, Juanita, 219 (ill.)

Abernathy, Ralph, 104, 119, 124, 211, 214–16, 236, 239, 247, 302 (n. 29); Charleston strike and, 14, 217–19; Chavez and, 127, 222; criticism of, 132, 139, 150, 164, 166–67, 180, 247, 284 (n. 63); fashion of, 221; Corky Gonzales and, 222; Jesse Jackson and, 223, 225, 229, 238, 270 (n. 26); leadership of, 123, 139, 221–23, 247, 304 (n. 48); Poor People's Campaign and, 130, 133–34, 136, 146–47, 152, 154, 167–68, 170, 173–75, 182–84, 279 (n. 6); succeeds King, 122; Supreme Court protest and, 161–62, 164–65; Tijerina and, 110, 157–58, 168, 179, 183, 276 (n. 86)

Adams, Hank, 109–10, 114, 143, 161, 176, 179, 183, 197; background of, 162; fishing rights and, 162, 189, 295 (n. 11); Supreme Court protest and, 154, 162, 164–65

Adelitas de Aztlán, Las, 203

African Americans (term), 8. *See also* Black freedom struggle; Black power; Coalition building; Poor People's Campaign

Afro-American Patrolmen's League, 229

Agnew, Spiro, 301 (n. 13)

Agricultural Workers Organizing Committee (AWOC), 259 (n. 6)

Alabama, 183; civil rights movement in, 22, 28–29, 53, 73, 145, 221, 246, 309 (n. 116); Poor People's Campaign and, 113, 117, 133, 139, 182

Albany, Ga., 117, 193, 219

Albuquerque, 71–72; Chicano movement in, 69, 73–78, 88, 161, 186–89, 191, 193; Poor People's Campaign and, 142, 146; poverty in, 18 (ill.)

Albuquerque Journal, 188, 285 (n. 77), 294 (n. 8)

Alinsky, Saul, 25, 32, 43, 49

Allen, Ivan, 216

Allen, Karen, 132

Allen, Roxanne, 197

Alliance for Labor Action, 218

Alliance to End Repression, 237

American Federation of Labor–Congress of Industrial Organizations (AFL-CIO), 19, 82, 124, 302 (n. 29); civil rights and, 34–35, 47, 220; Vietnam War and, 106, 274 (n. 67), 275 (n. 69)

American Federation of Teachers, 106

American Friends Service Committee (AFSC), 40, 98, 124, 127, 273 (n. 51); American Indians and, 100, 272 (n. 42); Poor People's Campaign and, 55, 100–103; Vietnam War opposition by, 103

American GI Forum (AGIF), 17, 24–27, 38, 42, 80, 86, 300 (n. 70)

American Indian Movement (AIM), 197–98, 248

American Indians, 11, 50, 100, 134, 182–83, 186, 205, 213, 252 (n. 11); African Americans and, 149, 165; fishing rights and, 110, 143, 162–64, 272 (n. 42); Mexican Americans and, 3–4, 43, 72, 74, 143, 149, 176, 187, 193, 198; Poor People's Campaign and, 13, 97–100, 112, 114, 123, 129–31, 147, 153, 156–57, 170, 172

Amsterdam News, 239, 290 (n. 47)

Anderson, Mad Bear, 147, 157, 162, 177

Anderson, Marian, 37

Anderson, Roger, 191

Anticommunism, 23–24, 47, 50

Appalachia, 22, 99–100, 109–10, 193

Appalachians, 97, 120, 157, 159–60, 169, 171, 173, 176–77; in Chicago, 59, 208, 231, 233

Arcelis, Cruz, 56

Archuleta, Pedro, 170, 193

Mexican Americans (term), 8–9. *See also* Coalition building; *Mestizaje*

Mexican American Student Organization (MASO), 201

Mexican American Youth Organization (MAYO), 86–88, 107, 109, 112, 196, 201, 205

Mexican Independence Day, 202

Mexican Revolution, 72–73, 148

Miami Beach, Fla., 90, 214, 302 (n. 27)

Migrant Ministry, Texas Council of Churches, 143

"Militant nonviolence," 90, 93

Miller, Mike, 45–46

Milwaukee, Wis., 105, 125, 134, 161, 170, 174, 197

Mining, 31, 169

Minnesota, 142, 173

Minor, Ethel, 76–78

Minority Group Conference, 91, 103, 108–14, 129, 133, 179, 275 (n. 79)

Mississippi, 53, 68; civil rights movement, 16, 22, 31, 45–47, 71, 73, 94, 273 (n. 51); Poor People's Campaign and, 113–14, 117–18, 133–34, 176, 183, 210, 221; poverty, 19, 94–95, 100. *See also* Marks, Miss.

Mississippi Freedom Labor Union, 47

Mlot-Mroz, Josef, 134

Mobilization for Youth (MFY), 21, 32, 35

Model Cities, 204, 211

Moffett, Barbara, 100, 103

Monongye, Preston, 191

Montana, 142, 147, 157, 162, 213, 248, 282 (n. 31)

Montes, Carlos, 145–46, 148, 160, 161, 169, 176, 201, 203, 248

Montoya, Joseph, 71, 142

Moore, Cecil, 29

Morales, Oliverio, 109

Moreno, Luisa, 27

Morris, Calvin, 57, 224, 226, 262 (n. 61)

Moultrie, Mary, 216–17, 219–20. *See also* Hospital workers strike

Moyer, Bill, 151

Moyers, Bill, 51

Moynihan, Daniel Patrick, 212

Moynihan report, 255 (n. 15)

Muhammad, Elijah, 69, 72, 74, 77

Mule Train. *See* Caravans

Mulloy, Joseph, 169

Murray, Pauli, 37

Nabokov, Peter, 78

National Advisory Commission on Civil Disorders, 92, 96, 113–14

National Agricultural Workers Union, 17

National Association for the Advancement of Colored People (NAACP), 22–24, 29, 31, 37, 62, 199, 218, 236, 240; in Chicago, 49–50, 56, 230; Poor People's Campaign and, 94–95, 113, 182, 277 (n. 95); Youth Councils, 125, 197, 230

National Black Political Convention, 14, 209, 239–42

National Conference for New Politics (NCNP), 10, 65–68, 71, 98, 189, 266 (n. 30); black power and, 66; Corky Gonzales and, 12, 84, 98, 200; Martin Luther King and, 2, 98, 264 (n. 4); Tijerina and, 1–2, 6, 12, 84, 98

National Farm Labor Union (NFLU), 24–25

National Farm Workers Association (NFWA). *See* United Farm Workers of America

National Florist Workers Organization, 197

National Indian Youth Council (NIYC), 100, 131, 143, 162, 187, 193. *See also* American Indians; Fishing rights, American Indian

National Mobilization against the Vietnam War, 99

National Urban League, 35, 172

National Welfare Rights Organization (NWRO), 11, 129, 211–12, 222; FAP and, 212; guaranteed annual income and, 105–6; Mexican Americans and, 213; Mother's Day march of, 134–35; Poor People's Campaign and, 102–5, 162, 183, 272 (n. 45)

Nation of Islam, 68–69, 72, 74, 77

Native Americans. *See* American Indians

Nava, Julian, 85

Navajos, 193

Nebraska, 213

Negro American Labor Council, 34

Neighborhood Youth Corps, 80

Newark, N.J., 63, 92, 117, 264 (n. 6)

Newman, Grace Mora, 99, 109, 114, 177, 189

New politics. *See* National Conference for New Politics

Newsweek, 174

Newton, Huey, 79, 204

Newton, Quigg, 80

New York Times, 36, 62, 93, 119, 132, 134, 166–67, 173, 275 (n. 79)

New York Times Magazine, 108

Nieto, Leo, 109, 126, 143, 161, 168, 176, 248

Nieto-Gómez, Anna, 213

Nimetz, Matt, 128

Nixon, Richard, 212, 214–15, 221–22, 226, 231, 239–40, 301 (n. 13)

Nonviolent strategy, 29, 101–2, 112, 135, 174, 183, 215; Chavez and, 40, 45, 127; Martin Luther King and, 42, 55, 63, 95–96. *See also* "Militant nonviolence"

North Carolina, 22–23, 45, 231, 261 (n. 28)

North Carolina Fund, 32, 39

North Dakota, 100, 142, 147, 175, 213

Odetta, 37

Offenburger, Tom, 119, 137, 170, 270 (n. 17)

Office of Economic Opportunity (OEO), 52, 104, 131, 183–84

Ohio, 112, 127, 218

Ohlin, Lloyd, 21, 35

Omeja, Aleah, 141

O'Neal, William, 236

Open housing, 2, 7, 16, 37, 97, 102, 125, 130, 209; in California, 20, 27; in Chicago, 20, 42, 49–50, 53, 57, 59, 233; Mexican Americans and, 24, 26, 130, 144, 172; in Milwaukee, 197; in New York, 32; in Philadelphia, 23, 29; Poor People's Campaign and, 126, 129, 167

Operation Breadbasket, 42, 216, 218, 223, 229, 232–33, 244; background of, 57; hunger tour of, 226; Mexican Americans and, 42, 57, 226–28; success of, 57–58, 224–27, 229; tactics of, 96, 238–39. *See also* Boycotts, economic; Chicago Freedom Movement

Orange, James, 57, 103, 174, 217

Orendain, Tony, 58–59

"Orientals." *See* Asian Americans

Orr, Eleanor and Alexander, 158. *See also* Hawthorne School

Ortiz, José, 132

Otto, Doug, 283 (n. 49)

Padilla, Piedad, 144

Palladino, Moiece, 213

Papel, El, 186–87

Park Hill (Denver), 199

Paschal's Motor Lodge, 108

Paternalism. *See* Southern Christian Leadership Conference: paternalism of

Peace and Freedom Party, 183, 189–90

Peña, Albert, Jr., 26

Peña, Federico, 246

Penney, Marjorie, 103

Pentecostalism, 1, 68

People's Constitutional Party (PCP), 190 (ill.), 190–91, 295 (n. 17)

Pepper, William, 65

Peretz, Martin, 264 (n. 4)

Perez, Ignacio "Nacho," 196, 277 (n. 91)

Perez, Jeannie, 199

Peterson, James Edward, 123–24

Philadelphia, Pa., 23, 34, 52, 57, 103; Poor People's Campaign and, 113, 132, 172; selective patronage campaigns and, 16, 28–29

Phoenix, Ariz., 145–46, 297 (n. 35)

Pilsen (Chicago), 234

Pinedo, Louis, 84

Pitts Motor Hotel, 137, 150

Plan de Aztlán, El, 13, 202–3, 205, 299 (n. 56)

Plan de La Raza, El, 79

Plan del Barrio, El, 172, 181, 196, 201

Police brutality, 2, 9, 16, 23, 28, 56, 67, 182; in Albuquerque, 188; in California, 20, 24, 26, 86; in Chicago, 20, 54, 56, 231, 234, 237; in Denver, 80, 83, 197, 204; in Detroit, 29; in Houston, 87; in Los Angeles, 20, 86; in Philadelphia, 23; Poor People's Campaign and, 110, 130, 144, 154, 167

Political Association of Spanish-Speaking Organizations, 38

Poor People's Campaign: Abernathy and, 130, 133–34, 136, 146–47, 152, 154, 167–68, 170, 173–75, 182–84, 279 (n. 6); American Indians and, 13, 97–100, 112, 114, 123, 129–31, 147, 153, 156–57, 170, 172; announcement of, 89–91; black critics of, 95–96, 98, 101, 113, 277 (n. 95); caravans, 125, 133–34, 136, 142–45, 147, 149–50, 152–53, 157, 196, 210–11, 214–15, 283 (nn. 49, 51), 284 (n. 75); Committee of 100, 111, 120, 130–33, 153; congressional critics of, 118, 122, 128; demography of, 287 (n. 121); formal demands of, 114, 129–30; historiography of, 5; Martin Luther King's goals for, 101–3, 106–8, 247; legacy of, 5, 179–81, 183–89, 192–97, 200–201,

209–12, 216; media criticism of, 93, 97, 118, 122, 136–37, 139–40, 164, 167–68, 170, 174–75; Mexican Americans and, 114–15, 129–33, 162–66, 168–69, 172–73; origins of, 92–96; planning for, 103–6, 116, 123, 150–51, 222, 252 (n. 9); poor whites and, 97, 100, 109–10, 112, 114, 131, 134, 156–57, 159–60, 169, 171, 173, 176–77; Puerto Ricans, 97–99, 109–10, 114–15, 130, 132, 134, 158, 160–61, 171–72; recruitment for, 79, 91, 97–108, 113–14; Solidarity Day, 166–68, 172–74, 282 (n. 48), 290 (n. 47); weather and, 13, 123, 150–51. *See also* Caravans; Committee of 100; Hawthorne School; King, Martin Luther, Jr.; Media; Minority Group Conference; Resurrection City; Solidarity Day

Poor People's Coalition (PPC), 176–77

Poor People's Coalition of Lincoln Park, 209, 234

Poor People's Development Foundation, 192

Poor People's Embassy, 176–78, 182, 189, 192–93, 292 (n. 92), 295 (n. 11)

Poor People's University, 140

Poverty, 3–6, 10, 47, 65, 134; American Indians and, 100; black freedom struggle and, 22–23, 28–32, 34–39, 212–15, 224, 241; "culture of," 20–21; explanations for, 20–21; Martin Luther King and, 42, 46, 90–93, 95, 97, 105, 114; Mexican Americans and, 23–27, 67–69, 74, 81, 88, 143–44, 160, 172, 180–81, 188–89, 202; rates of, 2, 18 (ill.), 19; "rediscovery" of, 12, 15–17, 21–22, 32; women and, 104–5, 135, 173. *See also* Justice; Poor People's Campaign; War on Poverty

Powell, Adam Clayton, 264 (n. 6)

Prayer Pilgrimage for Freedom, 30, 33, 35

Presbyterian Church, 188, 294 (n. 8)

Price, Dempsey, 141

P Stone Nation. *See* Blackstone Rangers

Pucinski, Roman, 58

Puerto Ricans, 4, 6, 38, 213, 252 (n. 11); African Americans and, 30, 38, 46–47, 68, 72, 97–98, 106, 236, 246; in Chicago, 49–50, 55–59, 114, 201, 209, 231–34, 246; Chicano Youth Liberation Conference and, 201–2; civil rights movement, 10; as Latino, 9; Mexican Americans and, 43, 56–57, 72, 84, 158, 160–61, 171–72, 176,

197; as migrant workers, 19; in New York City, 189, 192; Poor People's Campaign and, 97–99, 109–10, 114–15, 130, 132, 134, 158, 160–61, 171–72; poor whites and, 59; poverty, 21

Quaker Action Group, 182

Raby, Al, 50, 52, 58, 61 (ill.), 246

Rainbow Coalition (1969), 10, 230 (ill.), 231, 233, 247; demise of, 209, 237; Hampton and, 6, 10, 14, 231; Latinos in, 233–34; origins of, 208, 230; police and, 9, 231, 234–36; political button of, 231 (ill.); whites in, 231–33. *See also* Black Panthers; Fesperman, Bill "Preacherman"; Hampton, Fred; Jimenez, Jose "Cha-Cha"; Young Lords; Young Patriots

Rainbow Coalition (1984), 10

Ramirez, Ralph, 85, 145, 147–48, 150, 160, 176, 201, 203

Ramos, Manuel, 234

Randolph, A. Philip, 17, 32–38, 65, 264 (n. 2)

Reagan, Ronald, 213, 247

Reagon, Bernice Johnson, 140, 248

Redcorn, Jim, 194

Reddick, L. D., 47

Red Rooster food stores, 225

Red Squad (Chicago), 9, 49, 60, 235, 307 (n. 99)

Republican National Convention (1968), 183, 214–15

Republican Party, 189, 191, 204, 206, 212, 214, 239, 243, 260 (n. 28), 295 (n. 17), 308 (n. 105)

Resurrection City, 105, 128, 135, 138 (ill.), 159, 162, 170, 193, 211, 221; American Indians and, 157, 175; construction of, 136–37, 149; culture in, 139–41, 175–76, 195, 211, 233, 288 (n. 14), 296 (n. 23); demise of, 13, 175–76; disorganization of, 13, 122–23, 136–37, 151–52, 177, 221; gang members in, 125, 174, 229, 232; health worries in, 150–52; idea of, 13, 97, 122, 268 (n. 2); Jesse Jackson and, 223, 270 (n. 26); media criticism of, 137–39, 170, 175–76, 182, 221, 223, 288 (n. 12); Mexican Americans, 149–50, 152, 157–58; as racialized space, 13, 123, 150, 152, 158, 168, 211; violence in, 174–75; weather and, 13, 123, 140, 150, 151 (ill.), 171, 287 (n. 114); whites

127, 181; courthouse raid and, 12, 70–71, 131, 142; criticism of, 70–71, 180–81, 285 (n. 77); Corky Gonzales and, 3, 78–79, 83–84, 87–88, 180–81, 206; governor's race and, 13, 190 (ill.), 190–91; *indohispano* and, 8, 72–74, 149, 244; justice, 1–2, 7; Martin Luther King and, 2–3, 72, 76, 79, 90, 98, 107, 115, 126–27, 276 (n. 86); land-grant rights and, 1, 69–70, 73, 76, 82, 131, 143, 152, 156, 180–81, 245, 294 (n. 8); leadership style of, 78, 148, 156–57, 178–79; media and, 158, 164–65, 171, 179–80; Mexican Americans and, 3, 71, 74, 78, 148, 161, 178–81, 189, 206; Minority Group Conference and, 109–11; National Conference for New Politics and, 1, 66–67, 71–73, 98; Poor People's Campaign and, 79, 115, 142, 145–49, 152, 156–58, 164–65, 176, 179 (ill.), 183; Poor People's Embassy and, 176–78, 192, 292 (n. 92); Puerto Ricans and, 172; trouble with law, 131, 142, 191–92, 245, 282 (n. 36); whites and, 193
Tillmon, Johnnie, 104, 211–13, 222
Time, 67, 94–95
Trade Union Leadership Council (TULC), 30–31
Treaty of Guadalupe Hidalgo, 69, 88, 110, 130, 181, 190, 265 (n. 14)
Treaty of Peace, Harmony, and Mutual Assistance, 75, 77
Tresjan, Lares, 115, 131
True Unity News, 140
Tucker, Sterling, 123, 168, 172
Turco, Art, 209, 233

Udall, Stewart, 128, 131
United Auto Workers (UAW), 23, 30, 47, 173, 218, 259 (n. 14)
United Church of Christ, 100
United Farm Workers of America (UFW), 12, 63, 65, 82; AFSC and, 100; background of, 41, 43–44; in Chicago, 41–42, 58–59, 226–28; CORE and, 12, 41, 44–46; Delano-to-Sacramento march, 46, 133; grape boycotts by, 12, 41, 58, 127, 226, 228; lettuce boycotts by, 227–28; naming of, 259 (n. 6); NWRO and, 213; Poor People's Campaign and, 40, 106, 127, 131, 161; SCLC and, 40–41, 44, 46, 98, 222, 226; SNCC and, 12, 41, 44–46, 76. *See* Chavez, Cesar

United Farm Workers Organizing Committee (UFWOC). *See* United Farm Workers of America
United Mexican American Students (UMAS), 85, 88, 187–88, 201, 203
United Migrant Opportunity Services, 285 (n. 83)
United Nations Association, 123
United Packinghouse Workers of America, 23, 30, 35, 49–50, 59, 275 (n. 69)
United Scholarship Service, 100
U.S. Capitol, 93, 118, 175, 182
U.S. Congress, 126, 211–12, 226, 261 (n. 28); activist runs for, 189, 211, 223, 295 (n. 11); Chicago and, 49, 51, 58; conservatism of, 93, 96; critics of Poor People's Campaign, 118, 122, 126–28; March on Washington, 34; poverty hearings, 19, 51, 94, 131–32, 212; as target of Poor People's Campaign, 90, 108, 111, 114, 117, 128–29, 139, 141, 143, 166, 178, 211–12; War on Poverty, 51, 58, 92, 114, 183, 224, 274 (n. 58), 301 (n. 13)
U.S. Department of Agriculture, 94, 130, 164, 175, 184
U.S. Department of Health, Education, and Welfare (HEW), 184, 211, 301 (n. 13)
U.S. Department of Interior, 169, 174
U.S. News & World Report, 122
U.S. Senate Subcommittee on Employment, Manpower, and Poverty, 94, 131
U.S. Supreme Court, 152, 154–56, 161–65, 170–71, 199
University of New Mexico (UNM), 187
Uptown (Chicago), 50, 55, 59, 111, 114, 208, 226, 231–33, 245, 282 (n. 48)
Urban renewal, 2, 172; in Chicago, 51, 55, 192, 209, 231, 234–35, 245, 300 (n. 70); in Santa Fe, 144
Urban uprisings. *See* Violence
US Organization, 3, 75–76, 244. *See also* Karenga, Ron

Valdez, Andres, 195
Valley of Peace (Arizona), 68
Varela, Maria, 5, 193, 201–2, 248; Alianza convention and, 76, 78; background of, 73, 99; National Conference for New Politics and, 3, 72–73; Poor People's Campaign and, 11, 131, 145–46; SNCC and, 71–73, 76, 78, 152, 161, 170; Tijerina and, 72–74, 78, 131, 148, 179–81

Vargas, Roberto "Beto," 201

Velásquez, Baldemar, 111–12, 127

Vietnam Summer, 84

Vietnam Veterans against the War, 275 (n. 69)

Vietnam War, 1, 204, 215, 270 (n. 24); African Americans and, 62–63, 83–84, 97–98, 204, 263 (n. 70); farmworkers and, 44, 63; general opposition to, 12, 65, 264 (n. 6); Corky Gonzales and, 81, 83–84, 205; Johnson and, 1, 3, 61–62; Martin Luther King and, 3, 42, 60–63, 91, 97–99, 106, 109, 263 (n. 75); labor and, 106, 274 (n. 67), 275 (n. 69); Mexican Americans and, 87–88, 168, 205, 300 (n. 75); Poor People's Campaign and, 103, 112, 130, 167–68, 172–73; poverty funding and, 62, 65, 97, 101, 109, 172; Rustin and, 65, 167, 264 (n. 2); Tijerina and, 84, 88

Vigil, Ernesto, 83, 185, 201, 248; Poor People's Campaign and, 144, 147, 152, 159–61, 182; Supreme Court protest and, 154, 155 (ill.), 166

Villa, Pancho, 204

Violence: freedom struggle and, 28–29, 31–32, 36, 39, 47, 53–55, 117–18, 125; government fear of, 34, 36, 118, 122, 127–28; Martin Luther King on, 57, 62–63, 92, 119; media obsession with, 36, 93, 112, 122, 126, 134, 164–65, 174; by police, 4, 9, 14, 67, 83–84, 93, 154–55, 165–66, 200, 209, 231–32, 234–36; Poor People's Campaign and, 164–66, 174–75, 184; by state, 2, 4, 9, 62, 83–84, 93; Tijerina on, 110; urban uprisings, 2, 48, 57, 62–63, 92, 116, 121–22, 126, 200, 214, 223, 278 (n. 99), 280 (n. 7). *See also* Police brutality; Vietnam War

Viva Kennedy, 80, 267 (n. 45)

Vivian, C. T., 58

Voluntarios, Los. *See* Crusade for Justice

Wachtel, Harry, 269 (n. 16)

Walgreens drug store, 225

Walker, David, 68

Walker, Tillie, 100, 109, 114, 147, 175, 192

Wallace, David, 57

Wallace, Lurleen, 133

Ware, Flo, 211

War on Poverty, 11, 33, 39, 41, 58, 60–61, 64, 189, 247; in Chicago, 50–52, 55, 233; in Denver, 80–81, 131; in Los Angeles, 85;

"origins" of, 12, 15–17, 21–22, 254 (n. 4); and Poor People's Campaign, 3, 5, 90–91, 101, 285 (n. 83); in Texas, 26. *See also* Poverty

Warrior, Clyde, 100, 162

Washington (state), 110, 162, 182, 189, 196–97

Washington, Booker T., 229

Washington, D.C., 5, 11, 34–35, 38, 94, 112–13, 123, 158, 232. *See also* March on Washington for Jobs and Freedom; Poor People's Campaign; U.S. Congress

Washington, George, 204

Washington, Harold, 10, 237, 246

Washington Post, 62–63, 97, 122, 132, 164, 166, 171, 175

Waters, Muddy, 140

Watson, Lauren, 83, 124–25, 149–50, 166, 198, 204

Watts (Los Angeles), 20, 48, 53, 62, 85, 121, 145, 278 (n. 99)

Welfare (AFDC), 19, 29, 32, 37, 101, 116, 184

Welfare rights, 2, 5, 21–23, 94; in Albuquerque, 187, 191; in Chicago, 50, 59, 114, 189, 223, 225–26, 232; Chicanas and, 144, 161, 197, 201, 213; NWRO and, 11, 101–6, 108, 129, 135, 211–13; Poor People's Campaign and, 108, 114, 120, 129, 131–32, 134, 140, 144, 167, 172–73; SCLC and, 104–6, 129, 214, 218, 223, 239. *See also* Guaranteed annual income; National Welfare Rights Organization

West Side (Chicago), 20, 49–51, 53–54, 56, 59, 229–35

Westside (Denver), 199–200, 300 (n. 70)

Westside Coalition (Denver), 300 (n. 70)

West Side Organization (WSO), 51, 53, 59, 229, 235

West Virginia, 21, 118, 122, 128, 132, 169, 171

White, George, 261 (n. 28)

White Citizens Council, 297 (n. 27)

White House Conference on Hunger and Malnutrition, 212

Whiteness, 8, 24, 27, 73, 87, 199, 202, 253 (n. 19)

Whites, 3–4, 9, 50, 252 (n. 11); civil rights movement and, 102; in Hawthorne School, 159–60, 171; Minority Group Conference, 110–12; Poor People's Campaign and middle class, 123, 141, 173; Poor People's Campaign and poor, 97,

Index ◆ 361